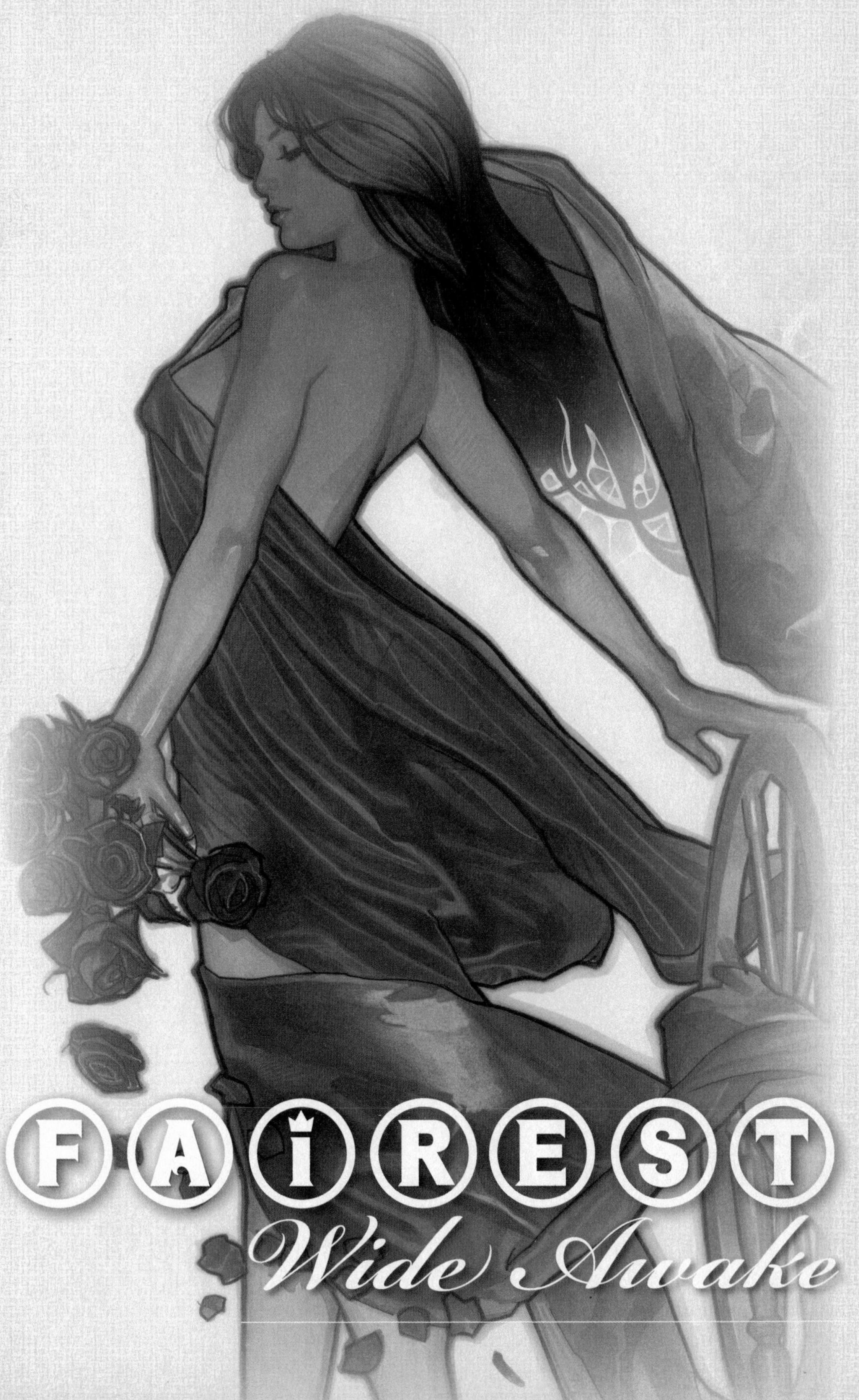

FAiREST
Wide Awake

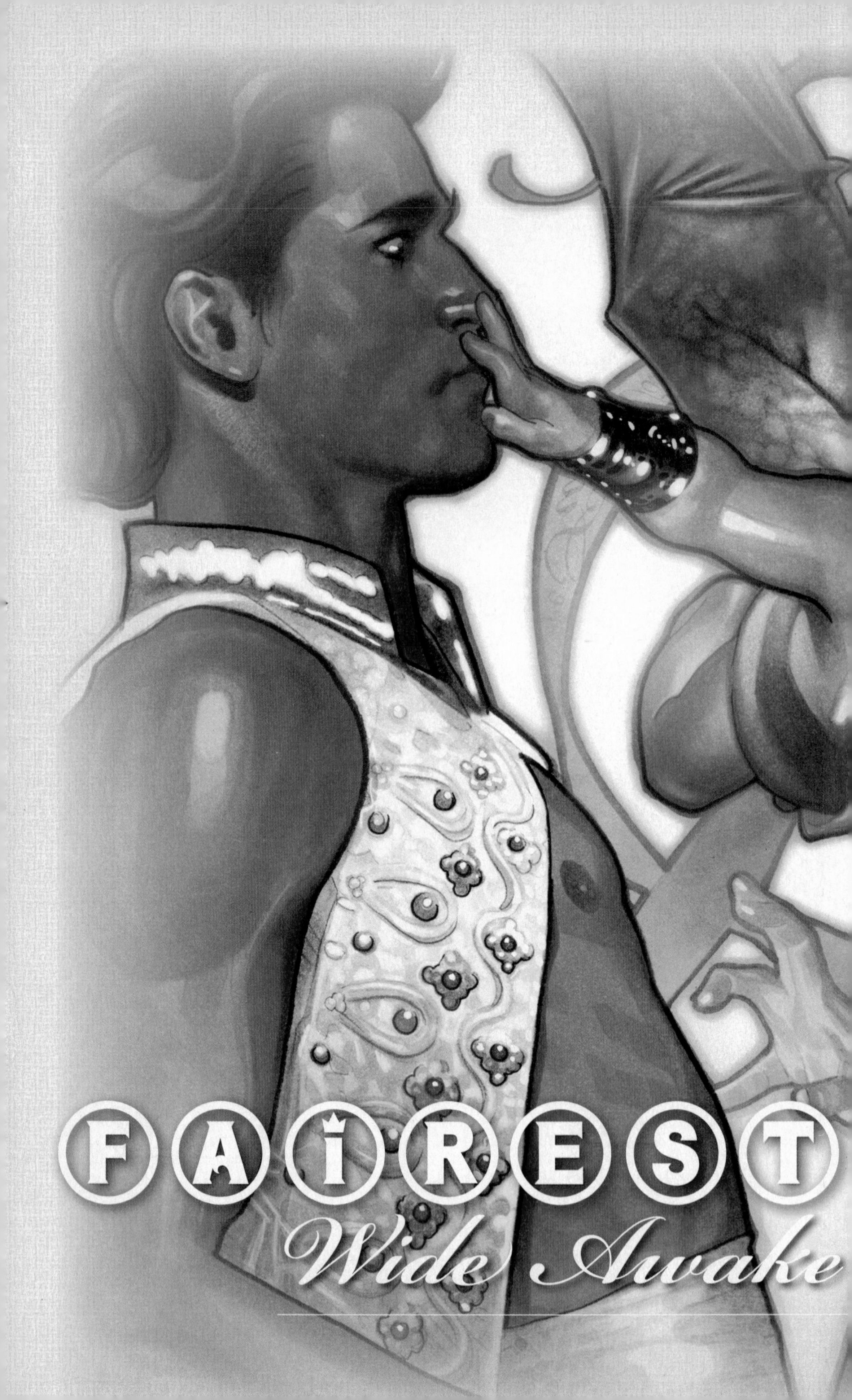
FAIREST
Wide Awake

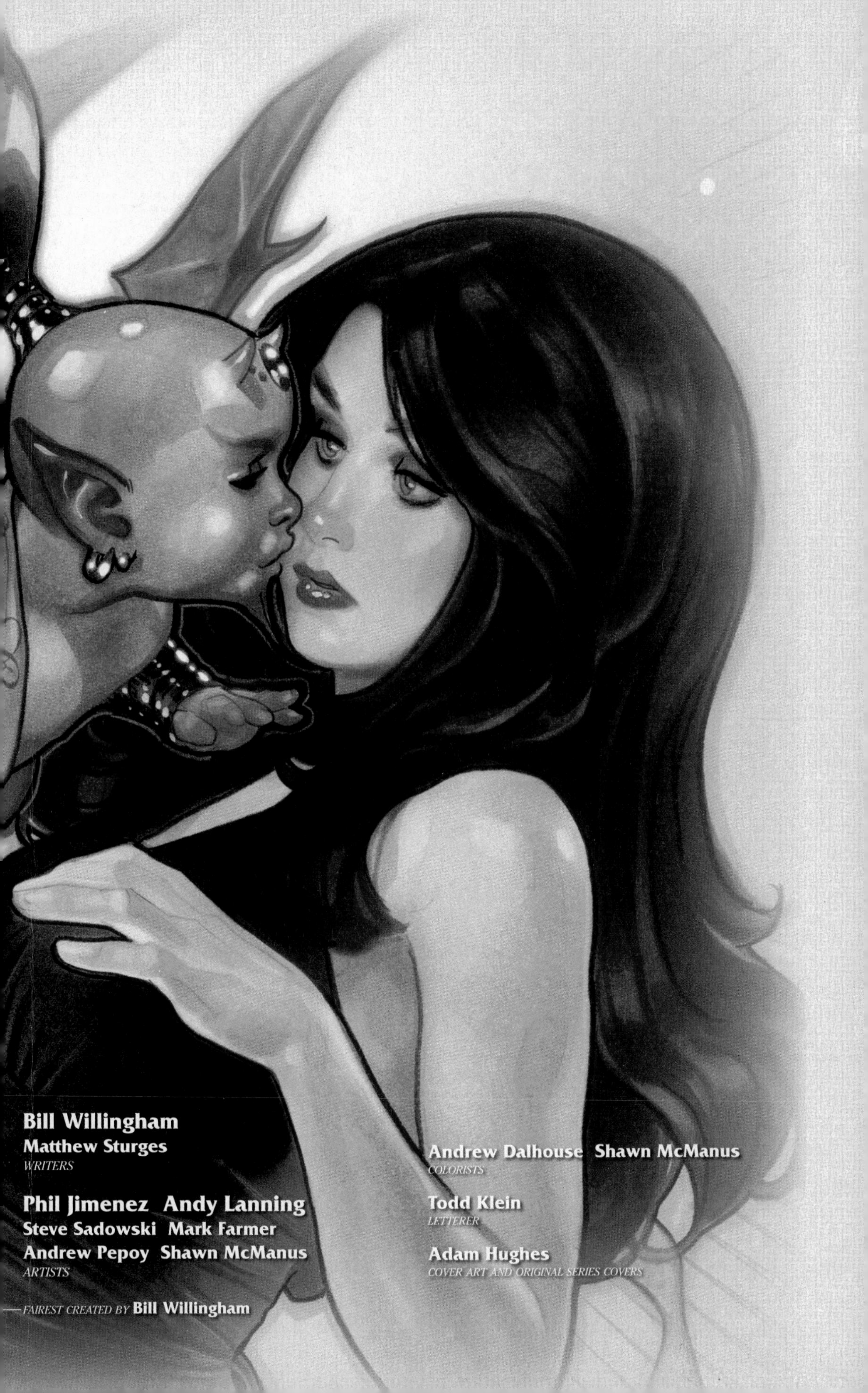

Bill Willingham
Matthew Sturges
WRITERS

Phil Jimenez Andy Lanning
Steve Sadowski Mark Farmer
Andrew Pepoy Shawn McManus
ARTISTS

Andrew Dalhouse Shawn McManus
COLORISTS

Todd Klein
LETTERER

Adam Hughes
COVER ART AND ORIGINAL SERIES COVERS

FAIREST CREATED BY **Bill Willingham**

Shelly Bond
EDITOR – ORIGINAL SERIES

Gregory Lockard
ASSISTANT EDITOR – ORIGINAL SERIES

Scott Nybakken
EDITOR

Robbin Brosterman
DESIGN DIRECTOR – BOOKS

Curtis King Jr.
PUBLICATION DESIGN

Karen Berger
SENIOR VP – EXECUTIVE EDITOR, VERTIGO

Bob Harras
VP – EDITOR-IN-CHIEF

Diane Nelson
PRESIDENT

Dan DiDio and **Jim Lee**
CO-PUBLISHERS

Geoff Johns
CHIEF CREATIVE OFFICER

John Rood
EXECUTIVE VP – SALES, MARKETING AND BUSINESS DEVELOPMENT

Amy Genkins
SENIOR VP – BUSINESS AND LEGAL AFFAIRS

Nairi Gardiner
SENIOR VP – FINANCE

Jeff Boison
VP – PUBLISHING OPERATIONS

Mark Chiarello
VP – ART DIRECTION AND DESIGN

John Cunningham
VP – MARKETING

Terri Cunningham
VP – TALENT RELATIONS AND SERVICES

Alison Gill
SENIOR VP – MANUFACTURING AND OPERATIONS

Hank Kanalz
SENIOR VP – DIGITAL

Jay Kogan
VP – BUSINESS AND LEGAL AFFAIRS, PUBLISHING

Jack Mahan
VP – BUSINESS AFFAIRS, TALENT

Nick Napolitano
VP – MANUFACTURING ADMINISTRATION

Sue Pohja
VP – BOOK SALES

Courtney Simmons
SENIOR VP – PUBLICITY

Bob Wayne
SENIOR VP – SALES

DC Comics, 1700 Broadway, New York, NY 10019
A Warner Bros. Entertainment Company
Printed in the U.S.A. First Printing. ISBN: 978-1-4012-3550-5

Willingham, Bill.
  Fairest. Volume 1, Wide awake / Bill Willingham, Phil Jimenez, Andy
Lanning.
    p. cm.
  "Originally published in single magazine form in Fairest 1-7."
  ISBN 978-1-4012-3550-5 (alk. paper)
  1. Graphic novels. I. Jimenez, Phil. II. Lanning, Andy. III. Title. IV. Title:
Wide awake.
  PN6727.W52F55 2012
  741.5'973—dc23
                              2012030614

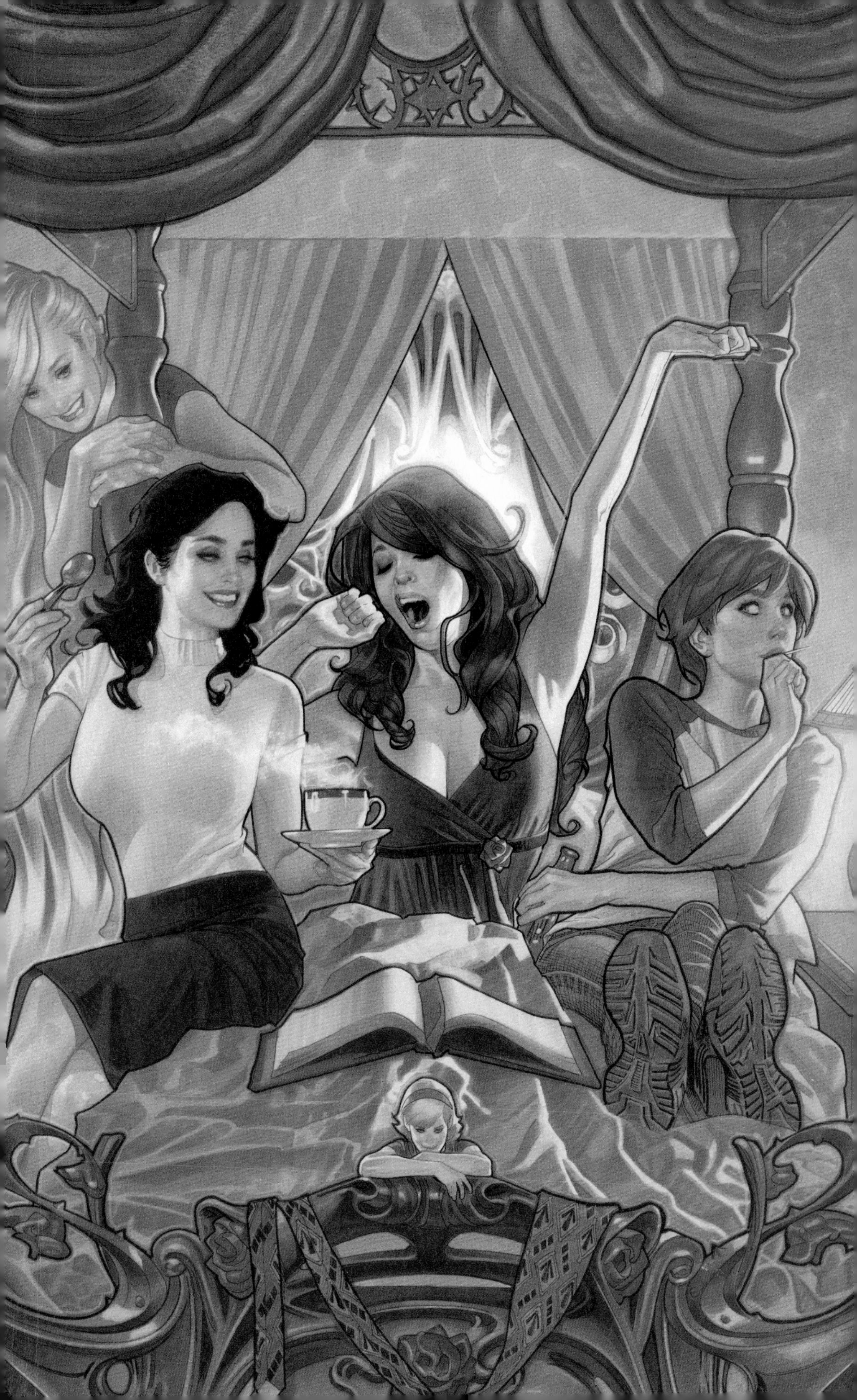

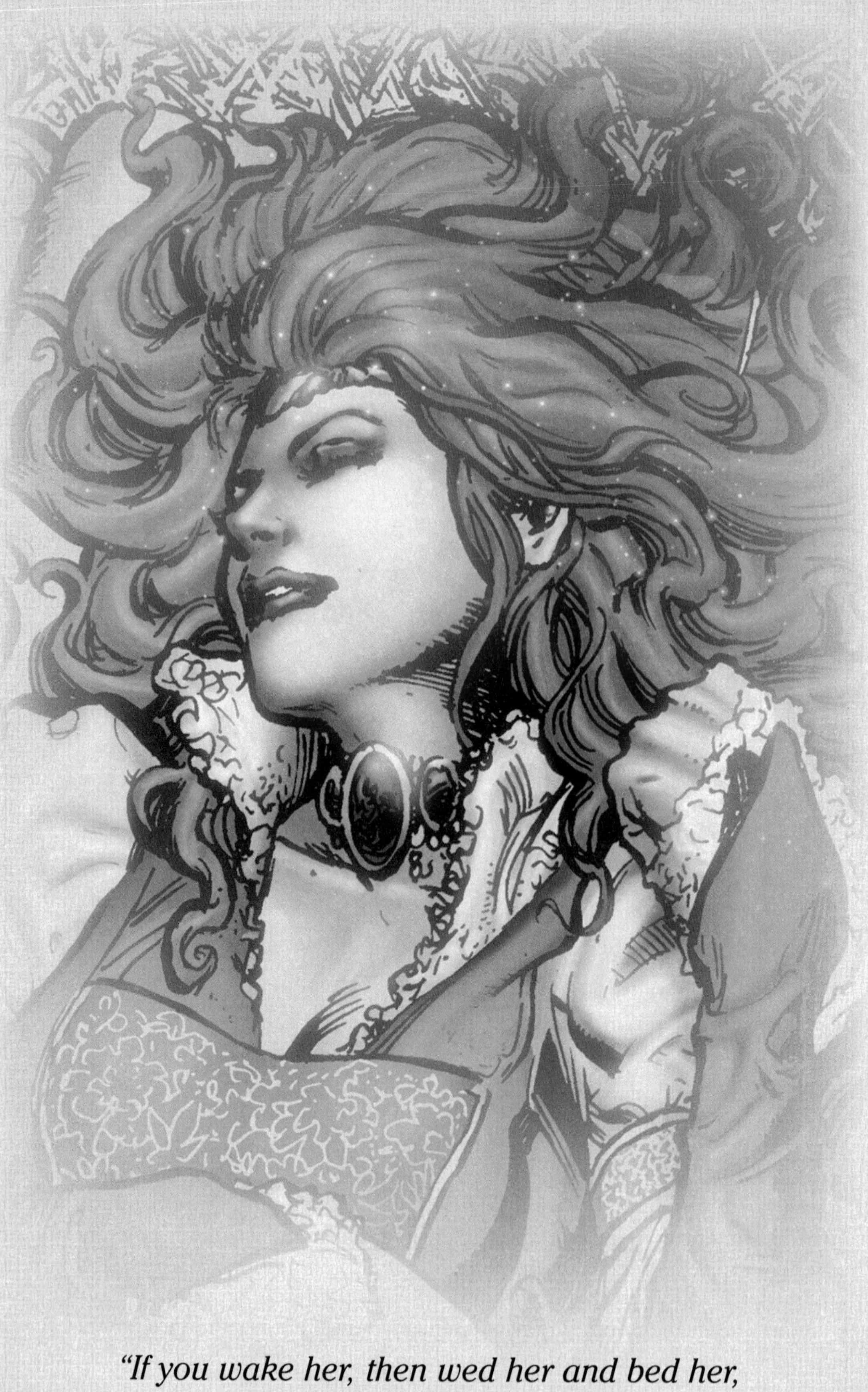

"If you wake her, then wed her and bed her, you get everything she gets."

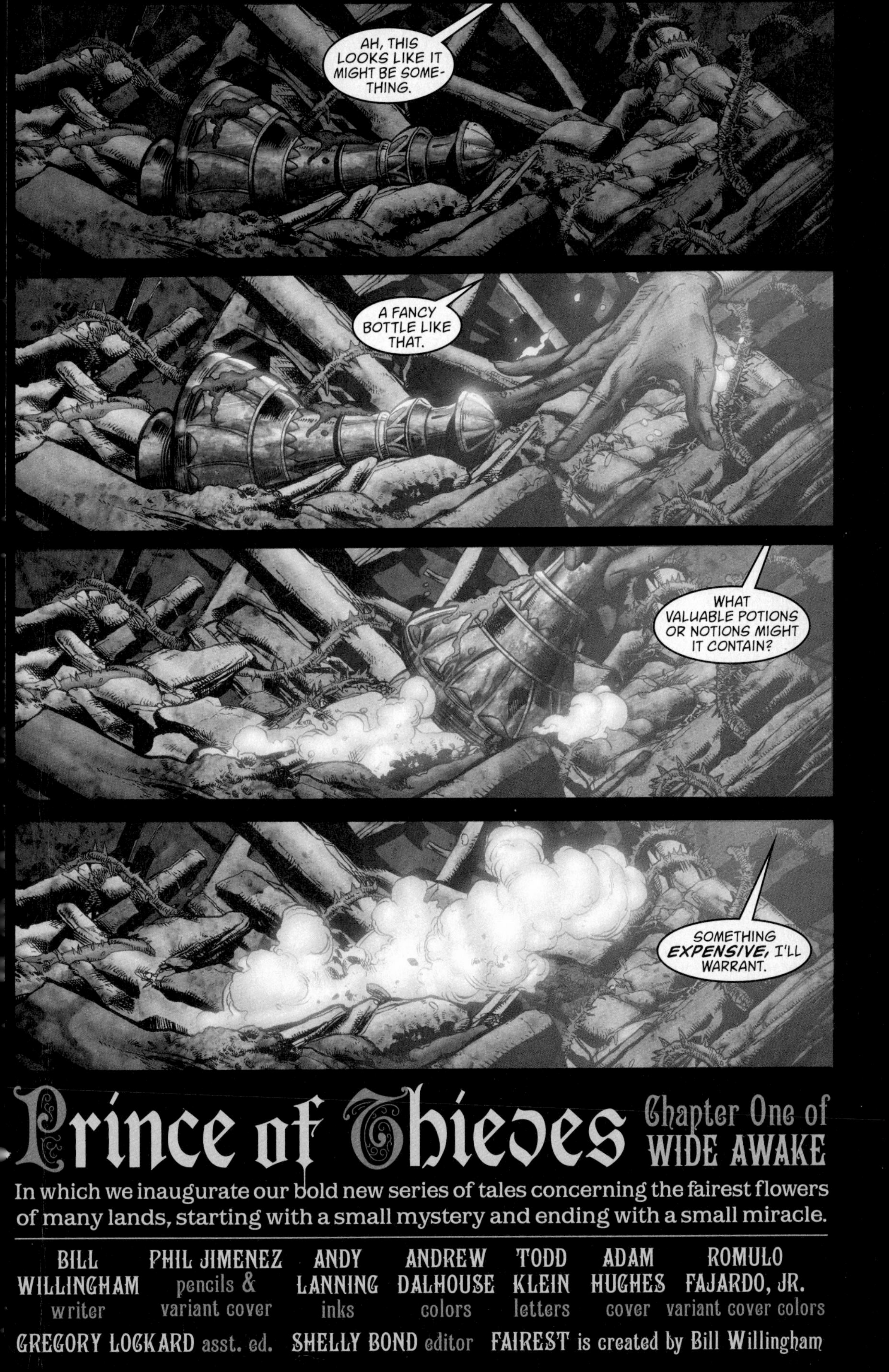
AH, THIS LOOKS LIKE IT MIGHT BE SOMETHING.
A FANCY BOTTLE LIKE THAT.
WHAT VALUABLE POTIONS OR NOTIONS MIGHT IT CONTAIN?
SOMETHING *EXPENSIVE,* I'LL WARRANT.

Prince of Thieves

Chapter One of WIDE AWAKE

In which we inaugurate our bold new series of tales concerning the fairest flowers of many lands, starting with a small mystery and ending with a small miracle.

BILL WILLINGHAM writer — PHIL JIMENEZ pencils & variant cover — ANDY LANNING inks — ANDREW DALHOUSE colors — TODD KLEIN letters — ADAM HUGHES cover — ROMULO FAJARDO, JR. variant cover colors

GREGORY LOCKARD asst. ed. SHELLY BOND editor FAIREST is created by Bill Willingham

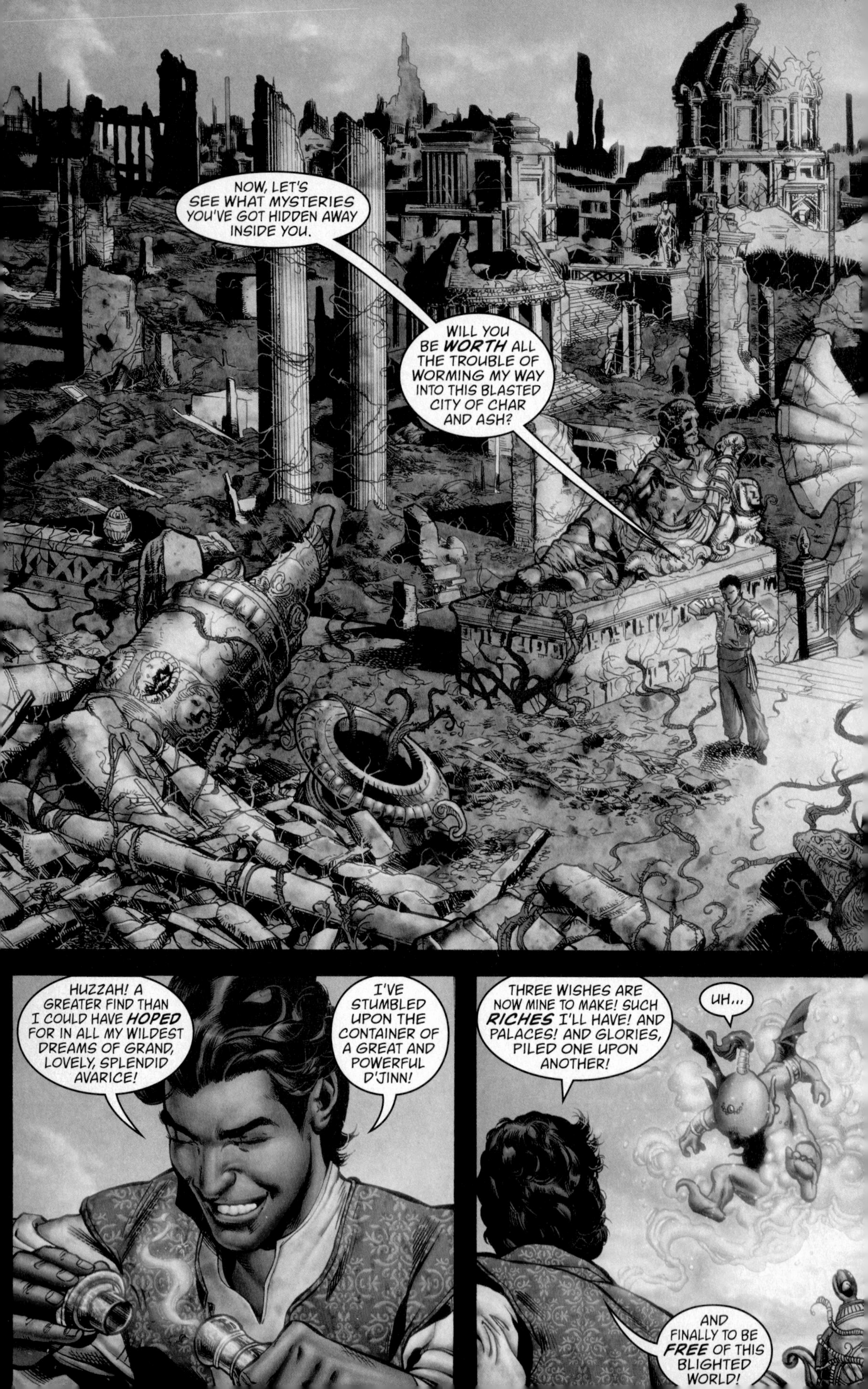
NOW, LET'S SEE WHAT MYSTERIES YOU'VE GOT HIDDEN AWAY INSIDE YOU.
WILL YOU BE WORTH ALL THE TROUBLE OF WORMING MY WAY INTO THIS BLASTED CITY OF CHAR AND ASH?
HUZZAH! A GREATER FIND THAN I COULD HAVE HOPED FOR IN ALL MY WILDEST DREAMS OF GRAND, LOVELY, SPLENDID AVARICE!
I'VE STUMBLED UPON THE CONTAINER OF A GREAT AND POWERFUL D'JINN!
THREE WISHES ARE NOW MINE TO MAKE! SUCH RICHES I'LL HAVE! AND PALACES! AND GLORIES, PILED ONE UPON ANOTHER!
UH...
AND FINALLY TO BE FREE OF THIS BLIGHTED WORLD!

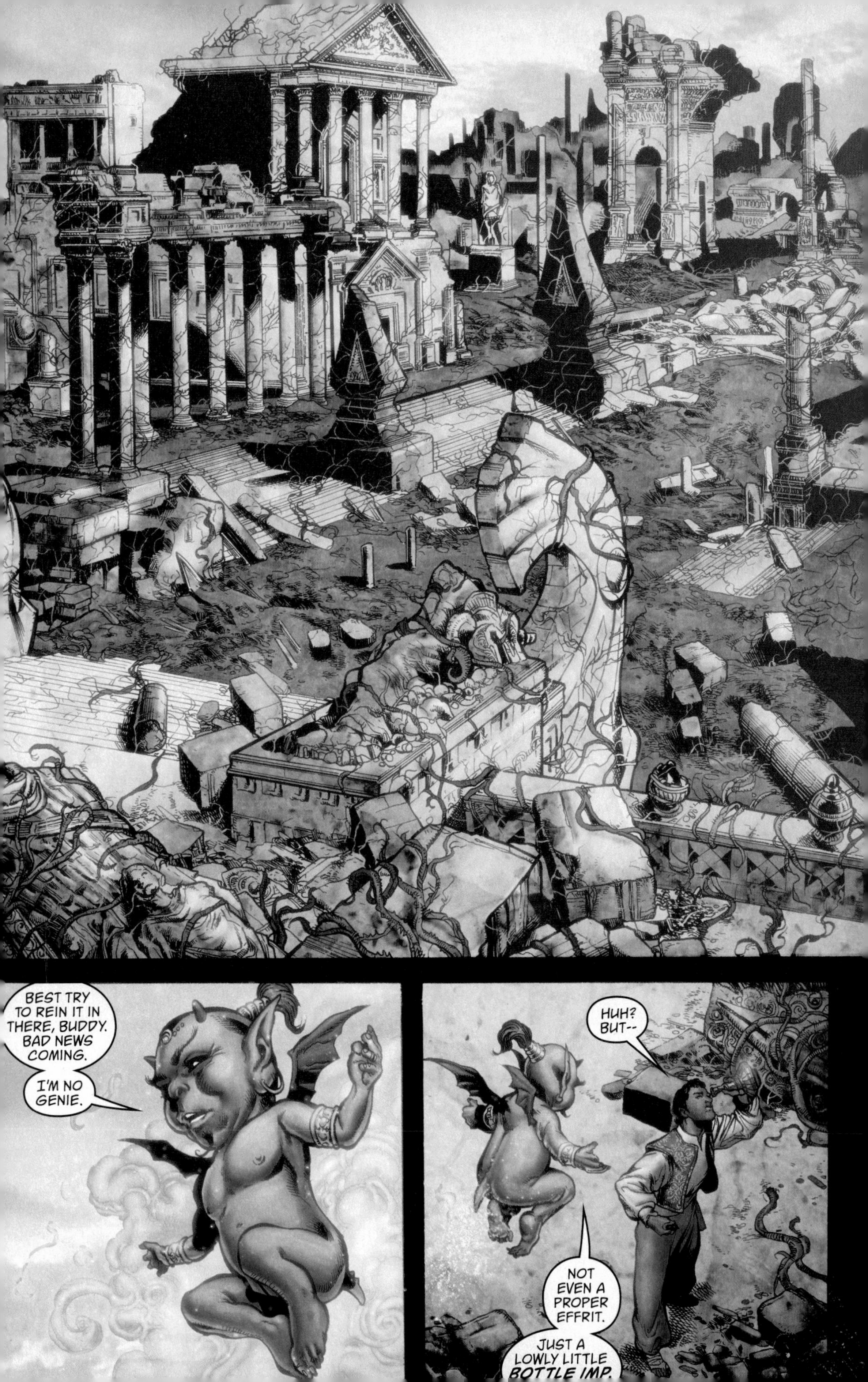
BEST TRY TO REIN IT IN THERE, BUDDY. BAD NEWS COMING.
I'M NO GENIE.
HUH? BUT--
NOT EVEN A PROPER EFFRIT.
JUST A LOWLY LITTLE BOTTLE IMP.

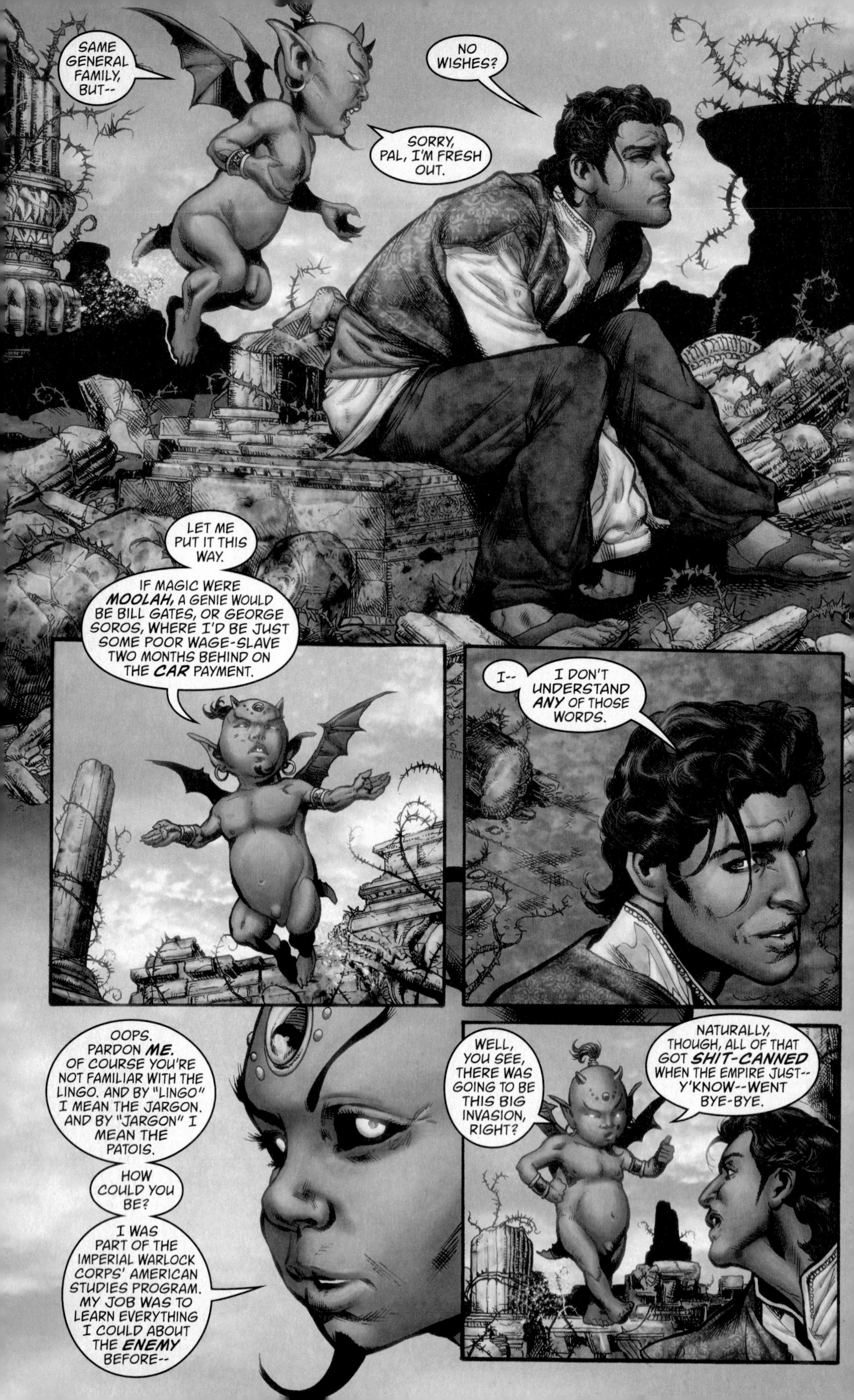
SAME GENERAL FAMILY, BUT--
NO WISHES?
SORRY, PAL, I'M FRESH OUT.
LET ME PUT IT THIS WAY.
IF MAGIC WERE MOOLAH, A GENIE WOULD BE BILL GATES, OR GEORGE SOROS, WHERE I'D BE JUST SOME POOR WAGE-SLAVE TWO MONTHS BEHIND ON THE CAR PAYMENT.
I--
I DON'T UNDERSTAND ANY OF THOSE WORDS.
OOPS. PARDON ME. OF COURSE YOU'RE NOT FAMILIAR WITH THE LINGO. AND BY "LINGO" I MEAN THE JARGON. AND BY "JARGON" I MEAN THE PATOIS.
HOW COULD YOU BE?
I WAS PART OF THE IMPERIAL WARLOCK CORPS' AMERICAN STUDIES PROGRAM. MY JOB WAS TO LEARN EVERYTHING I COULD ABOUT THE ENEMY BEFORE--
WELL, YOU SEE, THERE WAS GOING TO BE THIS BIG INVASION, RIGHT?
NATURALLY, THOUGH, ALL OF THAT GOT SHIT-CANNED WHEN THE EMPIRE JUST-- Y'KNOW--WENT BYE-BYE.

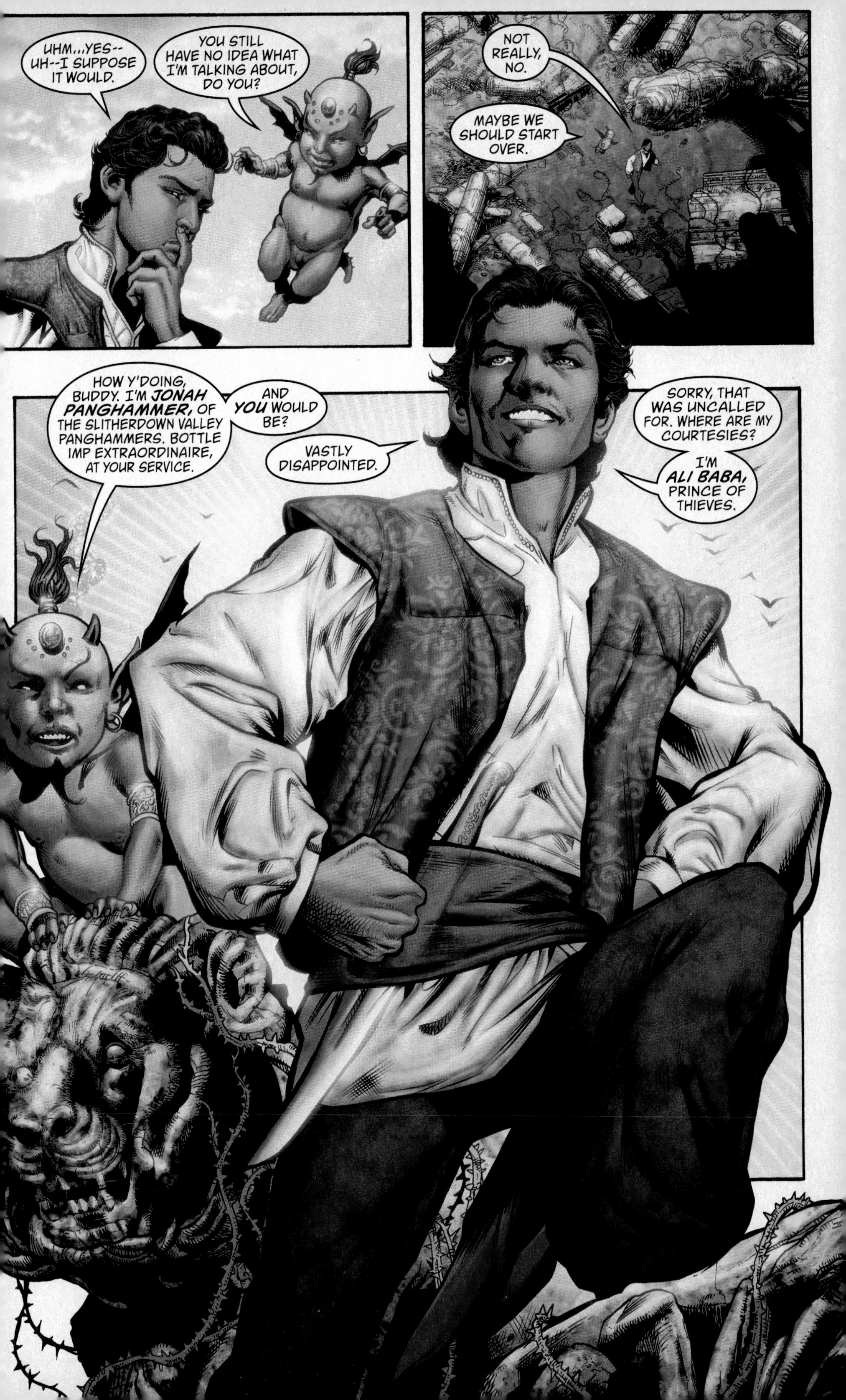
UHM...YES--
UH--I SUPPOSE IT WOULD.
YOU STILL HAVE NO IDEA WHAT I'M TALKING ABOUT, DO YOU?
NOT REALLY, NO.
MAYBE WE SHOULD START OVER.
HOW Y'DOING, BUDDY. I'M JONAH PANGHAMMER, OF THE SLITHERDOWN VALLEY PANGHAMMERS. BOTTLE IMP EXTRAORDINAIRE, AT YOUR SERVICE.
AND YOU WOULD BE?
VASTLY DISAPPOINTED.
SORRY, THAT WAS UNCALLED FOR. WHERE ARE MY COURTESIES?
I'M ALI BABA, PRINCE OF THIEVES.

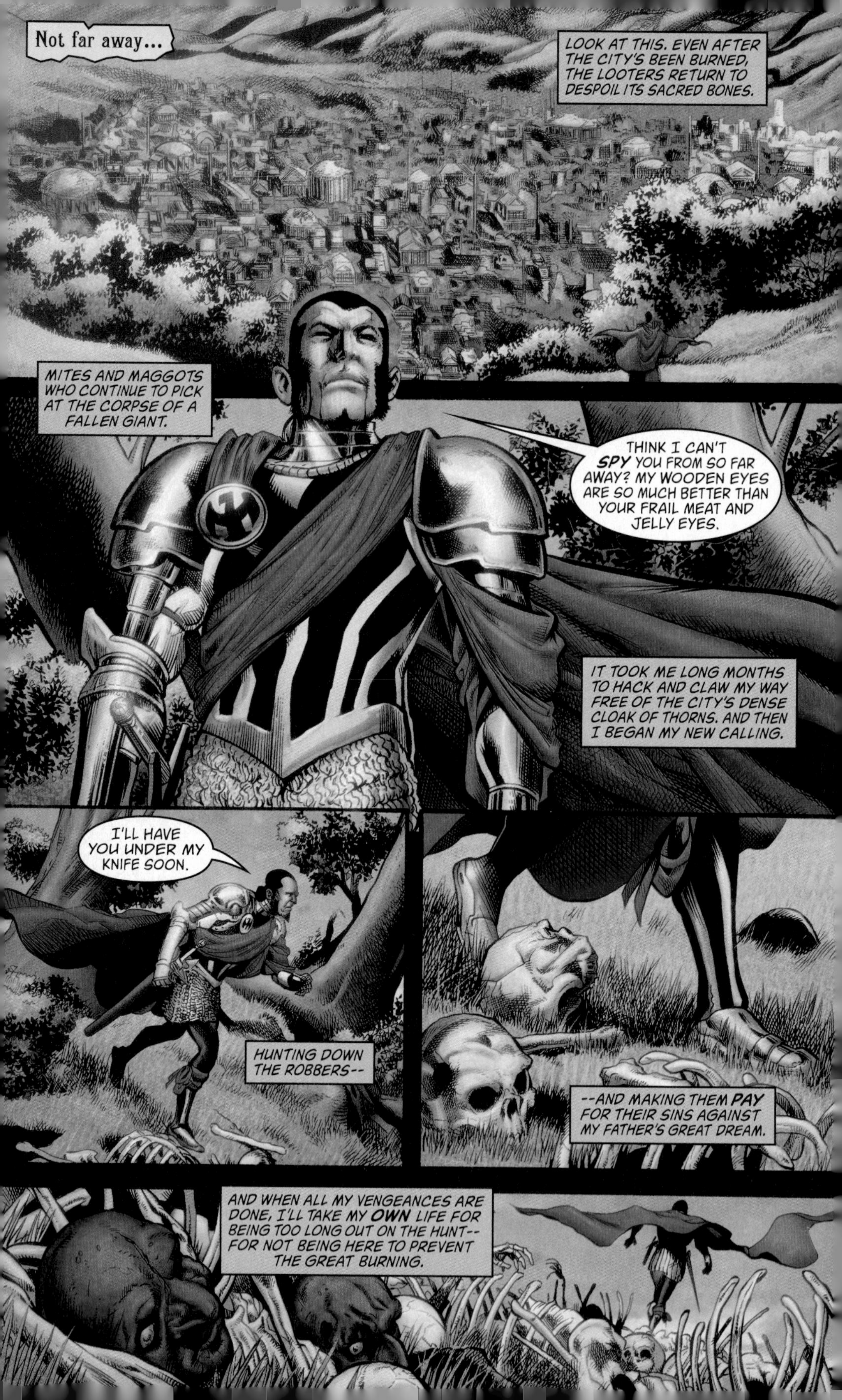
Not far away...
LOOK AT THIS. EVEN AFTER THE CITY'S BEEN BURNED, THE LOOTERS RETURN TO DESPOIL ITS SACRED BONES.
MITES AND MAGGOTS WHO CONTINUE TO PICK AT THE CORPSE OF A FALLEN GIANT.
THINK I CAN'T SPY YOU FROM SO FAR AWAY? MY WOODEN EYES ARE SO MUCH BETTER THAN YOUR FRAIL MEAT AND JELLY EYES.
IT TOOK ME LONG MONTHS TO HACK AND CLAW MY WAY FREE OF THE CITY'S DENSE CLOAK OF THORNS. AND THEN I BEGAN MY NEW CALLING.
I'LL HAVE YOU UNDER MY KNIFE SOON.
HUNTING DOWN THE ROBBERS--
--AND MAKING THEM PAY FOR THEIR SINS AGAINST MY FATHER'S GREAT DREAM.
AND WHEN ALL MY VENGEANCES ARE DONE, I'LL TAKE MY OWN LIFE FOR BEING TOO LONG OUT ON THE HUNT--FOR NOT BEING HERE TO PREVENT THE GREAT BURNING.

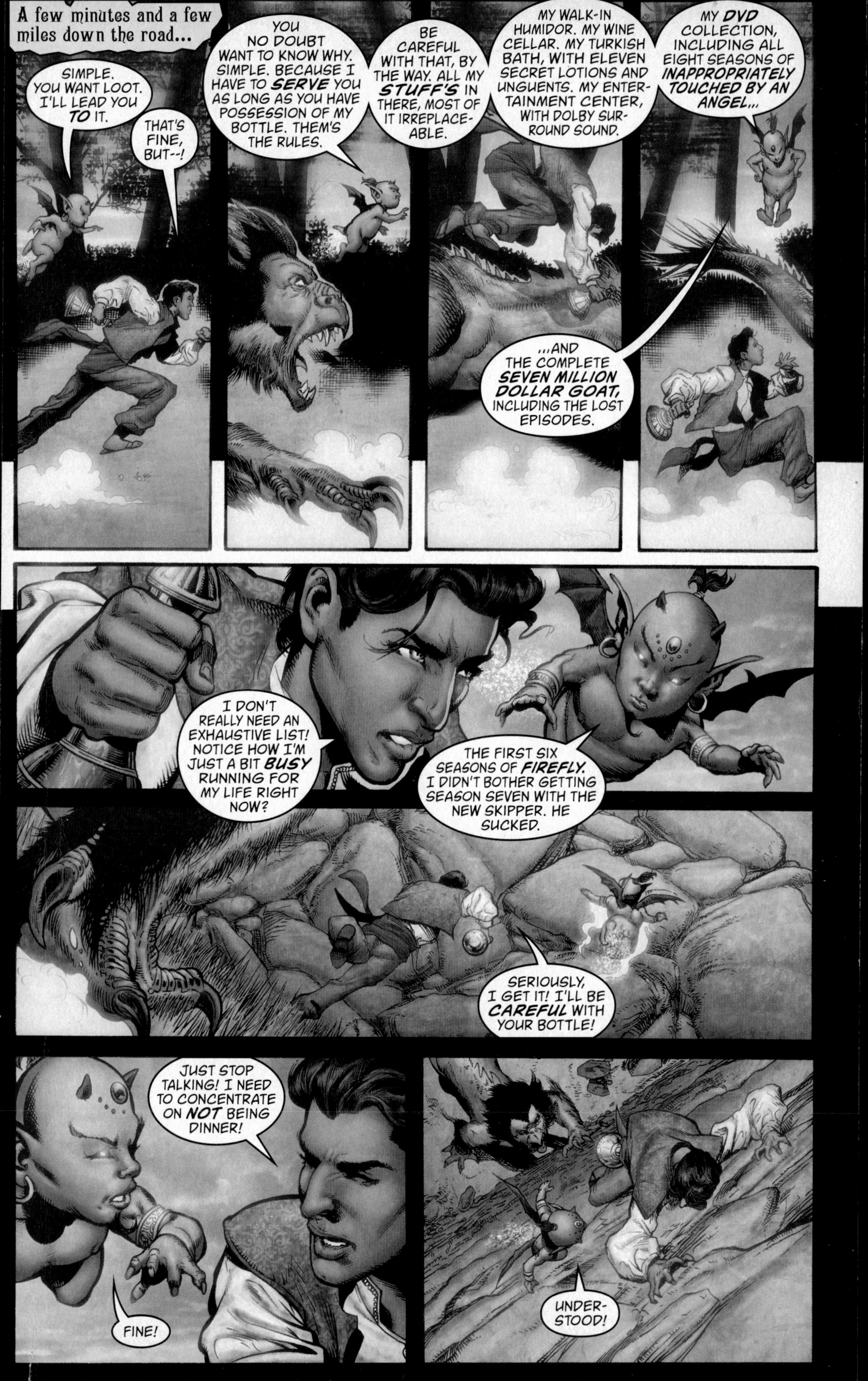
A few minutes and a few miles down the road...
SIMPLE. YOU WANT LOOT. I'LL LEAD YOU TO IT.
THAT'S FINE, BUT--!
YOU NO DOUBT WANT TO KNOW WHY. SIMPLE. BECAUSE I HAVE TO SERVE YOU AS LONG AS YOU HAVE POSSESSION OF MY BOTTLE. THEM'S THE RULES.
BE CAREFUL WITH THAT, BY THE WAY. ALL MY STUFF'S IN THERE, MOST OF IT IRREPLACE-ABLE.
MY WALK-IN HUMIDOR. MY WINE CELLAR. MY TURKISH BATH, WITH ELEVEN SECRET LOTIONS AND UNGUENTS. MY ENTER-TAINMENT CENTER, WITH DOLBY SUR-ROUND SOUND.
MY DVD COLLECTION, INCLUDING ALL EIGHT SEASONS OF INAPPROPRIATELY TOUCHED BY AN ANGEL...
...AND THE COMPLETE SEVEN MILLION DOLLAR GOAT, INCLUDING THE LOST EPISODES.
I DON'T REALLY NEED AN EXHAUSTIVE LIST! NOTICE HOW I'M JUST A BIT BUSY RUNNING FOR MY LIFE RIGHT NOW?
THE FIRST SIX SEASONS OF FIREFLY. I DIDN'T BOTHER GETTING SEASON SEVEN WITH THE NEW SKIPPER. HE SUCKED.
SERIOUSLY, I GET IT! I'LL BE CAREFUL WITH YOUR BOTTLE!
JUST STOP TALKING! I NEED TO CONCENTRATE ON NOT BEING DINNER!
FINE!
UNDER-STOOD!

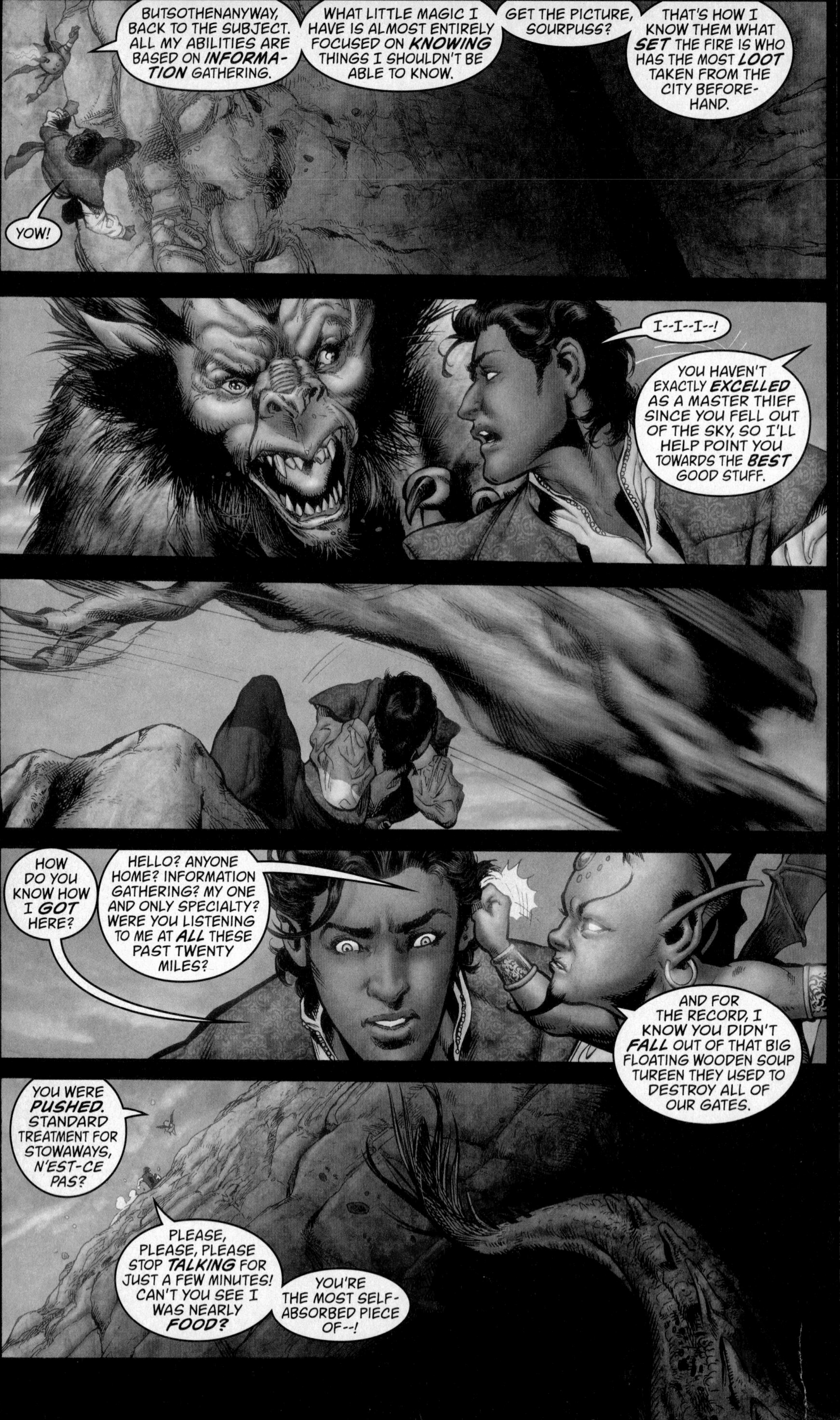

BUTSOTHENANYWAY, BACK TO THE SUBJECT. ALL MY ABILITIES ARE BASED ON INFORMATION GATHERING.
WHAT LITTLE MAGIC I HAVE IS ALMOST ENTIRELY FOCUSED ON KNOWING THINGS I SHOULDN'T BE ABLE TO KNOW.
GET THE PICTURE, SOURPUSS?
THAT'S HOW I KNOW THEM WHAT SET THE FIRE IS WHO HAS THE MOST LOOT TAKEN FROM THE CITY BEFOREHAND.
YOW!
I--I--I--!
YOU HAVEN'T EXACTLY EXCELLED AS A MASTER THIEF SINCE YOU FELL OUT OF THE SKY, SO I'LL HELP POINT YOU TOWARDS THE BEST GOOD STUFF.
HOW DO YOU KNOW HOW I GOT HERE?
HELLO? ANYONE HOME? INFORMATION GATHERING? MY ONE AND ONLY SPECIALTY? WERE YOU LISTENING TO ME AT ALL THESE PAST TWENTY MILES?
AND FOR THE RECORD, I KNOW YOU DIDN'T FALL OUT OF THAT BIG FLOATING WOODEN SOUP TUREEN THEY USED TO DESTROY ALL OF OUR GATES.
YOU WERE PUSHED. STANDARD TREATMENT FOR STOWAWAYS, N'EST-CE PAS?
PLEASE, PLEASE, PLEASE STOP TALKING FOR JUST A FEW MINUTES! CAN'T YOU SEE I WAS NEARLY FOOD?
YOU'RE THE MOST SELF-ABSORBED PIECE OF--!

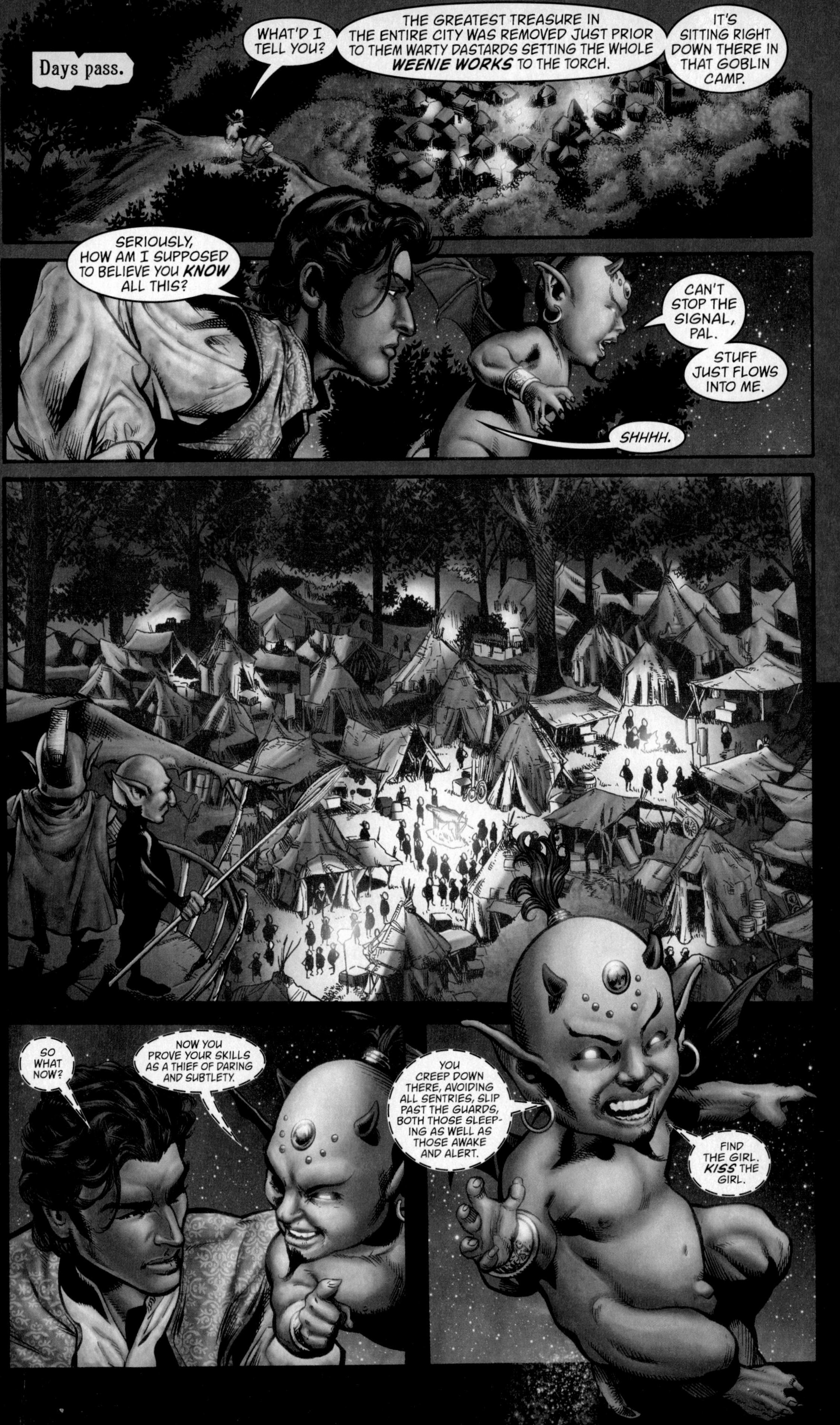
Days pass.
WHAT'D I TELL YOU?
THE GREATEST TREASURE IN THE ENTIRE CITY WAS REMOVED JUST PRIOR TO THEM WARTY DASTARDS SETTING THE WHOLE WEENIE WORKS TO THE TORCH.
IT'S SITTING RIGHT DOWN THERE IN THAT GOBLIN CAMP.
SERIOUSLY, HOW AM I SUPPOSED TO BELIEVE YOU KNOW ALL THIS?
CAN'T STOP THE SIGNAL, PAL.
STUFF JUST FLOWS INTO ME.
SHHHH.
SO WHAT NOW?
NOW YOU PROVE YOUR SKILLS AS A THIEF OF DARING AND SUBTLETY.
YOU CREEP DOWN THERE, AVOIDING ALL SENTRIES, SLIP PAST THE GUARDS, BOTH THOSE SLEEPING AS WELL AS THOSE AWAKE AND ALERT.
FIND THE GIRL. KISS THE GIRL.

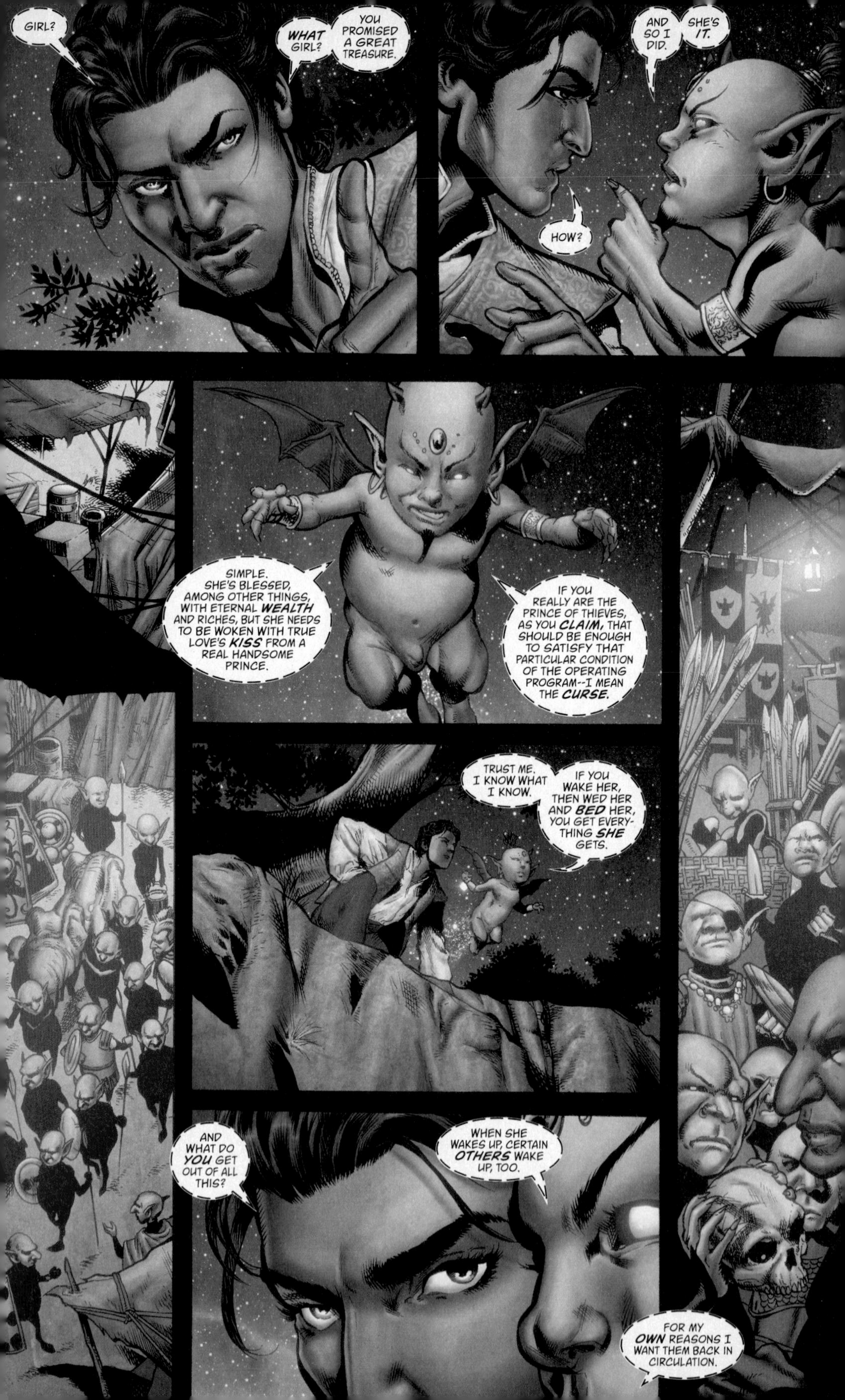
GIRL?
WHAT GIRL?
YOU PROMISED A GREAT TREASURE.
AND SO I DID.
SHE'S IT.
HOW?
SIMPLE. SHE'S BLESSED, AMONG OTHER THINGS, WITH ETERNAL WEALTH AND RICHES, BUT SHE NEEDS TO BE WOKEN WITH TRUE LOVE'S KISS FROM A REAL HANDSOME PRINCE.
IF YOU REALLY ARE THE PRINCE OF THIEVES, AS YOU CLAIM, THAT SHOULD BE ENOUGH TO SATISFY THAT PARTICULAR CONDITION OF THE OPERATING PROGRAM--I MEAN THE CURSE.
TRUST ME. I KNOW WHAT I KNOW.
IF YOU WAKE HER, THEN WED HER AND BED HER, YOU GET EVERY-THING SHE GETS.
AND WHAT DO YOU GET OUT OF ALL THIS?
WHEN SHE WAKES UP, CERTAIN OTHERS WAKE UP, TOO.
FOR MY OWN REASONS I WANT THEM BACK IN CIRCULATION.

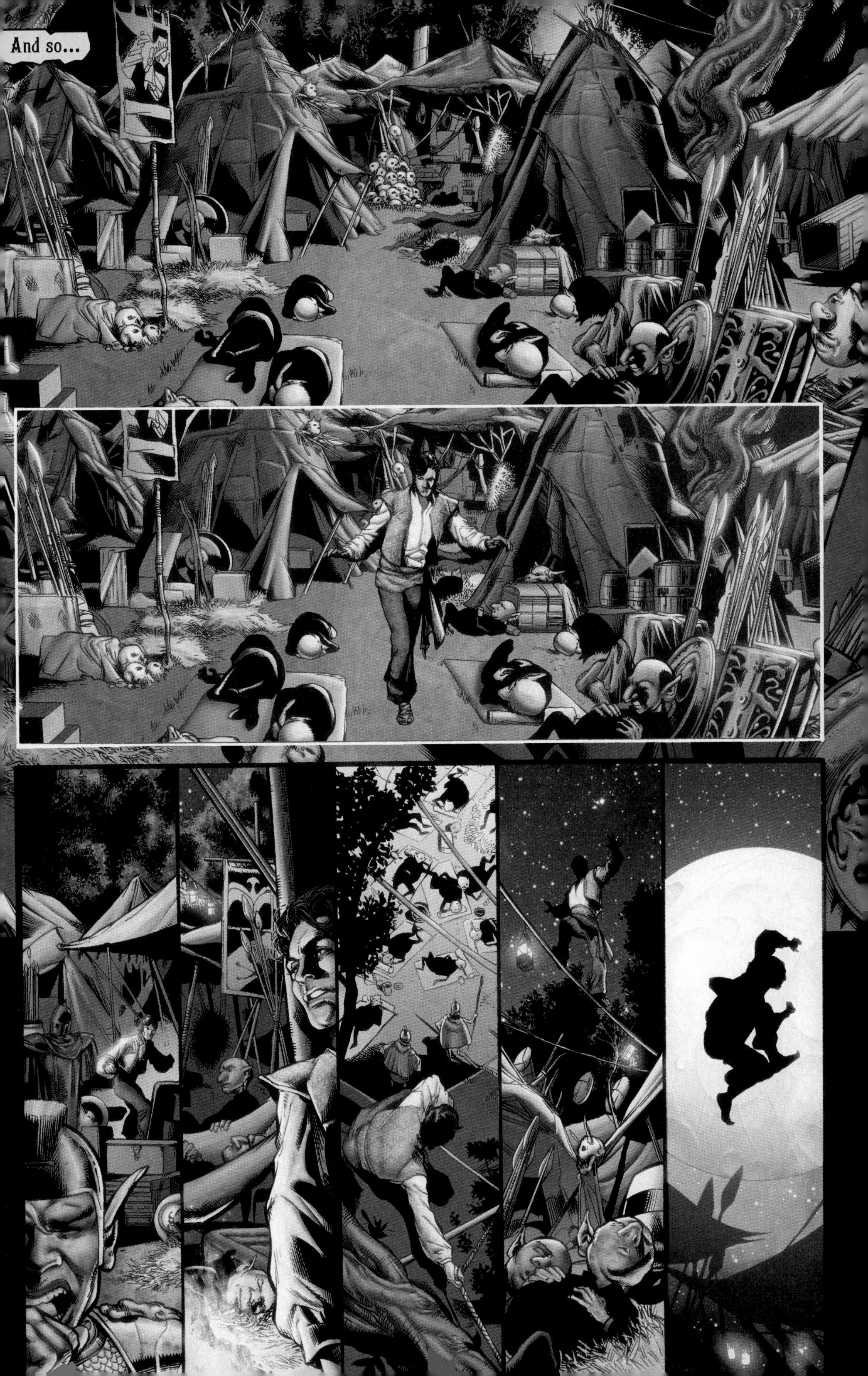
And so...

I FOLLOWED THE RAGAMUFFIN THIEF AND HIS BOTTLE IMP SERVANT FOR DAYS, HOPING THEY MIGHT LEAD ME TO MORE OF THEIR KIND.

MY PATIENCE AND FORBEARANCE PAID OFF HANDSOMELY. THEY BROUGHT ME DIRECTLY TO THE ENCAMPMENT OF THOSE WHO BURNED THE IMPERIAL CITY.

THIS MEAT BOY HAD SKILLS. HE'S SLY AND STEALTHY, ALMOST ADMIRABLE IN HIS ABILITY TO SLIP PAST THE GOBLINS. BUT HE'S NO SON OF THE SACRED GROVE.

THERE IS NO STEALTH LIKE THAT OF WOODKIND. WE BREATHE NOT. WE NEITHER STUMBLE NOR FALTER. PROVIDED OUR MAINTENANCE REGIMEN IS KEPT UP, OUR JOINTS SQUEAK NOT.

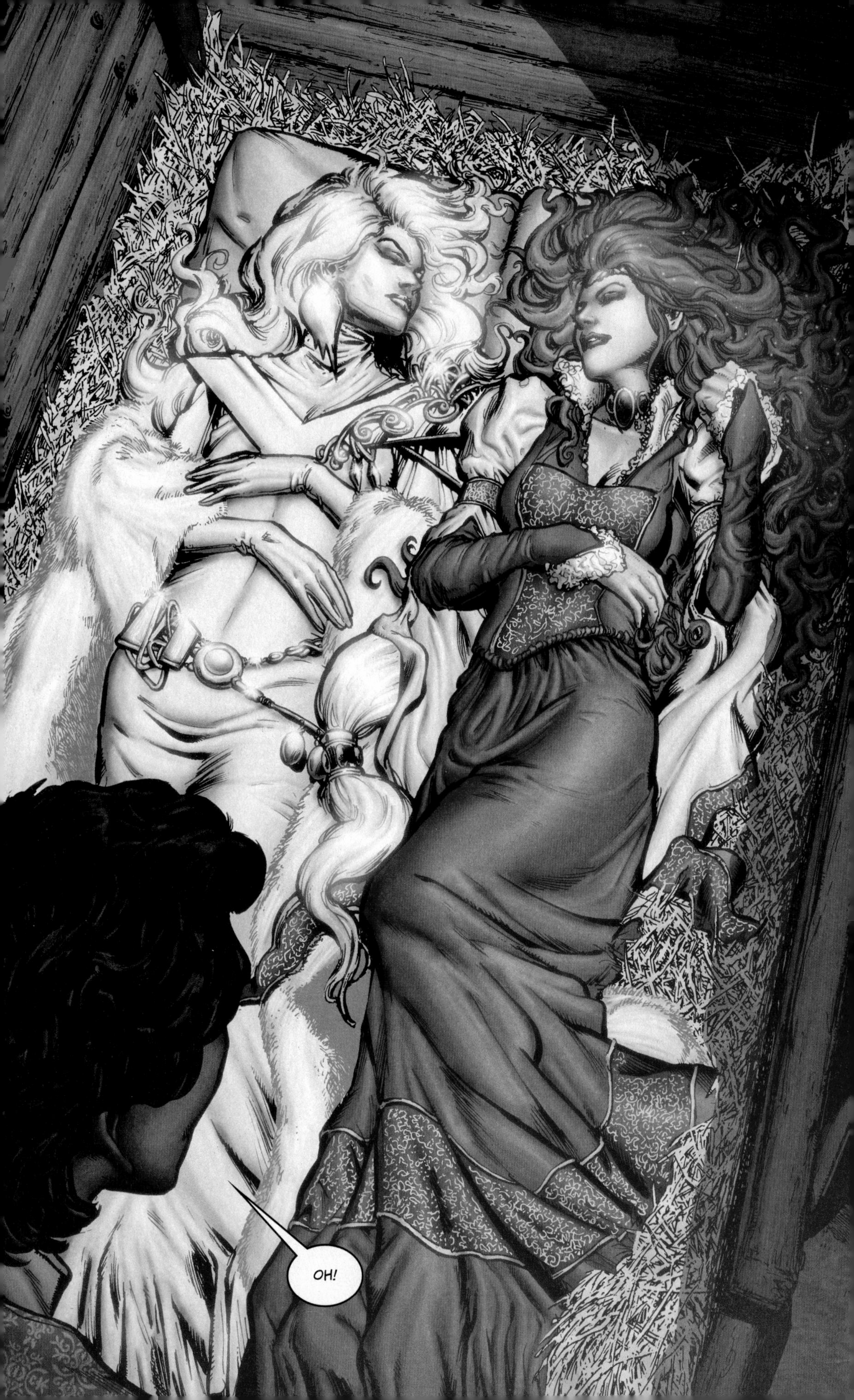
OH!

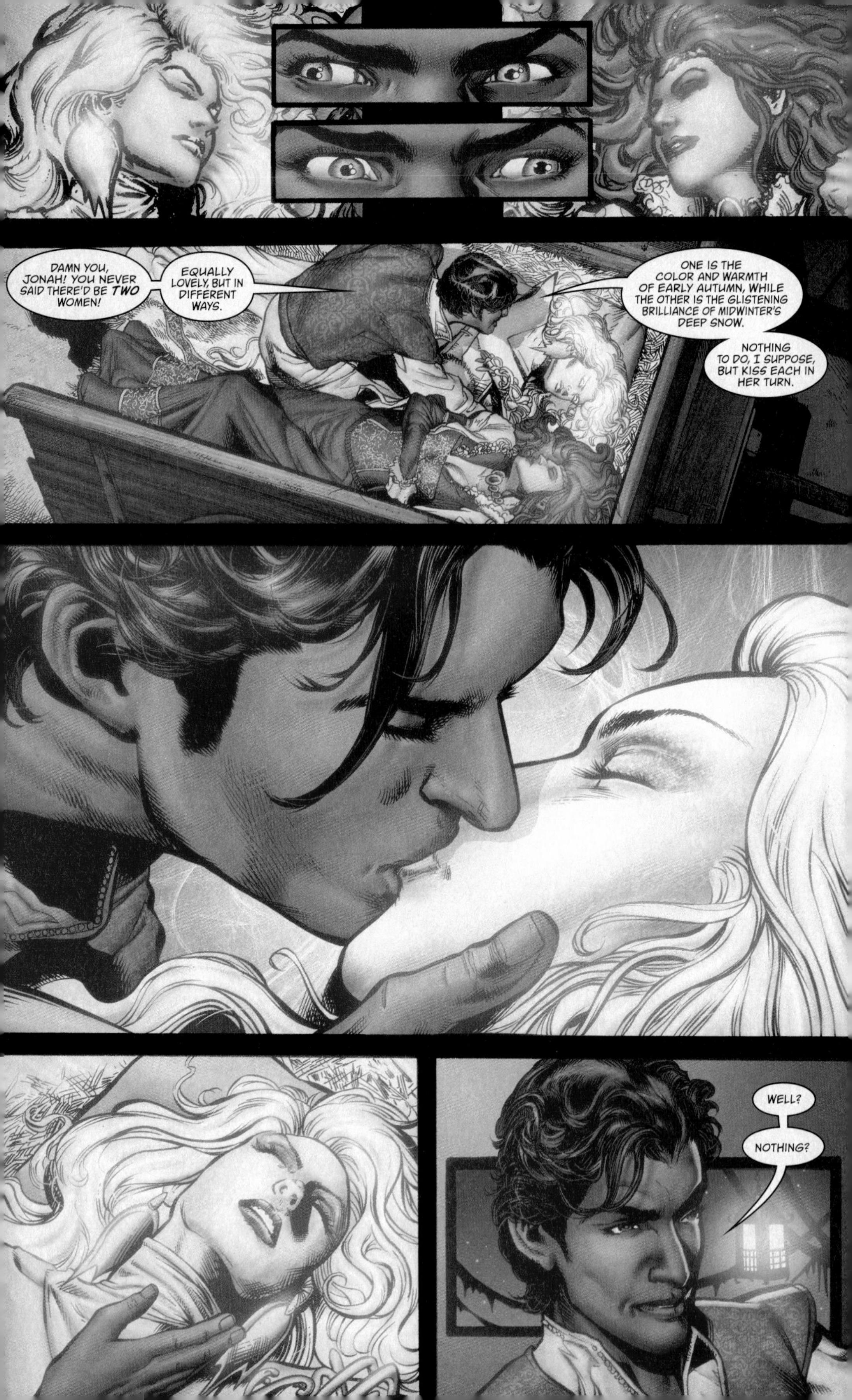
DAMN YOU, JONAH! YOU NEVER SAID THERE'D BE **TWO** WOMEN!
EQUALLY LOVELY, BUT IN DIFFERENT WAYS.
ONE IS THE COLOR AND WARMTH OF EARLY AUTUMN, WHILE THE OTHER IS THE GLISTENING BRILLIANCE OF MIDWINTER'S DEEP SNOW.
NOTHING TO DO, I SUPPOSE, BUT KISS EACH IN HER TURN.
WELL?
NOTHING?

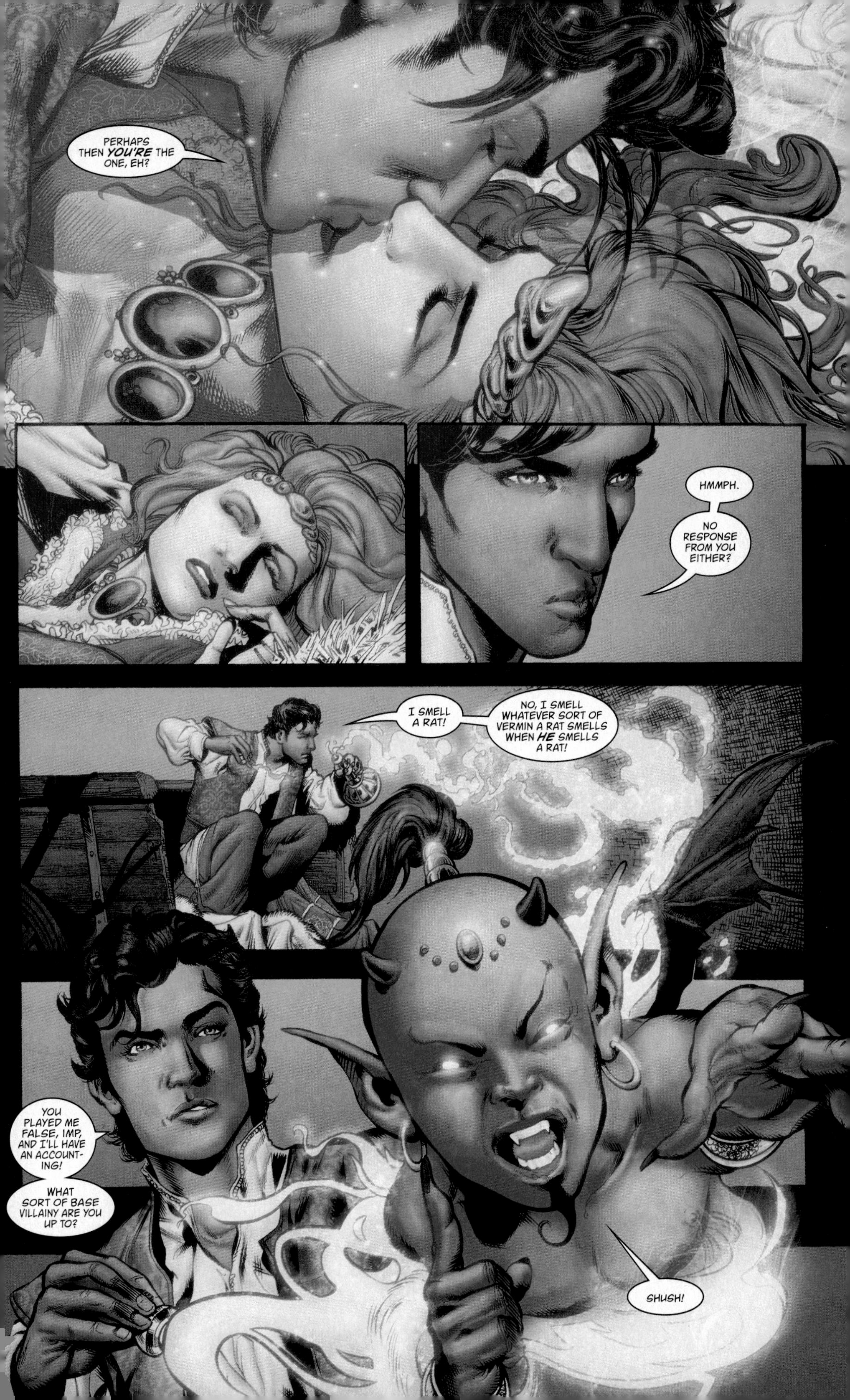
PERHAPS THEN *YOU'RE* THE ONE, EH?
HMMPH.
NO RESPONSE FROM YOU EITHER?
I SMELL A RAT!
NO, I SMELL WHATEVER SORT OF VERMIN A RAT SMELLS WHEN *HE* SMELLS A RAT!
YOU PLAYED ME FALSE, IMP, AND I'LL HAVE AN ACCOUNTING!
WHAT SORT OF BASE VILLAINY ARE YOU UP TO?
SHUSH!

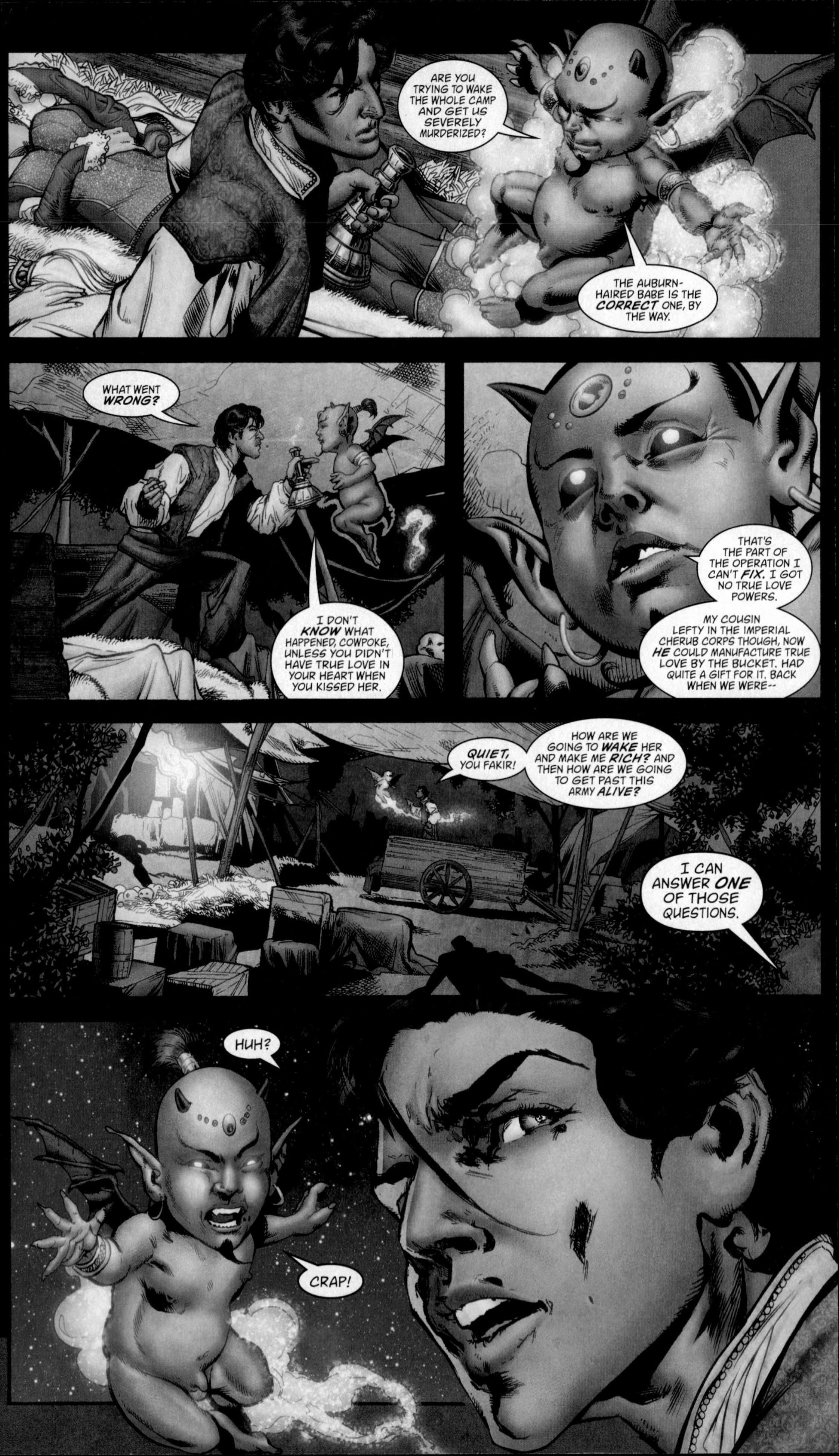
ARE YOU TRYING TO WAKE THE WHOLE CAMP AND GET US SEVERELY MURDERIZED?
THE AUBURN-HAIRED BABE IS THE CORRECT ONE, BY THE WAY.
WHAT WENT WRONG?
I DON'T KNOW WHAT HAPPENED, COWPOKE, UNLESS YOU DIDN'T HAVE TRUE LOVE IN YOUR HEART WHEN YOU KISSED HER.
THAT'S THE PART OF THE OPERATION I CAN'T FIX. I GOT NO TRUE LOVE POWERS.
MY COUSIN LEFTY IN THE IMPERIAL CHERUB CORPS THOUGH, NOW HE COULD MANUFACTURE TRUE LOVE BY THE BUCKET. HAD QUITE A GIFT FOR IT. BACK WHEN WE WERE--
QUIET, YOU FAKIR!
HOW ARE WE GOING TO WAKE HER AND MAKE ME RICH? AND THEN HOW ARE WE GOING TO GET PAST THIS ARMY ALIVE?
I CAN ANSWER ONE OF THOSE QUESTIONS.
HUH?
CRAP!

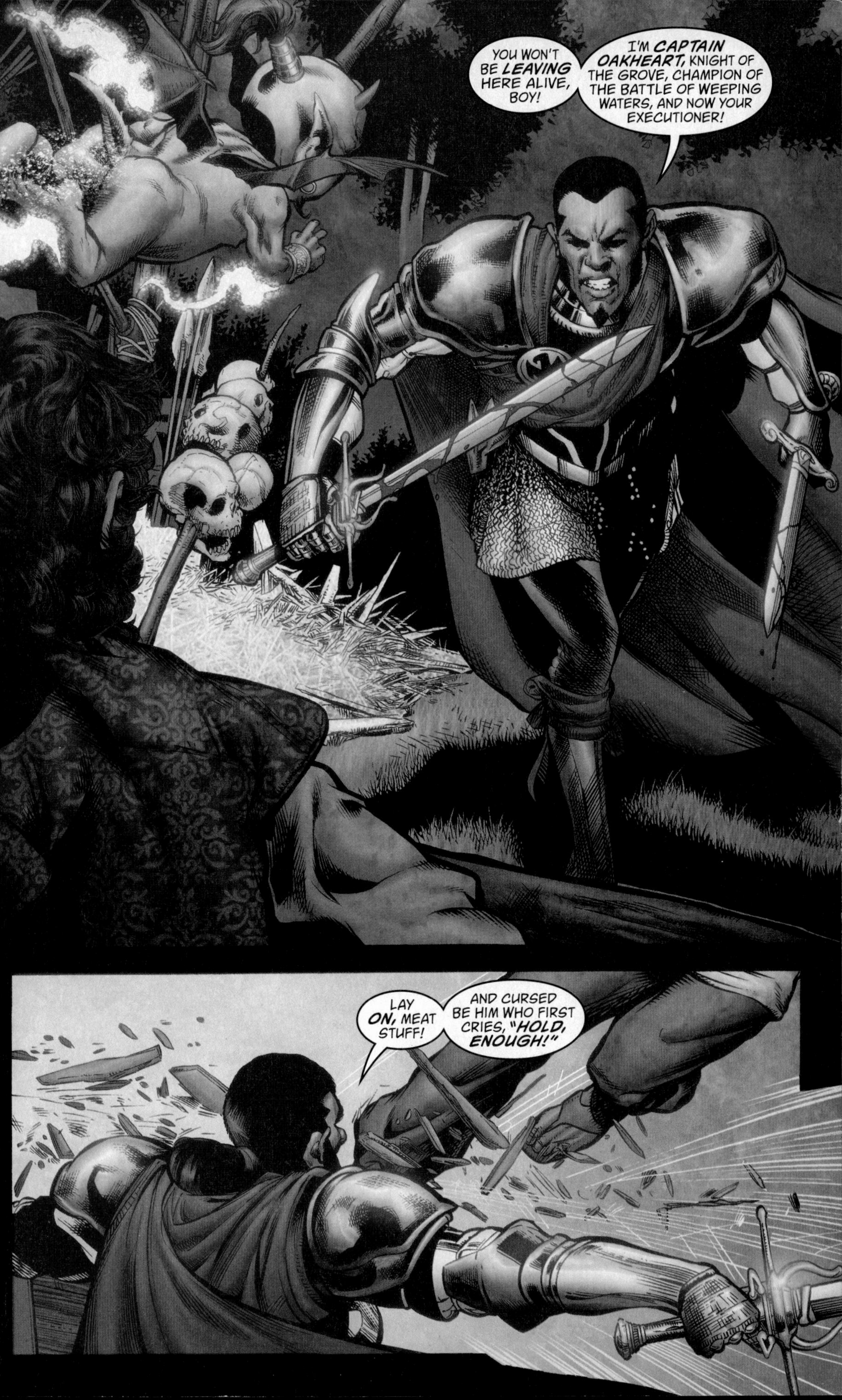
YOU WON'T BE LEAVING HERE ALIVE, BOY!
I'M CAPTAIN OAKHEART, KNIGHT OF THE GROVE, CHAMPION OF THE BATTLE OF WEEPING WATERS, AND NOW YOUR EXECUTIONER!
LAY ON, MEAT STUFF!
AND CURSED BE HIM WHO FIRST CRIES, "HOLD, ENOUGH!"

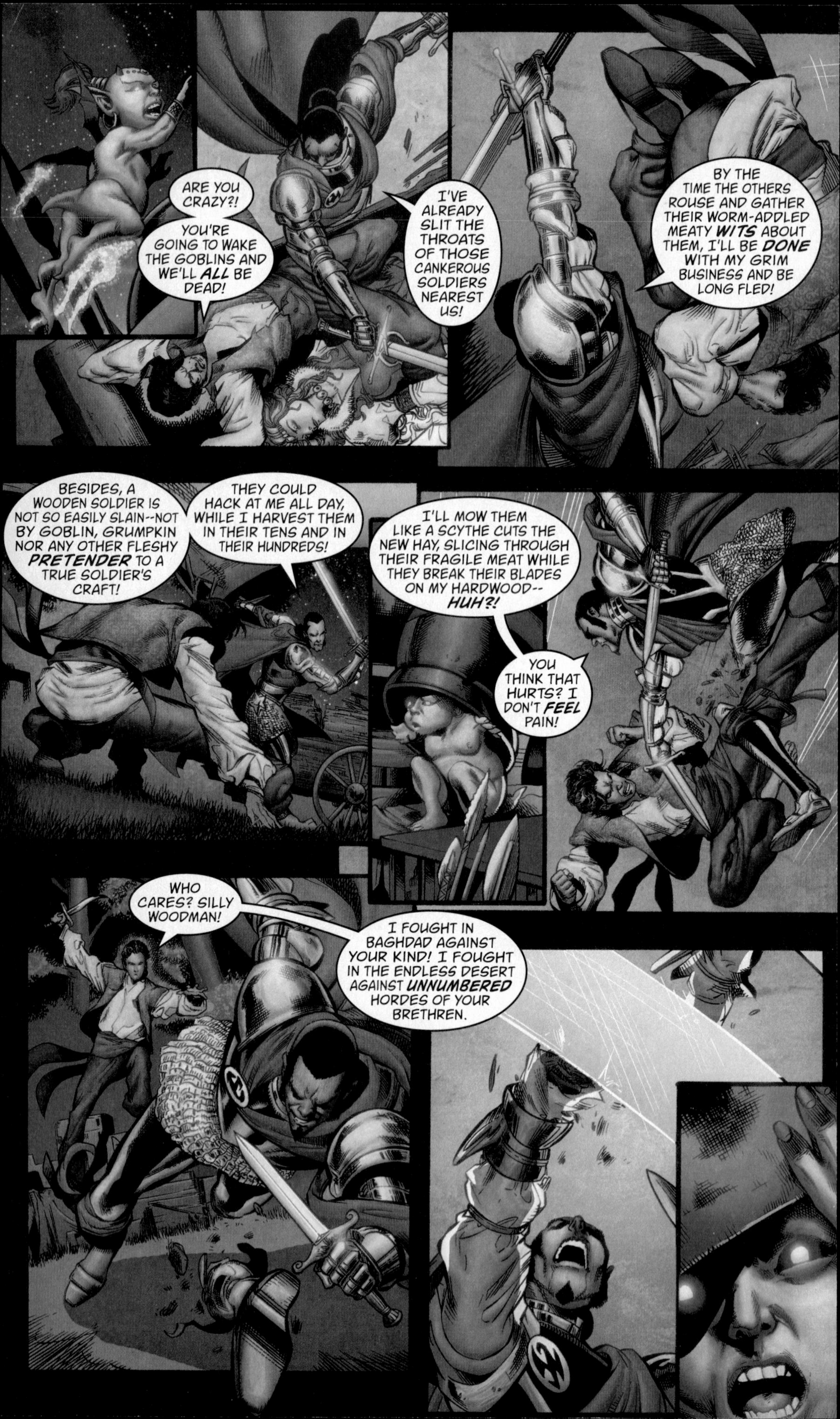
ARE YOU CRAZY?!
YOU'RE GOING TO WAKE THE GOBLINS AND WE'LL ALL BE DEAD!
I'VE ALREADY SLIT THE THROATS OF THOSE CANKEROUS SOLDIERS NEAREST US!
BY THE TIME THE OTHERS ROUSE AND GATHER THEIR WORM-ADDLED MEATY WITS ABOUT THEM, I'LL BE DONE WITH MY GRIM BUSINESS AND BE LONG FLED!
BESIDES, A WOODEN SOLDIER IS NOT SO EASILY SLAIN--NOT BY GOBLIN, GRUMPKIN NOR ANY OTHER FLESHY PRETENDER TO A TRUE SOLDIER'S CRAFT!
THEY COULD HACK AT ME ALL DAY, WHILE I HARVEST THEM IN THEIR TENS AND IN THEIR HUNDREDS!
I'LL MOW THEM LIKE A SCYTHE CUTS THE NEW HAY, SLICING THROUGH THEIR FRAGILE MEAT WHILE THEY BREAK THEIR BLADES ON MY HARDWOOD-- HUH?!
YOU THINK THAT HURTS? I DON'T FEEL PAIN!
WHO CARES? SILLY WOODMAN!
I FOUGHT IN BAGHDAD AGAINST YOUR KIND! I FOUGHT IN THE ENDLESS DESERT AGAINST UNNUMBERED HORDES OF YOUR BRETHREN.

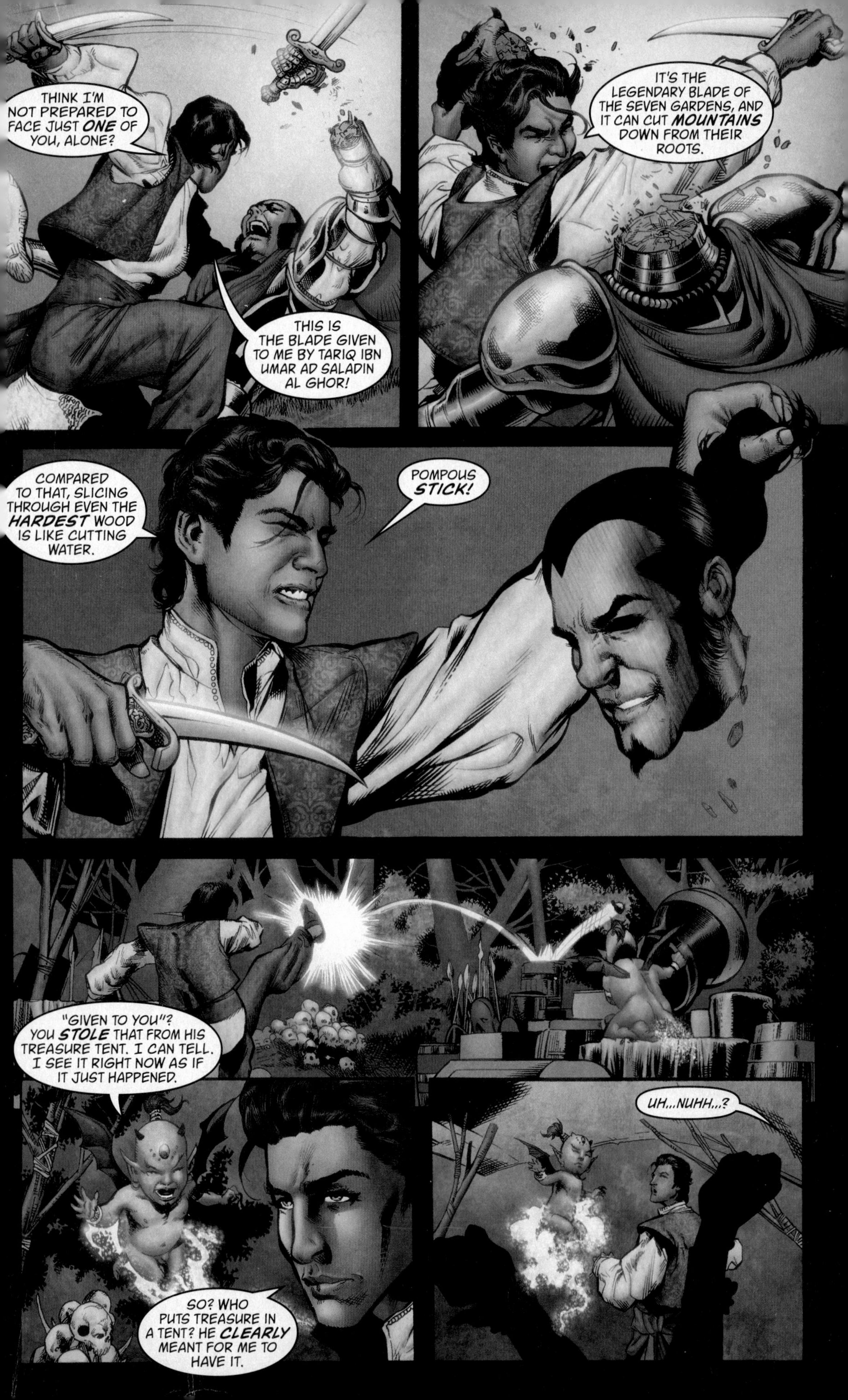
THINK I'M NOT PREPARED TO FACE JUST ONE OF YOU, ALONE?
THIS IS THE BLADE GIVEN TO ME BY TARIQ IBN UMAR AD SALADIN AL GHOR!
IT'S THE LEGENDARY BLADE OF THE SEVEN GARDENS, AND IT CAN CUT MOUNTAINS DOWN FROM THEIR ROOTS.
COMPARED TO THAT, SLICING THROUGH EVEN THE HARDEST WOOD IS LIKE CUTTING WATER.
POMPOUS STICK!
"GIVEN TO YOU"? YOU STOLE THAT FROM HIS TREASURE TENT. I CAN TELL. I SEE IT RIGHT NOW AS IF IT JUST HAPPENED.
SO? WHO PUTS TREASURE IN A TENT? HE CLEARLY MEANT FOR ME TO HAVE IT.
UH...NUHH...?

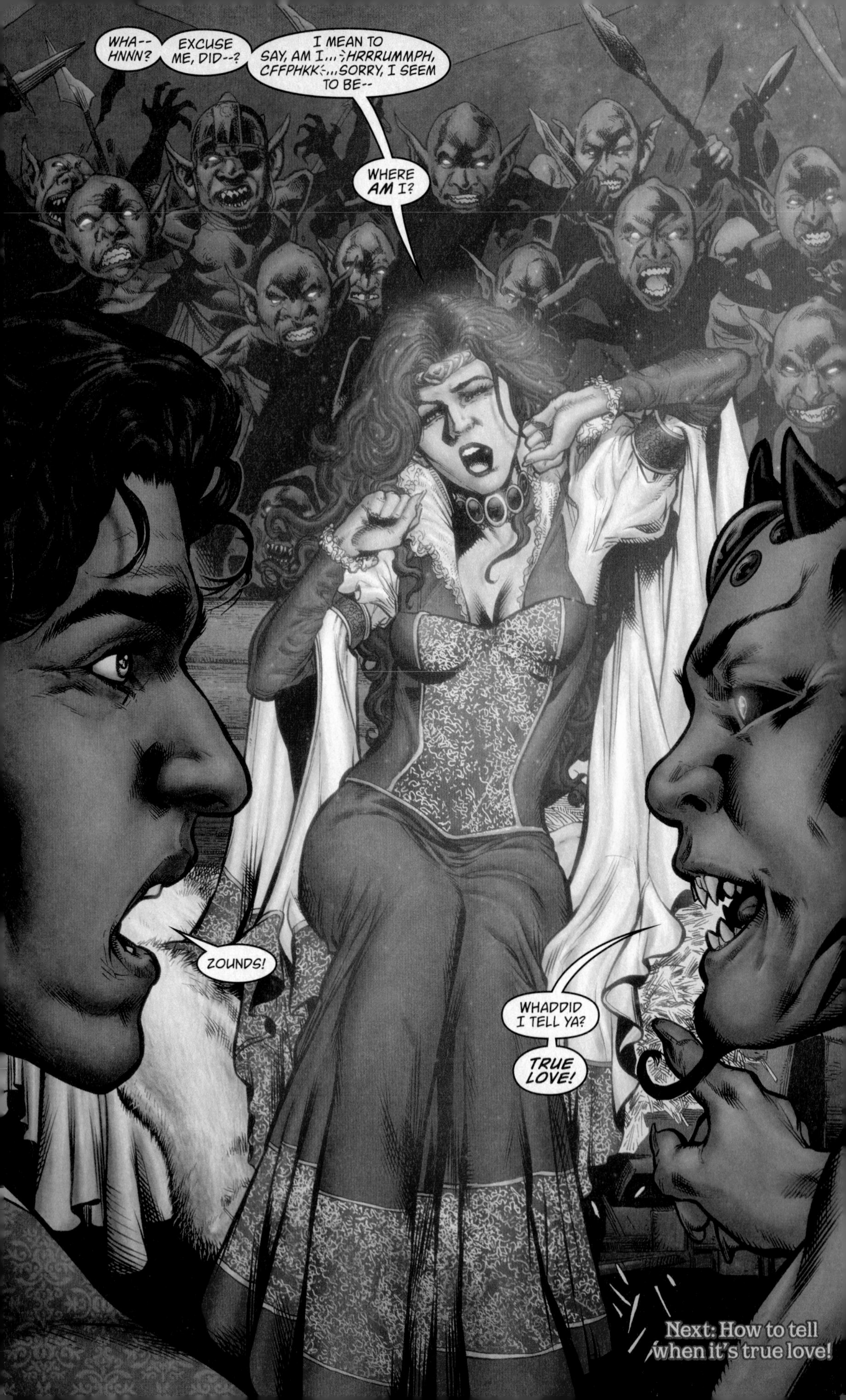
WHA-- HNNN?
EXCUSE ME, DID--?
I MEAN TO SAY, AM I... HRRRUMMPH, CFFPHKK... SORRY, I SEEM TO BE--
WHERE *AM* I?
ZOUNDS!
WHADDID I TELL YA?
TRUE LOVE!
Next: How to tell when it's true love!

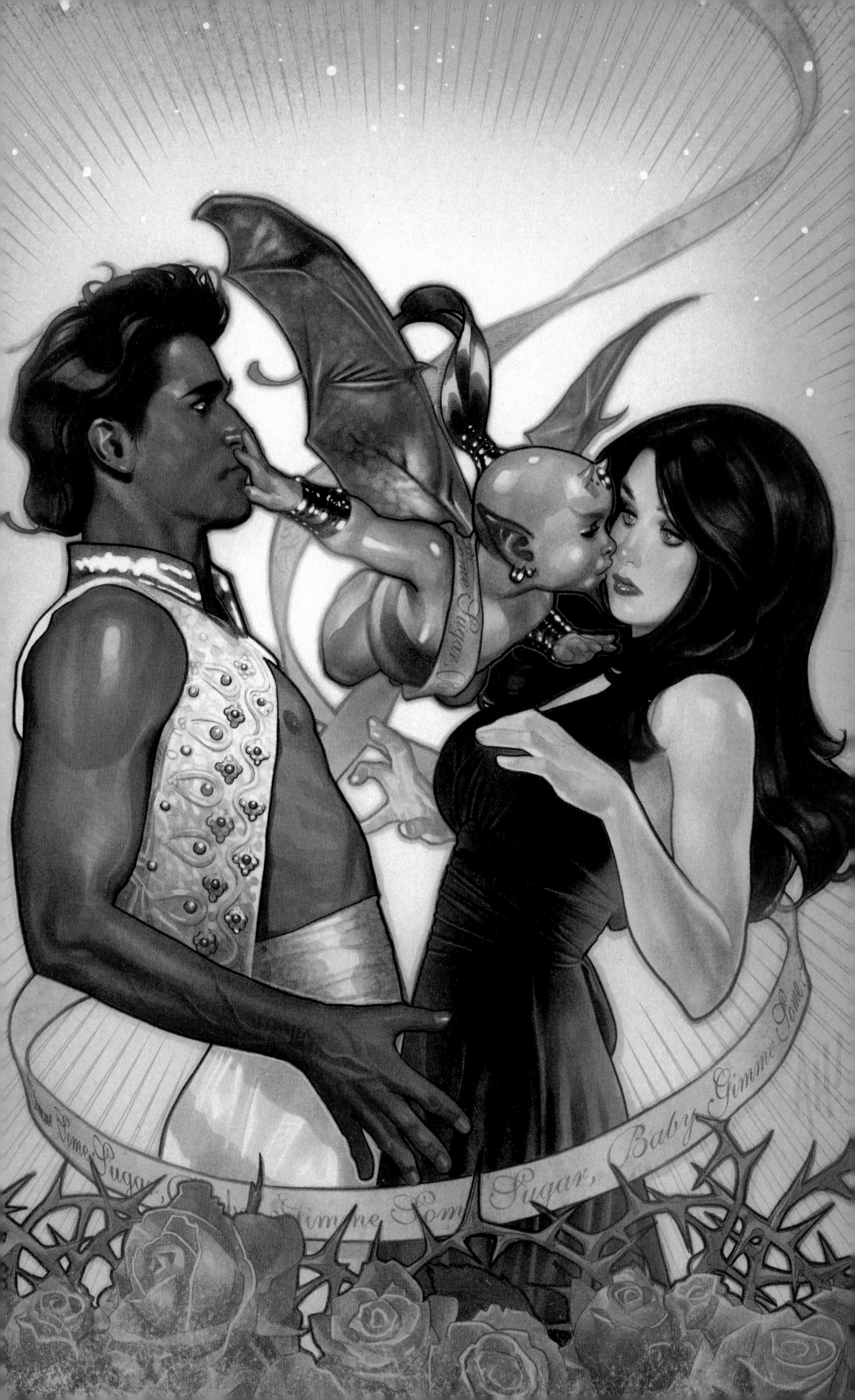
Gimme Some Sugar,
Sugar, Baby Gimme Some

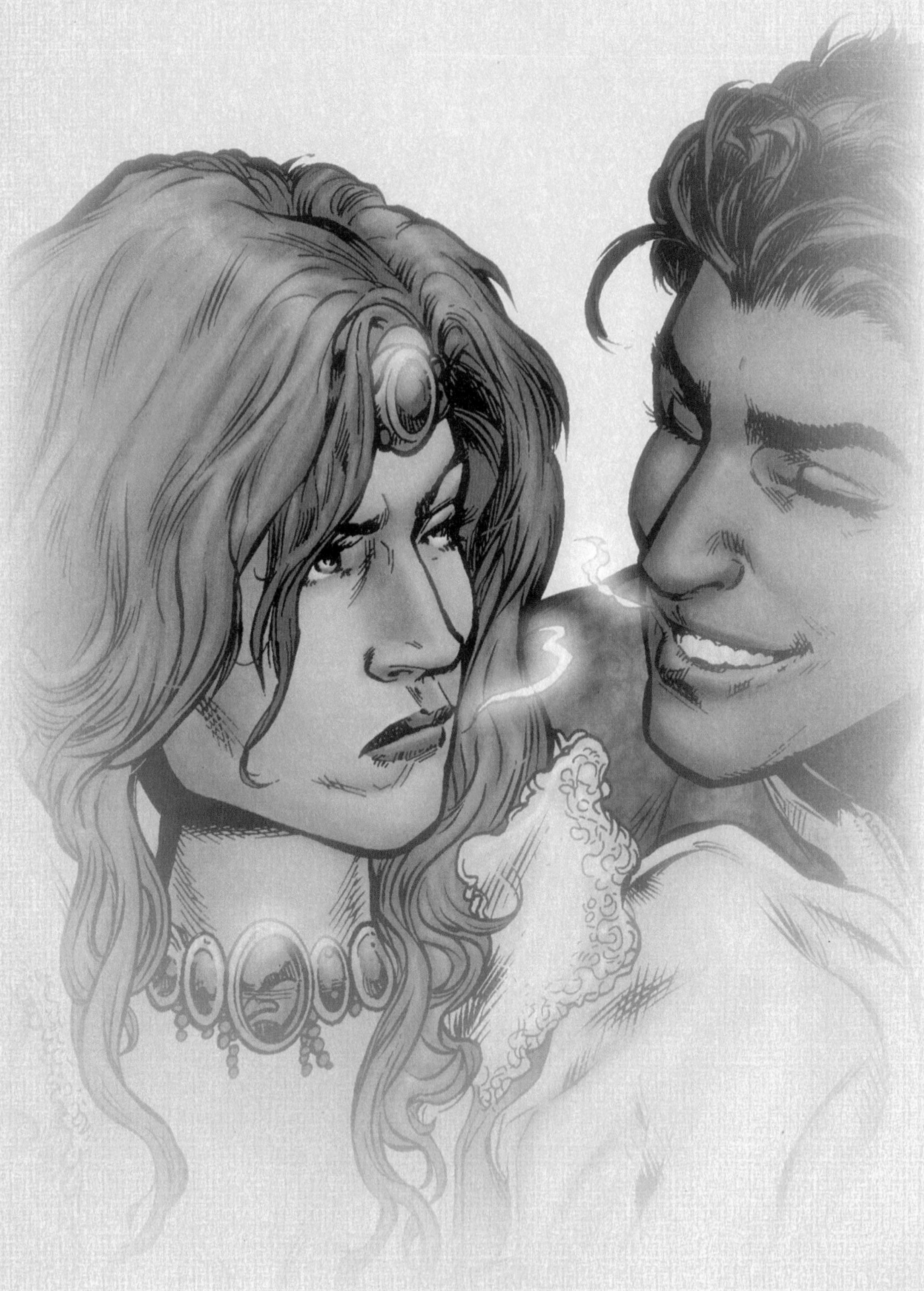

"Don't get fresh."

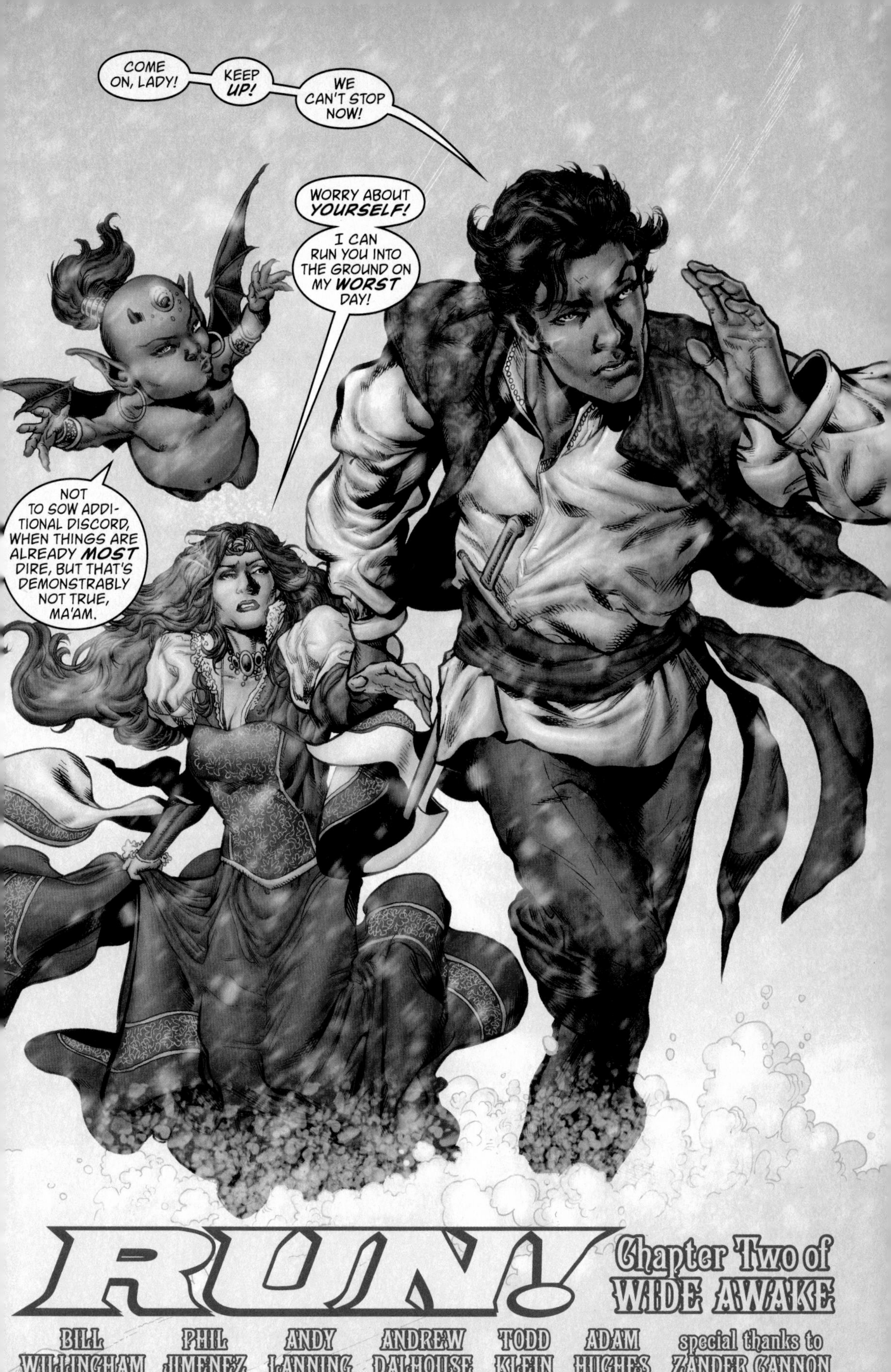
COME ON, LADY!
KEEP UP!
WE CAN'T STOP NOW!
WORRY ABOUT YOURSELF!
I CAN RUN YOU INTO THE GROUND ON MY WORST DAY!
NOT TO SOW ADDI-TIONAL DISCORD, WHEN THINGS ARE ALREADY MOST DIRE, BUT THAT'S DEMONSTRABLY NOT TRUE, MA'AM.

RUN!

Chapter Two of WIDE AWAKE

BILL WILLINGHAM writer
PHIL JIMENEZ pencils
ANDY LANNING inks
ANDREW DALHOUSE colors
TODD KLEIN letters
ADAM HUGHES cover
special thanks to ZANDER CANNON

GREGORY LOCKARD asst. ed. SHELLY BOND editor FAIREST is created by Bill Willingham

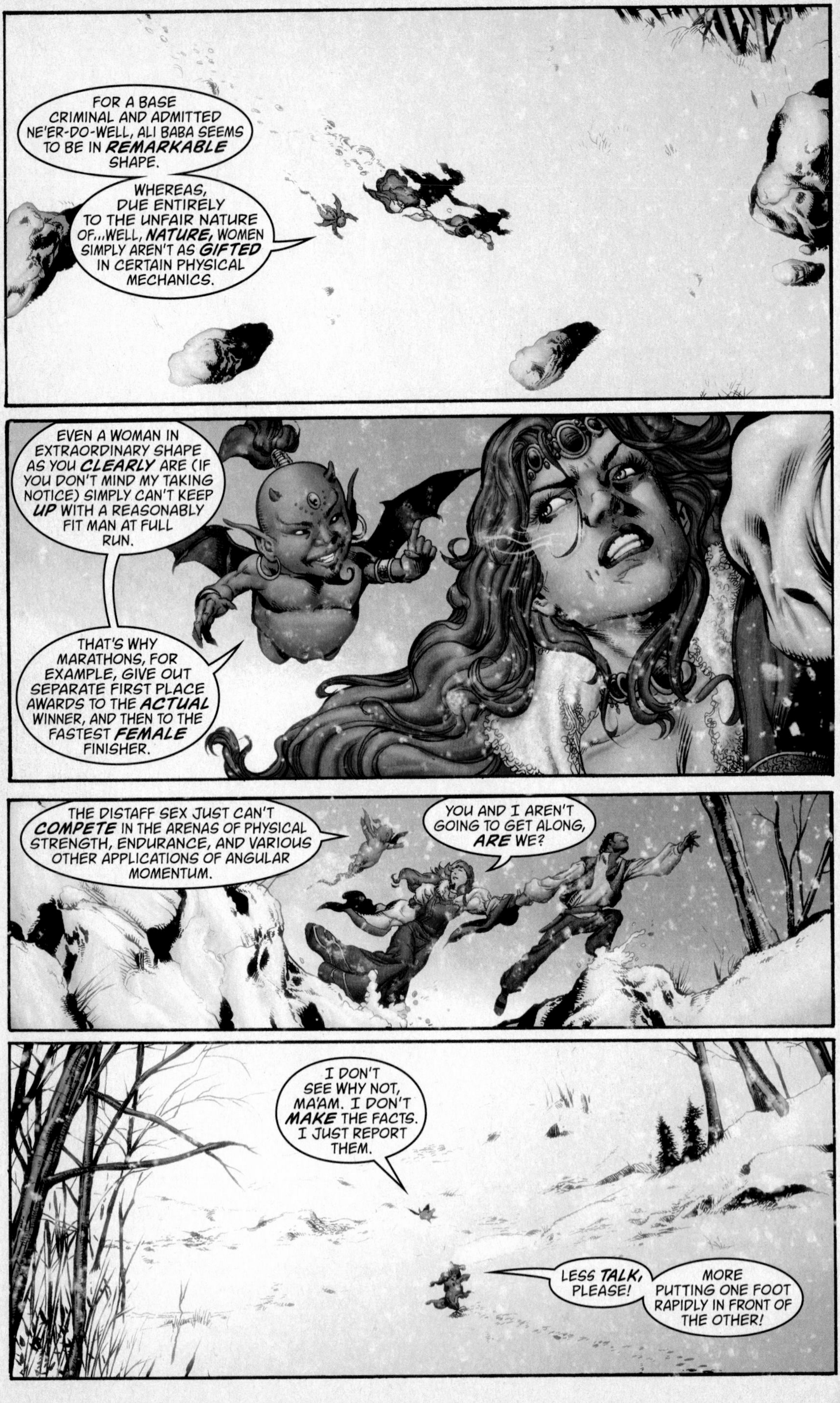
FOR A BASE CRIMINAL AND ADMITTED NE'ER-DO-WELL, ALI BABA SEEMS TO BE IN REMARKABLE SHAPE.
WHEREAS, DUE ENTIRELY TO THE UNFAIR NATURE OF...WELL, NATURE, WOMEN SIMPLY AREN'T AS GIFTED IN CERTAIN PHYSICAL MECHANICS.
EVEN A WOMAN IN EXTRAORDINARY SHAPE AS YOU CLEARLY ARE (IF YOU DON'T MIND MY TAKING NOTICE) SIMPLY CAN'T KEEP UP WITH A REASONABLY FIT MAN AT FULL RUN.
THAT'S WHY MARATHONS, FOR EXAMPLE, GIVE OUT SEPARATE FIRST PLACE AWARDS TO THE ACTUAL WINNER, AND THEN TO THE FASTEST FEMALE FINISHER.
THE DISTAFF SEX JUST CAN'T COMPETE IN THE ARENAS OF PHYSICAL STRENGTH, ENDURANCE, AND VARIOUS OTHER APPLICATIONS OF ANGULAR MOMENTUM.
YOU AND I AREN'T GOING TO GET ALONG, ARE WE?
I DON'T SEE WHY NOT, MA'AM. I DON'T MAKE THE FACTS. I JUST REPORT THEM.
LESS TALK, PLEASE!
MORE PUTTING ONE FOOT RAPIDLY IN FRONT OF THE OTHER!

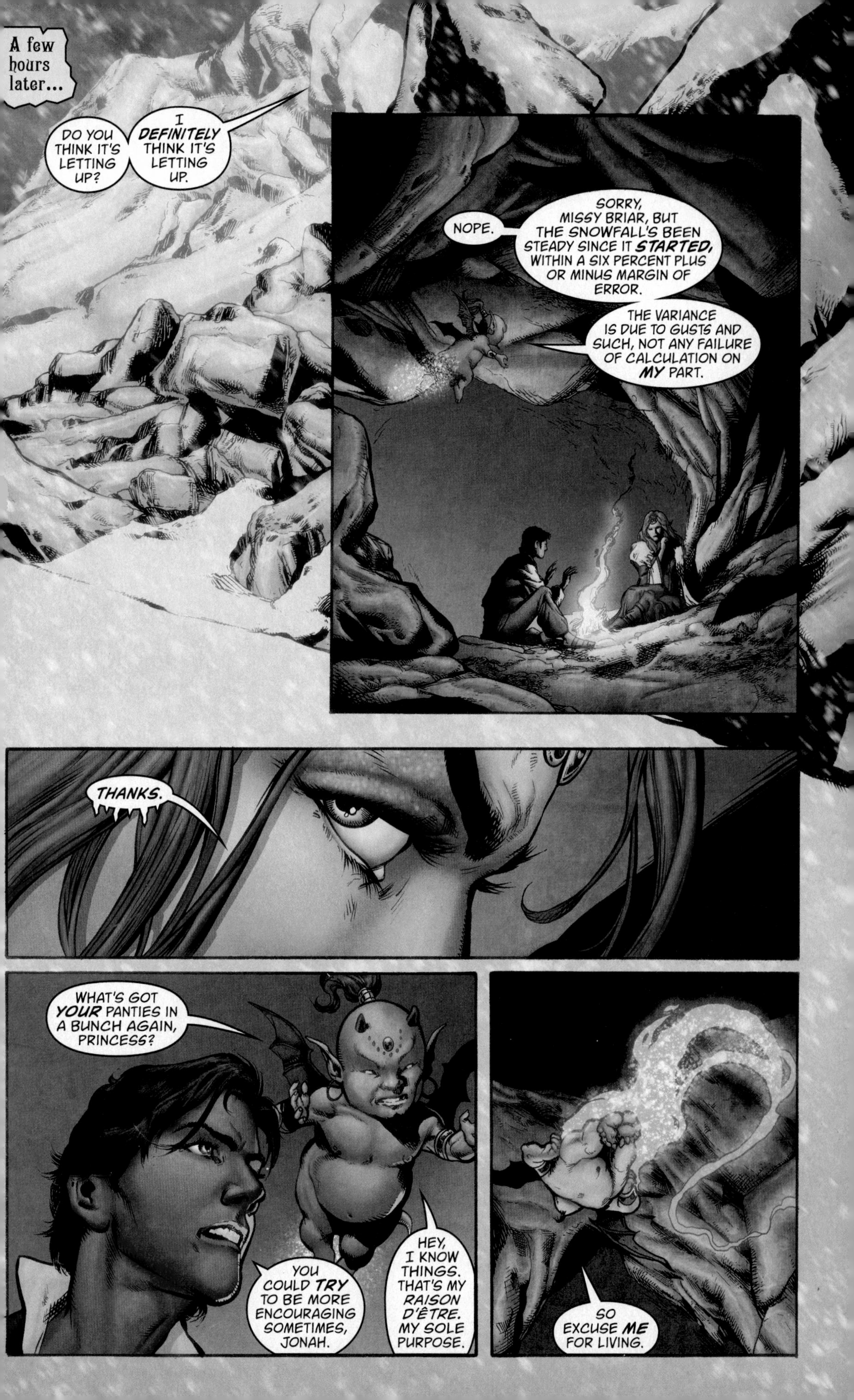
A few hours later...
DO YOU THINK IT'S LETTING UP?
I DEFINITELY THINK IT'S LETTING UP.
NOPE.
SORRY, MISSY BRIAR, BUT THE SNOWFALL'S BEEN STEADY SINCE IT STARTED, WITHIN A SIX PERCENT PLUS OR MINUS MARGIN OF ERROR.
THE VARIANCE IS DUE TO GUSTS AND SUCH, NOT ANY FAILURE OF CALCULATION ON MY PART.
THANKS.
WHAT'S GOT YOUR PANTIES IN A BUNCH AGAIN, PRINCESS?
YOU COULD TRY TO BE MORE ENCOURAGING SOMETIMES, JONAH.
HEY, I KNOW THINGS. THAT'S MY RAISON D'ÊTRE. MY SOLE PURPOSE.
SO EXCUSE ME FOR LIVING.

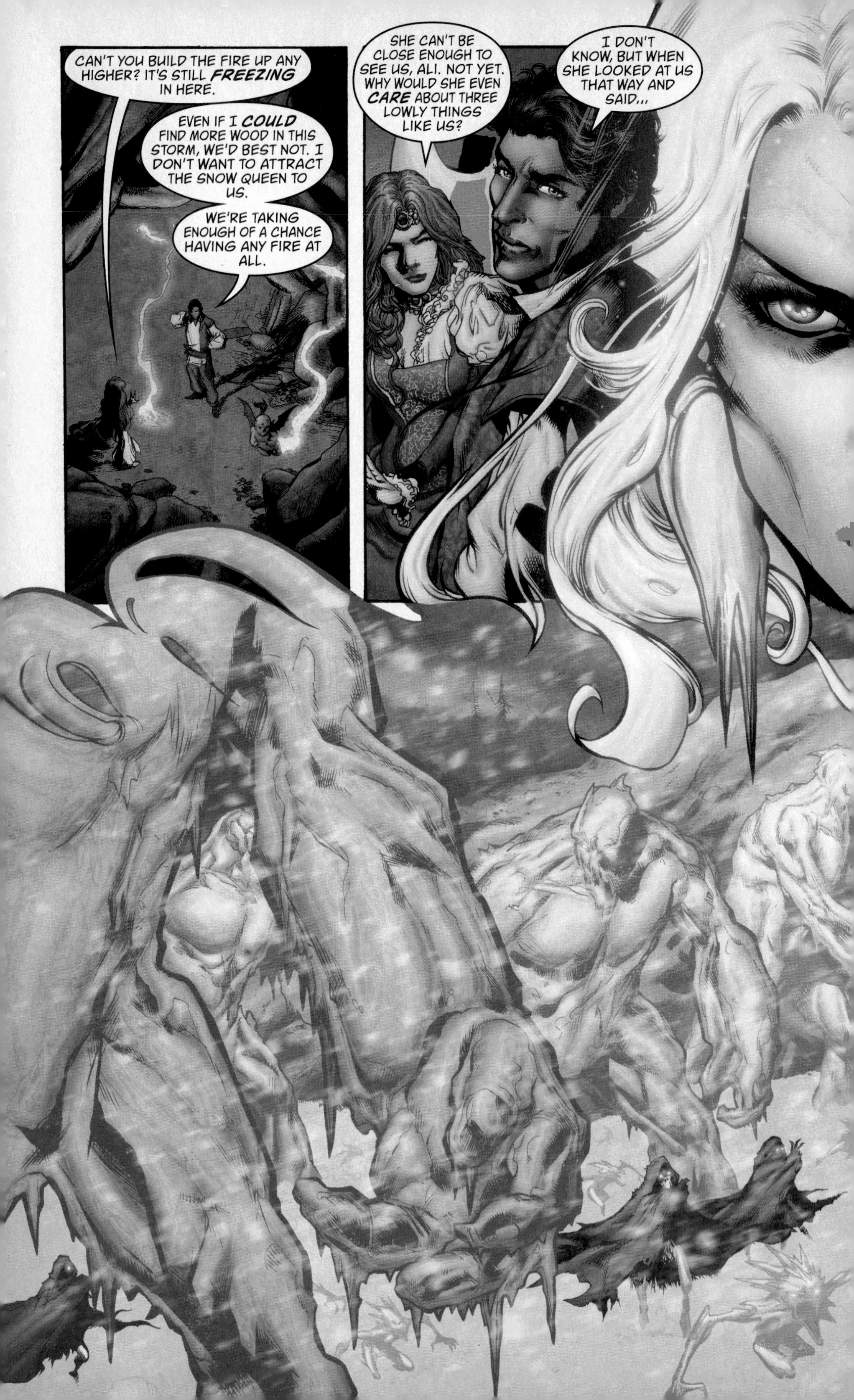
CAN'T YOU BUILD THE FIRE UP ANY HIGHER? IT'S STILL FREEZING IN HERE.
EVEN IF I COULD FIND MORE WOOD IN THIS STORM, WE'D BEST NOT. I DON'T WANT TO ATTRACT THE SNOW QUEEN TO US.
WE'RE TAKING ENOUGH OF A CHANCE HAVING ANY FIRE AT ALL.
SHE CAN'T BE CLOSE ENOUGH TO SEE US, ALI. NOT YET. WHY WOULD SHE EVEN CARE ABOUT THREE LOWLY THINGS LIKE US?
I DON'T KNOW, BUT WHEN SHE LOOKED AT US THAT WAY AND SAID...

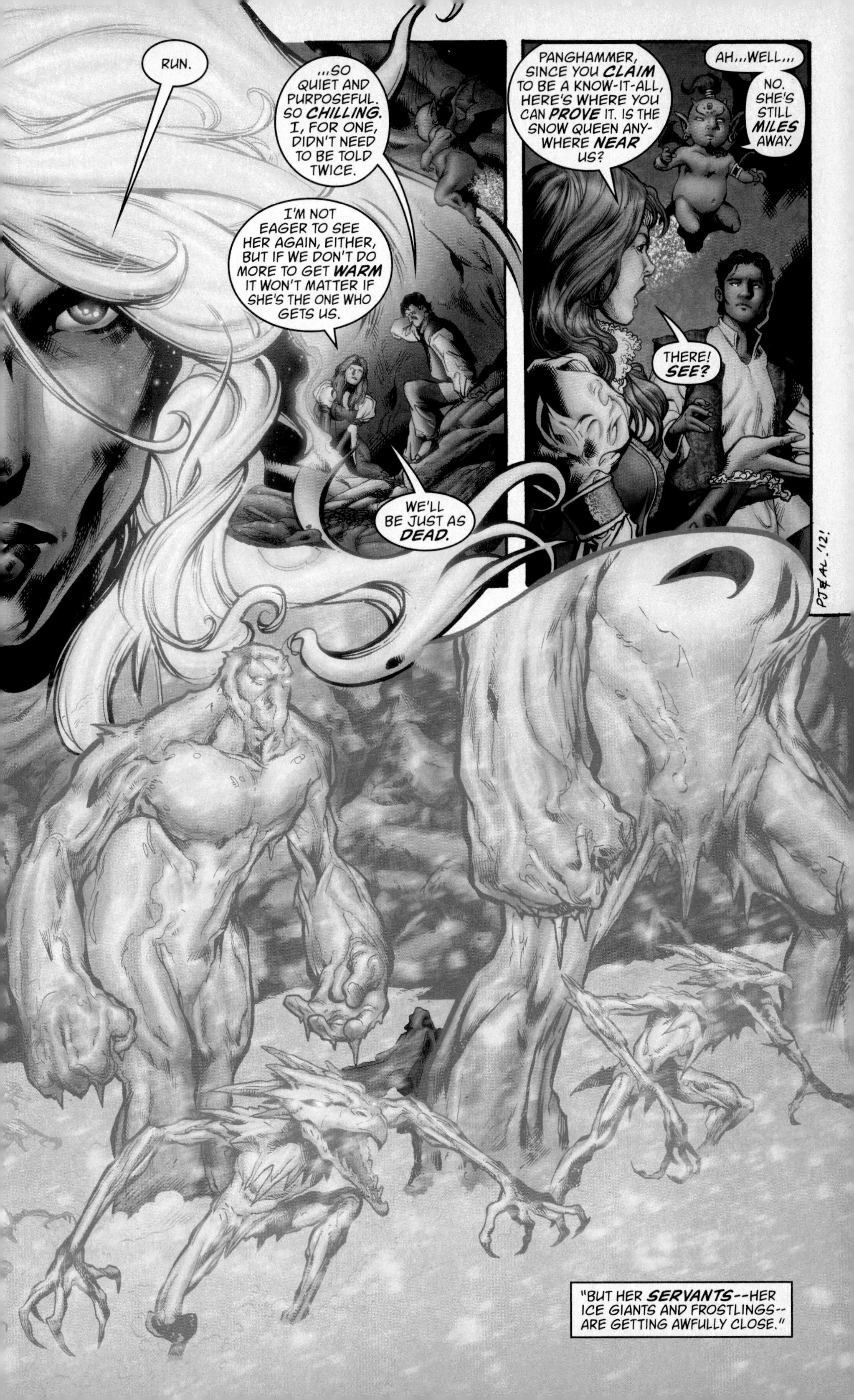
RUN.
...SO QUIET AND PURPOSEFUL. SO CHILLING. I, FOR ONE, DIDN'T NEED TO BE TOLD TWICE.
I'M NOT EAGER TO SEE HER AGAIN, EITHER, BUT IF WE DON'T DO MORE TO GET WARM IT WON'T MATTER IF SHE'S THE ONE WHO GETS US.
WE'LL BE JUST AS DEAD.
PANGHAMMER, SINCE YOU CLAIM TO BE A KNOW-IT-ALL, HERE'S WHERE YOU CAN PROVE IT. IS THE SNOW QUEEN ANYWHERE NEAR US?
AH...WELL...
NO. SHE'S STILL MILES AWAY.
THERE! SEE?
PJ & AL '12!
"BUT HER SERVANTS--HER ICE GIANTS AND FROSTLINGS--ARE GETTING AWFULLY CLOSE."

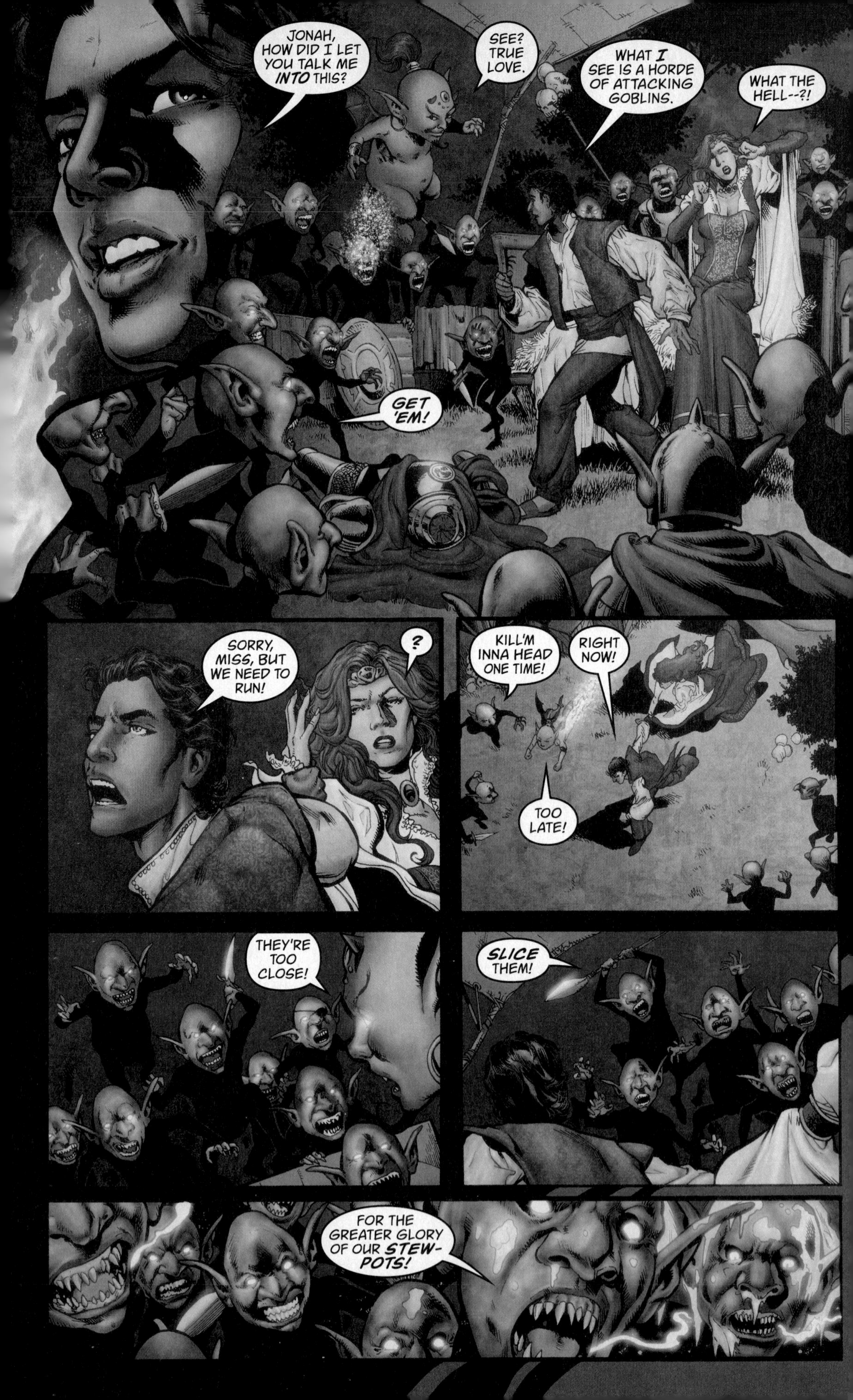
JONAH, HOW DID I LET YOU TALK ME INTO THIS?
SEE? TRUE LOVE.
WHAT I SEE IS A HORDE OF ATTACKING GOBLINS.
WHAT THE HELL--?!
GET 'EM!
SORRY, MISS, BUT WE NEED TO RUN!
?
KILL'M INNA HEAD ONE TIME!
RIGHT NOW!
TOO LATE!
THEY'RE TOO CLOSE!
SLICE THEM!
FOR THE GREATER GLORY OF OUR STEW-POTS!

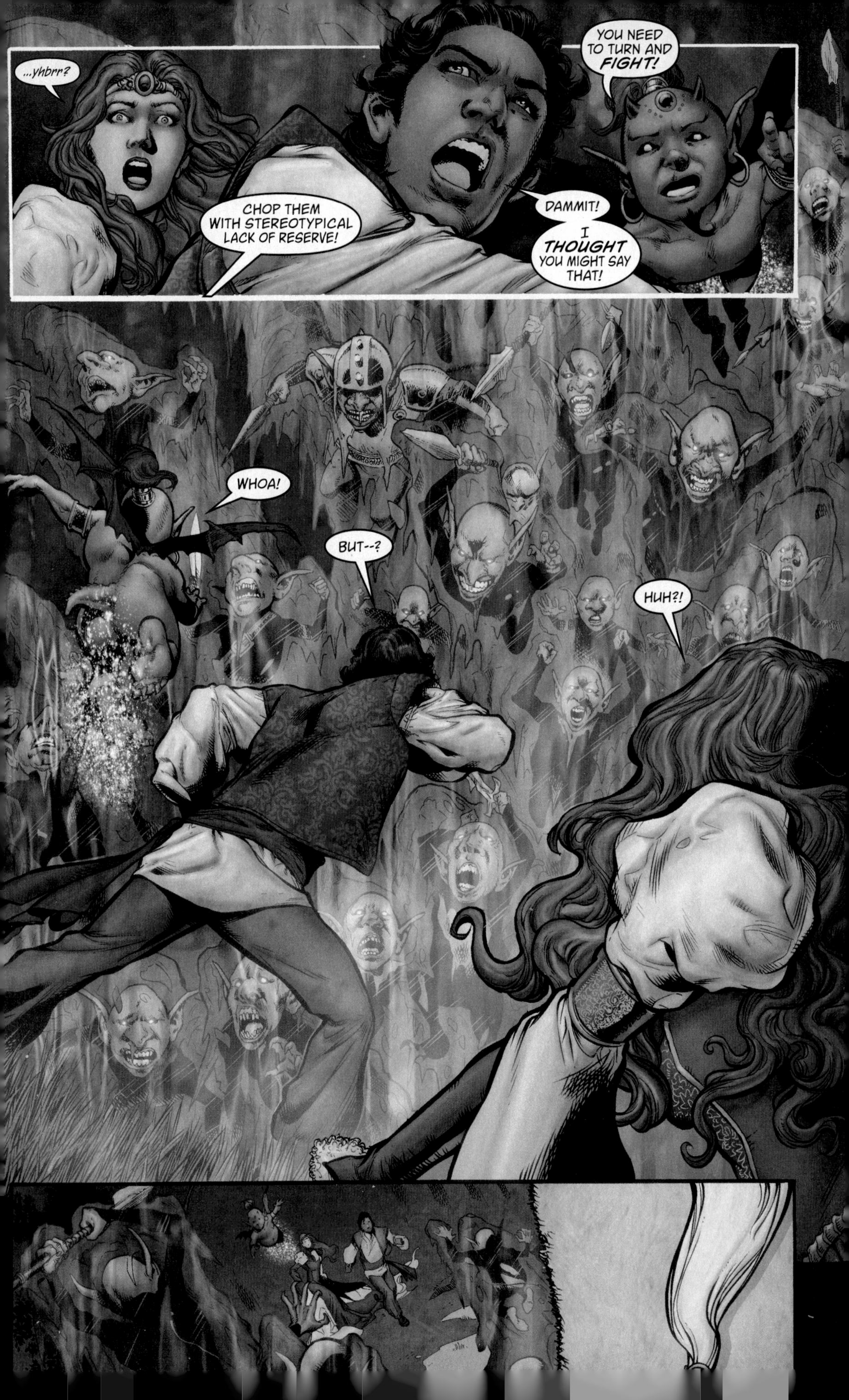
...yhbrr?
CHOP THEM WITH STEREOTYPICAL LACK OF RESERVE!
YOU NEED TO TURN AND FIGHT!
DAMMIT!
I THOUGHT YOU MIGHT SAY THAT!
WHOA!
BUT--?
HUH?!

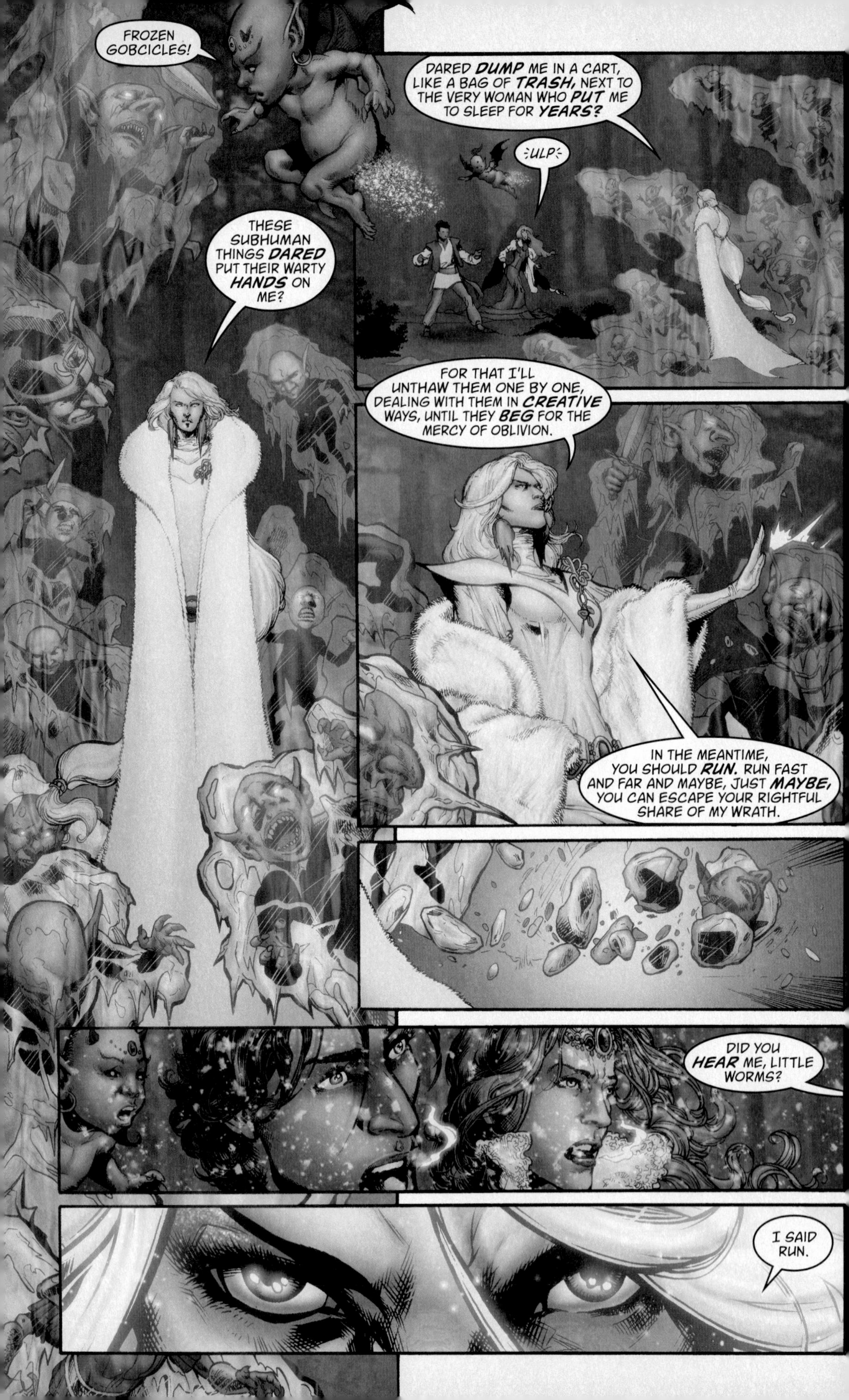
FROZEN GOBCICLES!
DARED DUMP ME IN A CART, LIKE A BAG OF TRASH, NEXT TO THE VERY WOMAN WHO PUT ME TO SLEEP FOR YEARS?
ULP
THESE SUBHUMAN THINGS DARED PUT THEIR WARTY HANDS ON ME?
FOR THAT I'LL UNTHAW THEM ONE BY ONE, DEALING WITH THEM IN CREATIVE WAYS, UNTIL THEY BEG FOR THE MERCY OF OBLIVION.
IN THE MEANTIME, YOU SHOULD RUN. RUN FAST AND FAR AND MAYBE, JUST MAYBE, YOU CAN ESCAPE YOUR RIGHTFUL SHARE OF MY WRATH.
DID YOU HEAR ME, LITTLE WORMS?
I SAID RUN.

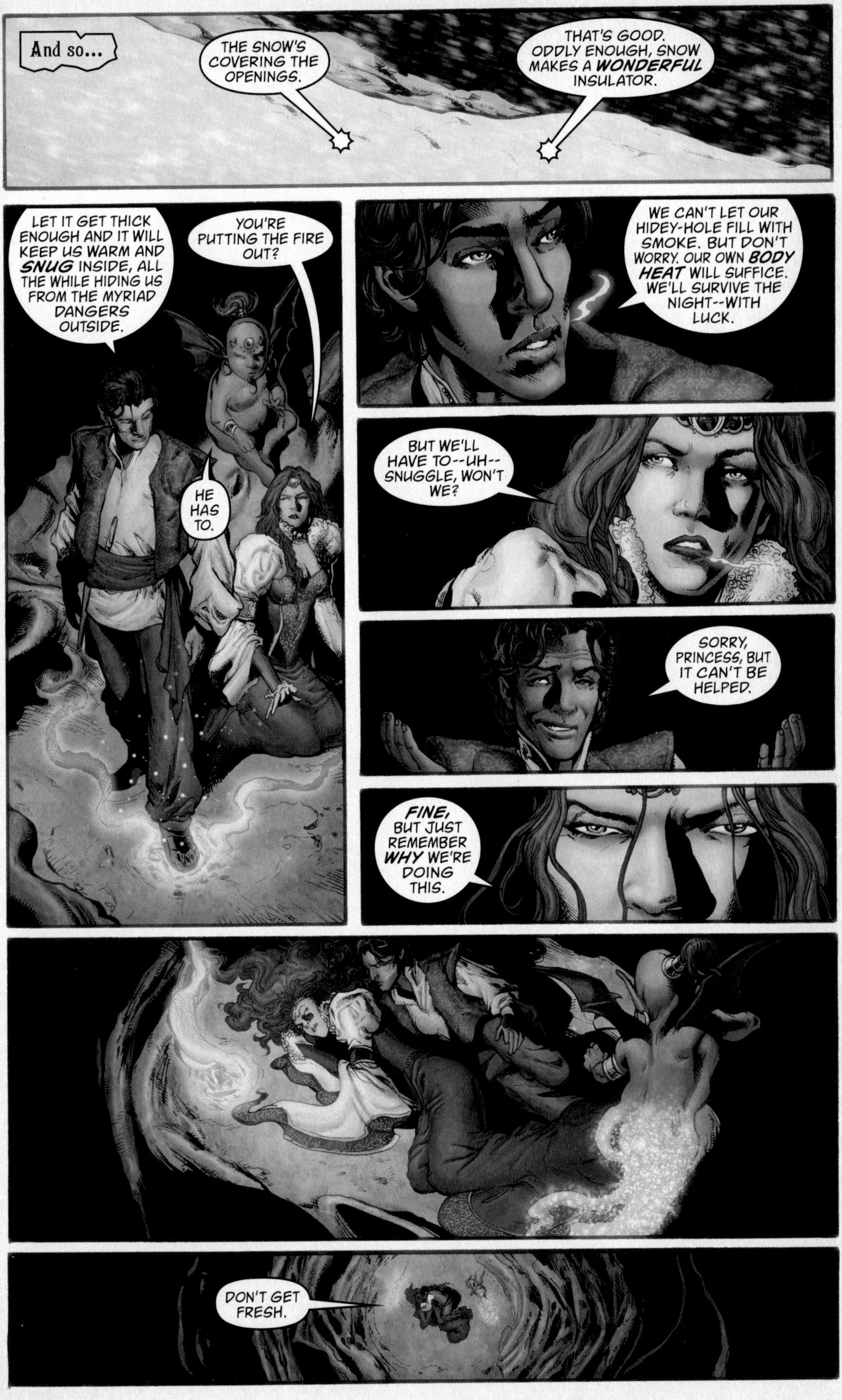
And so...
THE SNOW'S COVERING THE OPENINGS.
THAT'S GOOD. ODDLY ENOUGH, SNOW MAKES A WONDERFUL INSULATOR.
LET IT GET THICK ENOUGH AND IT WILL KEEP US WARM AND SNUG INSIDE, ALL THE WHILE HIDING US FROM THE MYRIAD DANGERS OUTSIDE.
YOU'RE PUTTING THE FIRE OUT?
HE HAS TO.
WE CAN'T LET OUR HIDEY-HOLE FILL WITH SMOKE. BUT DON'T WORRY. OUR OWN BODY HEAT WILL SUFFICE. WE'LL SURVIVE THE NIGHT--WITH LUCK.
BUT WE'LL HAVE TO--UH--SNUGGLE, WON'T WE?
SORRY, PRINCESS, BUT IT CAN'T BE HELPED.
FINE, BUT JUST REMEMBER WHY WE'RE DOING THIS.
DON'T GET FRESH.

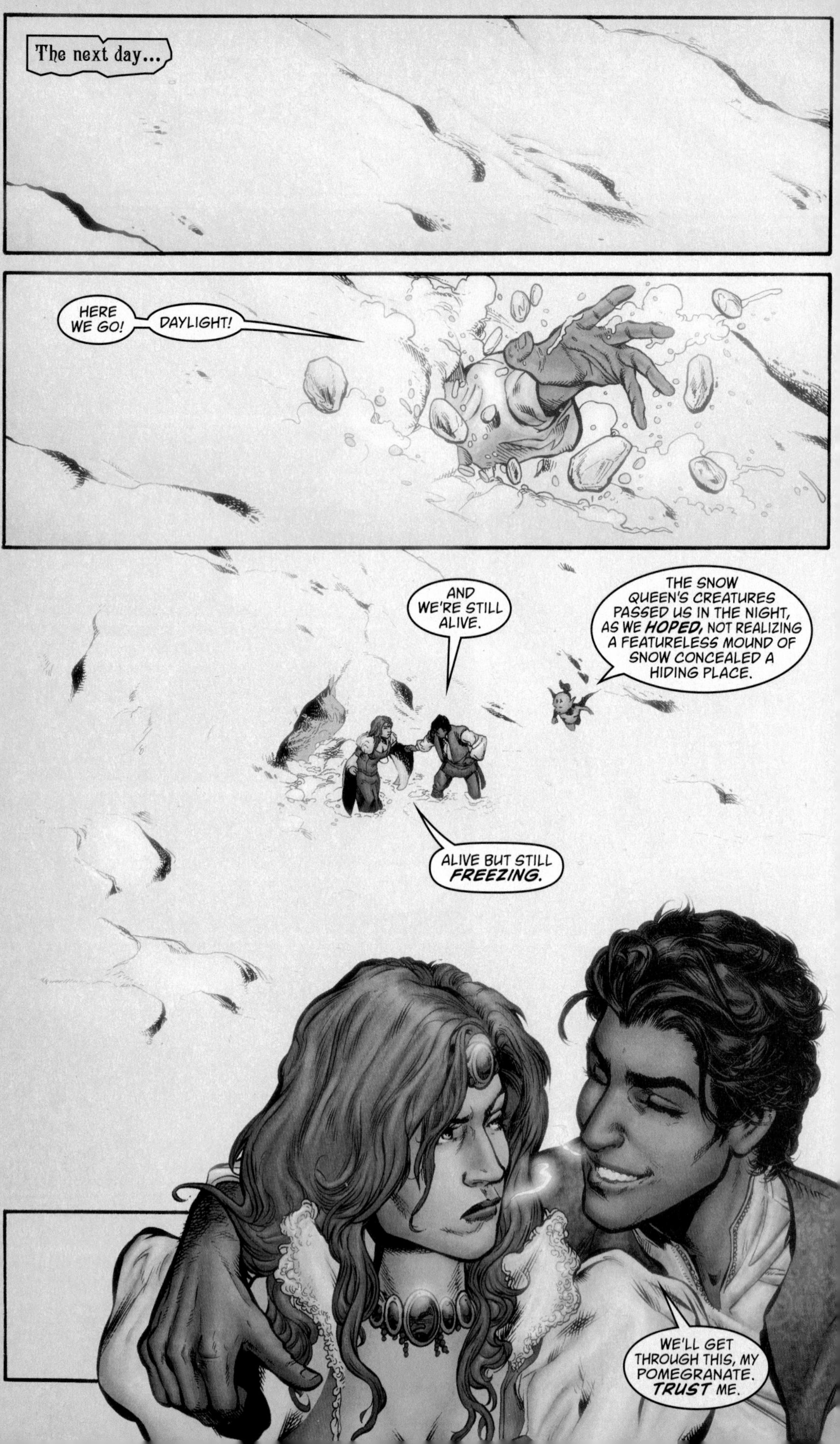
The next day...
HERE WE GO!
DAYLIGHT!
AND WE'RE STILL ALIVE.
THE SNOW QUEEN'S CREATURES PASSED US IN THE NIGHT, AS WE HOPED, NOT REALIZING A FEATURELESS MOUND OF SNOW CONCEALED A HIDING PLACE.
ALIVE BUT STILL FREEZING.
WE'LL GET THROUGH THIS, MY POMEGRANATE. TRUST ME.

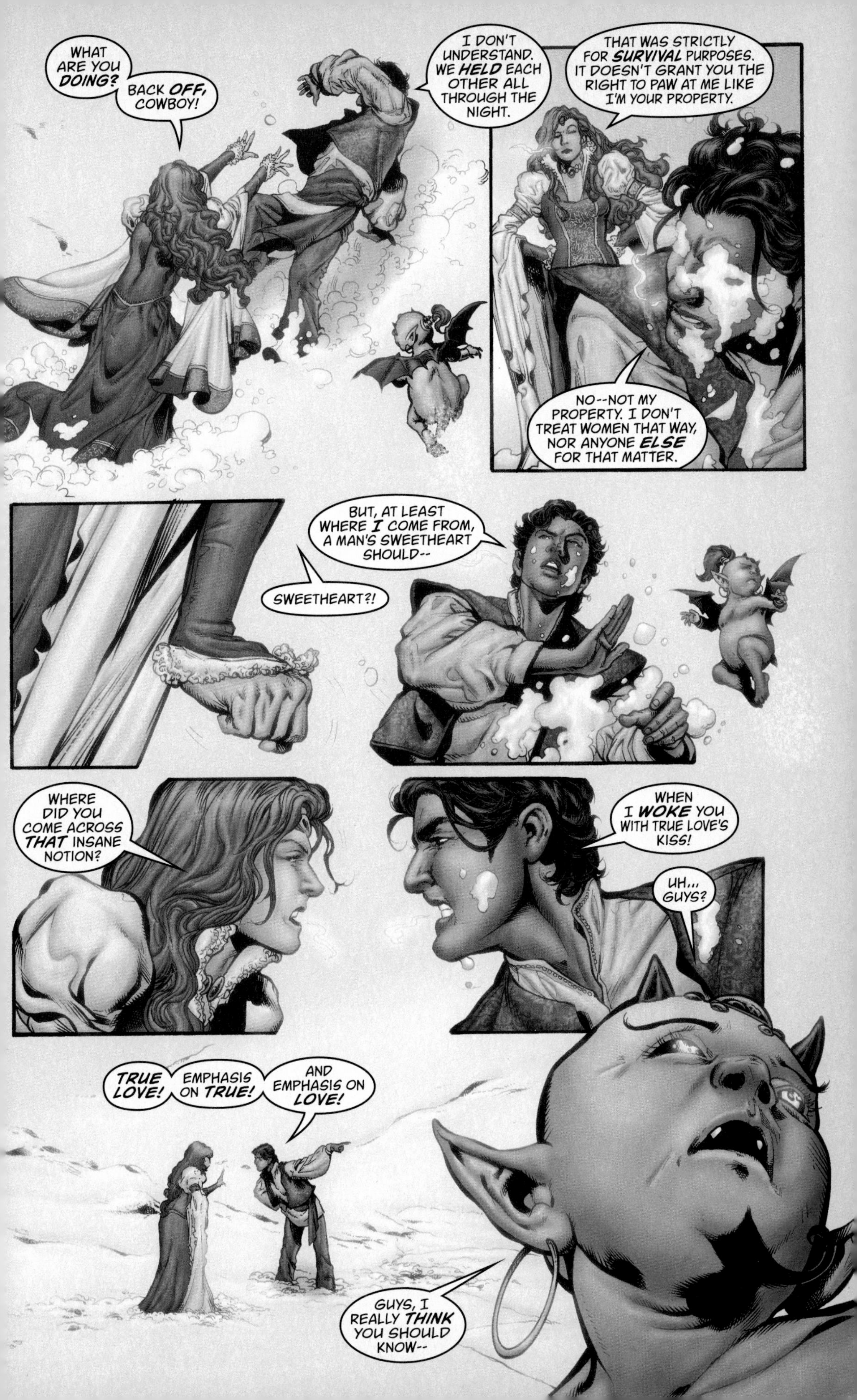
WHAT ARE YOU DOING?
BACK OFF, COWBOY!
I DON'T UNDERSTAND. WE HELD EACH OTHER ALL THROUGH THE NIGHT.
THAT WAS STRICTLY FOR SURVIVAL PURPOSES. IT DOESN'T GRANT YOU THE RIGHT TO PAW AT ME LIKE I'M YOUR PROPERTY.
NO--NOT MY PROPERTY. I DON'T TREAT WOMEN THAT WAY, NOR ANYONE ELSE FOR THAT MATTER.
BUT, AT LEAST WHERE I COME FROM, A MAN'S SWEETHEART SHOULD--
SWEETHEART?!
WHERE DID YOU COME ACROSS THAT INSANE NOTION?
WHEN I WOKE YOU WITH TRUE LOVE'S KISS!
UH... GUYS?
TRUE LOVE!
EMPHASIS ON TRUE!
AND EMPHASIS ON LOVE!
GUYS, I REALLY THINK YOU SHOULD KNOW--

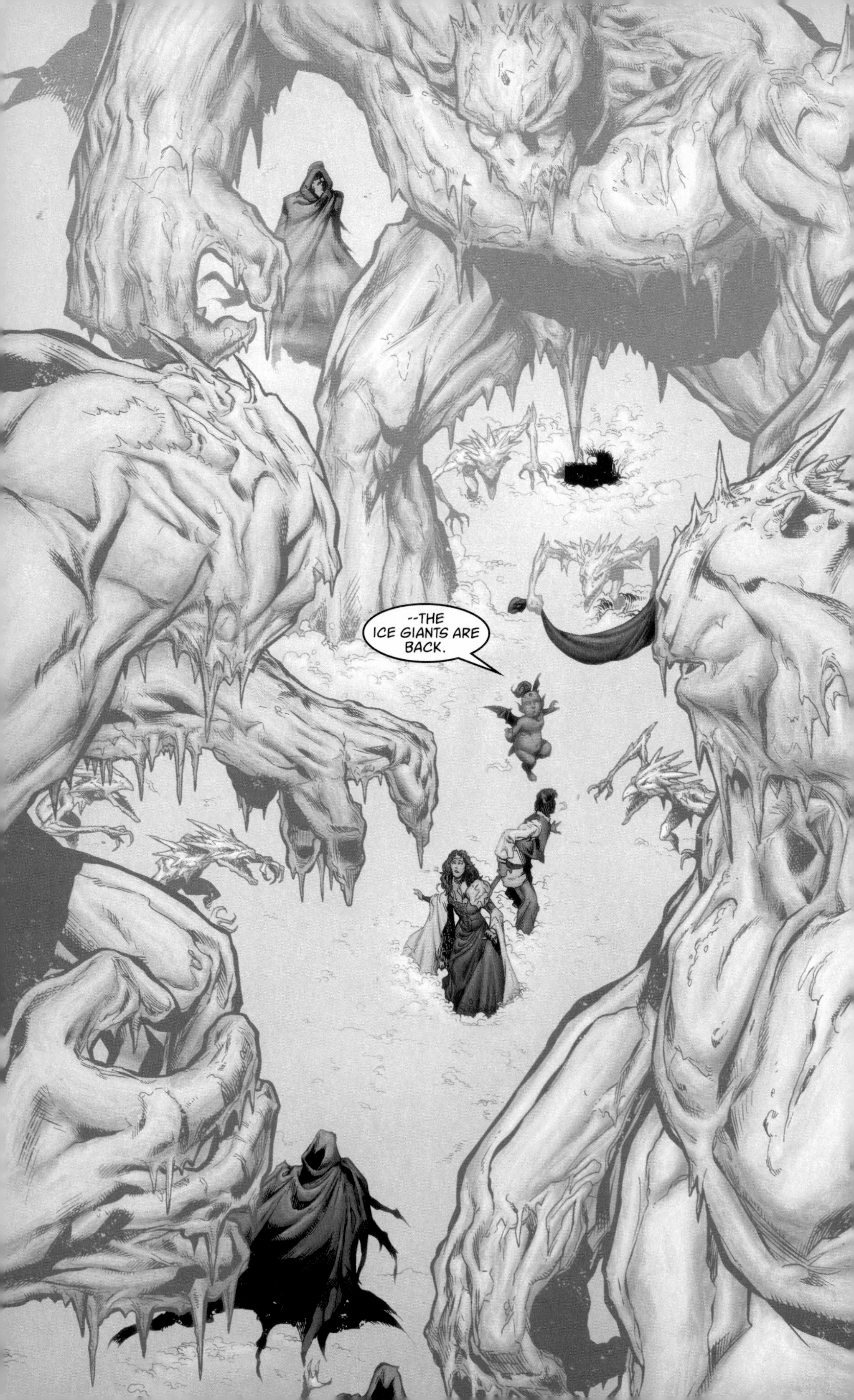
--THE ICE GIANTS ARE BACK.

AS NEAR AS I CAN TELL, THE VERY **ACT** OF PLACING HIMSELF IN SUCH GREAT DANGER, SNEAKING PAST AN ARMY OF GOBLINS JUST TO **REACH** YOU, QUALIFIES AS TRUE LOVE.

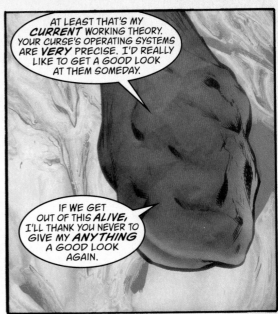

AT LEAST THAT'S MY **CURRENT** WORKING THEORY. YOUR CURSE'S OPERATING SYSTEMS ARE **VERY** PRECISE. I'D REALLY LIKE TO GET A GOOD LOOK AT THEM SOMEDAY.

IF WE GET OUT OF THIS **ALIVE,** I'LL THANK YOU NEVER TO GIVE MY **ANYTHING** A GOOD LOOK AGAIN.

NOW, NOW. NO NEED TO BE **SNIPPY,** PRINCESS. WE'RE ALIVE, AND AS THE FAMOUS ADVENTURER SAID, "AS LONG AS THERE'S LIFE, THERE'S HOPE."

AT LEAST IT'S **WARM** IN THIS GUNNYSACK. THAT'S SOMETHING.

SURE, IT'S A COMPLETE **JOY.**

MR. PANGHAMMER, CAN YOU PLEASE **EXPLAIN** TO ME HOW YOU LET THESE GIANTS COMPLETELY SNEAK UP ON US LIKE THAT?

EASY. THEY WERE QUIET AND YOU TWO WERE SCREAMING LIKE... UH...LIKE A COUPLE OF VERY LOUD **SCREAMY** THINGS.

FINE, BUT YOU'RE SUPPOSED TO **KNOW** THINGS.

AS I EXPLAINED **FAR** TOO MANY TIMES BEFORE...

...MY TRAINING WAS IN AMERICAN STUDIES. I KNOW EVERYTHING ABOUT THAT.

OTHER STUFF CAN BE HIT OR MISS.

DEAR LORD ABOVE, HOW DID I GET **INTO** THIS MESS?

OH, THAT I CAN EXPLAIN EASILY!

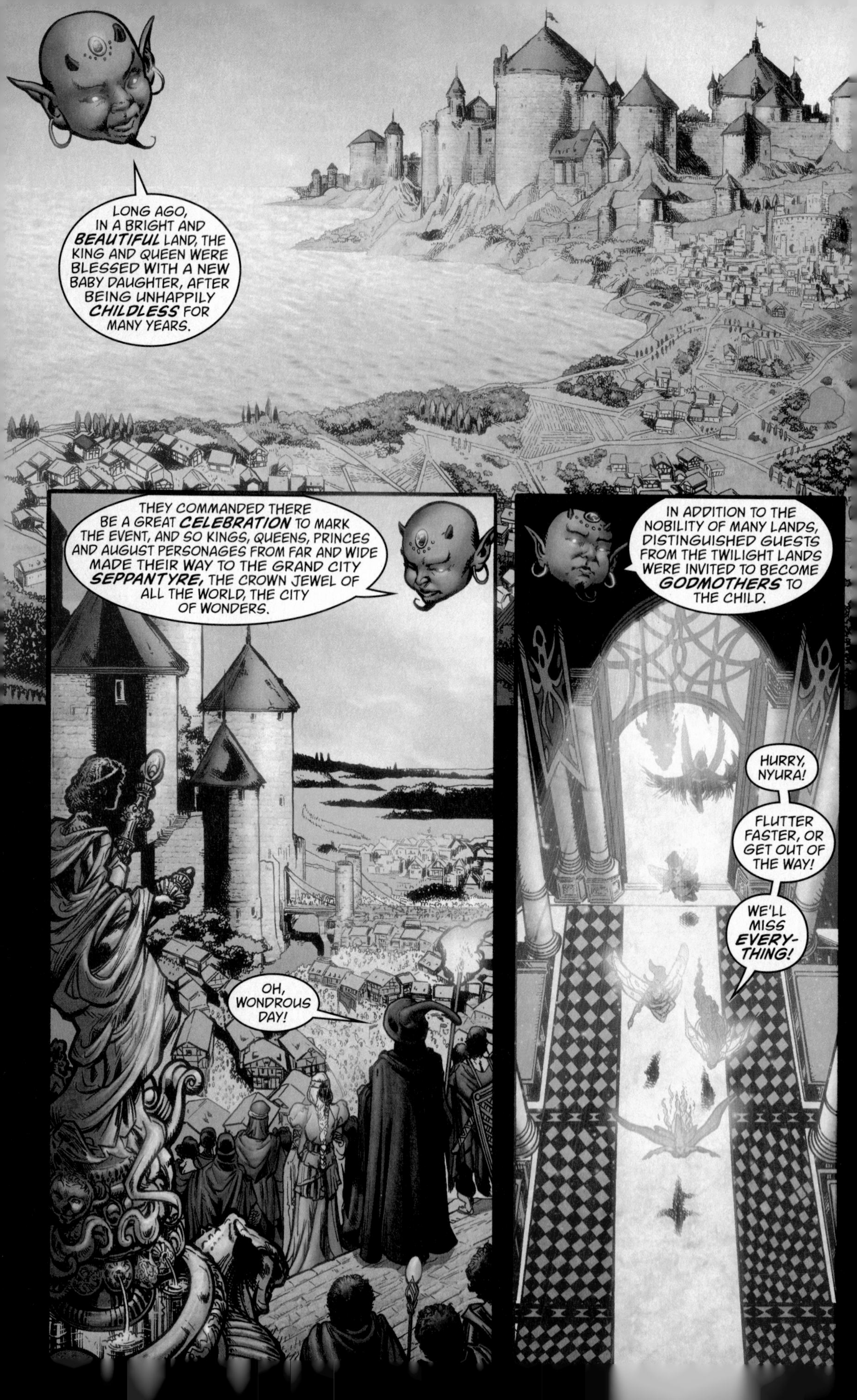
LONG AGO, IN A BRIGHT AND BEAUTIFUL LAND, THE KING AND QUEEN WERE BLESSED WITH A NEW BABY DAUGHTER, AFTER BEING UNHAPPILY CHILDLESS FOR MANY YEARS.
THEY COMMANDED THERE BE A GREAT CELEBRATION TO MARK THE EVENT, AND SO KINGS, QUEENS, PRINCES AND AUGUST PERSONAGES FROM FAR AND WIDE MADE THEIR WAY TO THE GRAND CITY SEPPANTYRE, THE CROWN JEWEL OF ALL THE WORLD, THE CITY OF WONDERS.
OH, WONDROUS DAY!
IN ADDITION TO THE NOBILITY OF MANY LANDS, DISTINGUISHED GUESTS FROM THE TWILIGHT LANDS WERE INVITED TO BECOME GODMOTHERS TO THE CHILD.
HURRY, NYURA!
FLUTTER FASTER, OR GET OUT OF THE WAY!
WE'LL MISS EVERYTHING!

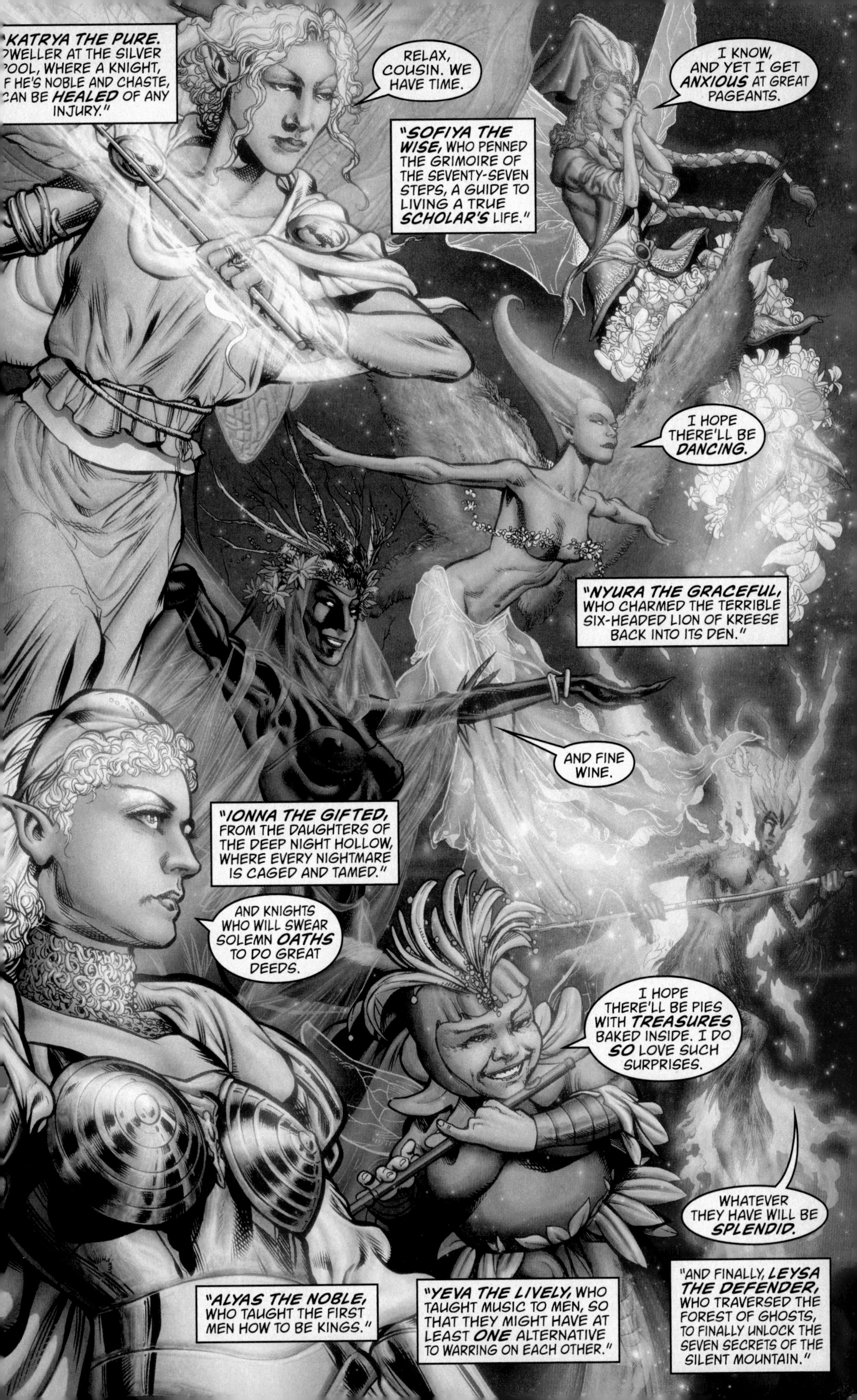
"KATRYA THE PURE. DWELLER AT THE SILVER POOL, WHERE A KNIGHT, IF HE'S NOBLE AND CHASTE, CAN BE HEALED OF ANY INJURY."
RELAX, COUSIN. WE HAVE TIME.
"SOFIYA THE WISE, WHO PENNED THE GRIMOIRE OF THE SEVENTY-SEVEN STEPS, A GUIDE TO LIVING A TRUE SCHOLAR'S LIFE."
I KNOW, AND YET I GET ANXIOUS AT GREAT PAGEANTS.
I HOPE THERE'LL BE DANCING.
"NYURA THE GRACEFUL, WHO CHARMED THE TERRIBLE SIX-HEADED LION OF KREESE BACK INTO ITS DEN."
AND FINE WINE.
"IONNA THE GIFTED, FROM THE DAUGHTERS OF THE DEEP NIGHT HOLLOW, WHERE EVERY NIGHTMARE IS CAGED AND TAMED."
AND KNIGHTS WHO WILL SWEAR SOLEMN OATHS TO DO GREAT DEEDS.
I HOPE THERE'LL BE PIES WITH TREASURES BAKED INSIDE. I DO SO LOVE SUCH SURPRISES.
WHATEVER THEY HAVE WILL BE SPLENDID.
"ALYAS THE NOBLE, WHO TAUGHT THE FIRST MEN HOW TO BE KINGS."
"YEVA THE LIVELY, WHO TAUGHT MUSIC TO MEN, SO THAT THEY MIGHT HAVE AT LEAST ONE ALTERNATIVE TO WARRING ON EACH OTHER."
"AND FINALLY, LEYSA THE DEFENDER, WHO TRAVERSED THE FOREST OF GHOSTS, TO FINALLY UNLOCK THE SEVEN SECRETS OF THE SILENT MOUNTAIN."

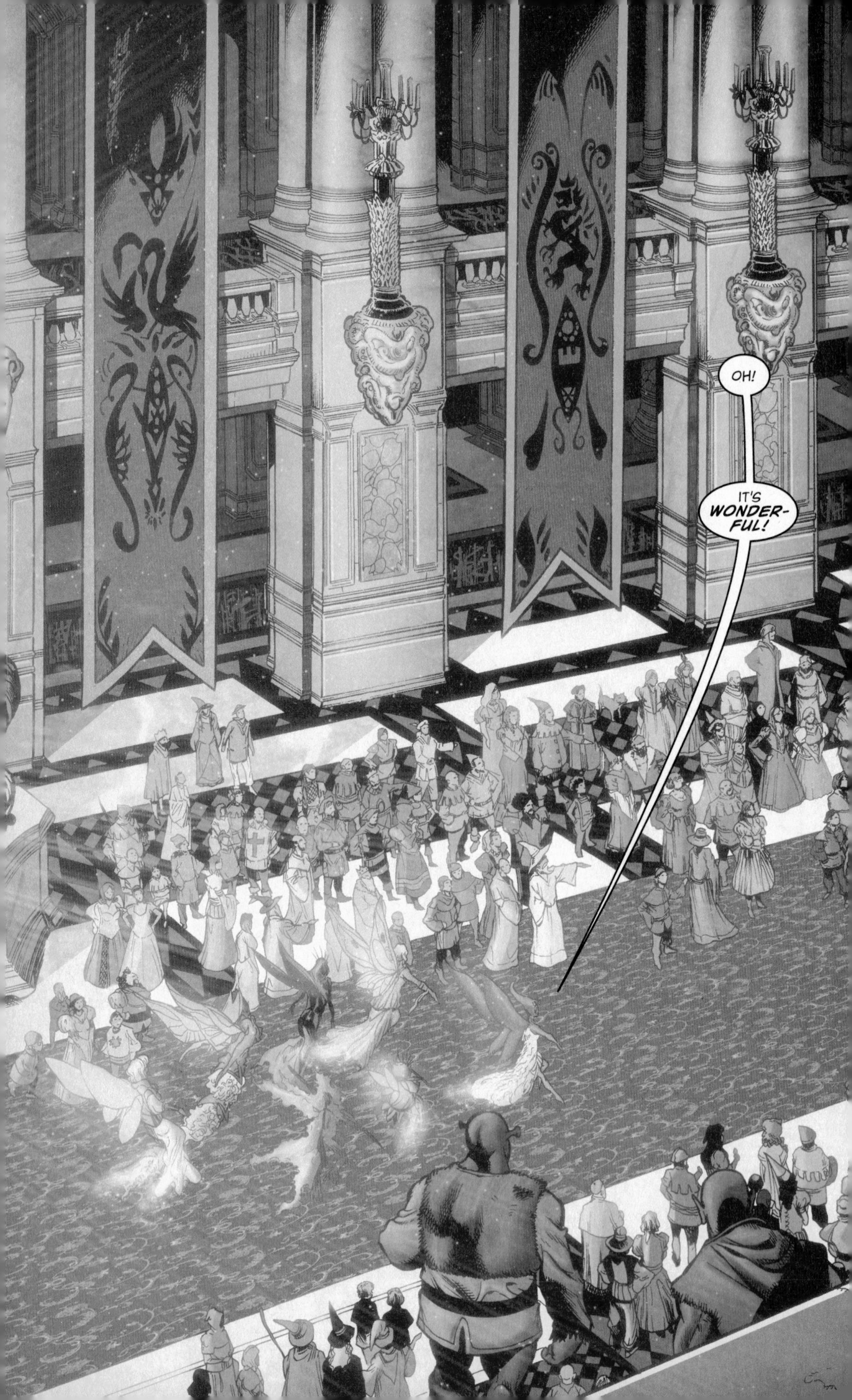
OH!
IT'S WONDER-FUL!

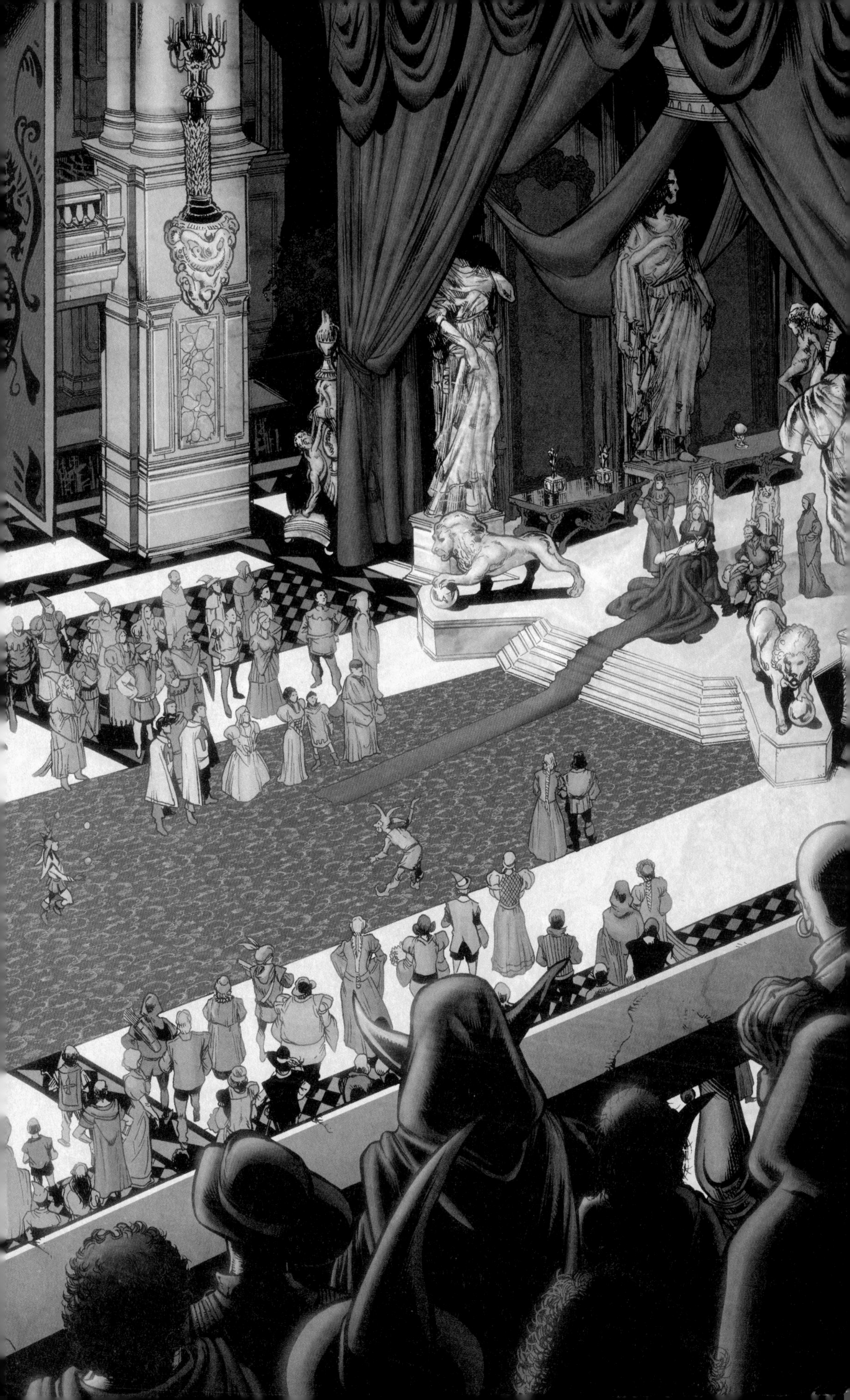

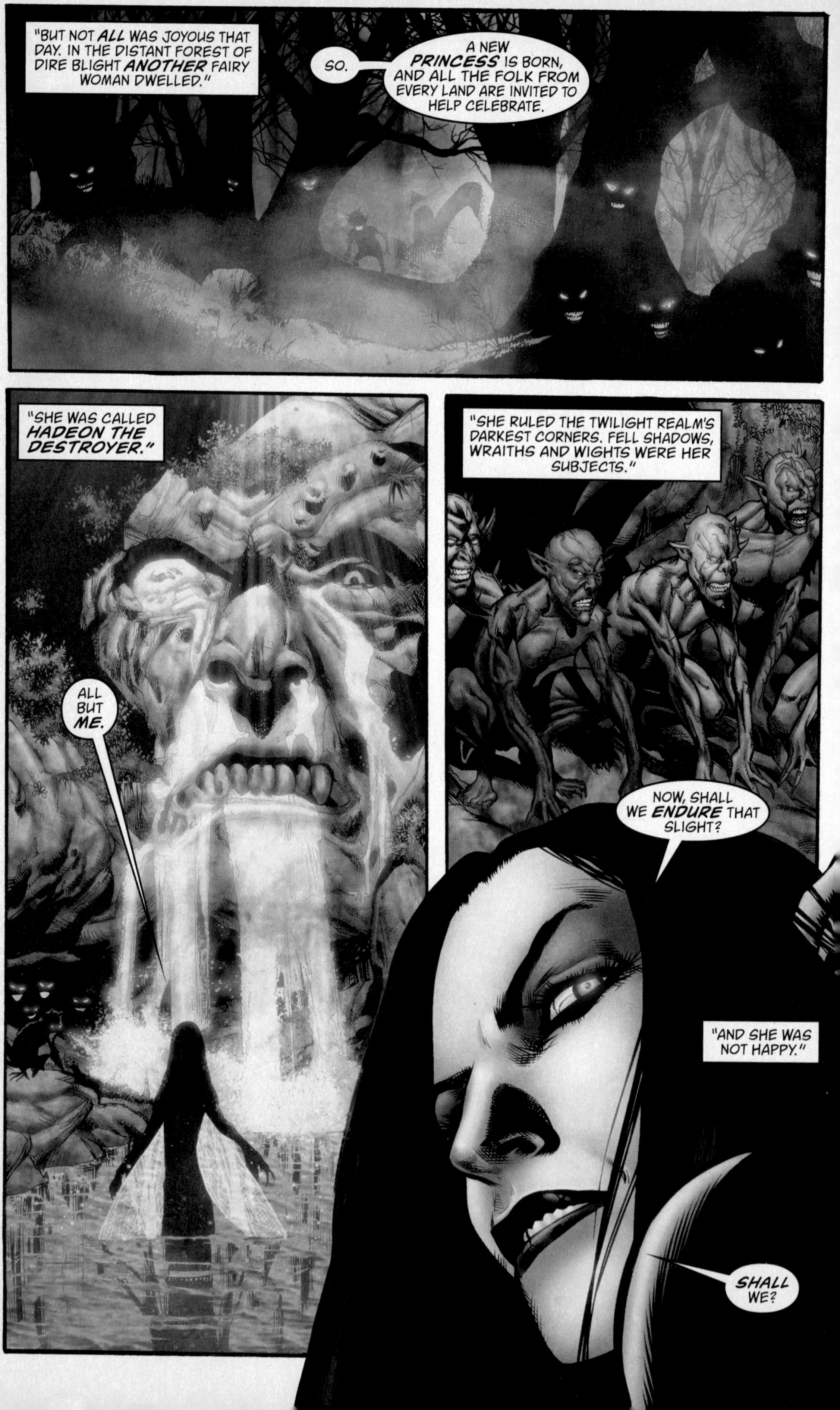
"BUT NOT ALL WAS JOYOUS THAT DAY. IN THE DISTANT FOREST OF DIRE BLIGHT ANOTHER FAIRY WOMAN DWELLED."
SO.
A NEW PRINCESS IS BORN, AND ALL THE FOLK FROM EVERY LAND ARE INVITED TO HELP CELEBRATE.
"SHE WAS CALLED HADEON THE DESTROYER."
ALL BUT ME.
"SHE RULED THE TWILIGHT REALM'S DARKEST CORNERS. FELL SHADOWS, WRAITHS AND WIGHTS WERE HER SUBJECTS."
NOW, SHALL WE ENDURE THAT SLIGHT?
"AND SHE WAS NOT HAPPY."
SHALL WE?

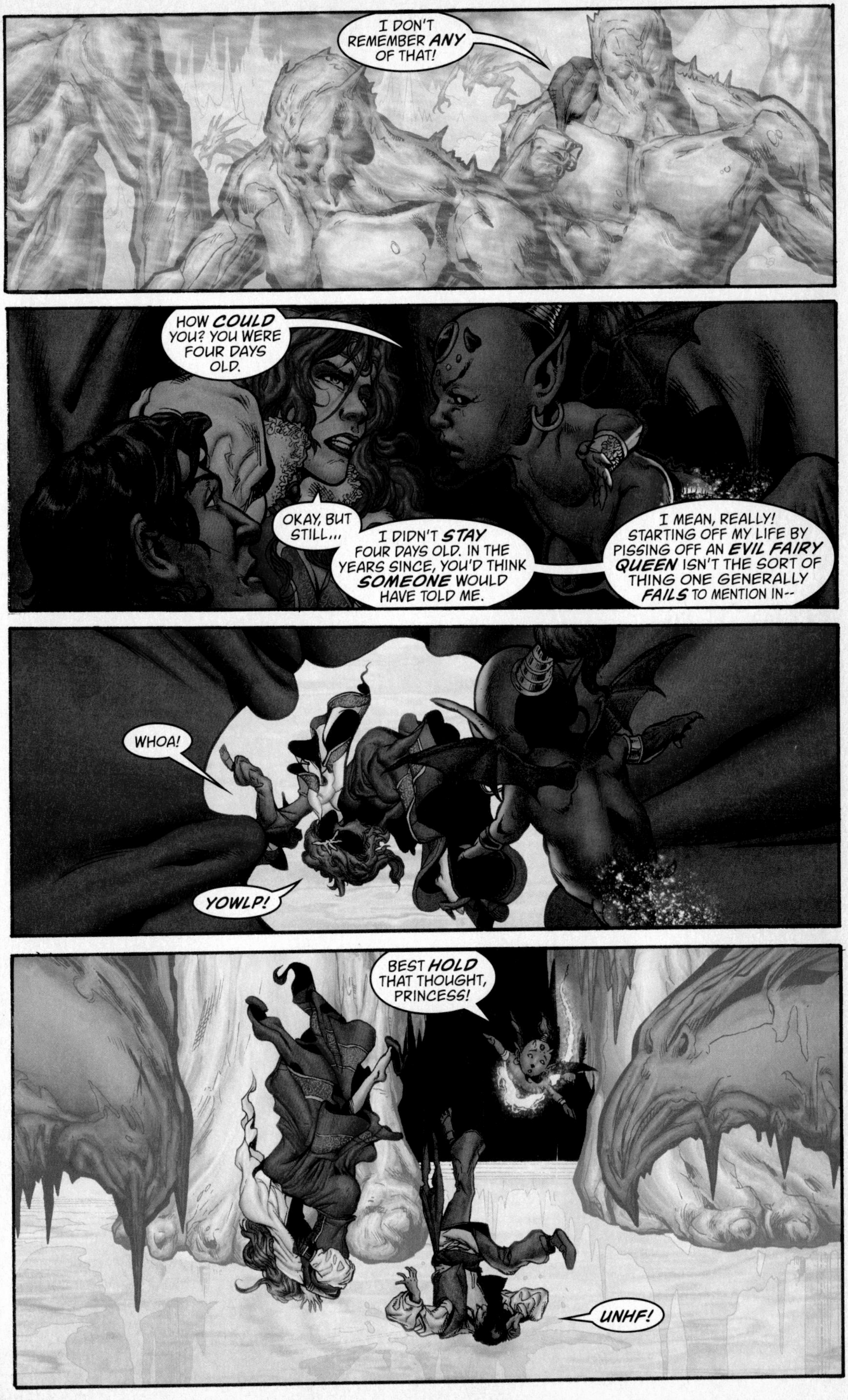
I DON'T REMEMBER ANY OF THAT!
HOW COULD YOU? YOU WERE FOUR DAYS OLD.
OKAY, BUT STILL...
I DIDN'T STAY FOUR DAYS OLD. IN THE YEARS SINCE, YOU'D THINK SOMEONE WOULD HAVE TOLD ME.
I MEAN, REALLY! STARTING OFF MY LIFE BY PISSING OFF AN EVIL FAIRY QUEEN ISN'T THE SORT OF THING ONE GENERALLY FAILS TO MENTION IN--
WHOA!
YOWLP!
BEST HOLD THAT THOUGHT, PRINCESS!
UNHF!

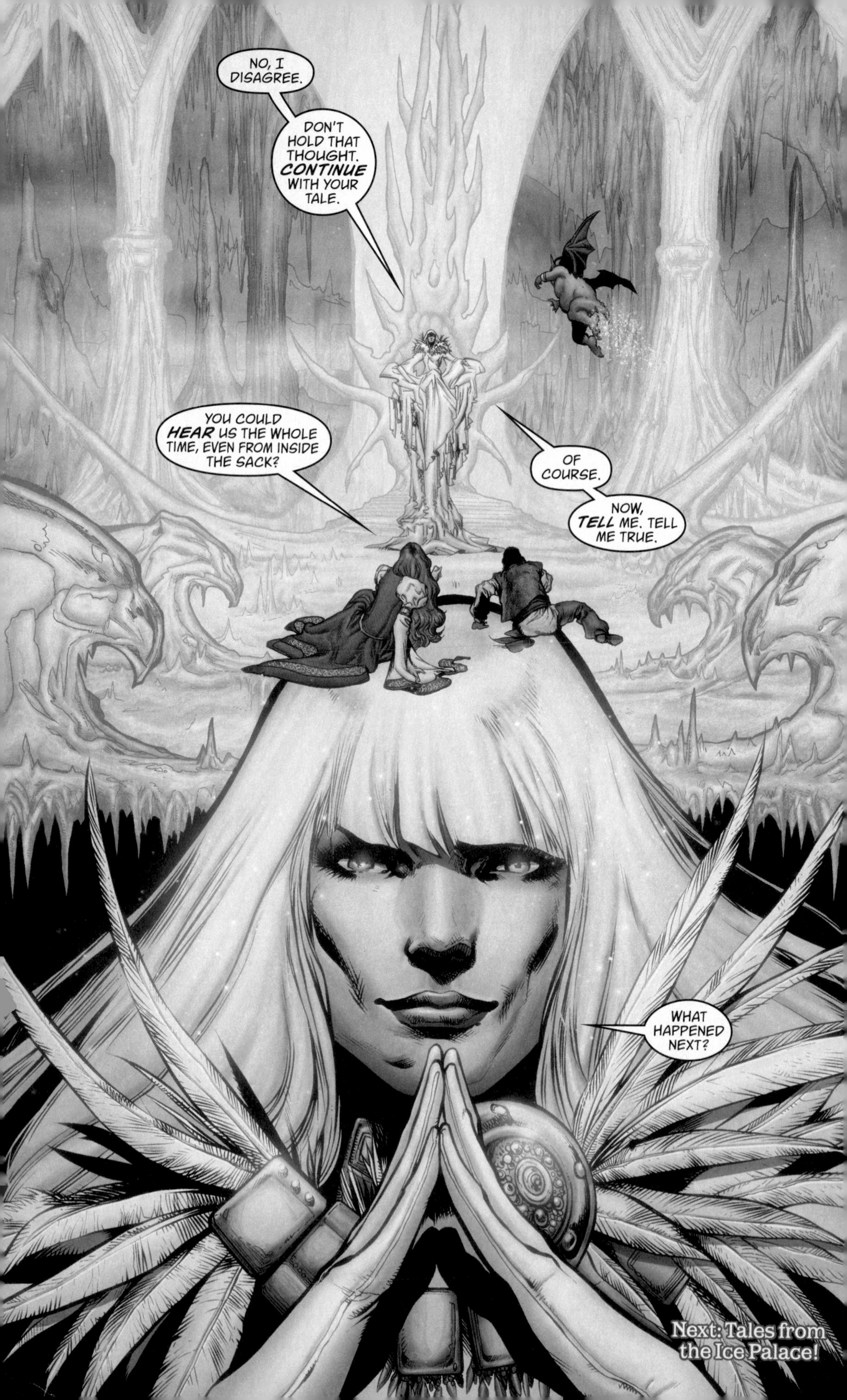
NO, I DISAGREE.
DON'T HOLD THAT THOUGHT. CONTINUE WITH YOUR TALE.
YOU COULD HEAR US THE WHOLE TIME, EVEN FROM INSIDE THE SACK?
OF COURSE.
NOW, TELL ME. TELL ME TRUE.
WHAT HAPPENED NEXT?
Next: Tales from the Ice Palace!

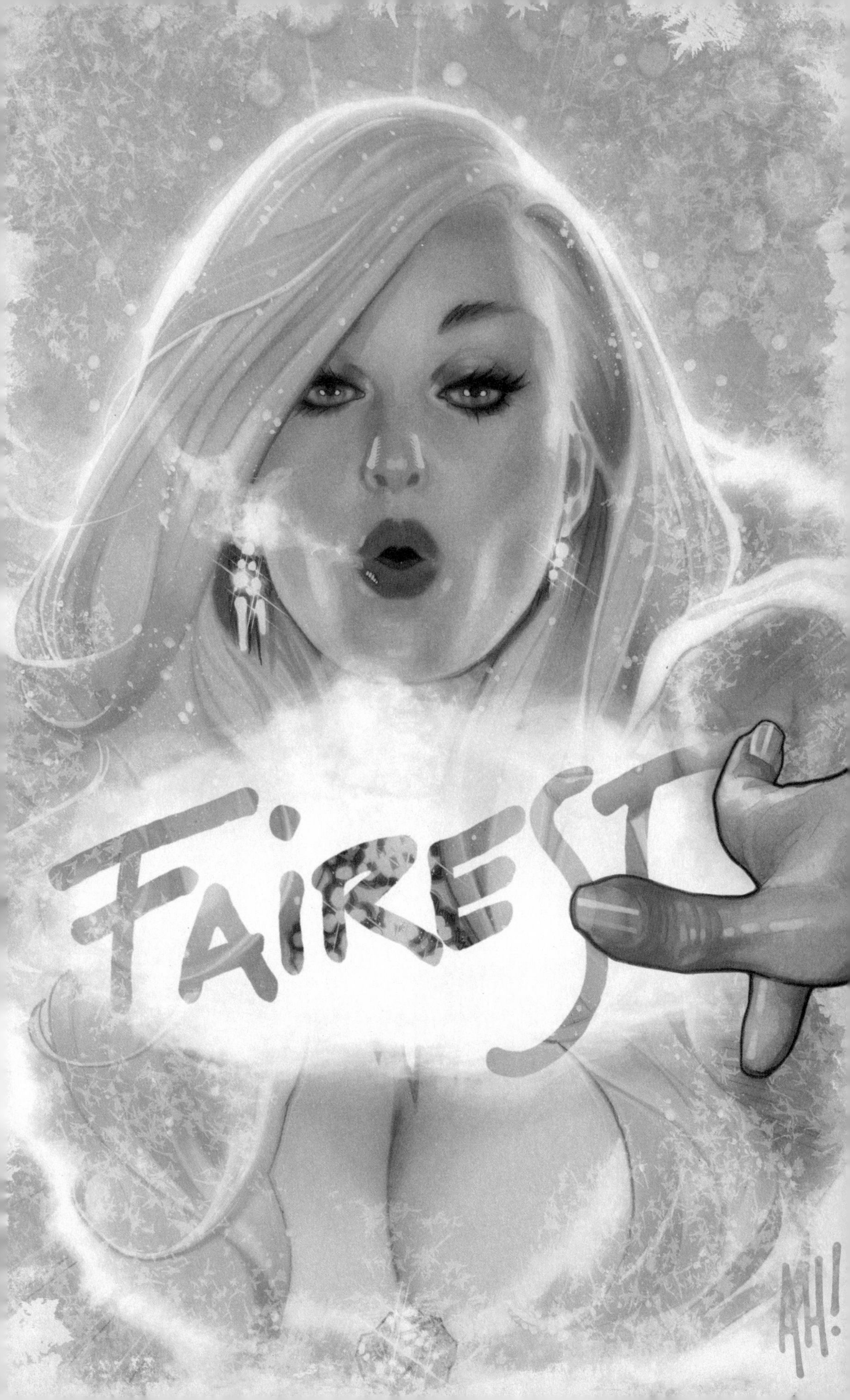
FAIREST
AH!

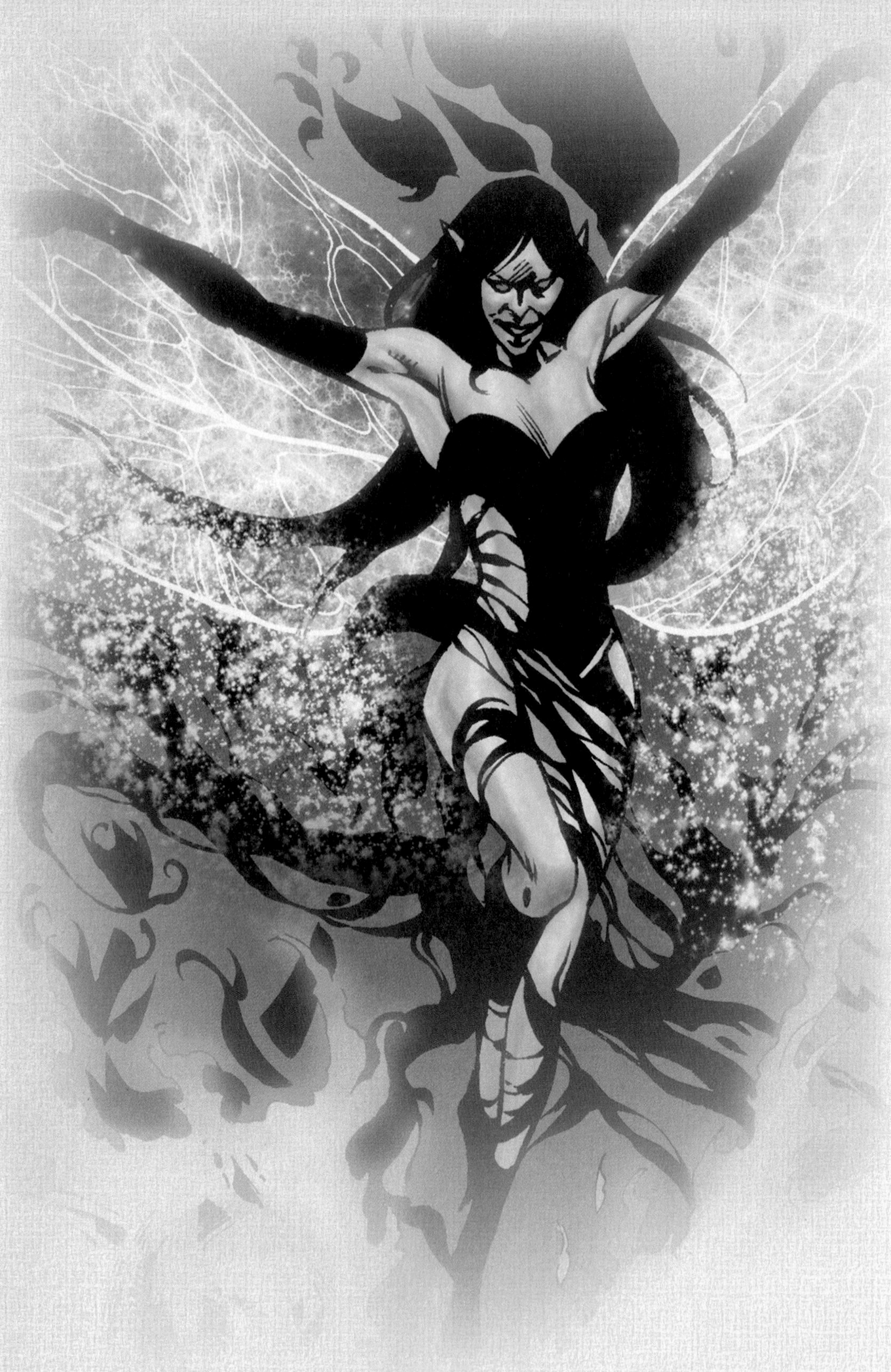

"So quickly our joy turns to ashes."

PARTY CRASHER

Chapter Three of WIDE AWAKE

BILL WILLINGHAM writer · PHIL JIMENEZ pencils · ANDY LANNING inks 1-7,13-20 · MARK FARMER inks 8-12 · ANDREW DALHOUSE colors · TODD KLEIN letters · ADAM HUGHES cover · GREGORY LOCKARD asst. ed. · SHELLY BOND editor · Special Thanks to ZANDER CANNON

FAIREST is created by Bill Willingham

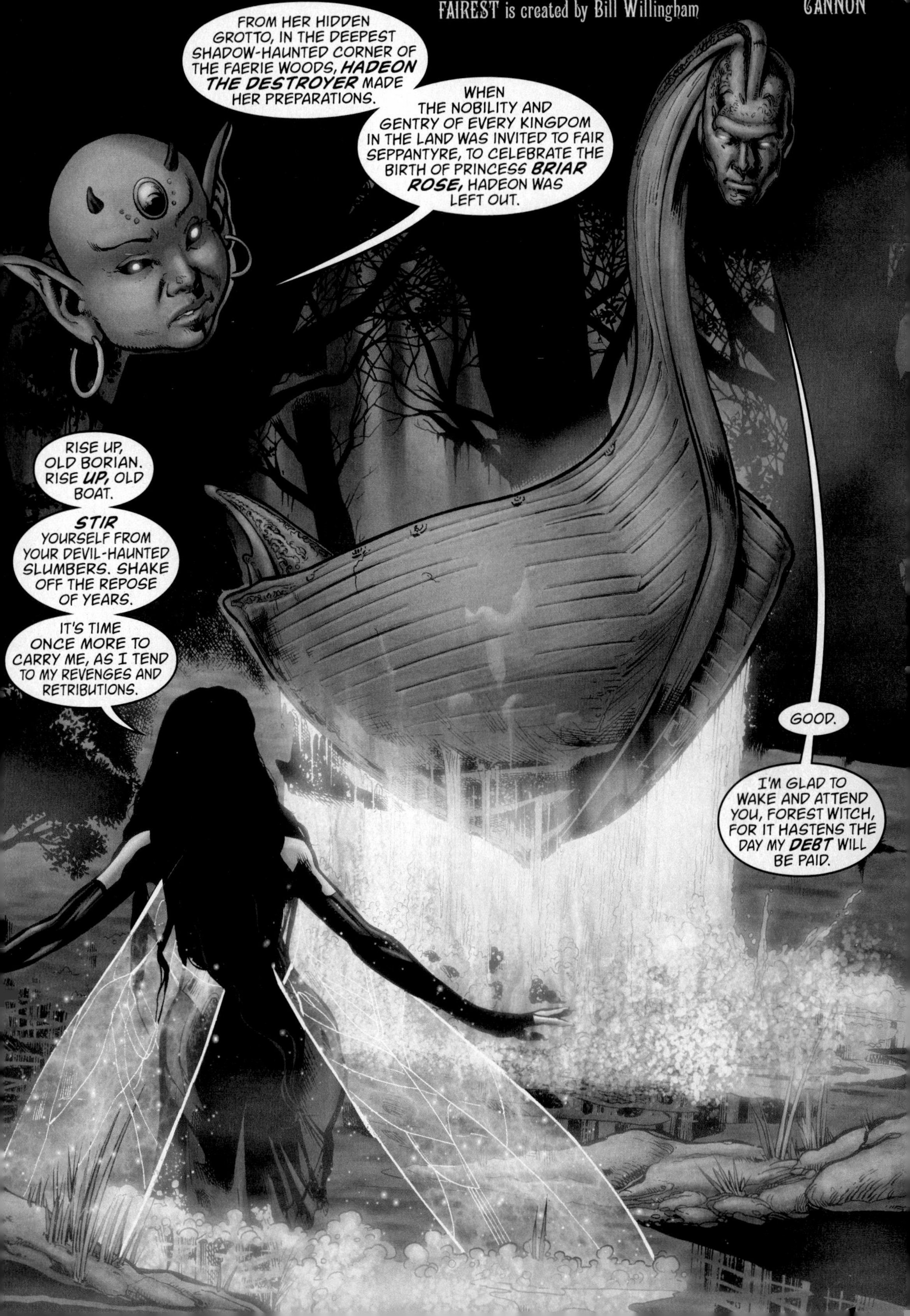

FROM HER HIDDEN GROTTO, IN THE DEEPEST SHADOW-HAUNTED CORNER OF THE FAERIE WOODS, HADEON THE DESTROYER MADE HER PREPARATIONS.
WHEN THE NOBILITY AND GENTRY OF EVERY KINGDOM IN THE LAND WAS INVITED TO FAIR SEPPANTYRE, TO CELEBRATE THE BIRTH OF PRINCESS BRIAR ROSE, HADEON WAS LEFT OUT.
RISE UP, OLD BORIAN. RISE UP, OLD BOAT.
STIR YOURSELF FROM YOUR DEVIL-HAUNTED SLUMBERS. SHAKE OFF THE REPOSE OF YEARS.
IT'S TIME ONCE MORE TO CARRY ME, AS I TEND TO MY REVENGES AND RETRIBUTIONS.
GOOD.
I'M GLAD TO WAKE AND ATTEND YOU, FOREST WITCH, FOR IT HASTENS THE DAY MY DEBT WILL BE PAID.

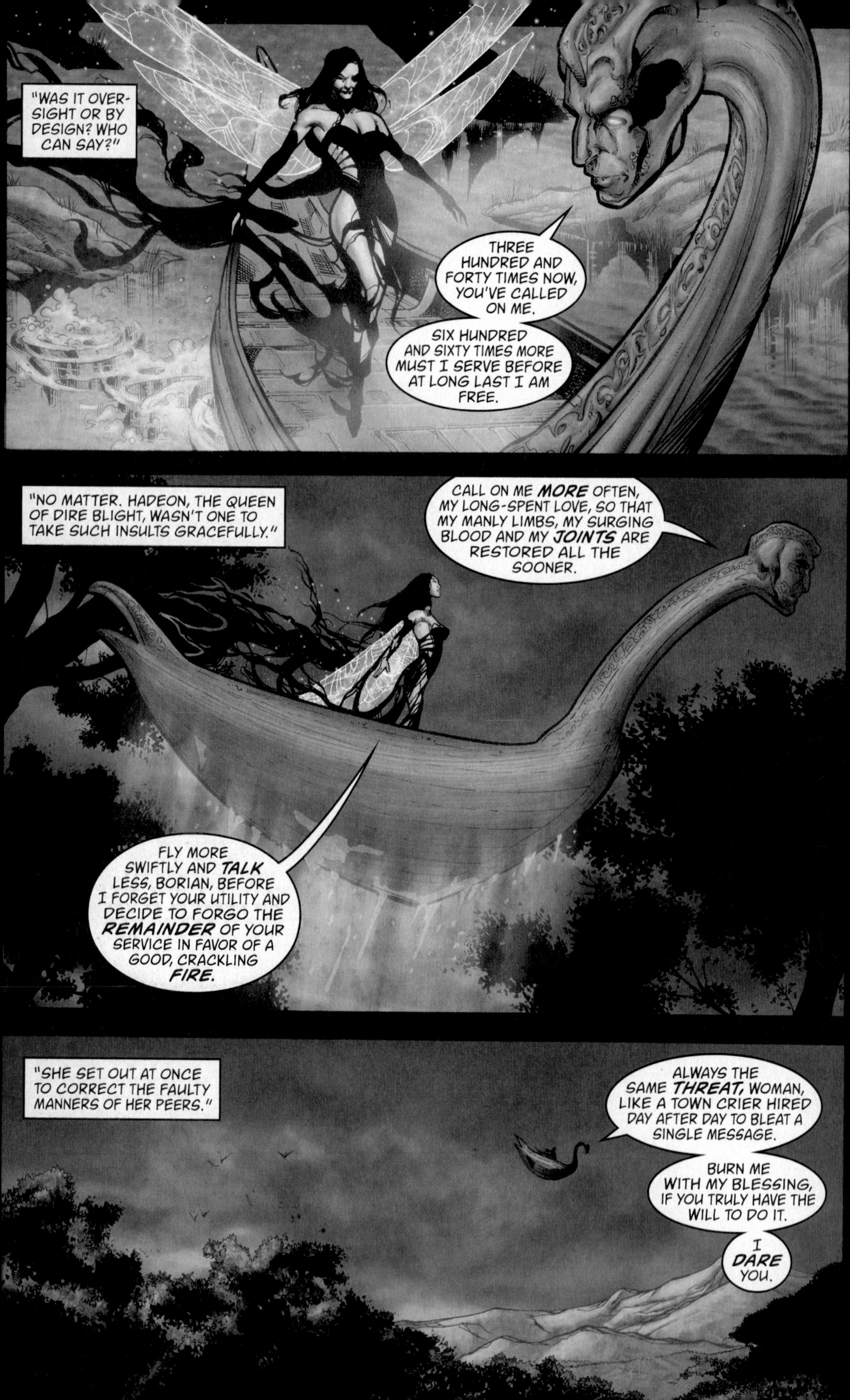
"WAS IT OVER-SIGHT OR BY DESIGN? WHO CAN SAY?"
THREE HUNDRED AND FORTY TIMES NOW, YOU'VE CALLED ON ME.
SIX HUNDRED AND SIXTY TIMES MORE MUST I SERVE BEFORE AT LONG LAST I AM FREE.
"NO MATTER. HADEON, THE QUEEN OF DIRE BLIGHT, WASN'T ONE TO TAKE SUCH INSULTS GRACEFULLY."
CALL ON ME MORE OFTEN, MY LONG-SPENT LOVE, SO THAT MY MANLY LIMBS, MY SURGING BLOOD AND MY JOINTS ARE RESTORED ALL THE SOONER.
FLY MORE SWIFTLY AND TALK LESS, BORIAN, BEFORE I FORGET YOUR UTILITY AND DECIDE TO FORGO THE REMAINDER OF YOUR SERVICE IN FAVOR OF A GOOD, CRACKLING FIRE.
"SHE SET OUT AT ONCE TO CORRECT THE FAULTY MANNERS OF HER PEERS."
ALWAYS THE SAME THREAT, WOMAN, LIKE A TOWN CRIER HIRED DAY AFTER DAY TO BLEAT A SINGLE MESSAGE.
BURN ME WITH MY BLESSING, IF YOU TRULY HAVE THE WILL TO DO IT.
I DARE YOU.

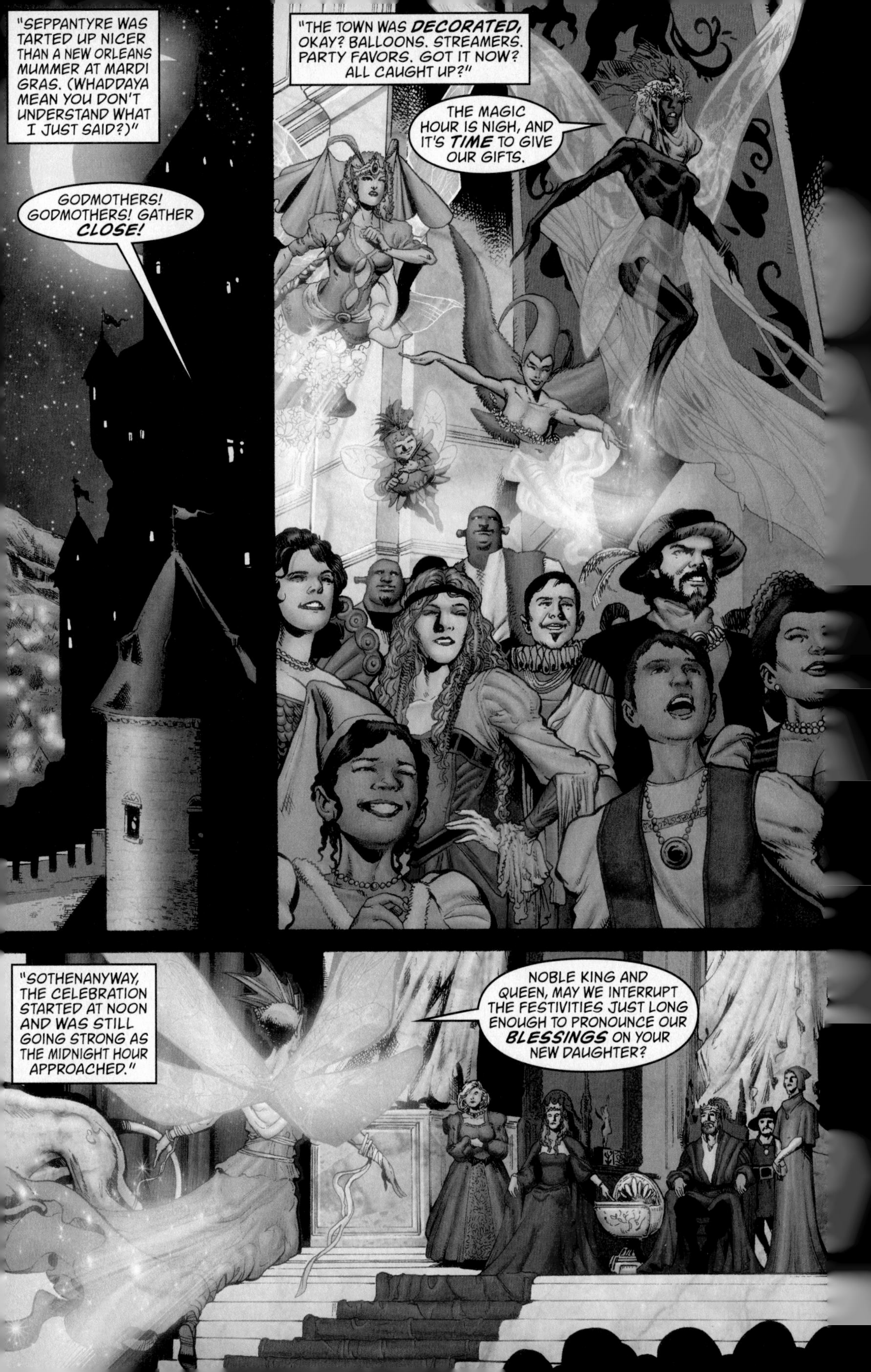
"SEPPANTYRE WAS TARTED UP NICER THAN A NEW ORLEANS MUMMER AT MARDI GRAS. (WHADDAYA MEAN YOU DON'T UNDERSTAND WHAT I JUST SAID?)"
"THE TOWN WAS DECORATED, OKAY? BALLOONS. STREAMERS. PARTY FAVORS. GOT IT NOW? ALL CAUGHT UP?"
GODMOTHERS! GODMOTHERS! GATHER CLOSE!
THE MAGIC HOUR IS NIGH, AND IT'S TIME TO GIVE OUR GIFTS.
"SOTHENANYWAY, THE CELEBRATION STARTED AT NOON AND WAS STILL GOING STRONG AS THE MIDNIGHT HOUR APPROACHED."
NOBLE KING AND QUEEN, MAY WE INTERRUPT THE FESTIVITIES JUST LONG ENOUGH TO PRONOUNCE OUR BLESSINGS ON YOUR NEW DAUGHTER?

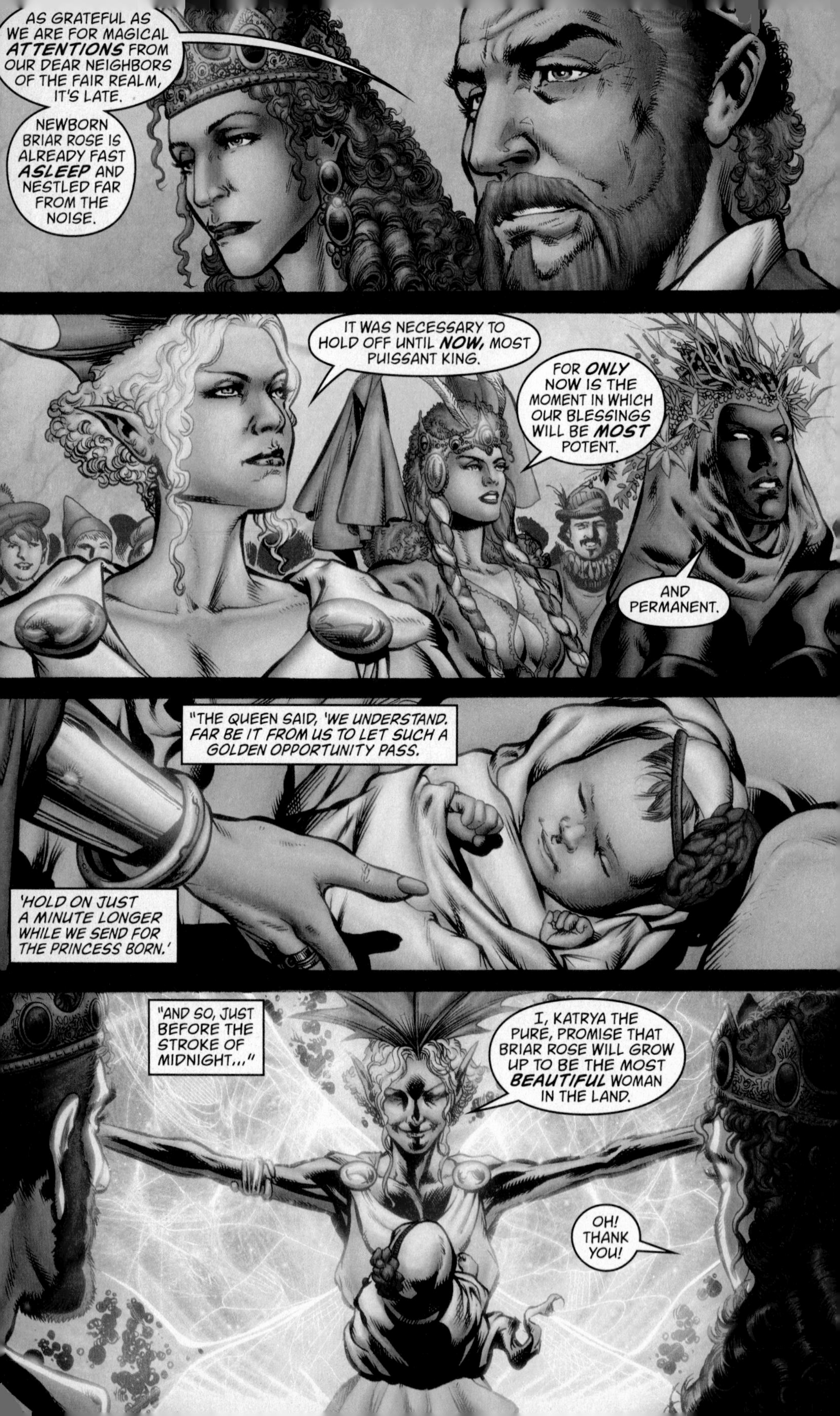
AS GRATEFUL AS WE ARE FOR MAGICAL ATTENTIONS FROM OUR DEAR NEIGHBORS OF THE FAIR REALM, IT'S LATE.
NEWBORN BRIAR ROSE IS ALREADY FAST ASLEEP AND NESTLED FAR FROM THE NOISE.
IT WAS NECESSARY TO HOLD OFF UNTIL NOW, MOST PUISSANT KING.
FOR ONLY NOW IS THE MOMENT IN WHICH OUR BLESSINGS WILL BE MOST POTENT.
AND PERMANENT.
"THE QUEEN SAID, 'WE UNDERSTAND. FAR BE IT FROM US TO LET SUCH A GOLDEN OPPORTUNITY PASS.
'HOLD ON JUST A MINUTE LONGER WHILE WE SEND FOR THE PRINCESS BORN.'
"AND SO, JUST BEFORE THE STROKE OF MIDNIGHT..."
I, KATRYA THE PURE, PROMISE THAT BRIAR ROSE WILL GROW UP TO BE THE MOST BEAUTIFUL WOMAN IN THE LAND.
OH! THANK YOU!

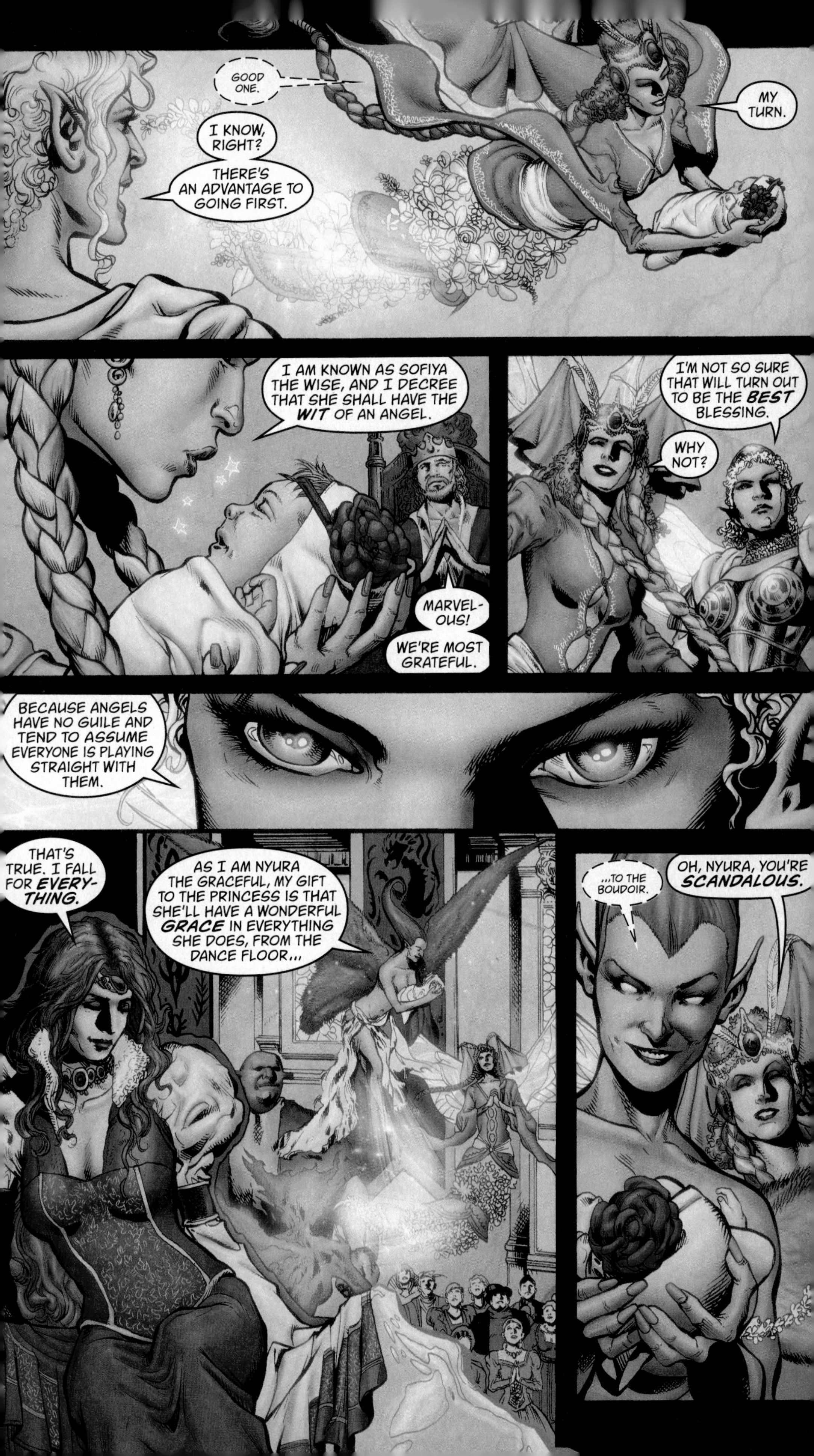
GOOD ONE.
I KNOW, RIGHT?
THERE'S AN ADVANTAGE TO GOING FIRST.
MY TURN.
I AM KNOWN AS SOFIYA THE WISE, AND I DECREE THAT SHE SHALL HAVE THE WIT OF AN ANGEL.
MARVEL-OUS!
WE'RE MOST GRATEFUL.
I'M NOT SO SURE THAT WILL TURN OUT TO BE THE BEST BLESSING.
WHY NOT?
BECAUSE ANGELS HAVE NO GUILE AND TEND TO ASSUME EVERYONE IS PLAYING STRAIGHT WITH THEM.
THAT'S TRUE. I FALL FOR EVERY-THING.
AS I AM NYURA THE GRACEFUL, MY GIFT TO THE PRINCESS IS THAT SHE'LL HAVE A WONDERFUL GRACE IN EVERYTHING SHE DOES, FROM THE DANCE FLOOR...
...TO THE BOUDOIR.
OH, NYURA, YOU'RE SCANDALOUS.

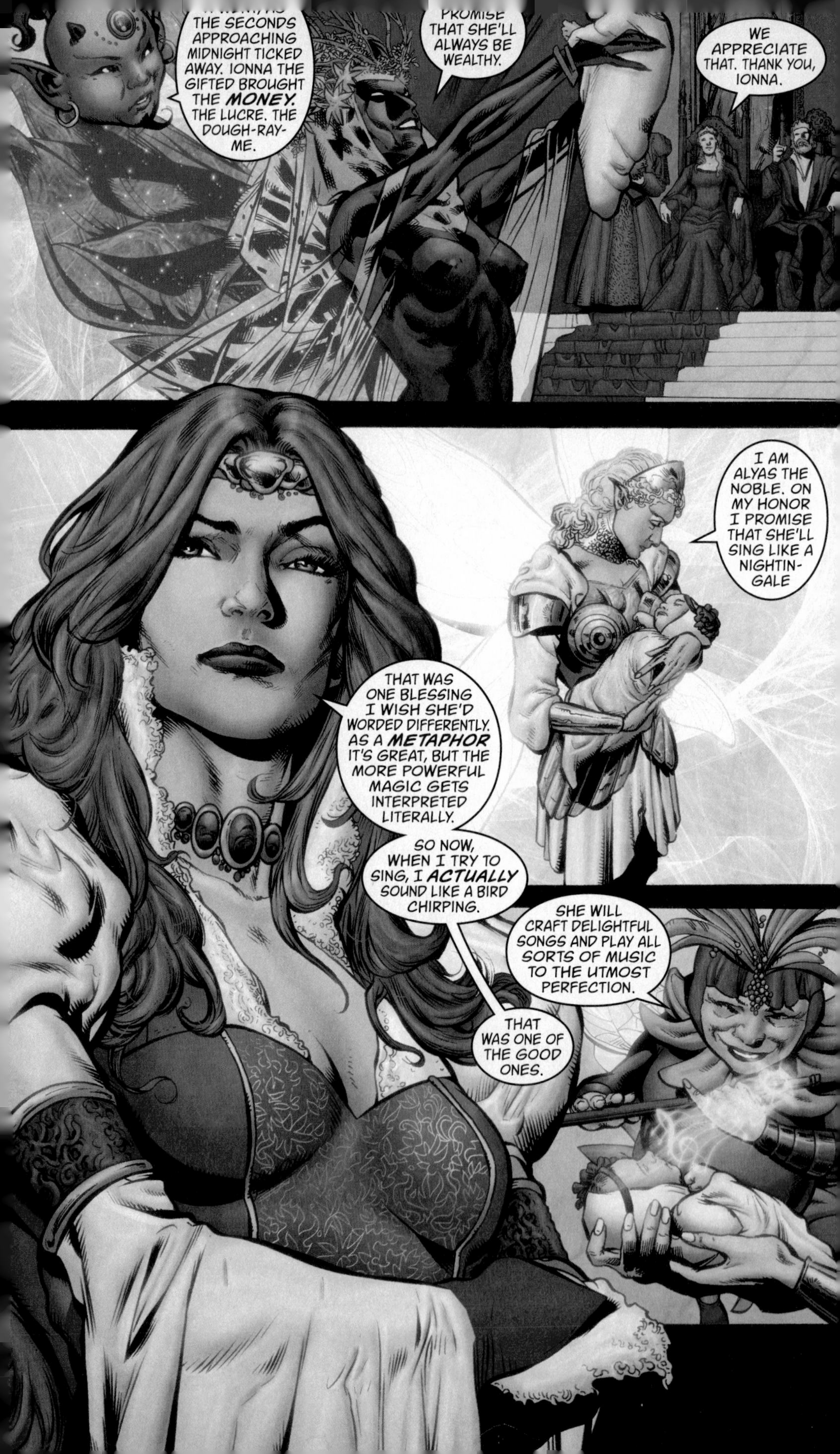

THE SECONDS APPROACHING MIDNIGHT TICKED AWAY. IONNA THE GIFTED BROUGHT THE **MONEY.** THE LUCRE. THE DOUGH-RAY-ME.
PROMISE THAT SHE'LL ALWAYS BE WEALTHY.
WE APPRECIATE THAT. THANK YOU, IONNA.
I AM ALYAS THE NOBLE. ON MY HONOR I PROMISE THAT SHE'LL SING LIKE A NIGHTIN-GALE
THAT WAS ONE BLESSING I WISH SHE'D WORDED DIFFERENTLY. AS A **METAPHOR** IT'S GREAT, BUT THE MORE POWERFUL MAGIC GETS INTERPRETED LITERALLY.
SO NOW, WHEN I TRY TO SING, I **ACTUALLY** SOUND LIKE A BIRD CHIRPING.
SHE WILL CRAFT DELIGHTFUL SONGS AND PLAY ALL SORTS OF MUSIC TO THE UTMOST PERFECTION.
THAT WAS ONE OF THE GOOD ONES.

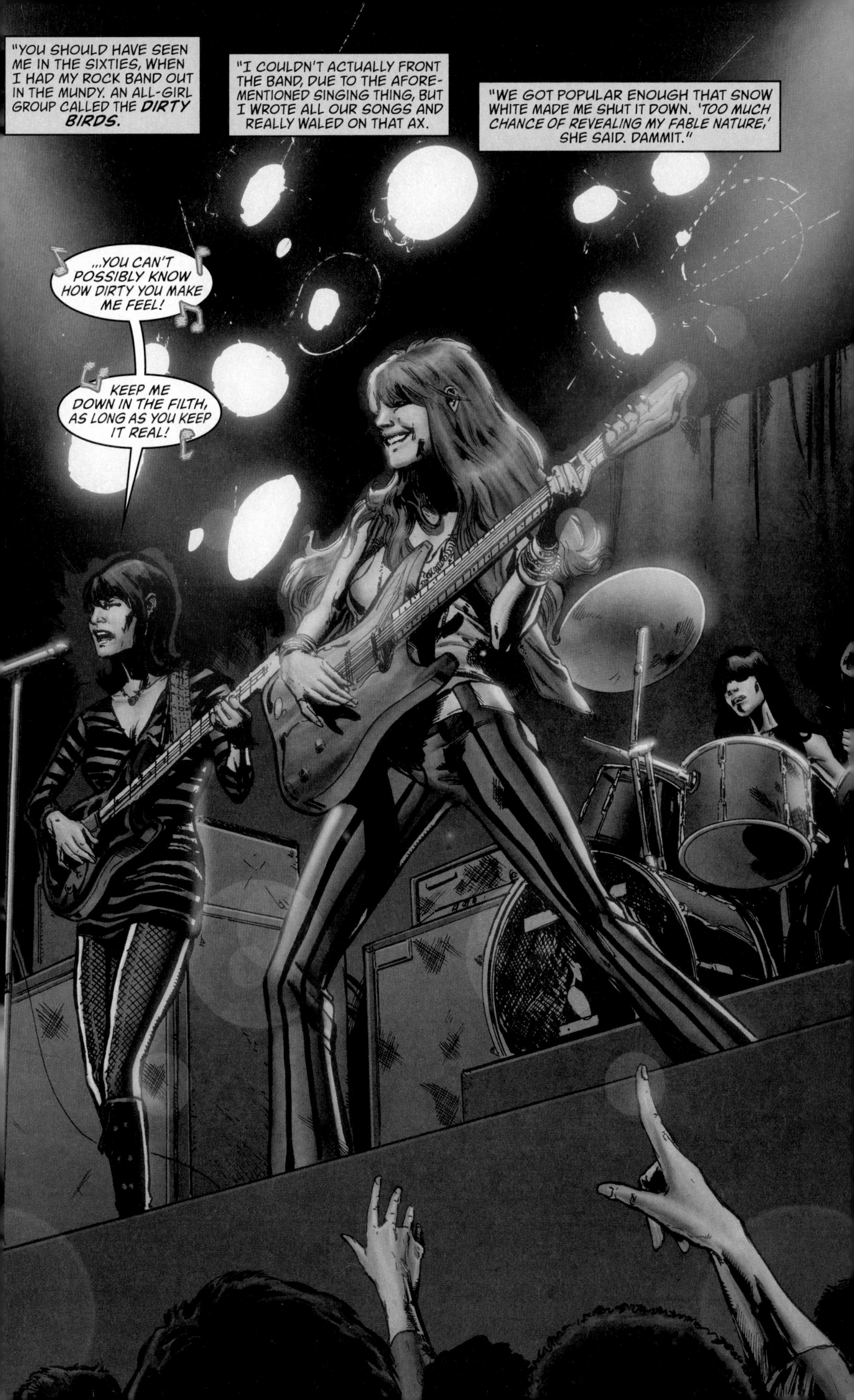
"YOU SHOULD HAVE SEEN ME IN THE SIXTIES, WHEN I HAD MY ROCK BAND OUT IN THE MUNDY. AN ALL-GIRL GROUP CALLED THE DIRTY BIRDS.
"I COULDN'T ACTUALLY FRONT THE BAND, DUE TO THE AFORE-MENTIONED SINGING THING, BUT I WROTE ALL OUR SONGS AND REALLY WALED ON THAT AX.
"WE GOT POPULAR ENOUGH THAT SNOW WHITE MADE ME SHUT IT DOWN. 'TOO MUCH CHANCE OF REVEALING MY FABLE NATURE,' SHE SAID. DAMMIT."
...YOU CAN'T POSSIBLY KNOW HOW DIRTY YOU MAKE ME FEEL!
KEEP ME DOWN IN THE FILTH, AS LONG AS YOU KEEP IT REAL!

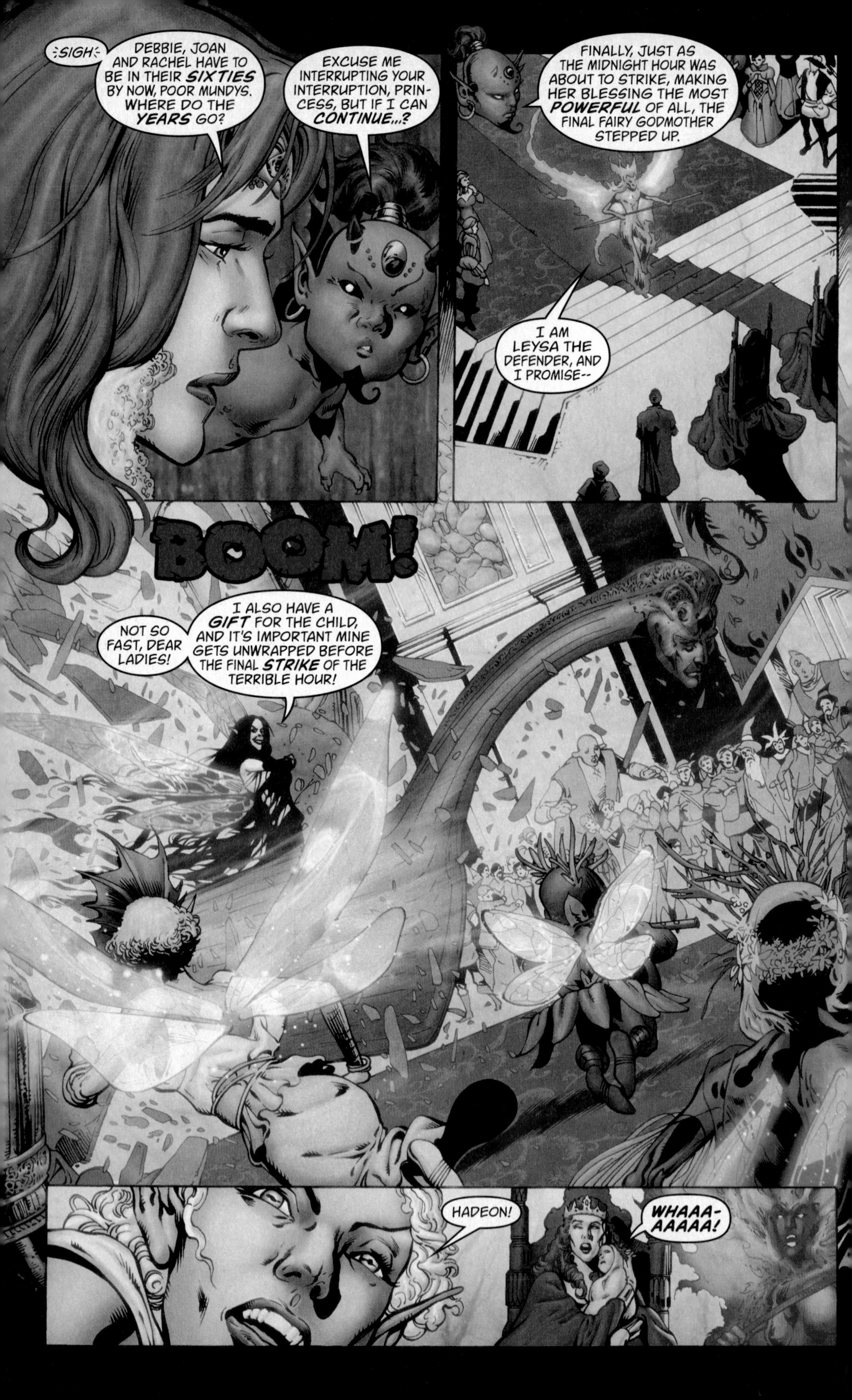

SIGH
DEBBIE, JOAN AND RACHEL HAVE TO BE IN THEIR SIXTIES BY NOW, POOR MUNDYS. WHERE DO THE YEARS GO?
EXCUSE ME INTERRUPTING YOUR INTERRUPTION, PRINCESS, BUT IF I CAN CONTINUE...?
FINALLY, JUST AS THE MIDNIGHT HOUR WAS ABOUT TO STRIKE, MAKING HER BLESSING THE MOST POWERFUL OF ALL, THE FINAL FAIRY GODMOTHER STEPPED UP.
I AM LEYSA THE DEFENDER, AND I PROMISE--
BOOM!
NOT SO FAST, DEAR LADIES!
I ALSO HAVE A GIFT FOR THE CHILD, AND IT'S IMPORTANT MINE GETS UNWRAPPED BEFORE THE FINAL STRIKE OF THE TERRIBLE HOUR!
HADEON!
WHAAAAAAAA!

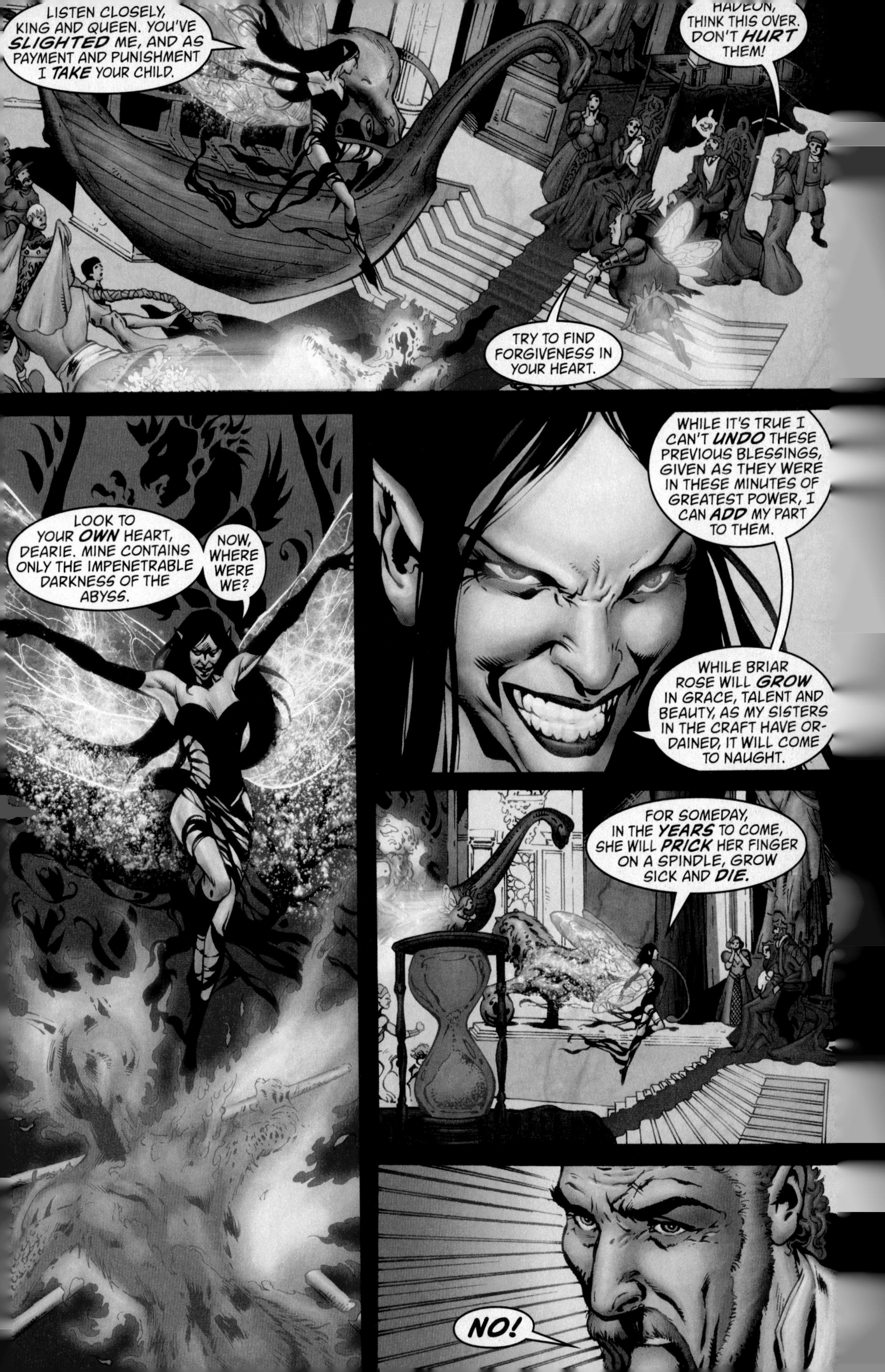

LISTEN CLOSELY, KING AND QUEEN. YOU'VE SLIGHTED ME, AND AS PAYMENT AND PUNISHMENT I TAKE YOUR CHILD.
HADEON, THINK THIS OVER. DON'T HURT THEM!
TRY TO FIND FORGIVENESS IN YOUR HEART.
LOOK TO YOUR OWN HEART, DEARIE. MINE CONTAINS ONLY THE IMPENETRABLE DARKNESS OF THE ABYSS.
NOW, WHERE WERE WE?
WHILE IT'S TRUE I CAN'T UNDO THESE PREVIOUS BLESSINGS, GIVEN AS THEY WERE IN THESE MINUTES OF GREATEST POWER, I CAN ADD MY PART TO THEM.
WHILE BRIAR ROSE WILL GROW IN GRACE, TALENT AND BEAUTY, AS MY SISTERS IN THE CRAFT HAVE ORDAINED, IT WILL COME TO NAUGHT.
FOR SOMEDAY, IN THE YEARS TO COME, SHE WILL PRICK HER FINGER ON A SPINDLE, GROW SICK AND DIE.
NO!

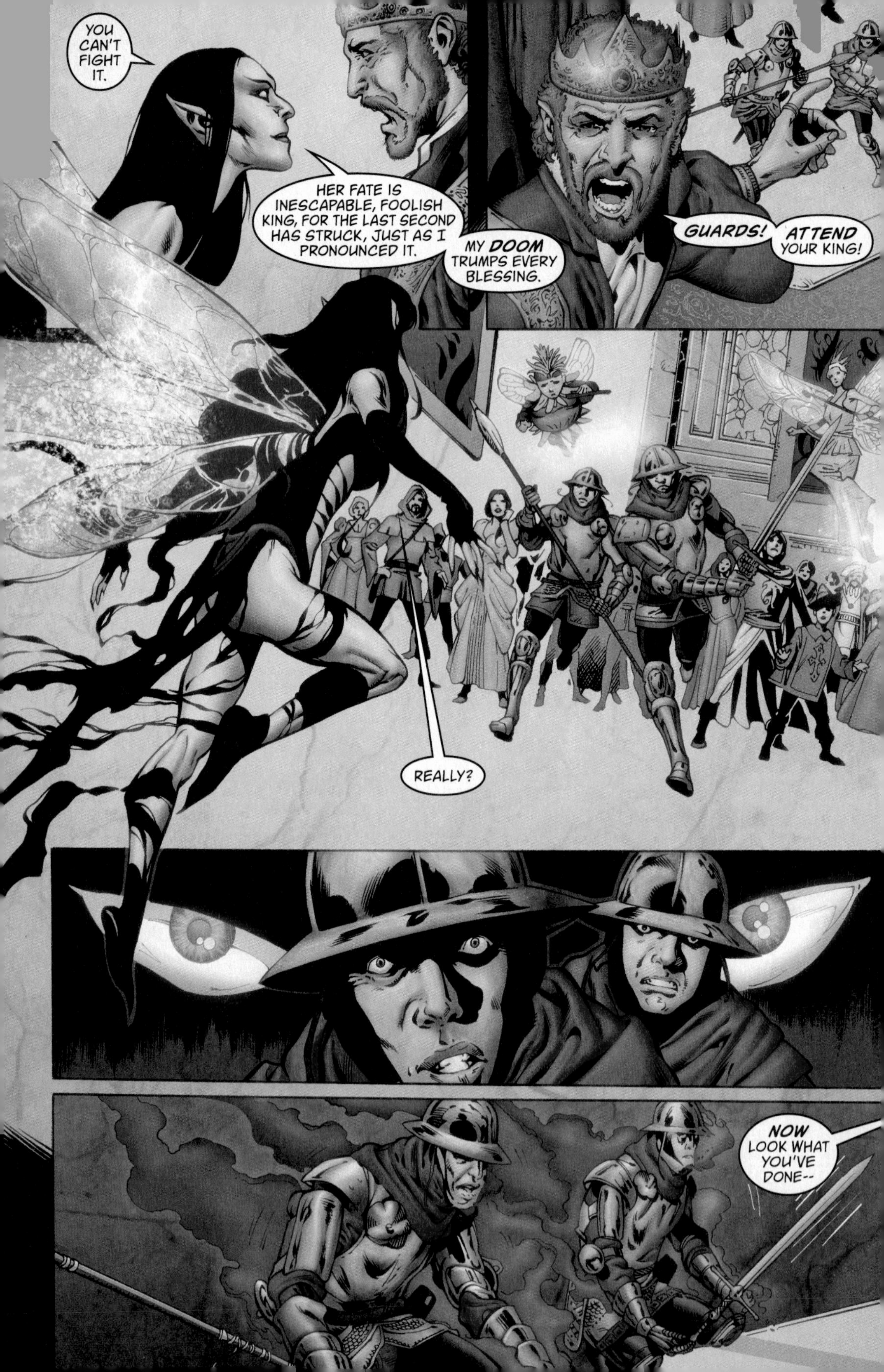
YOU CAN'T FIGHT IT.
HER FATE IS INESCAPABLE, FOOLISH KING, FOR THE LAST SECOND HAS STRUCK, JUST AS I PRONOUNCED IT.
MY DOOM TRUMPS EVERY BLESSING.
GUARDS!
ATTEND YOUR KING!
REALLY?
NOW LOOK WHAT YOU'VE DONE--

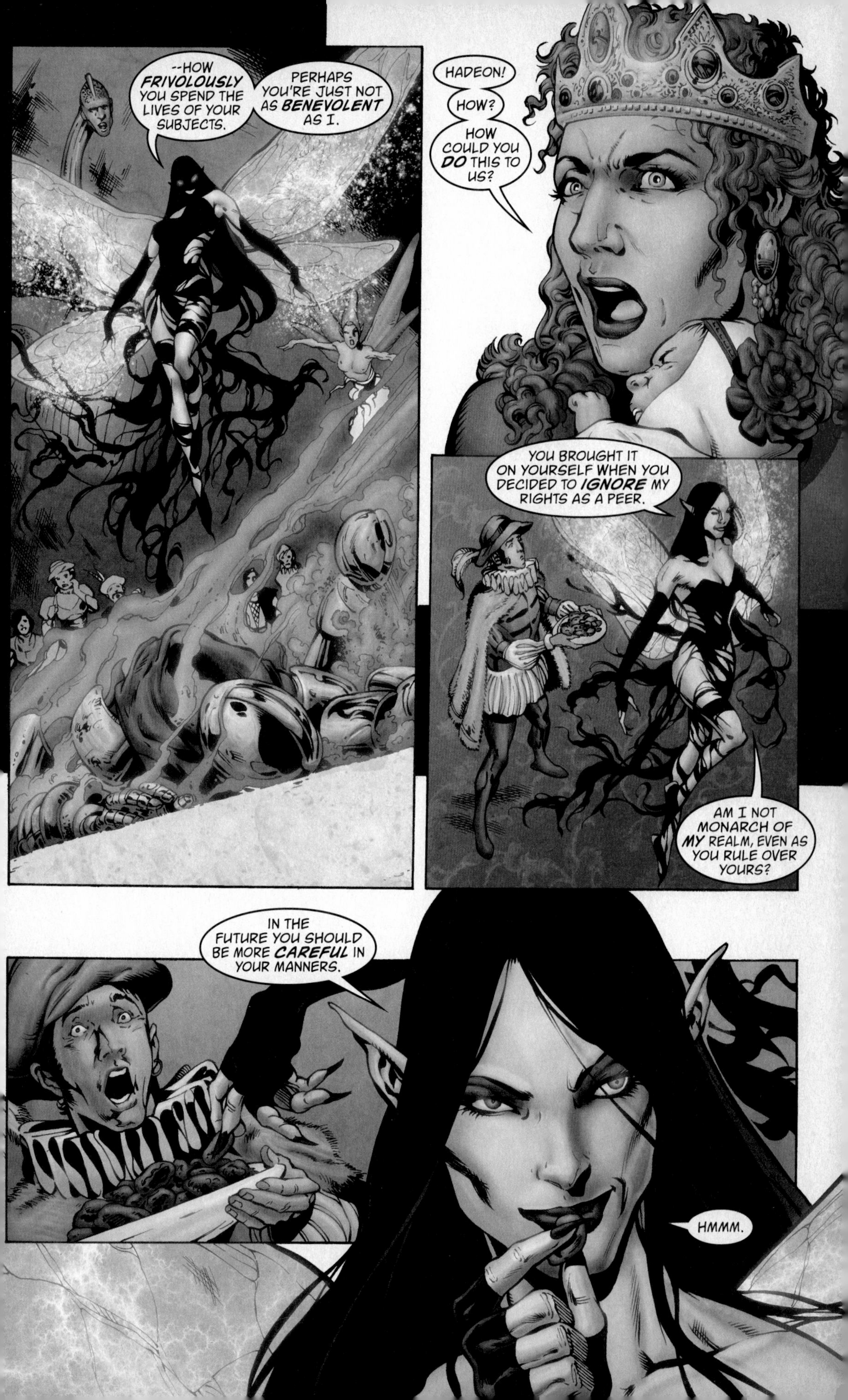
--HOW FRIVOLOUSLY YOU SPEND THE LIVES OF YOUR SUBJECTS.
PERHAPS YOU'RE JUST NOT AS BENEVOLENT AS I.
HADEON!
HOW?
HOW COULD YOU DO THIS TO US?
YOU BROUGHT IT ON YOURSELF WHEN YOU DECIDED TO IGNORE MY RIGHTS AS A PEER.
AM I NOT MONARCH OF MY REALM, EVEN AS YOU RULE OVER YOURS?
IN THE FUTURE YOU SHOULD BE MORE CAREFUL IN YOUR MANNERS.
HMMM.

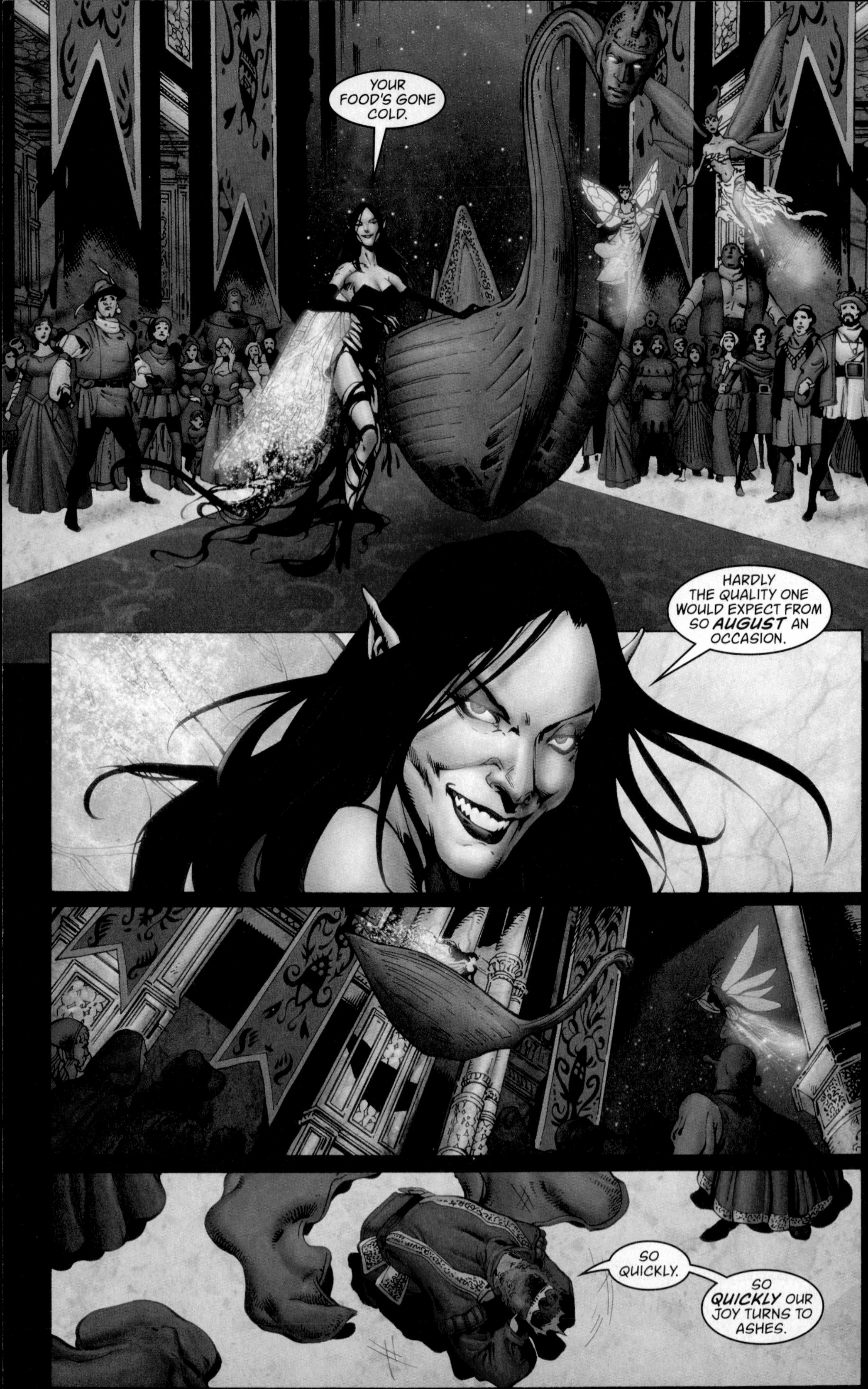
YOUR FOOD'S GONE COLD.
HARDLY THE QUALITY ONE WOULD EXPECT FROM SO **AUGUST** AN OCCASION.
SO QUICKLY.
SO **QUICKLY** OUR JOY TURNS TO ASHES.

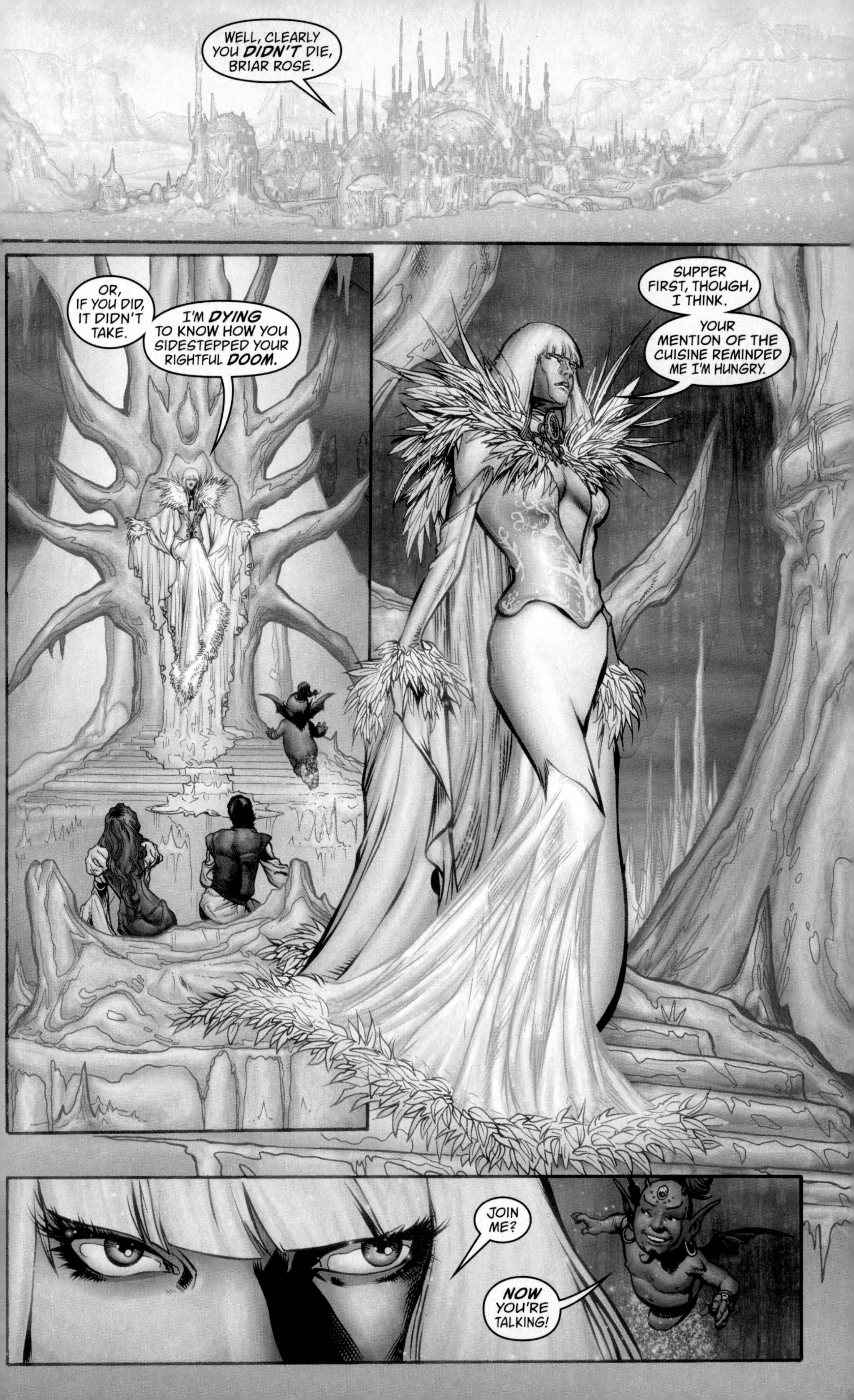
WELL, CLEARLY YOU DIDN'T DIE, BRIAR ROSE.
OR, IF YOU DID, IT DIDN'T TAKE.
I'M DYING TO KNOW HOW YOU SIDESTEPPED YOUR RIGHTFUL DOOM.
SUPPER FIRST, THOUGH, I THINK.
YOUR MENTION OF THE CUISINE REMINDED ME I'M HUNGRY.
JOIN ME?
NOW YOU'RE TALKING!

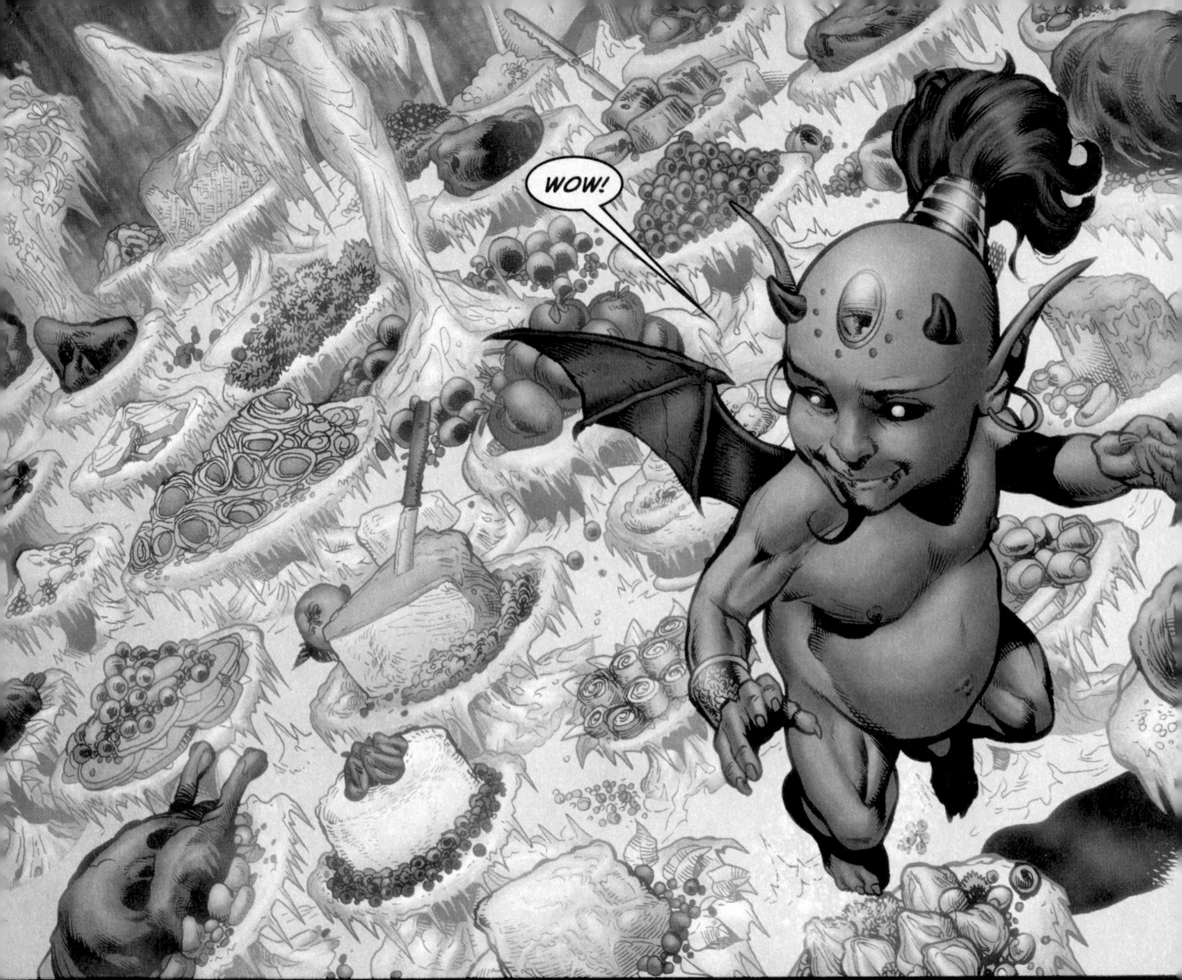
WOW!

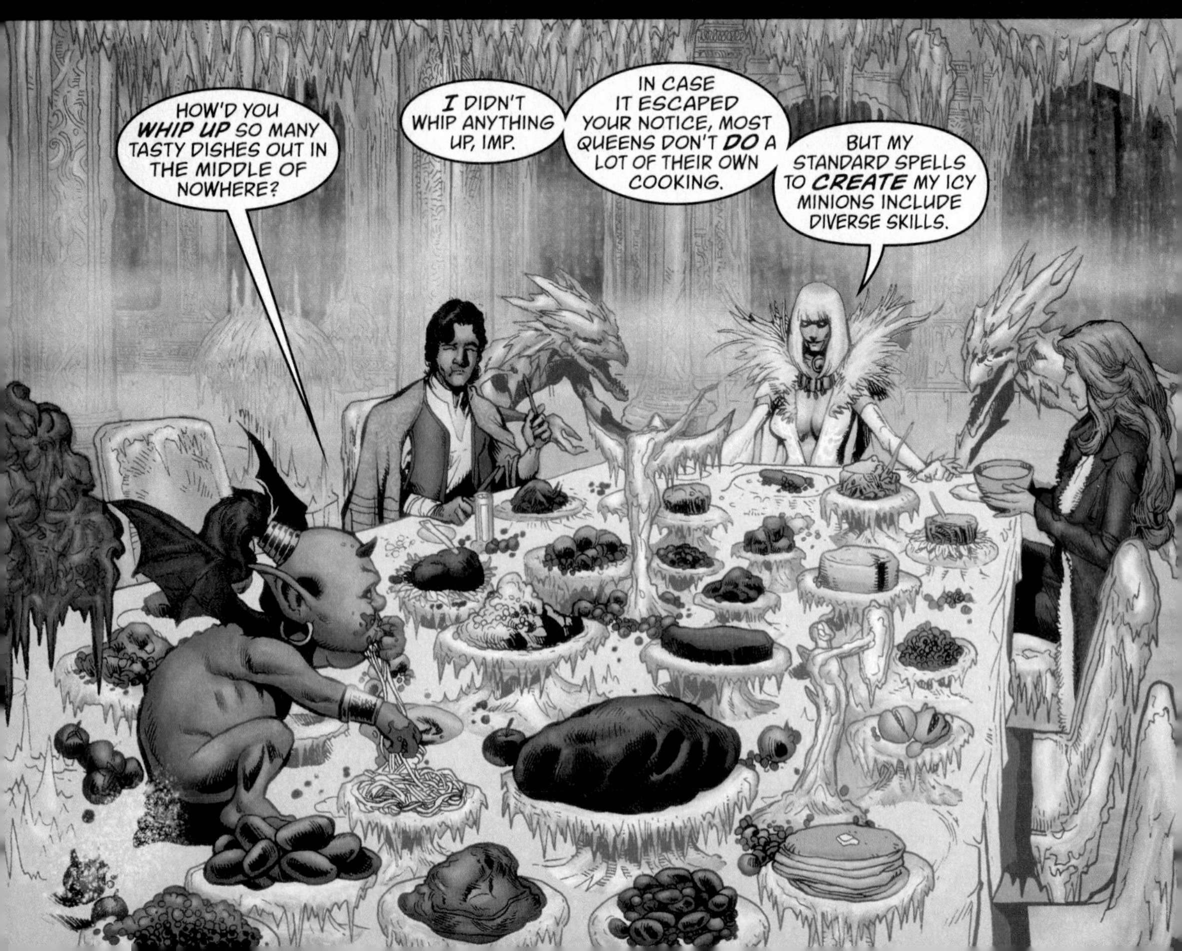
HOW'D YOU WHIP UP SO MANY TASTY DISHES OUT IN THE MIDDLE OF NOWHERE?
I DIDN'T WHIP ANYTHING UP, IMP.
IN CASE IT ESCAPED YOUR NOTICE, MOST QUEENS DON'T DO A LOT OF THEIR OWN COOKING.
BUT MY STANDARD SPELLS TO CREATE MY ICY MINIONS INCLUDE DIVERSE SKILLS.

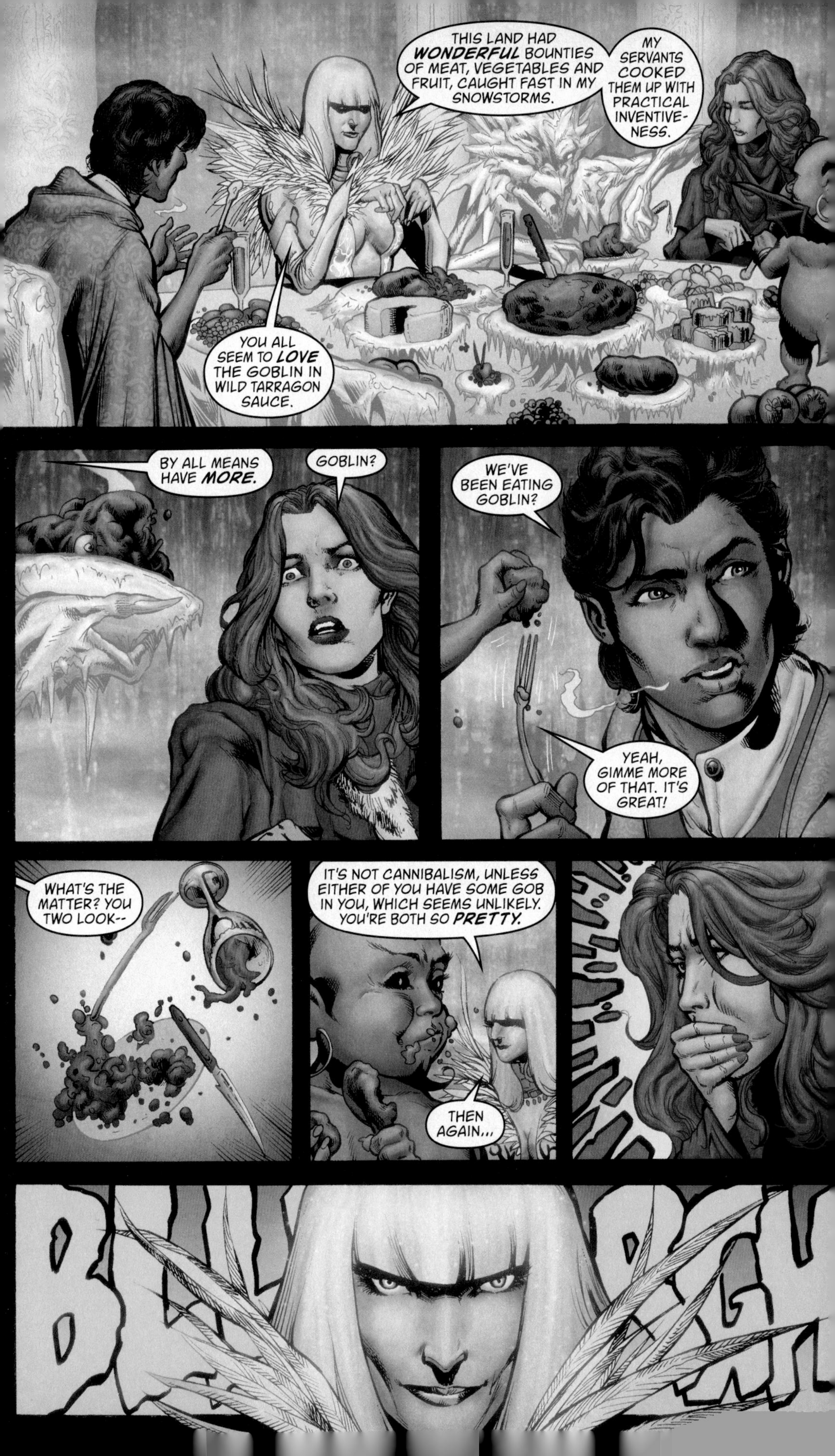
THIS LAND HAD WONDERFUL BOUNTIES OF MEAT, VEGETABLES AND FRUIT, CAUGHT FAST IN MY SNOWSTORMS.
MY SERVANTS COOKED THEM UP WITH PRACTICAL INVENTIVE-NESS.
YOU ALL SEEM TO LOVE THE GOBLIN IN WILD TARRAGON SAUCE.
BY ALL MEANS HAVE MORE.
GOBLIN?
WE'VE BEEN EATING GOBLIN?
YEAH, GIMME MORE OF THAT. IT'S GREAT!
WHAT'S THE MATTER? YOU TWO LOOK--
IT'S NOT CANNIBALISM, UNLESS EITHER OF YOU HAVE SOME GOB IN YOU, WHICH SEEMS UNLIKELY. YOU'RE BOTH SO PRETTY.
THEN AGAIN...

PERHAPS YOU TWO SHOULD *REST* A BIT, BEFORE WE CONTINUE YOUR TALE.

MR. FROST WILL ESCORT YOU TO YOUR CELLS-- *ah*--TO YOUR *ROOMS.*

GOOD.

I THOUGHT THOSE TWO WOULD *NEVER* LEAVE, YOUR WORSHIPFULNESS. NOW IT'S YOU AND ME, ALONE AT *LAST.*

DON'T GET *FRESH,* IMP.

I CAN CRUSH YOU LIKE A BUG, BUT NOT BEFORE I HAVE YOU FLAYED *ALIVE* FIRST.

DON'T WORRY, QUEENIE, YOU'RE NOT MY TYPE.

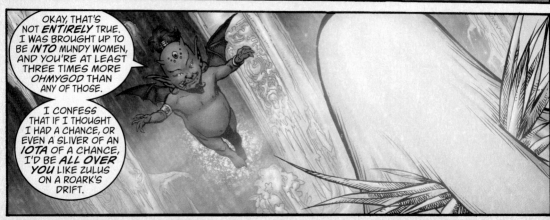

OKAY, THAT'S NOT *ENTIRELY* TRUE. I WAS BROUGHT UP TO BE *INTO* MUNDY WOMEN, AND YOU'RE AT LEAST THREE TIMES MORE *OHMYGOD* THAN ANY OF THOSE.

I CONFESS THAT IF I THOUGHT I HAD A CHANCE, OR EVEN A SLIVER OF AN *IOTA* OF A CHANCE, I'D BE *ALL OVER YOU* LIKE ZULUS ON A ROARK'S DRIFT.

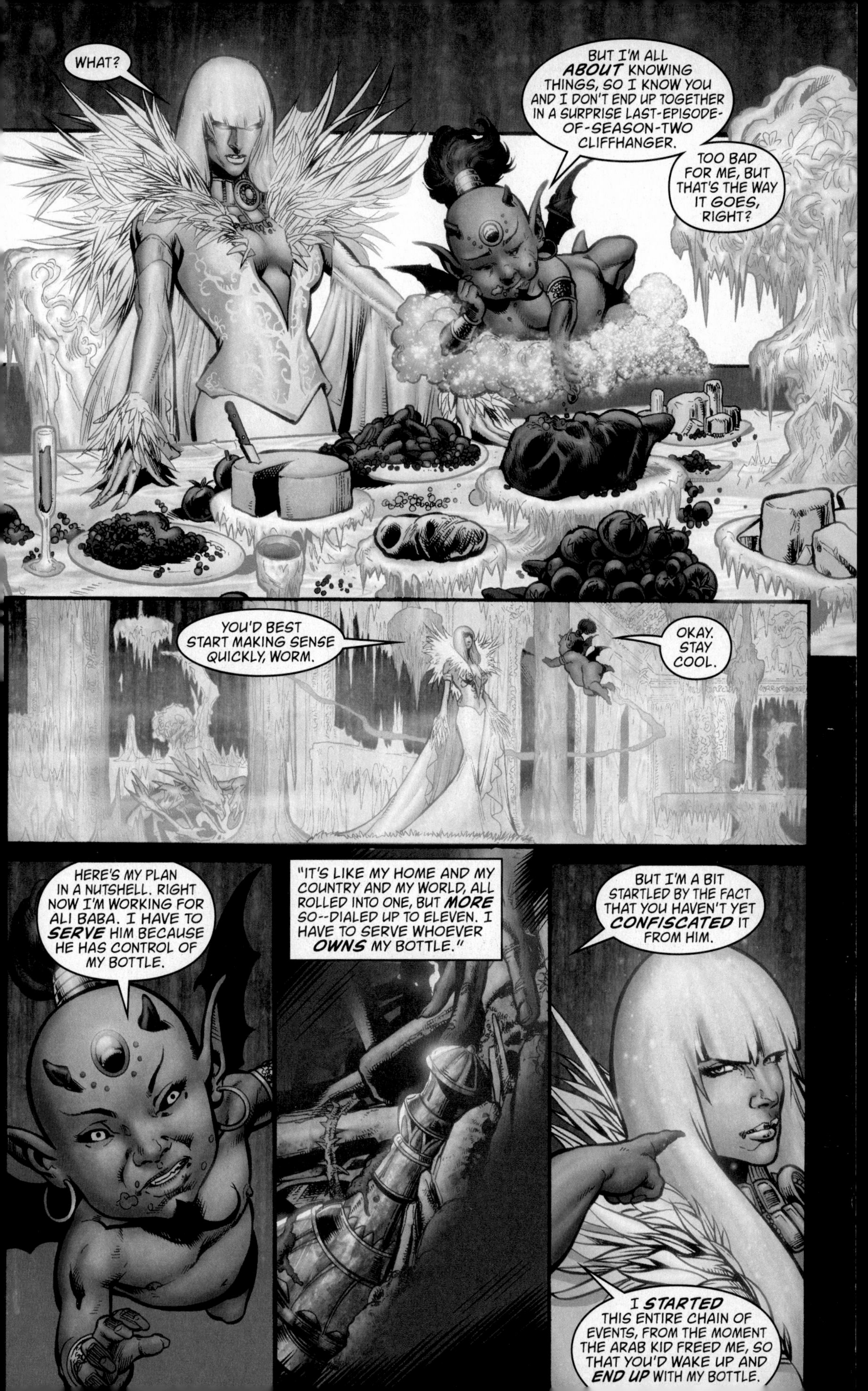
WHAT?
BUT I'M ALL ABOUT KNOWING THINGS, SO I KNOW YOU AND I DON'T END UP TOGETHER IN A SURPRISE LAST-EPISODE-OF-SEASON-TWO CLIFFHANGER.
TOO BAD FOR ME, BUT THAT'S THE WAY IT GOES, RIGHT?
YOU'D BEST START MAKING SENSE QUICKLY, WORM.
OKAY. STAY COOL.
HERE'S MY PLAN IN A NUTSHELL. RIGHT NOW I'M WORKING FOR ALI BABA. I HAVE TO SERVE HIM BECAUSE HE HAS CONTROL OF MY BOTTLE.
"IT'S LIKE MY HOME AND MY COUNTRY AND MY WORLD, ALL ROLLED INTO ONE, BUT MORE SO--DIALED UP TO ELEVEN. I HAVE TO SERVE WHOEVER OWNS MY BOTTLE."
BUT I'M A BIT STARTLED BY THE FACT THAT YOU HAVEN'T YET CONFISCATED IT FROM HIM.
I STARTED THIS ENTIRE CHAIN OF EVENTS, FROM THE MOMENT THE ARAB KID FREED ME, SO THAT YOU'D WAKE UP AND END UP WITH MY BOTTLE.

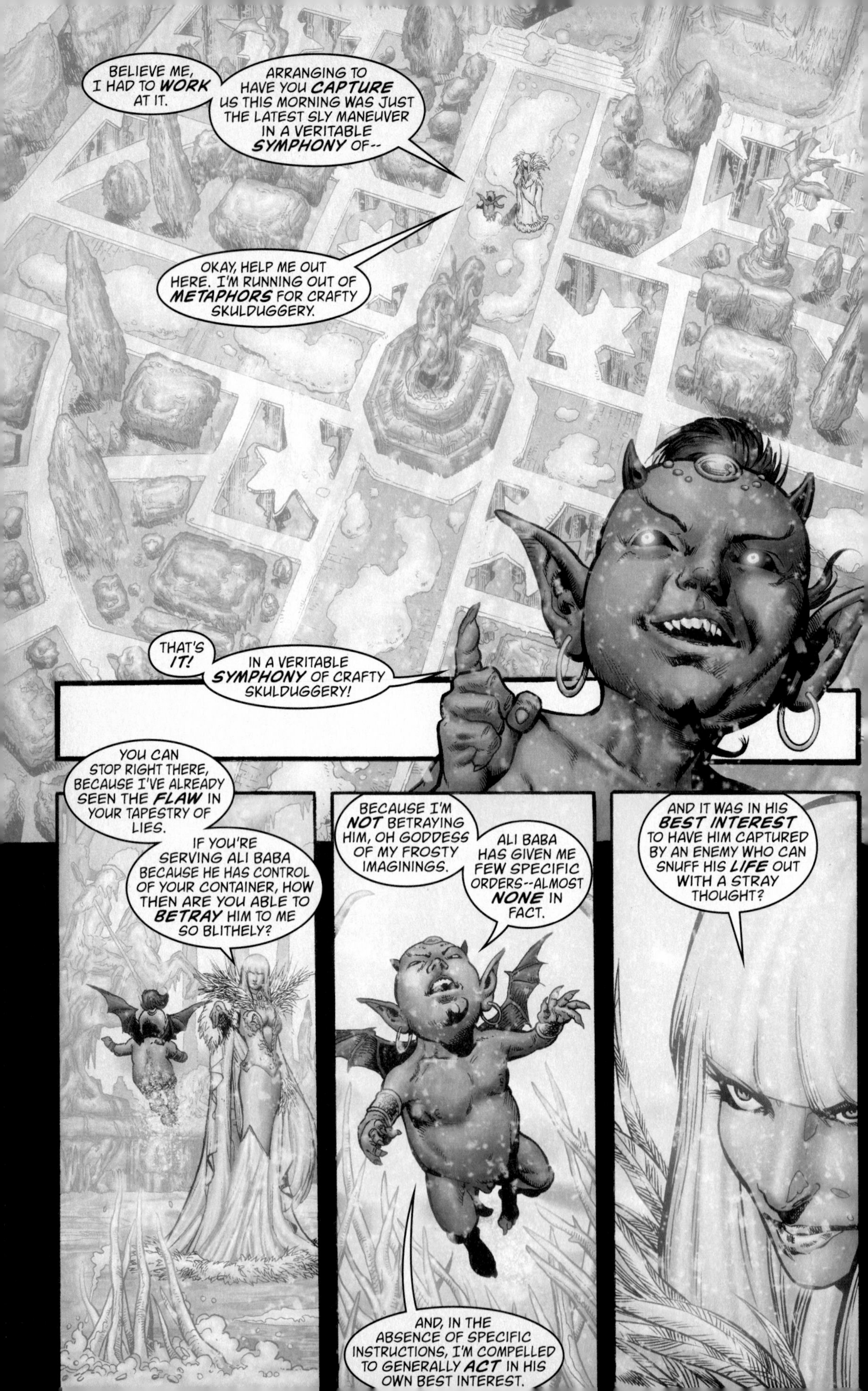

BELIEVE ME, I HAD TO WORK AT IT.
ARRANGING TO HAVE YOU CAPTURE US THIS MORNING WAS JUST THE LATEST SLY MANEUVER IN A VERITABLE SYMPHONY OF--
OKAY, HELP ME OUT HERE. I'M RUNNING OUT OF METAPHORS FOR CRAFTY SKULDUGGERY.
THAT'S IT!
IN A VERITABLE SYMPHONY OF CRAFTY SKULDUGGERY!
YOU CAN STOP RIGHT THERE, BECAUSE I'VE ALREADY SEEN THE FLAW IN YOUR TAPESTRY OF LIES.
IF YOU'RE SERVING ALI BABA BECAUSE HE HAS CONTROL OF YOUR CONTAINER, HOW THEN ARE YOU ABLE TO BETRAY HIM TO ME SO BLITHELY?
BECAUSE I'M NOT BETRAYING HIM, OH GODDESS OF MY FROSTY IMAGININGS.
ALI BABA HAS GIVEN ME FEW SPECIFIC ORDERS--ALMOST NONE IN FACT.
AND, IN THE ABSENCE OF SPECIFIC INSTRUCTIONS, I'M COMPELLED TO GENERALLY ACT IN HIS OWN BEST INTEREST.
AND IT WAS IN HIS BEST INTEREST TO HAVE HIM CAPTURED BY AN ENEMY WHO CAN SNUFF HIS LIFE OUT WITH A STRAY THOUGHT?

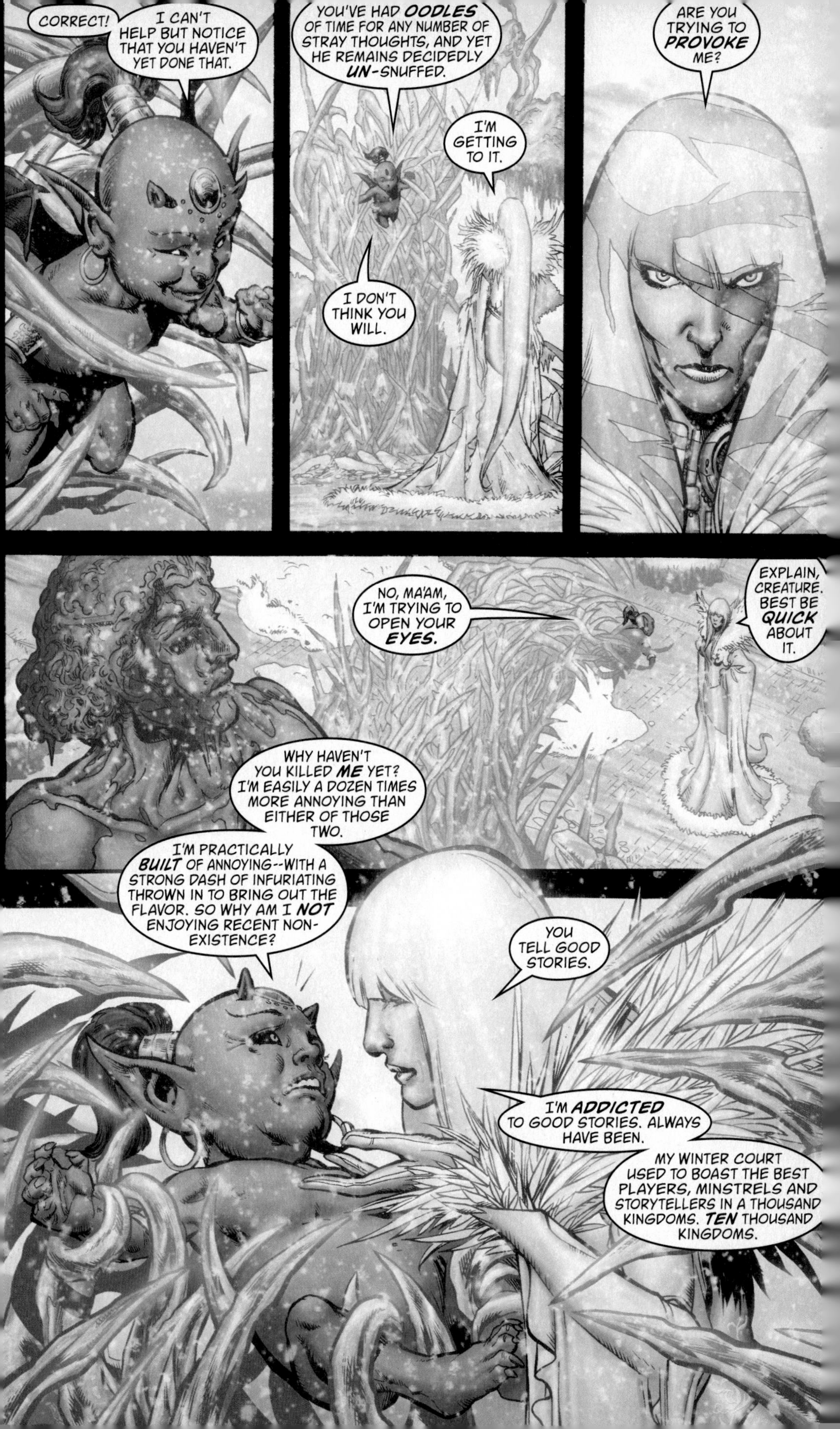

CORRECT!
I CAN'T HELP BUT NOTICE THAT YOU HAVEN'T YET DONE THAT.
YOU'VE HAD OODLES OF TIME FOR ANY NUMBER OF STRAY THOUGHTS, AND YET HE REMAINS DECIDEDLY UN-SNUFFED.
I'M GETTING TO IT.
I DON'T THINK YOU WILL.
ARE YOU TRYING TO PROVOKE ME?
NO, MA'AM, I'M TRYING TO OPEN YOUR EYES.
EXPLAIN, CREATURE. BEST BE QUICK ABOUT IT.
WHY HAVEN'T YOU KILLED ME YET? I'M EASILY A DOZEN TIMES MORE ANNOYING THAN EITHER OF THOSE TWO.
I'M PRACTICALLY BUILT OF ANNOYING--WITH A STRONG DASH OF INFURIATING THROWN IN TO BRING OUT THE FLAVOR. SO WHY AM I NOT ENJOYING RECENT NON-EXISTENCE?
YOU TELL GOOD STORIES.
I'M ADDICTED TO GOOD STORIES. ALWAYS HAVE BEEN.
MY WINTER COURT USED TO BOAST THE BEST PLAYERS, MINSTRELS AND STORYTELLERS IN A THOUSAND KINGDOMS. TEN THOUSAND KINGDOMS.

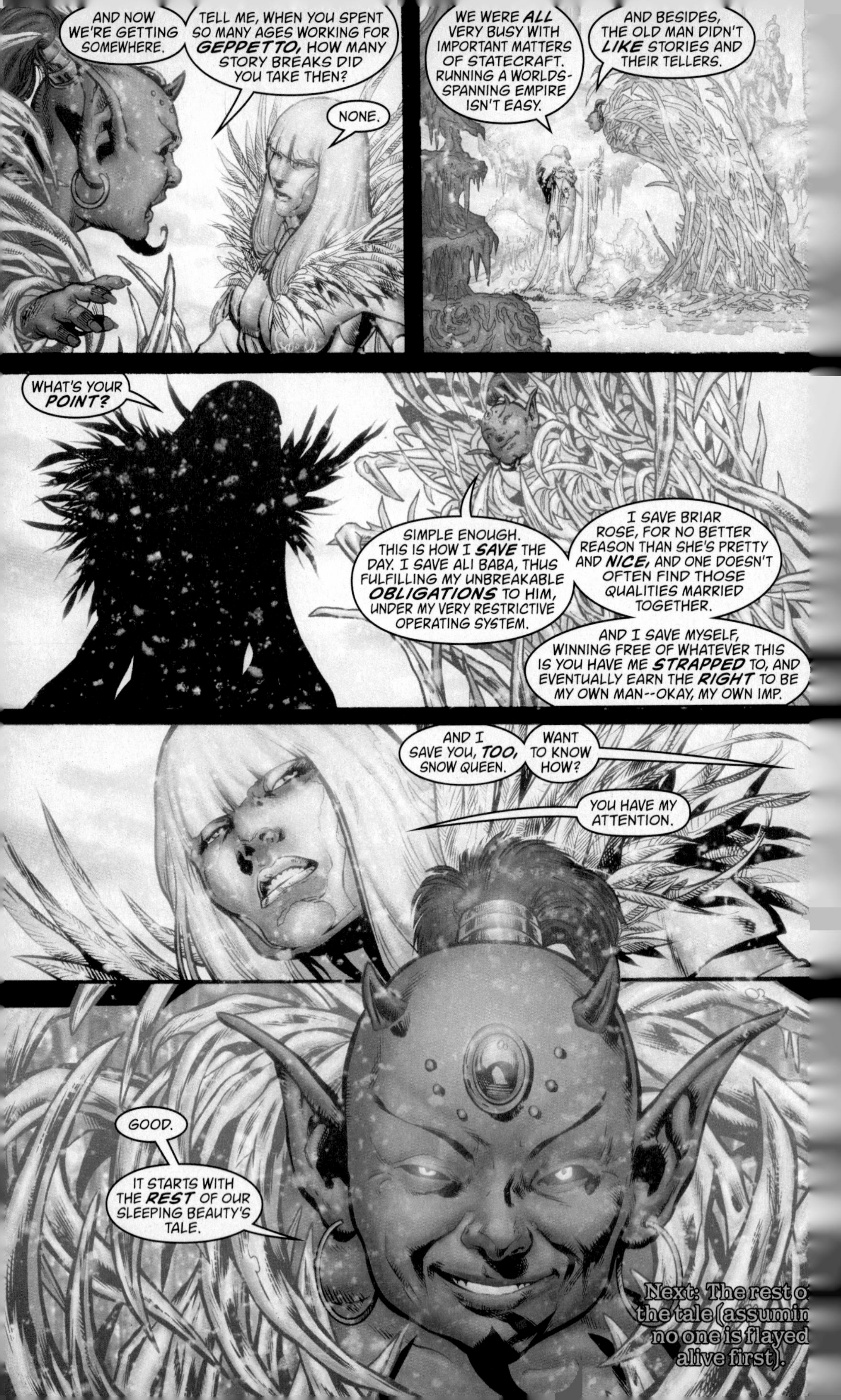
AND NOW WE'RE GETTING SOMEWHERE.
TELL ME, WHEN YOU SPENT SO MANY AGES WORKING FOR GEPPETTO, HOW MANY STORY BREAKS DID YOU TAKE THEN?
NONE.
WE WERE ALL VERY BUSY WITH IMPORTANT MATTERS OF STATECRAFT. RUNNING A WORLDS-SPANNING EMPIRE ISN'T EASY.
AND BESIDES, THE OLD MAN DIDN'T LIKE STORIES AND THEIR TELLERS.
WHAT'S YOUR POINT?
SIMPLE ENOUGH. THIS IS HOW I SAVE THE DAY. I SAVE ALI BABA, THUS FULFILLING MY UNBREAKABLE OBLIGATIONS TO HIM, UNDER MY VERY RESTRICTIVE OPERATING SYSTEM.
I SAVE BRIAR ROSE, FOR NO BETTER REASON THAN SHE'S PRETTY AND NICE, AND ONE DOESN'T OFTEN FIND THOSE QUALITIES MARRIED TOGETHER.
AND I SAVE MYSELF, WINNING FREE OF WHATEVER THIS IS YOU HAVE ME STRAPPED TO, AND EVENTUALLY EARN THE RIGHT TO BE MY OWN MAN--OKAY, MY OWN IMP.
AND I SAVE YOU, TOO, SNOW QUEEN.
WANT TO KNOW HOW?
YOU HAVE MY ATTENTION.
GOOD.
IT STARTS WITH THE REST OF OUR SLEEPING BEAUTY'S TALE.
Next: The rest o the tale (assumin no one is flayed alive first).

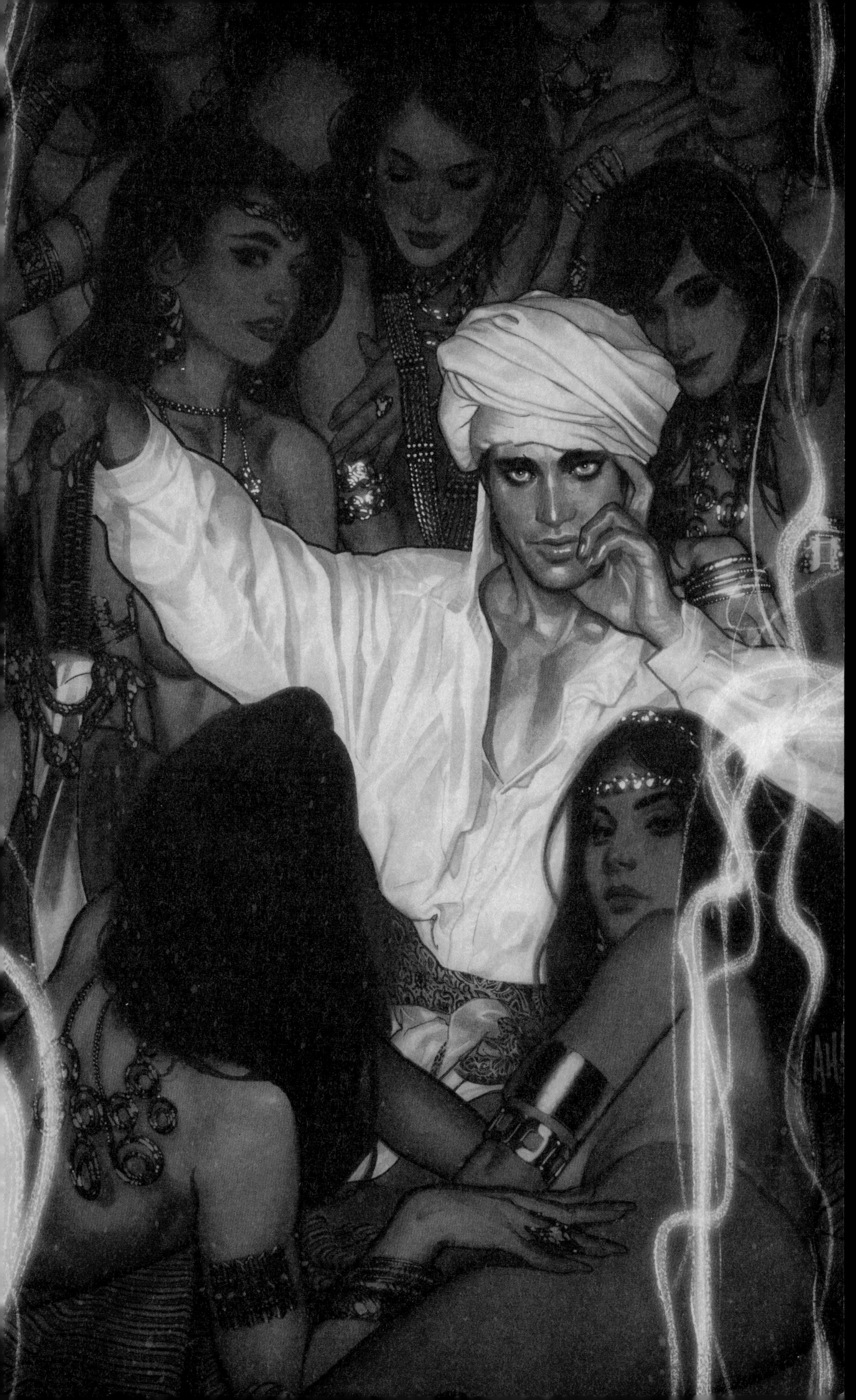

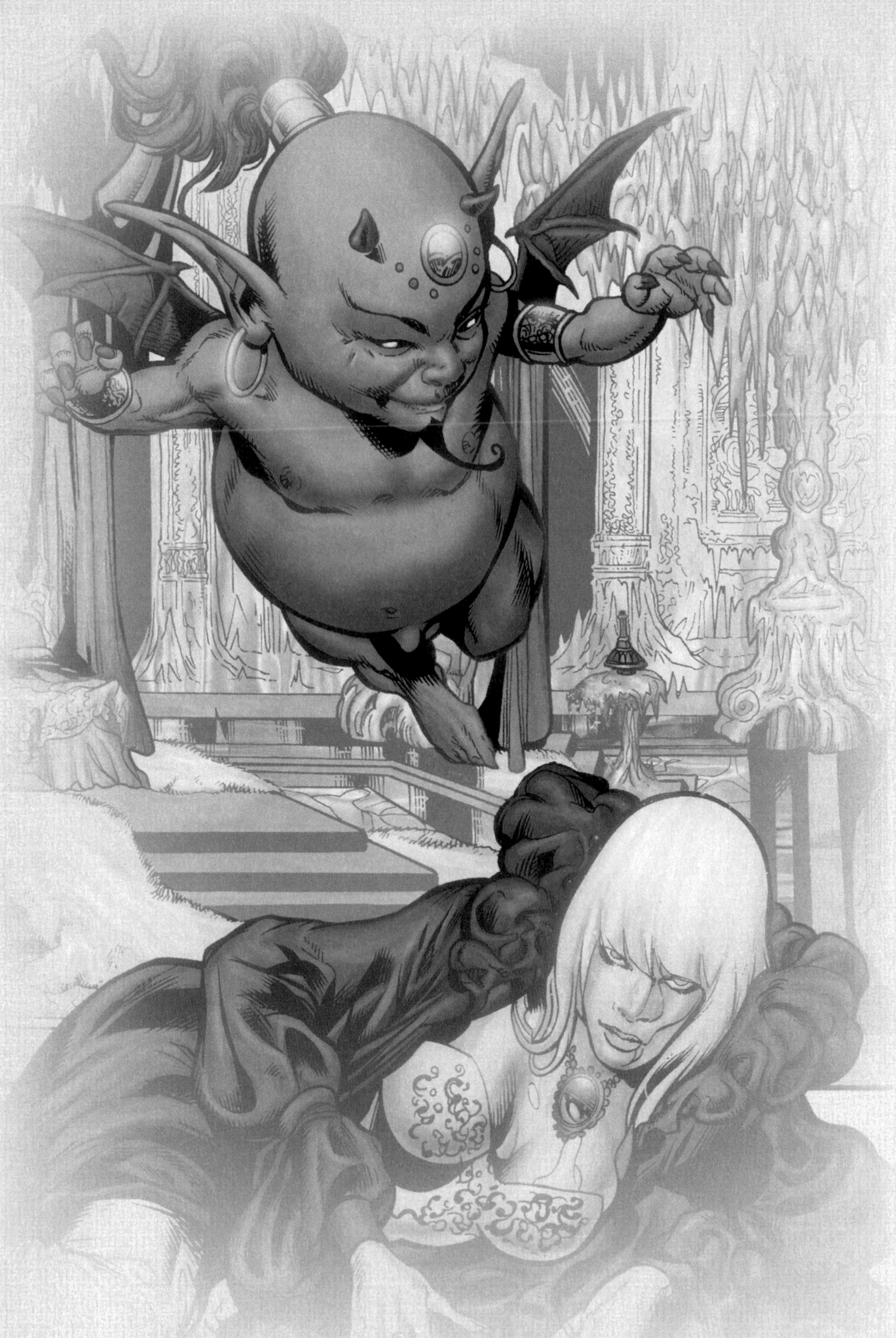

"You're an addict. You need stories the way the furrow needs the plow."

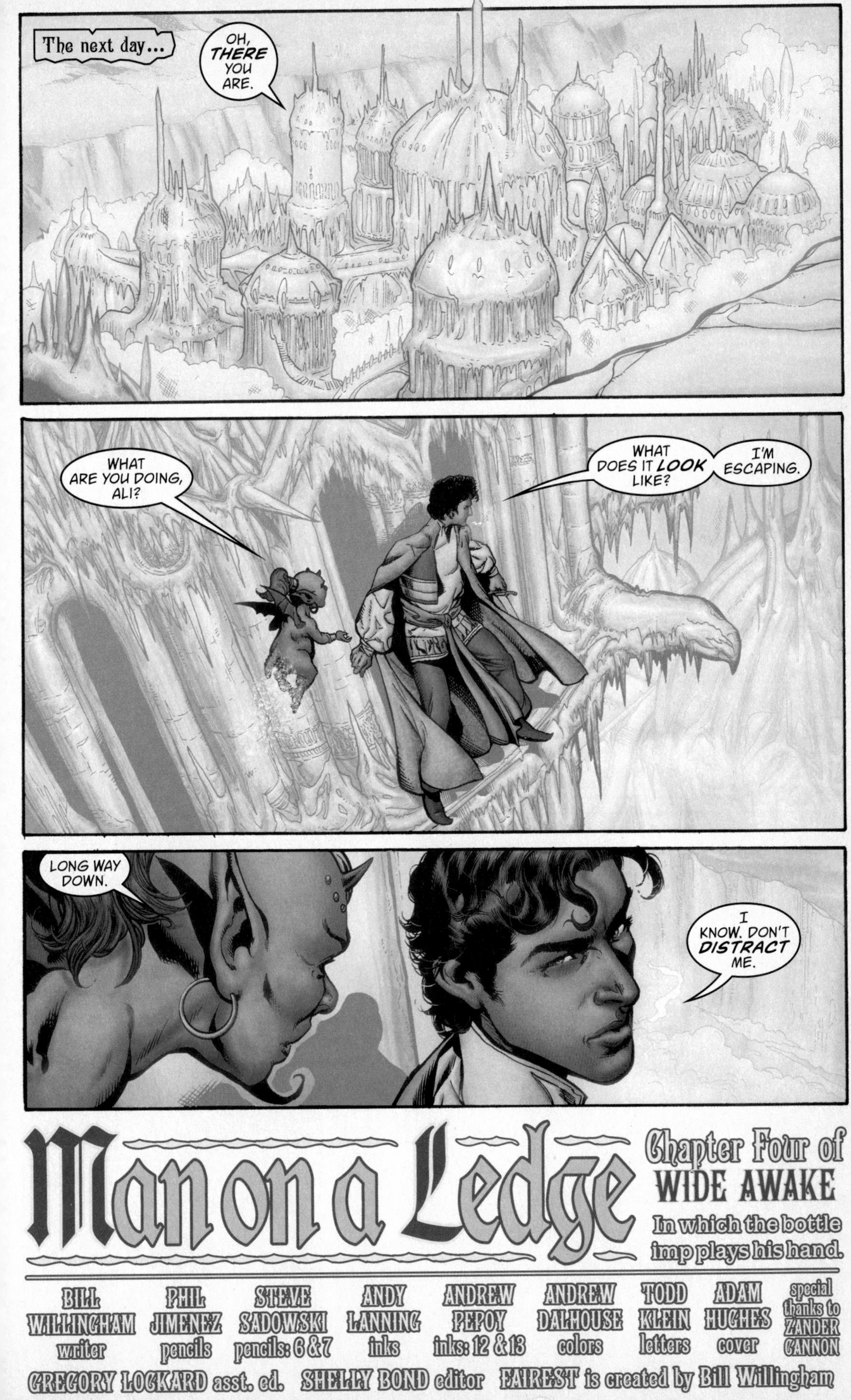
The next day...
OH, THERE YOU ARE.
WHAT ARE YOU DOING, ALI?
WHAT DOES IT LOOK LIKE?
I'M ESCAPING.
LONG WAY DOWN.
I KNOW. DON'T DISTRACT ME.

Man on a Ledge

Chapter Four of WIDE AWAKE

In which the bottle imp plays his hand.

BILL WILLINGHAM writer · PHIL JIMENEZ pencils · STEVE SADOWSKI pencils: 6 & 7 · ANDY LANNING inks · ANDREW PEPOY inks: 12 & 13 · ANDREW DALHOUSE colors · TODD KLEIN letters · ADAM HUGHES cover · special thanks to ZANDER CANNON

GREGORY LOCKARD asst. ed. · SHELLY BOND editor · FAIREST is created by Bill Willingham

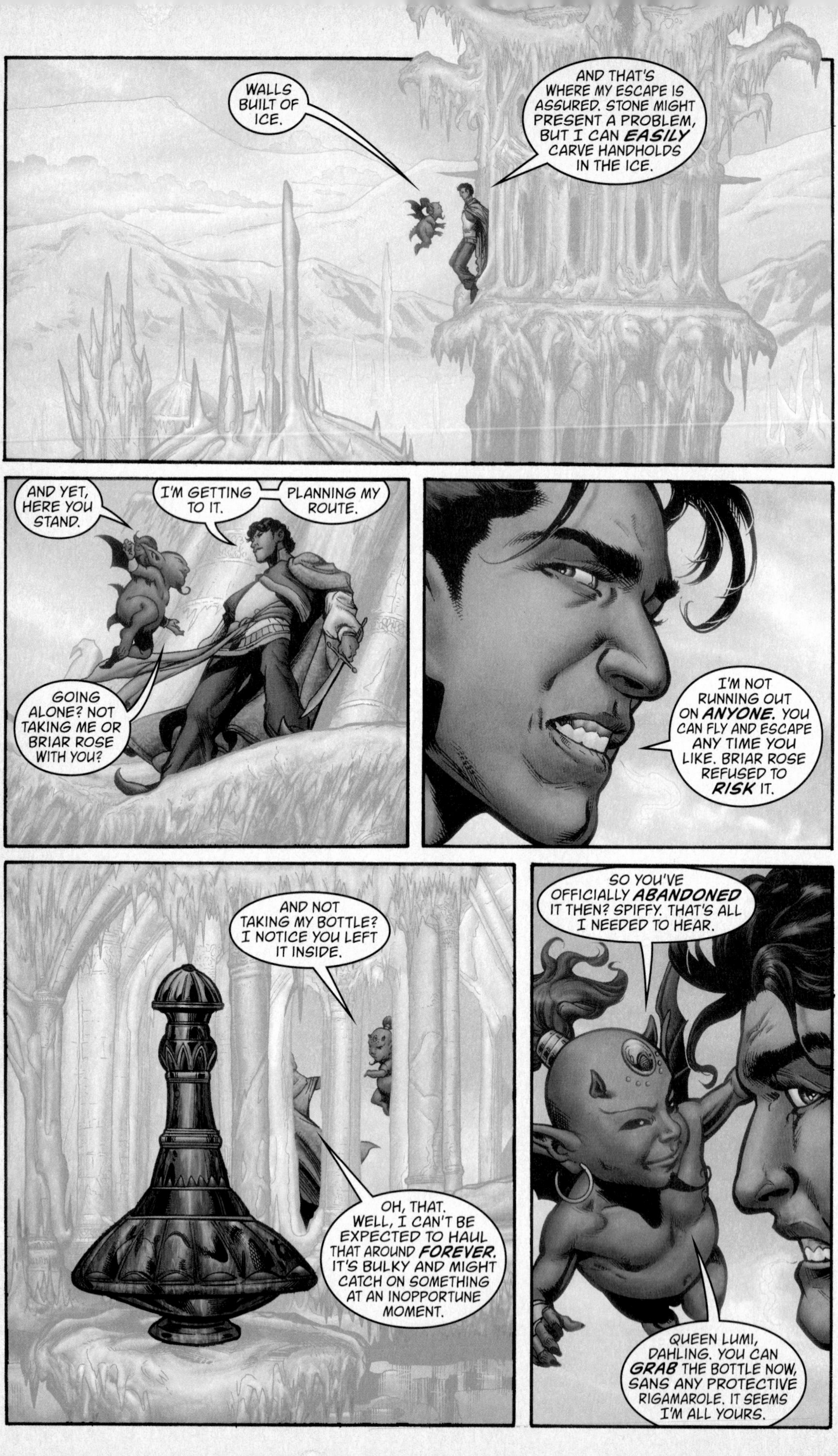
WALLS BUILT OF ICE.
AND THAT'S WHERE MY ESCAPE IS ASSURED. STONE MIGHT PRESENT A PROBLEM, BUT I CAN EASILY CARVE HANDHOLDS IN THE ICE.
AND YET, HERE YOU STAND.
I'M GETTING TO IT.
PLANNING MY ROUTE.
GOING ALONE? NOT TAKING ME OR BRIAR ROSE WITH YOU?
I'M NOT RUNNING OUT ON ANYONE. YOU CAN FLY AND ESCAPE ANY TIME YOU LIKE. BRIAR ROSE REFUSED TO RISK IT.
AND NOT TAKING MY BOTTLE? I NOTICE YOU LEFT IT INSIDE.
OH, THAT. WELL, I CAN'T BE EXPECTED TO HAUL THAT AROUND FOREVER. IT'S BULKY AND MIGHT CATCH ON SOMETHING AT AN INOPPORTUNE MOMENT.
SO YOU'VE OFFICIALLY ABANDONED IT THEN? SPIFFY. THAT'S ALL I NEEDED TO HEAR.
QUEEN LUMI, DAHLING. YOU CAN GRAB THE BOTTLE NOW, SANS ANY PROTECTIVE RIGAMAROLE. IT SEEMS I'M ALL YOURS.

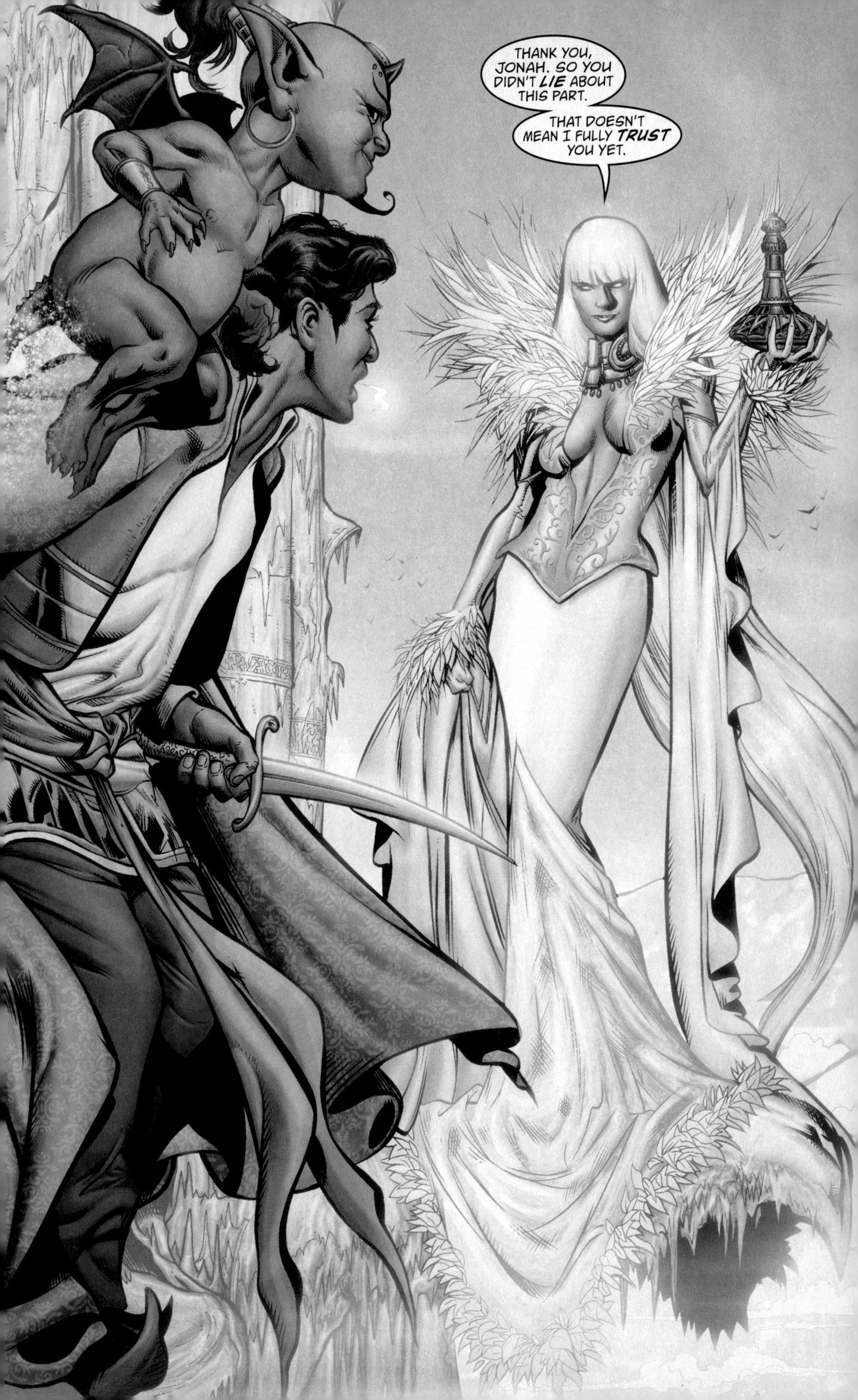
THANK YOU, JONAH. SO YOU DIDN'T LIE ABOUT THIS PART.
THAT DOESN'T MEAN I FULLY TRUST YOU YET.

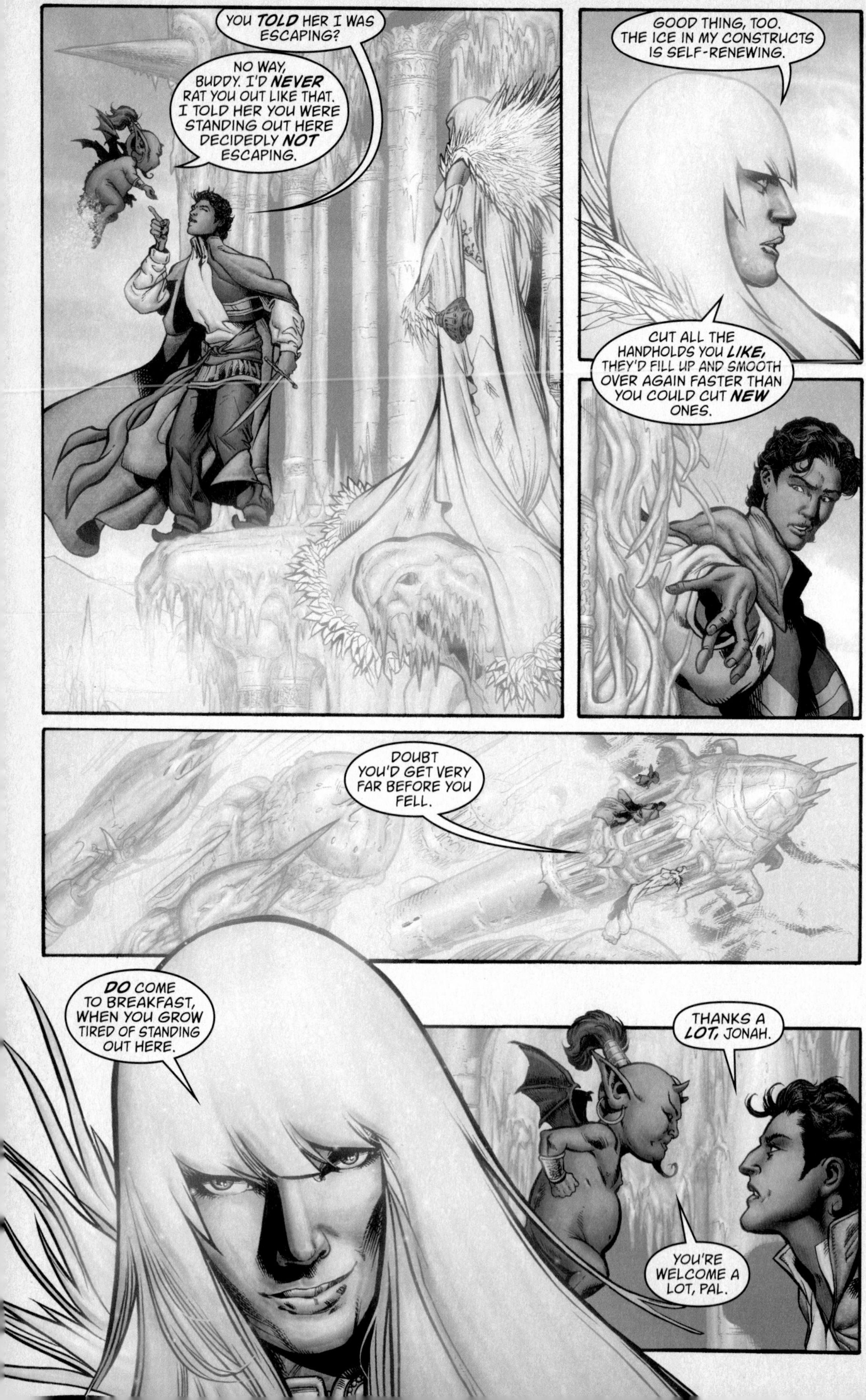
YOU TOLD HER I WAS ESCAPING?
NO WAY, BUDDY. I'D NEVER RAT YOU OUT LIKE THAT. I TOLD HER YOU WERE STANDING OUT HERE DECIDEDLY NOT ESCAPING.
GOOD THING, TOO. THE ICE IN MY CONSTRUCTS IS SELF-RENEWING.
CUT ALL THE HANDHOLDS YOU LIKE, THEY'D FILL UP AND SMOOTH OVER AGAIN FASTER THAN YOU COULD CUT NEW ONES.
DOUBT YOU'D GET VERY FAR BEFORE YOU FELL.
DO COME TO BREAKFAST, WHEN YOU GROW TIRED OF STANDING OUT HERE.
THANKS A LOT, JONAH.
YOU'RE WELCOME A LOT, PAL.

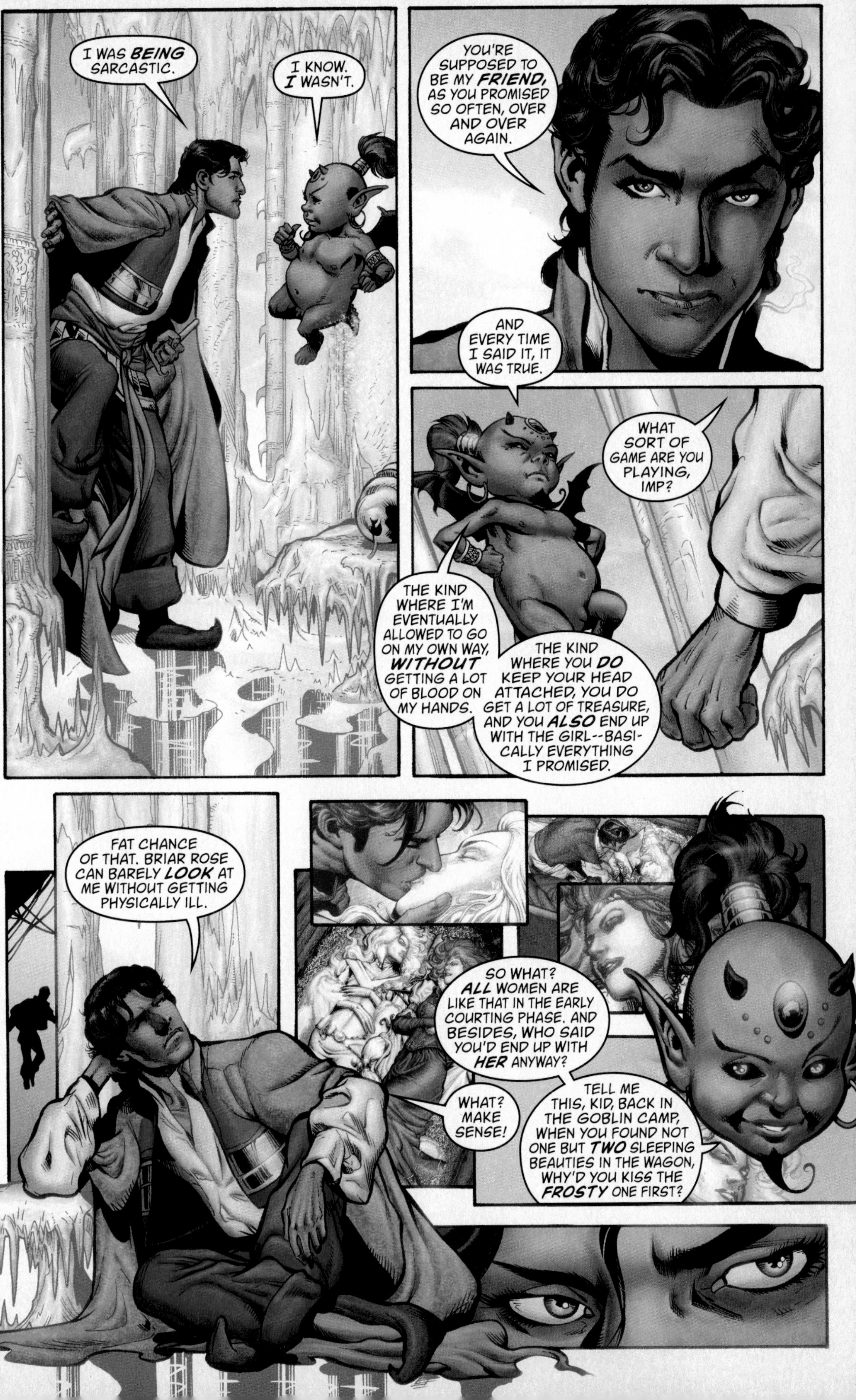

I WAS BEING SARCASTIC.
I KNOW. I WASN'T.
YOU'RE SUPPOSED TO BE MY FRIEND, AS YOU PROMISED SO OFTEN, OVER AND OVER AGAIN.
AND EVERY TIME I SAID IT, IT WAS TRUE.
WHAT SORT OF GAME ARE YOU PLAYING, IMP?
THE KIND WHERE I'M EVENTUALLY ALLOWED TO GO ON MY OWN WAY, WITHOUT GETTING A LOT OF BLOOD ON MY HANDS.
THE KIND WHERE YOU DO KEEP YOUR HEAD ATTACHED, YOU DO GET A LOT OF TREASURE, AND YOU ALSO END UP WITH THE GIRL--BASICALLY EVERYTHING I PROMISED.
FAT CHANCE OF THAT. BRIAR ROSE CAN BARELY LOOK AT ME WITHOUT GETTING PHYSICALLY ILL.
SO WHAT? ALL WOMEN ARE LIKE THAT IN THE EARLY COURTING PHASE. AND BESIDES, WHO SAID YOU'D END UP WITH HER ANYWAY?
WHAT? MAKE SENSE!
TELL ME THIS, KID, BACK IN THE GOBLIN CAMP, WHEN YOU FOUND NOT ONE BUT TWO SLEEPING BEAUTIES IN THE WAGON, WHY'D YOU KISS THE FROSTY ONE FIRST?

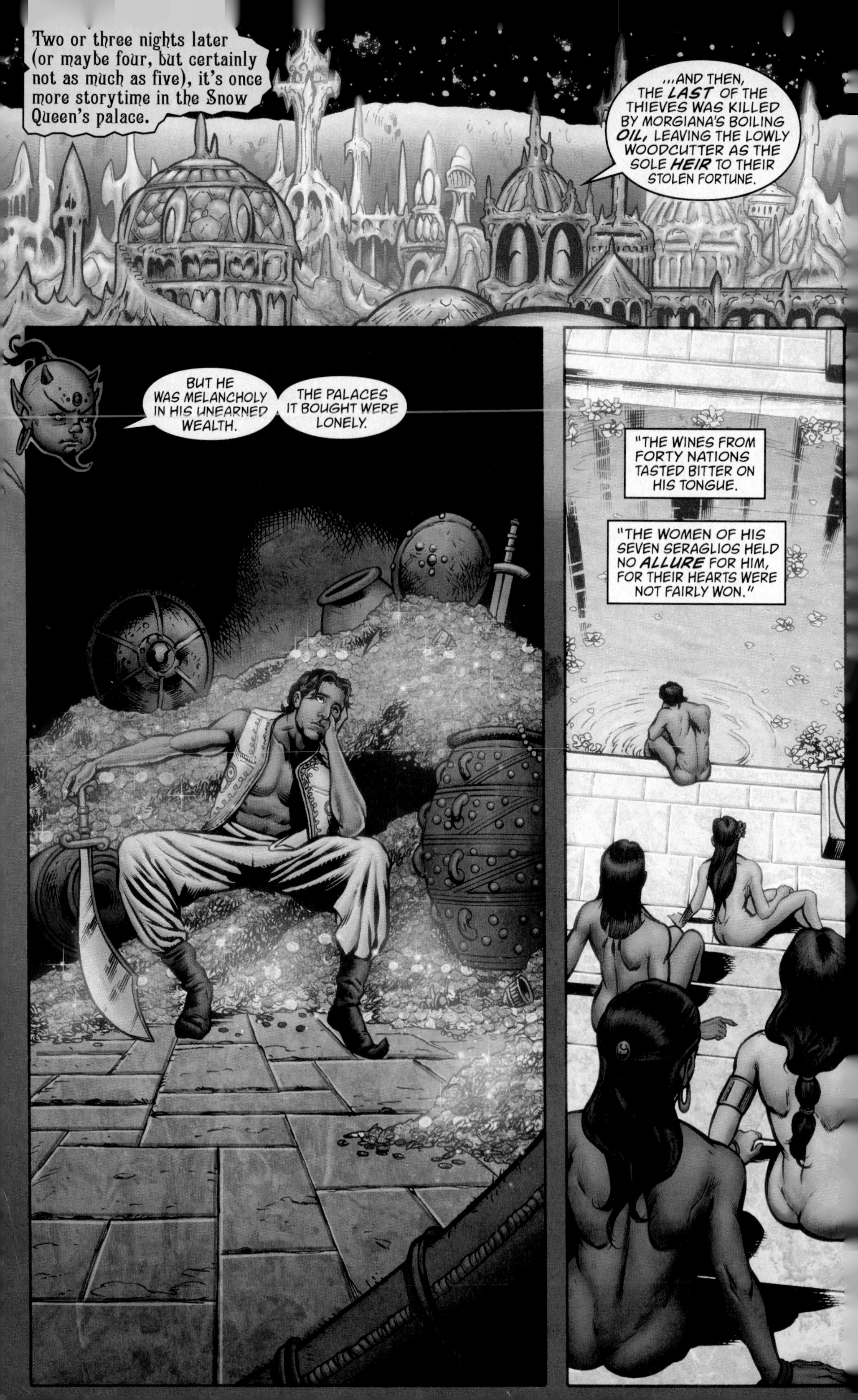
Two or three nights later (or maybe four, but certainly not as much as five), it's once more storytime in the Snow Queen's palace.
...AND THEN, THE LAST OF THE THIEVES WAS KILLED BY MORGIANA'S BOILING OIL, LEAVING THE LOWLY WOODCUTTER AS THE SOLE HEIR TO THEIR STOLEN FORTUNE.
BUT HE WAS MELANCHOLY IN HIS UNEARNED WEALTH.
THE PALACES IT BOUGHT WERE LONELY.
"THE WINES FROM FORTY NATIONS TASTED BITTER ON HIS TONGUE.
"THE WOMEN OF HIS SEVEN SERAGLIOS HELD NO ALLURE FOR HIM, FOR THEIR HEARTS WERE NOT FAIRLY WON."

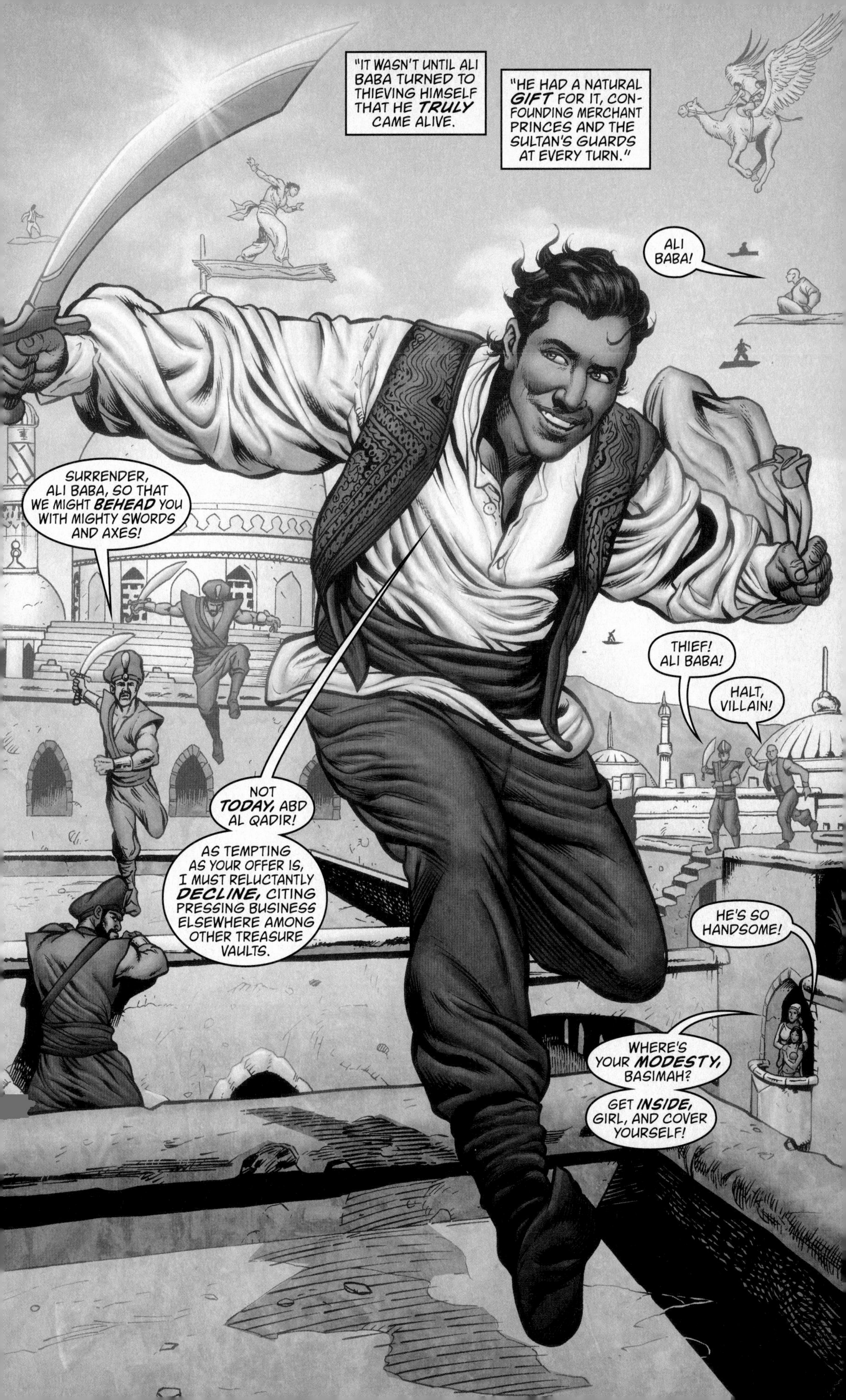
"IT WASN'T UNTIL ALI BABA TURNED TO THIEVING HIMSELF THAT HE TRULY CAME ALIVE.
"HE HAD A NATURAL GIFT FOR IT, CONFOUNDING MERCHANT PRINCES AND THE SULTAN'S GUARDS AT EVERY TURN."
ALI BABA!
SURRENDER, ALI BABA, SO THAT WE MIGHT BEHEAD YOU WITH MIGHTY SWORDS AND AXES!
THIEF! ALI BABA!
HALT, VILLAIN!
NOT TODAY, ABD AL QADIR!
AS TEMPTING AS YOUR OFFER IS, I MUST RELUCTANTLY DECLINE, CITING PRESSING BUSINESS ELSEWHERE AMONG OTHER TREASURE VAULTS.
HE'S SO HANDSOME!
WHERE'S YOUR MODESTY, BASIMAH?
GET INSIDE, GIRL, AND COVER YOURSELF!

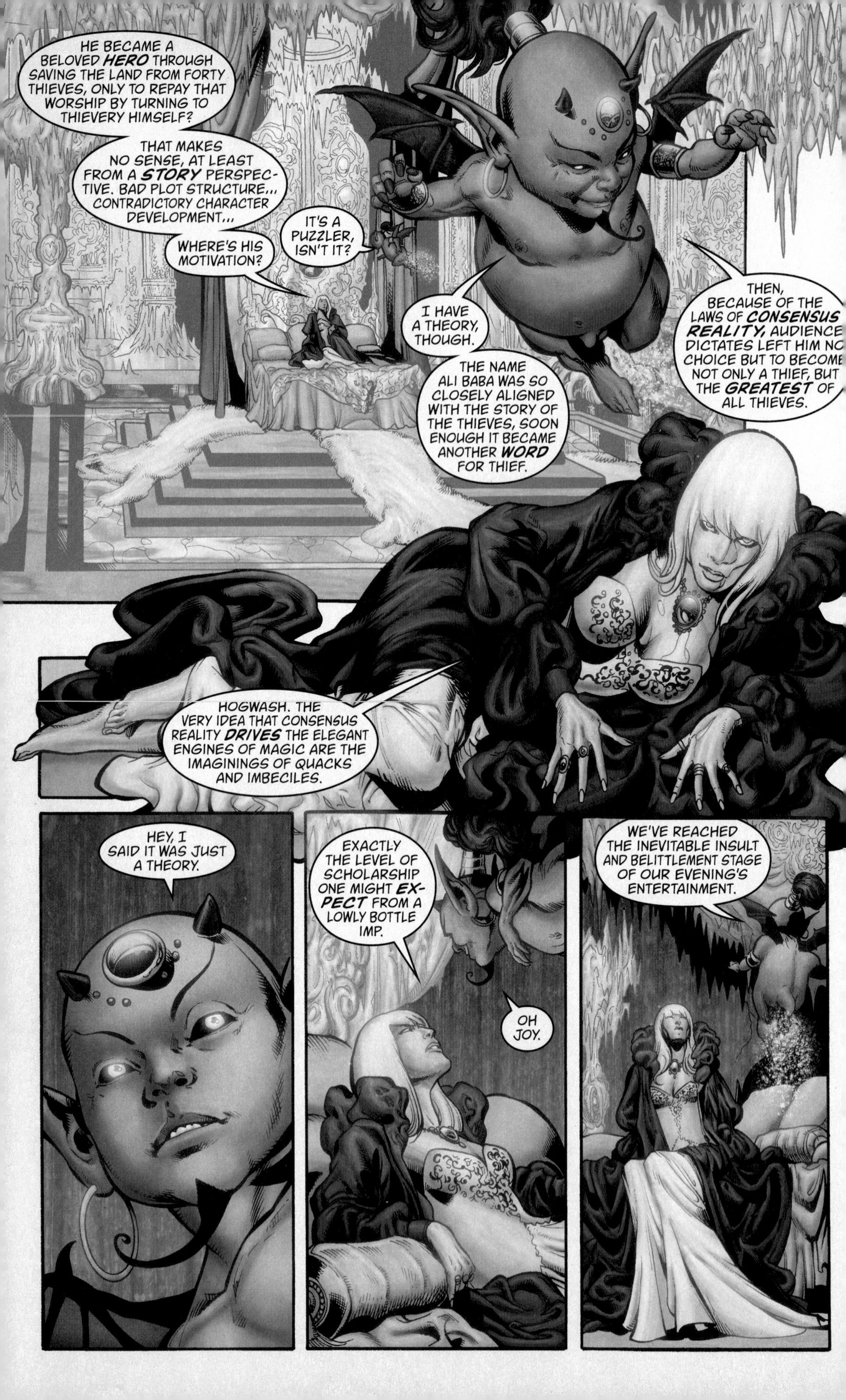
HE BECAME A BELOVED HERO THROUGH SAVING THE LAND FROM FORTY THIEVES, ONLY TO REPAY THAT WORSHIP BY TURNING TO THIEVERY HIMSELF?
THAT MAKES NO SENSE, AT LEAST FROM A STORY PERSPECTIVE. BAD PLOT STRUCTURE... CONTRADICTORY CHARACTER DEVELOPMENT...
WHERE'S HIS MOTIVATION?
IT'S A PUZZLER, ISN'T IT?
I HAVE A THEORY, THOUGH.
THE NAME ALI BABA WAS SO CLOSELY ALIGNED WITH THE STORY OF THE THIEVES, SOON ENOUGH IT BECAME ANOTHER WORD FOR THIEF.
THEN, BECAUSE OF THE LAWS OF CONSENSUS REALITY, AUDIENCE DICTATES LEFT HIM NO CHOICE BUT TO BECOME NOT ONLY A THIEF, BUT THE GREATEST OF ALL THIEVES.
HOGWASH. THE VERY IDEA THAT CONSENSUS REALITY DRIVES THE ELEGANT ENGINES OF MAGIC ARE THE IMAGININGS OF QUACKS AND IMBECILES.
HEY, I SAID IT WAS JUST A THEORY.
EXACTLY THE LEVEL OF SCHOLARSHIP ONE MIGHT EXPECT FROM A LOWLY BOTTLE IMP.
OH JOY.
WE'VE REACHED THE INEVITABLE INSULT AND BELITTLEMENT STAGE OF OUR EVENING'S ENTERTAINMENT.

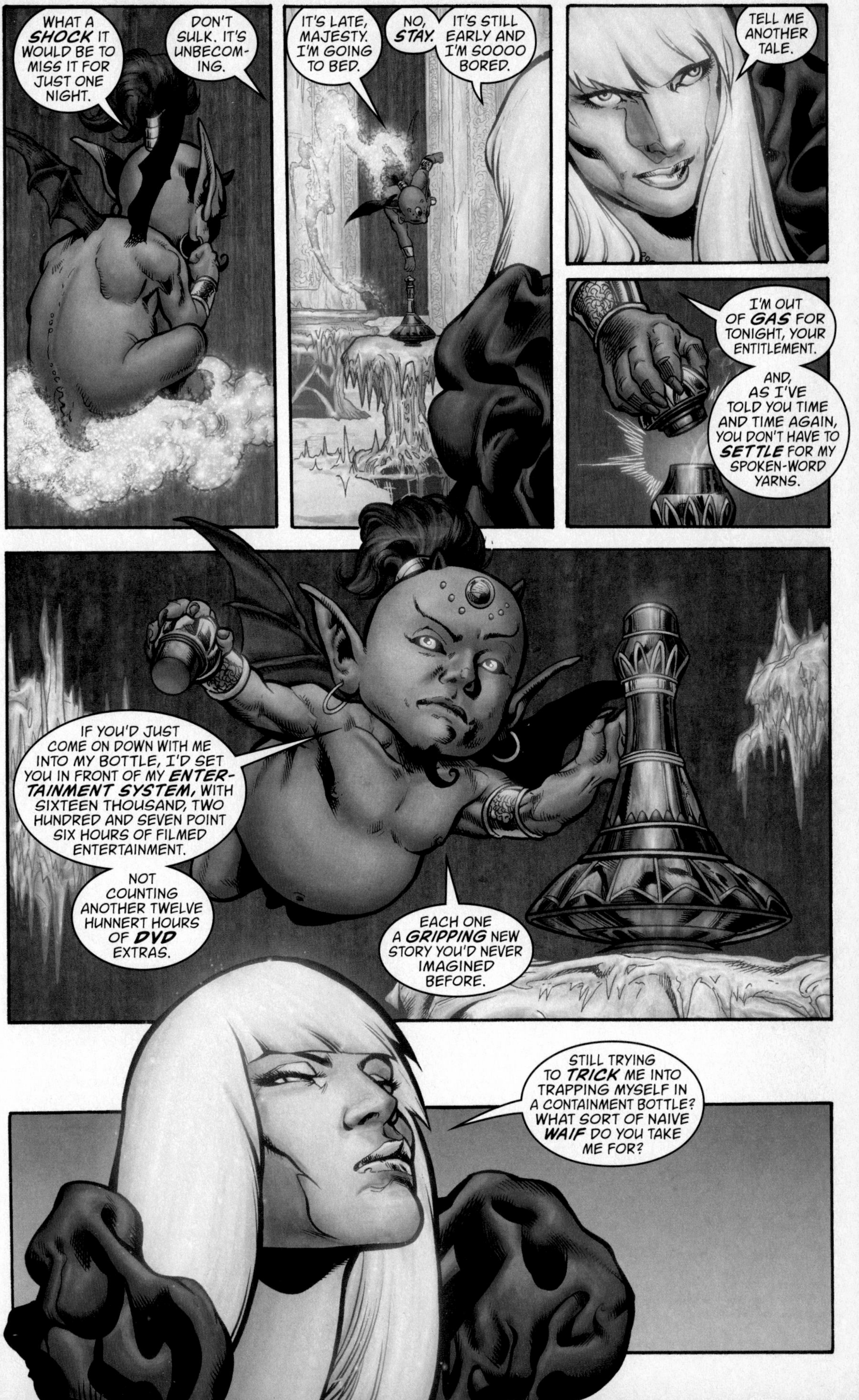
WHAT A SHOCK IT WOULD BE TO MISS IT FOR JUST ONE NIGHT.
DON'T SULK. IT'S UNBECOMING.
IT'S LATE, MAJESTY. I'M GOING TO BED.
NO, STAY.
IT'S STILL EARLY AND I'M SOOOO BORED.
TELL ME ANOTHER TALE.
I'M OUT OF GAS FOR TONIGHT, YOUR ENTITLEMENT.
AND, AS I'VE TOLD YOU TIME AND TIME AGAIN, YOU DON'T HAVE TO SETTLE FOR MY SPOKEN-WORD YARNS.
IF YOU'D JUST COME ON DOWN WITH ME INTO MY BOTTLE, I'D SET YOU IN FRONT OF MY ENTERTAINMENT SYSTEM, WITH SIXTEEN THOUSAND, TWO HUNDRED AND SEVEN POINT SIX HOURS OF FILMED ENTERTAINMENT.
NOT COUNTING ANOTHER TWELVE HUNNERT HOURS OF DVD EXTRAS.
EACH ONE A GRIPPING NEW STORY YOU'D NEVER IMAGINED BEFORE.
STILL TRYING TO TRICK ME INTO TRAPPING MYSELF IN A CONTAINMENT BOTTLE? WHAT SORT OF NAIVE WAIF DO YOU TAKE ME FOR?

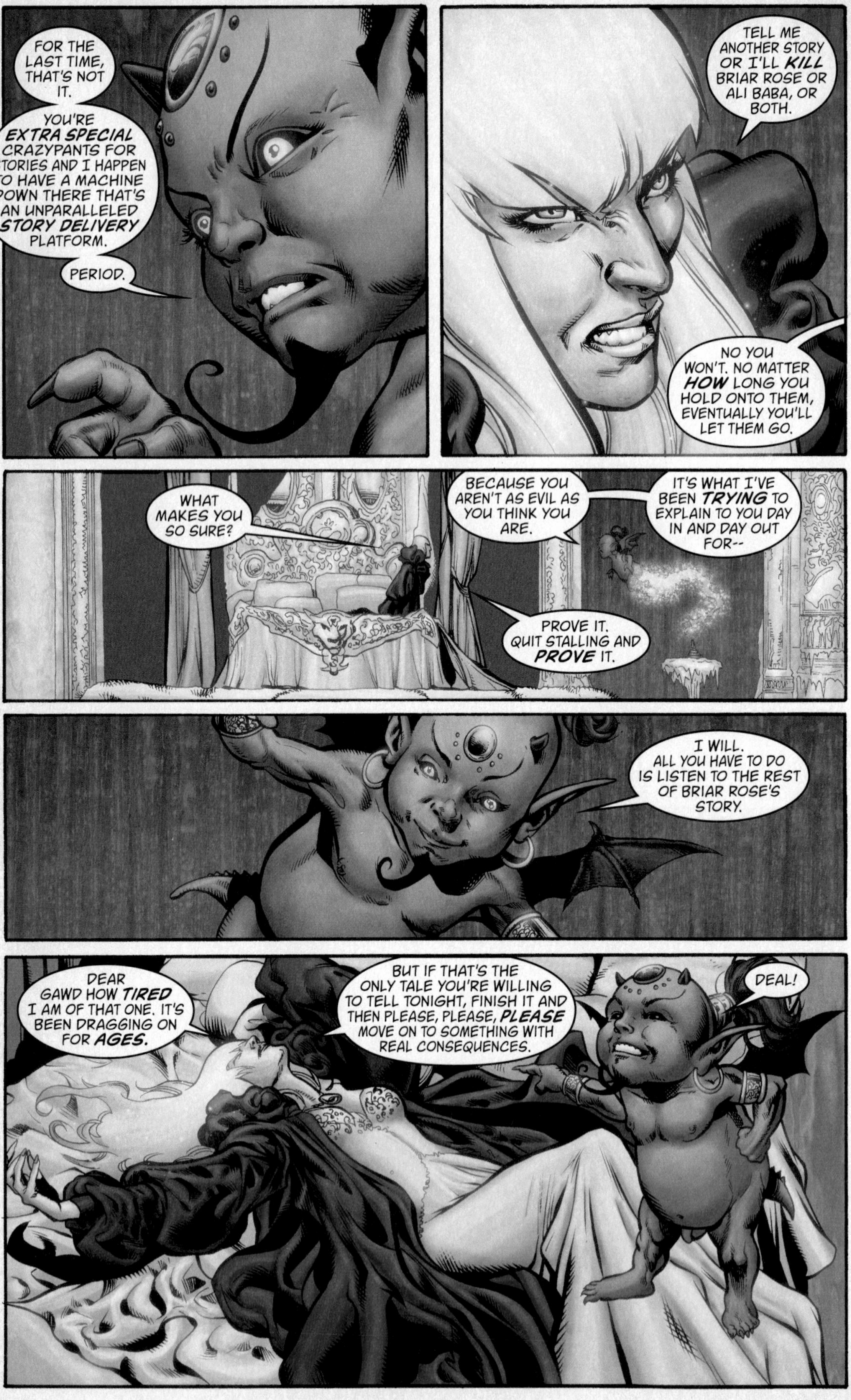

FOR THE LAST TIME, THAT'S NOT IT.
YOU'RE **EXTRA SPECIAL** CRAZYPANTS FOR STORIES AND I HAPPEN TO HAVE A MACHINE DOWN THERE THAT'S AN UNPARALLELED **STORY DELIVERY** PLATFORM.
PERIOD.
TELL ME ANOTHER STORY OR I'LL **KILL** BRIAR ROSE OR ALI BABA, OR BOTH.
NO YOU WON'T. NO MATTER **HOW** LONG YOU HOLD ONTO THEM, EVENTUALLY YOU'LL LET THEM GO.
WHAT MAKES YOU SO SURE?
BECAUSE YOU AREN'T AS EVIL AS YOU THINK YOU ARE.
IT'S WHAT I'VE BEEN **TRYING** TO EXPLAIN TO YOU DAY IN AND DAY OUT FOR--
PROVE IT. QUIT STALLING AND **PROVE** IT.
I WILL. ALL YOU HAVE TO DO IS LISTEN TO THE REST OF BRIAR ROSE'S STORY.
DEAR GAWD HOW **TIRED** I AM OF THAT ONE. IT'S BEEN DRAGGING ON FOR **AGES.**
BUT IF THAT'S THE ONLY TALE YOU'RE WILLING TO TELL TONIGHT, FINISH IT AND THEN PLEASE, PLEASE, **PLEASE** MOVE ON TO SOMETHING WITH REAL CONSEQUENCES.
DEAL!

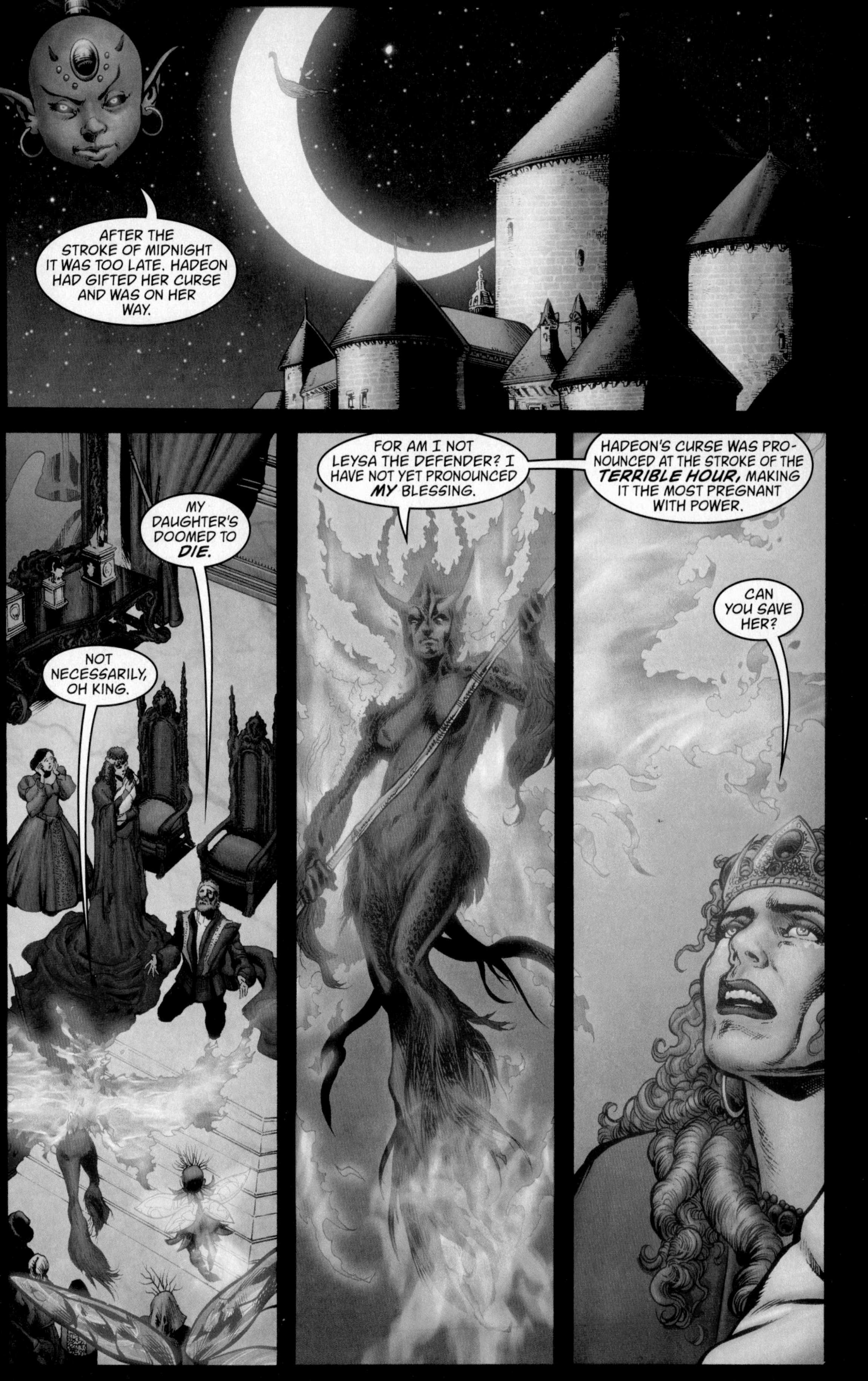
AFTER THE STROKE OF MIDNIGHT IT WAS TOO LATE. HADEON HAD GIFTED HER CURSE AND WAS ON HER WAY.
MY DAUGHTER'S DOOMED TO *DIE.*
NOT NECESSARILY, OH KING.
FOR AM I NOT LEYSA THE DEFENDER? I HAVE NOT YET PRONOUNCED *MY* BLESSING.
HADEON'S CURSE WAS PRONOUNCED AT THE STROKE OF THE *TERRIBLE HOUR,* MAKING IT THE MOST PREGNANT WITH POWER.
CAN YOU SAVE HER?

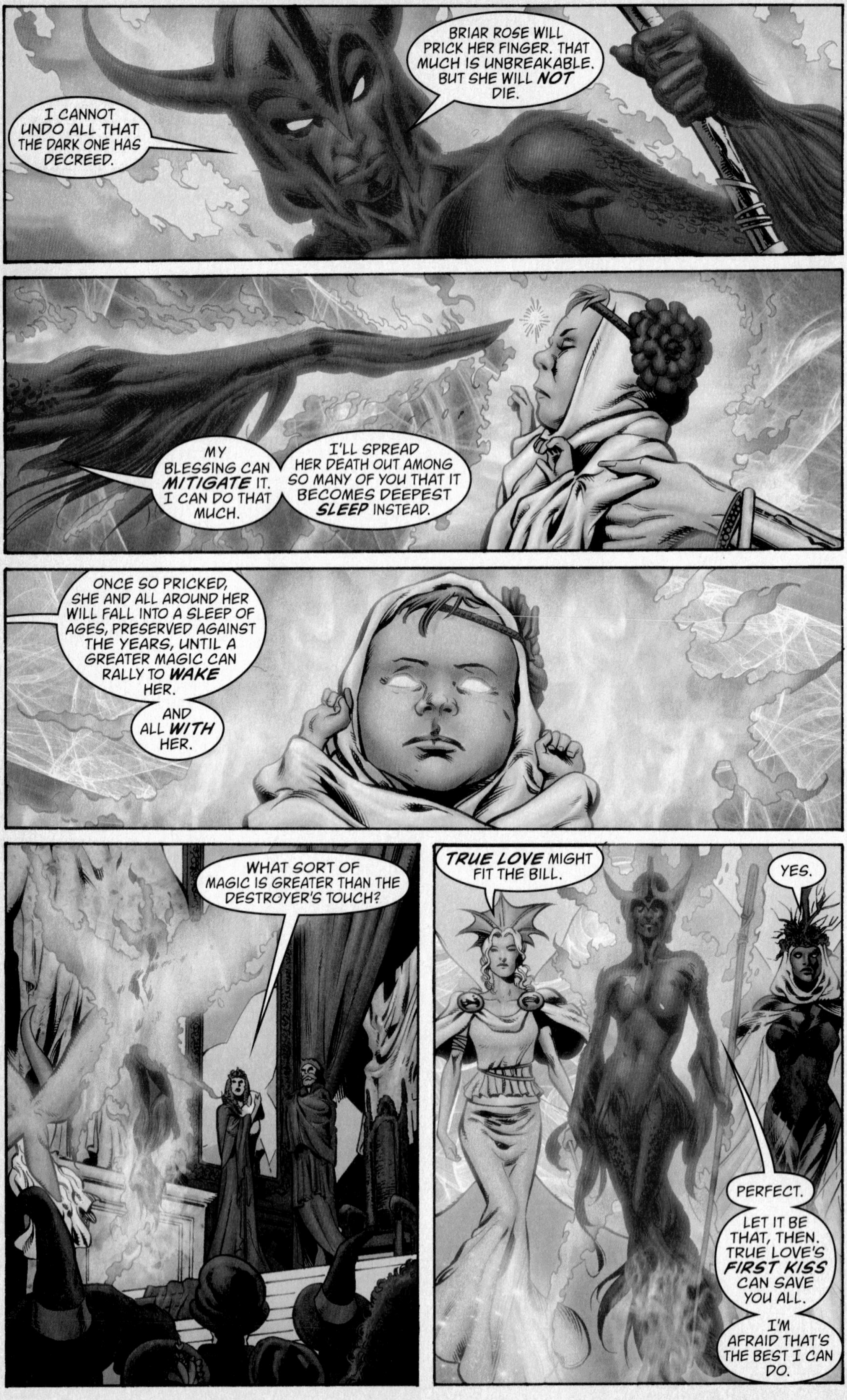
I CANNOT UNDO ALL THAT THE DARK ONE HAS DECREED.
BRIAR ROSE WILL PRICK HER FINGER. THAT MUCH IS UNBREAKABLE. BUT SHE WILL NOT DIE.
MY BLESSING CAN MITIGATE IT. I CAN DO THAT MUCH.
I'LL SPREAD HER DEATH OUT AMONG SO MANY OF YOU THAT IT BECOMES DEEPEST SLEEP INSTEAD.
ONCE SO PRICKED, SHE AND ALL AROUND HER WILL FALL INTO A SLEEP OF AGES, PRESERVED AGAINST THE YEARS, UNTIL A GREATER MAGIC CAN RALLY TO WAKE HER.
AND ALL WITH HER.
WHAT SORT OF MAGIC IS GREATER THAN THE DESTROYER'S TOUCH?
TRUE LOVE MIGHT FIT THE BILL.
YES.
PERFECT.
LET IT BE THAT, THEN. TRUE LOVE'S FIRST KISS CAN SAVE YOU ALL.
I'M AFRAID THAT'S THE BEST I CAN DO.

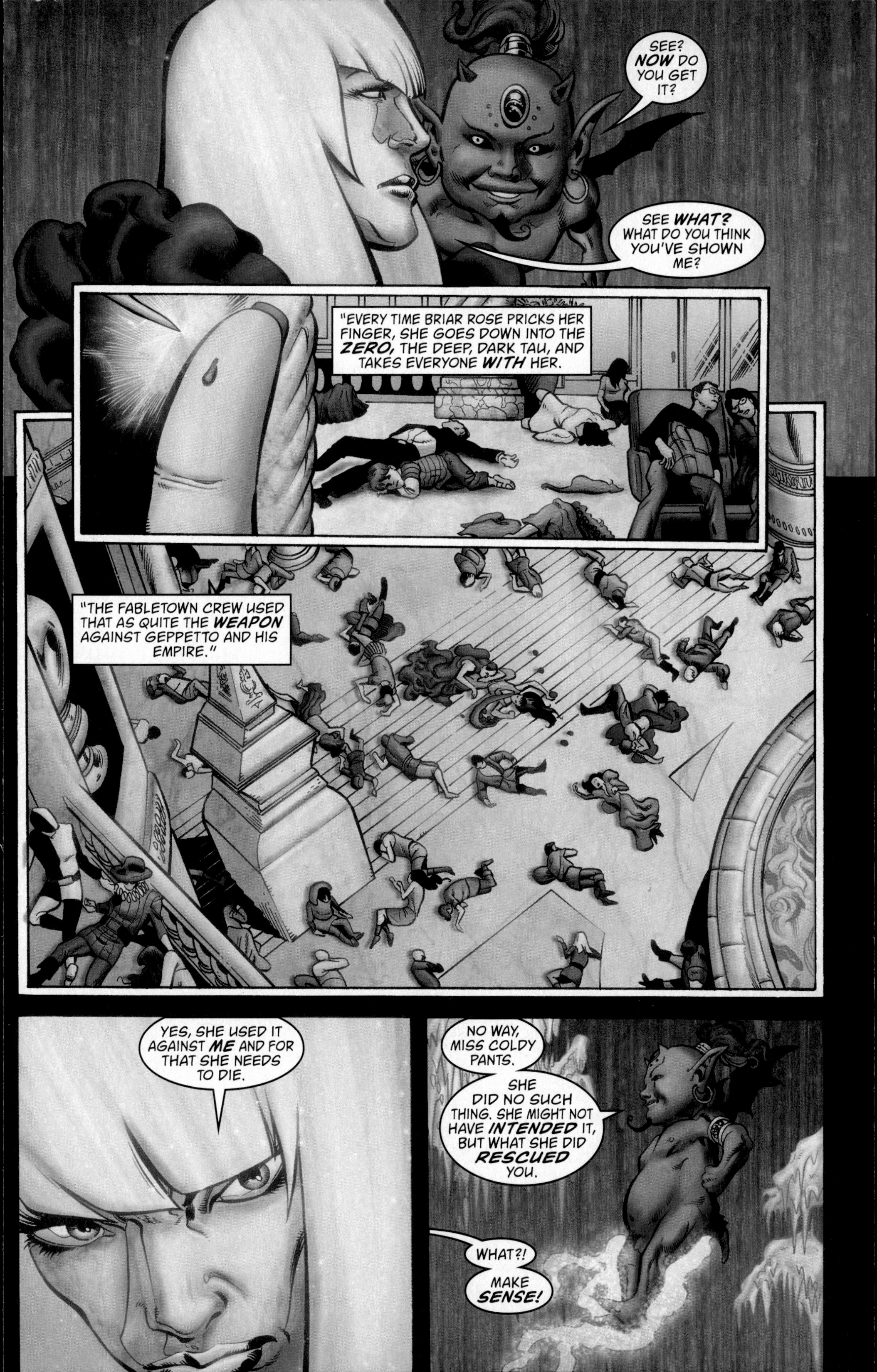
SEE? NOW DO YOU GET IT?
SEE WHAT? WHAT DO YOU THINK YOU'VE SHOWN ME?
"EVERY TIME BRIAR ROSE PRICKS HER FINGER, SHE GOES DOWN INTO THE ZERO, THE DEEP, DARK TAU, AND TAKES EVERYONE WITH HER.
"THE FABLETOWN CREW USED THAT AS QUITE THE WEAPON AGAINST GEPPETTO AND HIS EMPIRE."
YES, SHE USED IT AGAINST ME AND FOR THAT SHE NEEDS TO DIE.
NO WAY, MISS COLDY PANTS.
SHE DID NO SUCH THING. SHE MIGHT NOT HAVE INTENDED IT, BUT WHAT SHE DID RESCUED YOU.
WHAT?! MAKE SENSE!

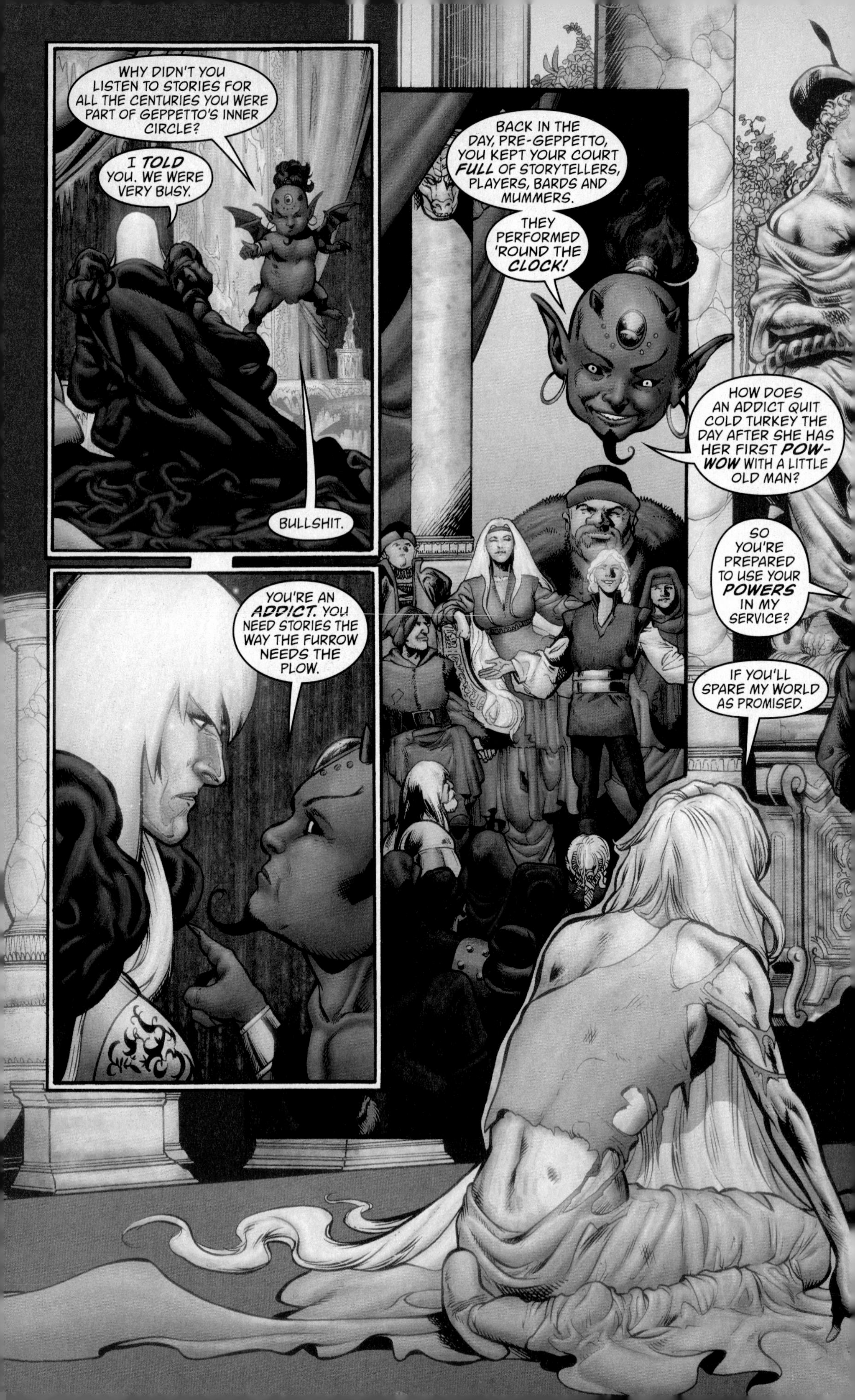
WHY DIDN'T YOU LISTEN TO STORIES FOR ALL THE CENTURIES YOU WERE PART OF GEPPETTO'S INNER CIRCLE?
I TOLD YOU. WE WERE VERY BUSY.
BULLSHIT.
YOU'RE AN ADDICT. YOU NEED STORIES THE WAY THE FURROW NEEDS THE PLOW.
BACK IN THE DAY, PRE-GEPPETTO, YOU KEPT YOUR COURT FULL OF STORYTELLERS, PLAYERS, BARDS AND MUMMERS.
THEY PERFORMED 'ROUND THE CLOCK!
HOW DOES AN ADDICT QUIT COLD TURKEY THE DAY AFTER SHE HAS HER FIRST POW-WOW WITH A LITTLE OLD MAN?
SO YOU'RE PREPARED TO USE YOUR POWERS IN MY SERVICE?
IF YOU'LL SPARE MY WORLD AS PROMISED.

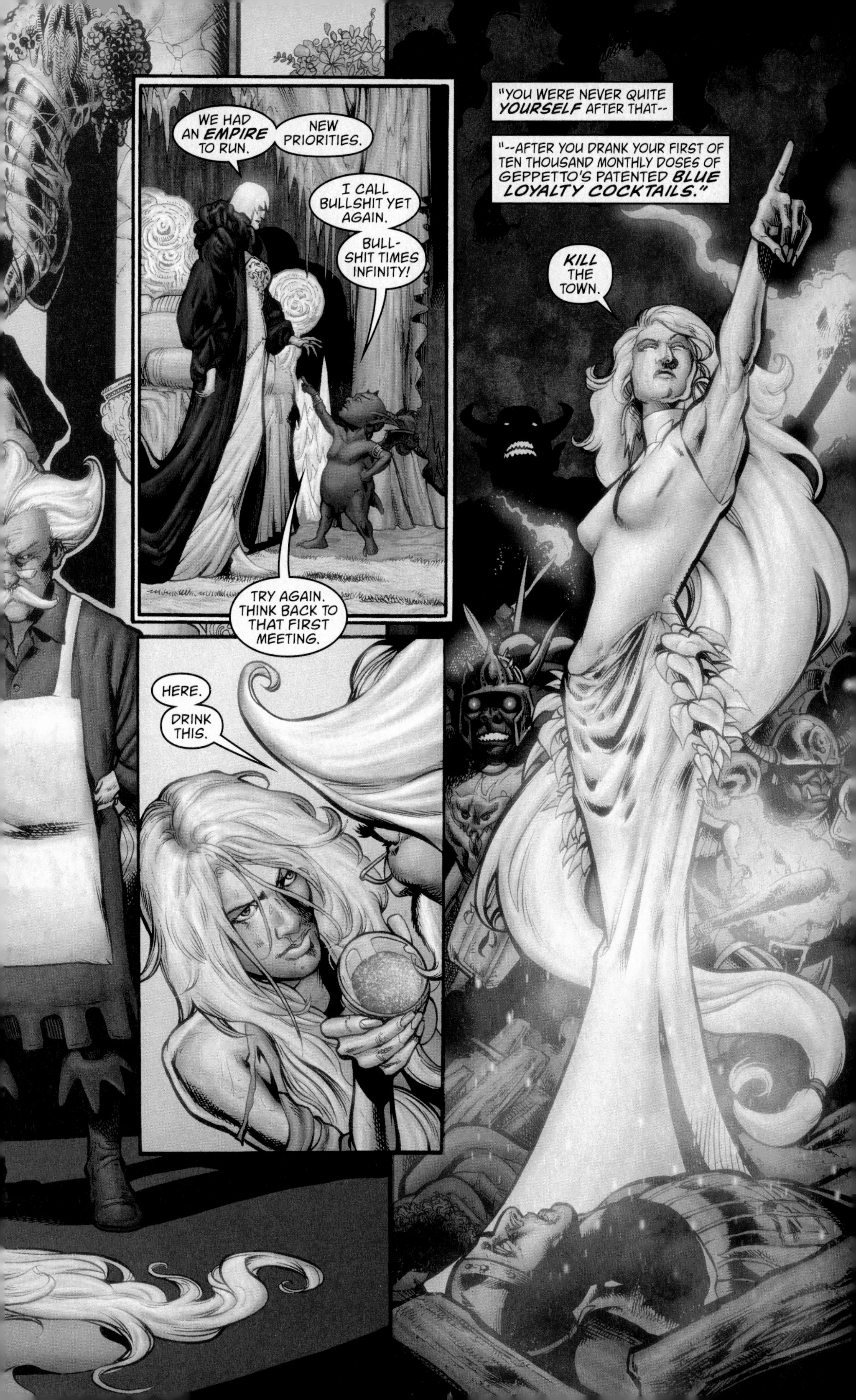

WE HAD AN EMPIRE TO RUN.
NEW PRIORITIES.
I CALL BULLSHIT YET AGAIN.
BULL-SHIT TIMES INFINITY!
TRY AGAIN. THINK BACK TO THAT FIRST MEETING.
HERE.
DRINK THIS.
"YOU WERE NEVER QUITE YOURSELF AFTER THAT--
"--AFTER YOU DRANK YOUR FIRST OF TEN THOUSAND MONTHLY DOSES OF GEPPETTO'S PATENTED BLUE LOYALTY COCKTAILS."
KILL THE TOWN.

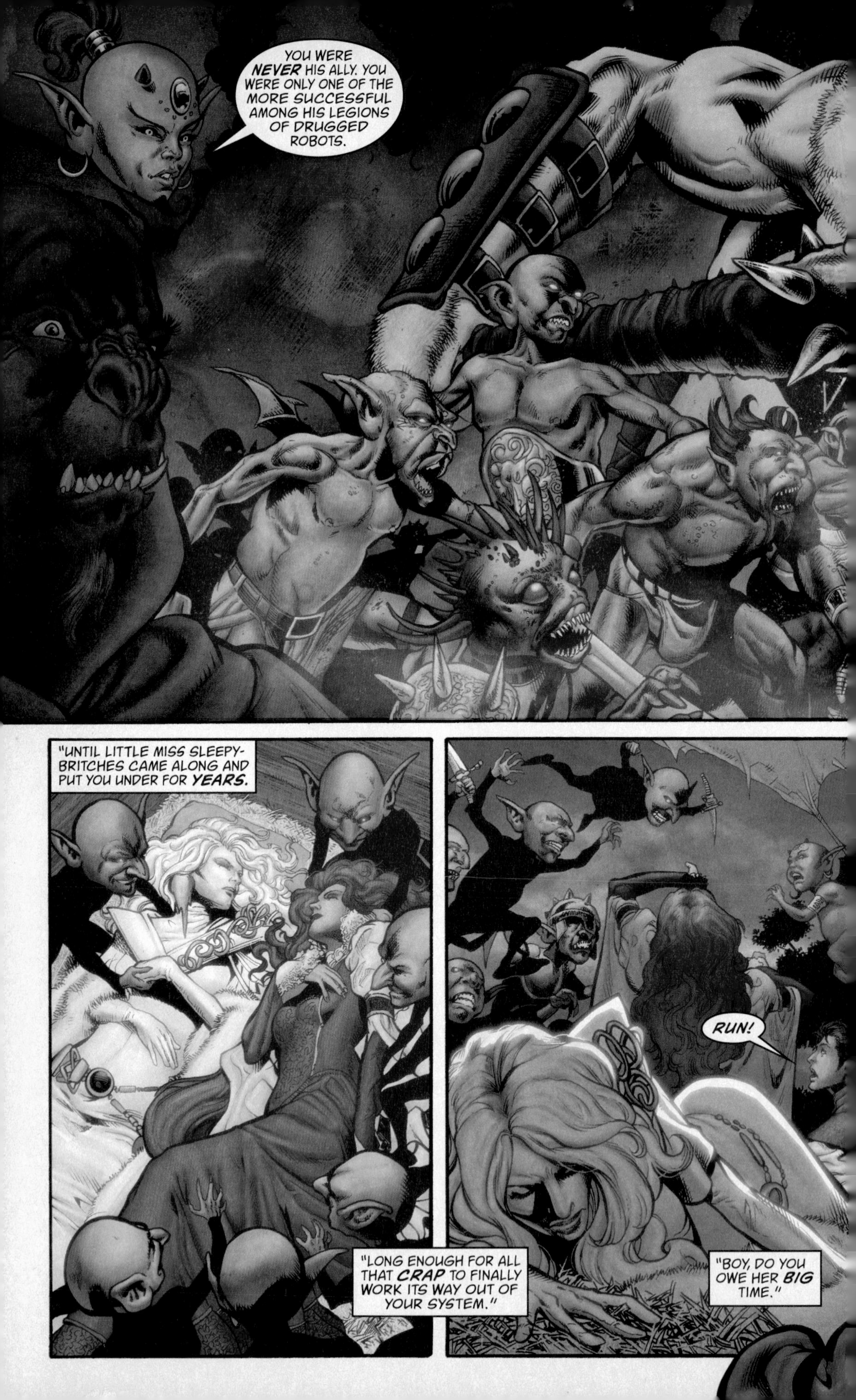
YOU WERE NEVER HIS ALLY. YOU WERE ONLY ONE OF THE MORE SUCCESSFUL AMONG HIS LEGIONS OF DRUGGED ROBOTS.
"UNTIL LITTLE MISS SLEEPY-BRITCHES CAME ALONG AND PUT YOU UNDER FOR YEARS.
"LONG ENOUGH FOR ALL THAT CRAP TO FINALLY WORK ITS WAY OUT OF YOUR SYSTEM."
RUN!
"BOY, DO YOU OWE HER BIG TIME."

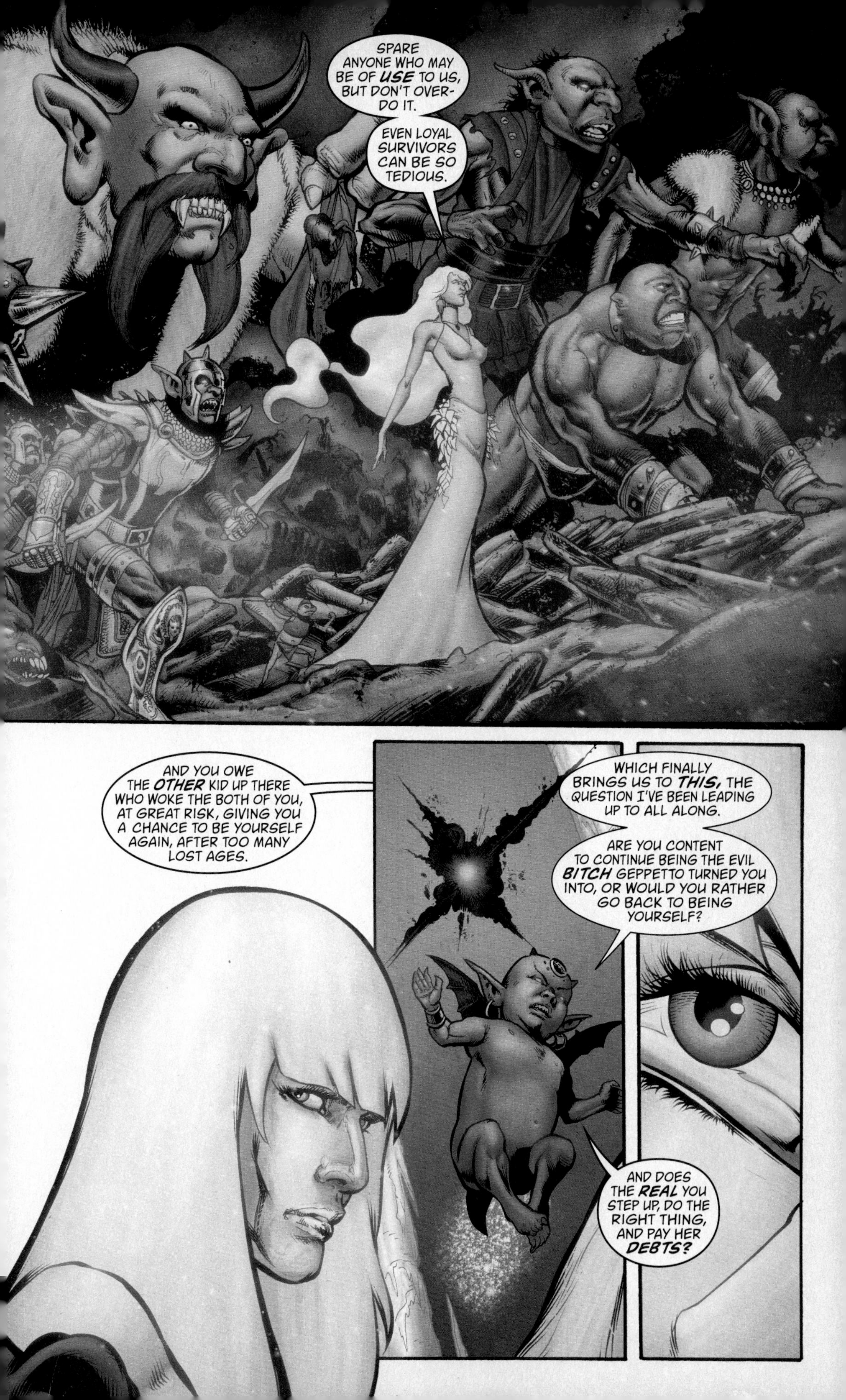
SPARE ANYONE WHO MAY BE OF USE TO US, BUT DON'T OVER-DO IT.
EVEN LOYAL SURVIVORS CAN BE SO TEDIOUS.
AND YOU OWE THE OTHER KID UP THERE WHO WOKE THE BOTH OF YOU, AT GREAT RISK, GIVING YOU A CHANCE TO BE YOURSELF AGAIN, AFTER TOO MANY LOST AGES.
WHICH FINALLY BRINGS US TO THIS, THE QUESTION I'VE BEEN LEADING UP TO ALL ALONG.
ARE YOU CONTENT TO CONTINUE BEING THE EVIL BITCH GEPPETTO TURNED YOU INTO, OR WOULD YOU RATHER GO BACK TO BEING YOURSELF?
AND DOES THE REAL YOU STEP UP, DO THE RIGHT THING, AND PAY HER DEBTS?

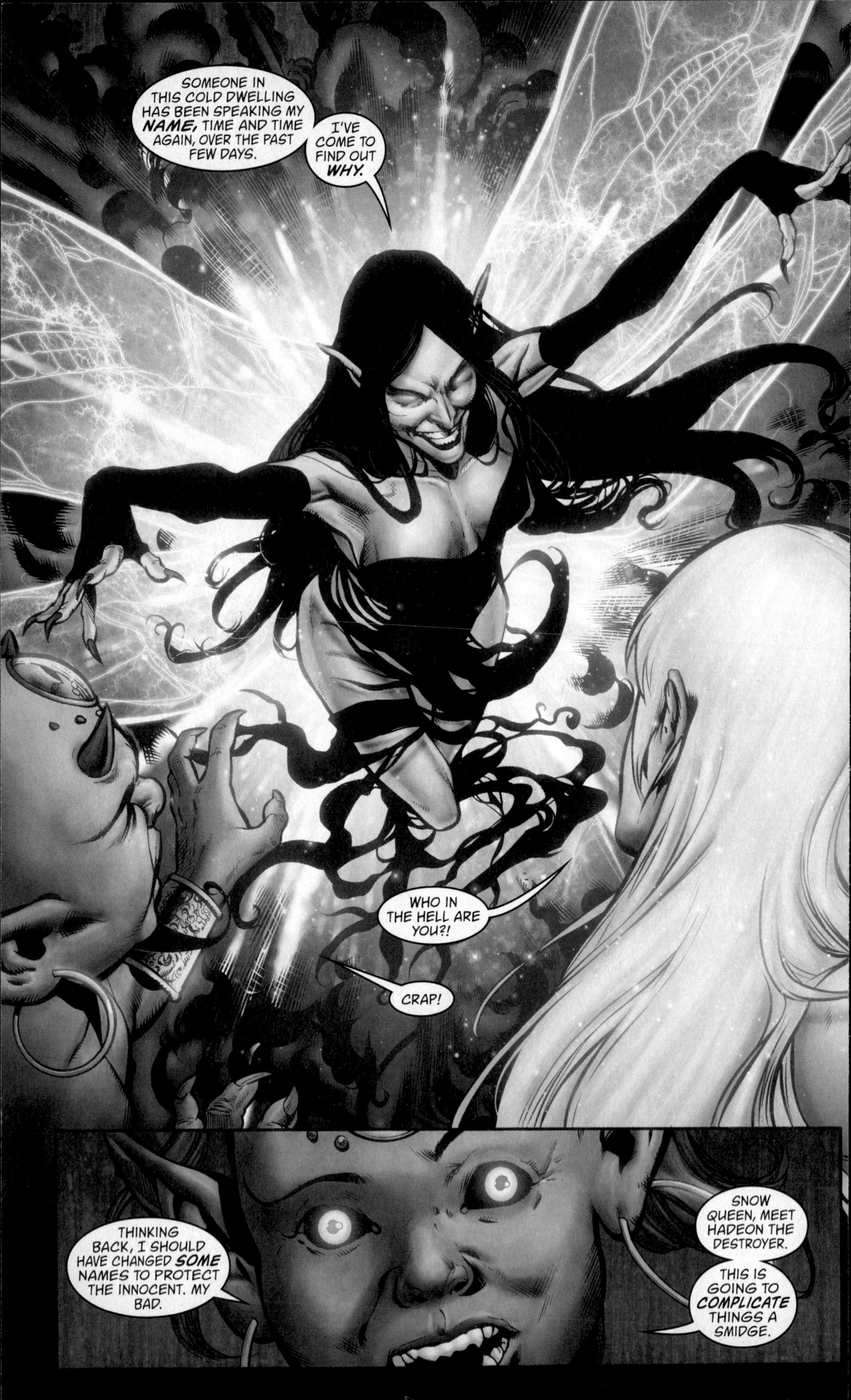
SOMEONE IN THIS COLD DWELLING HAS BEEN SPEAKING MY NAME, TIME AND TIME AGAIN, OVER THE PAST FEW DAYS.
I'VE COME TO FIND OUT WHY.
WHO IN THE HELL ARE YOU?!
CRAP!
THINKING BACK, I SHOULD HAVE CHANGED SOME NAMES TO PROTECT THE INNOCENT. MY BAD.
SNOW QUEEN, MEET HADEON THE DESTROYER.
THIS IS GOING TO COMPLICATE THINGS A SMIDGE.

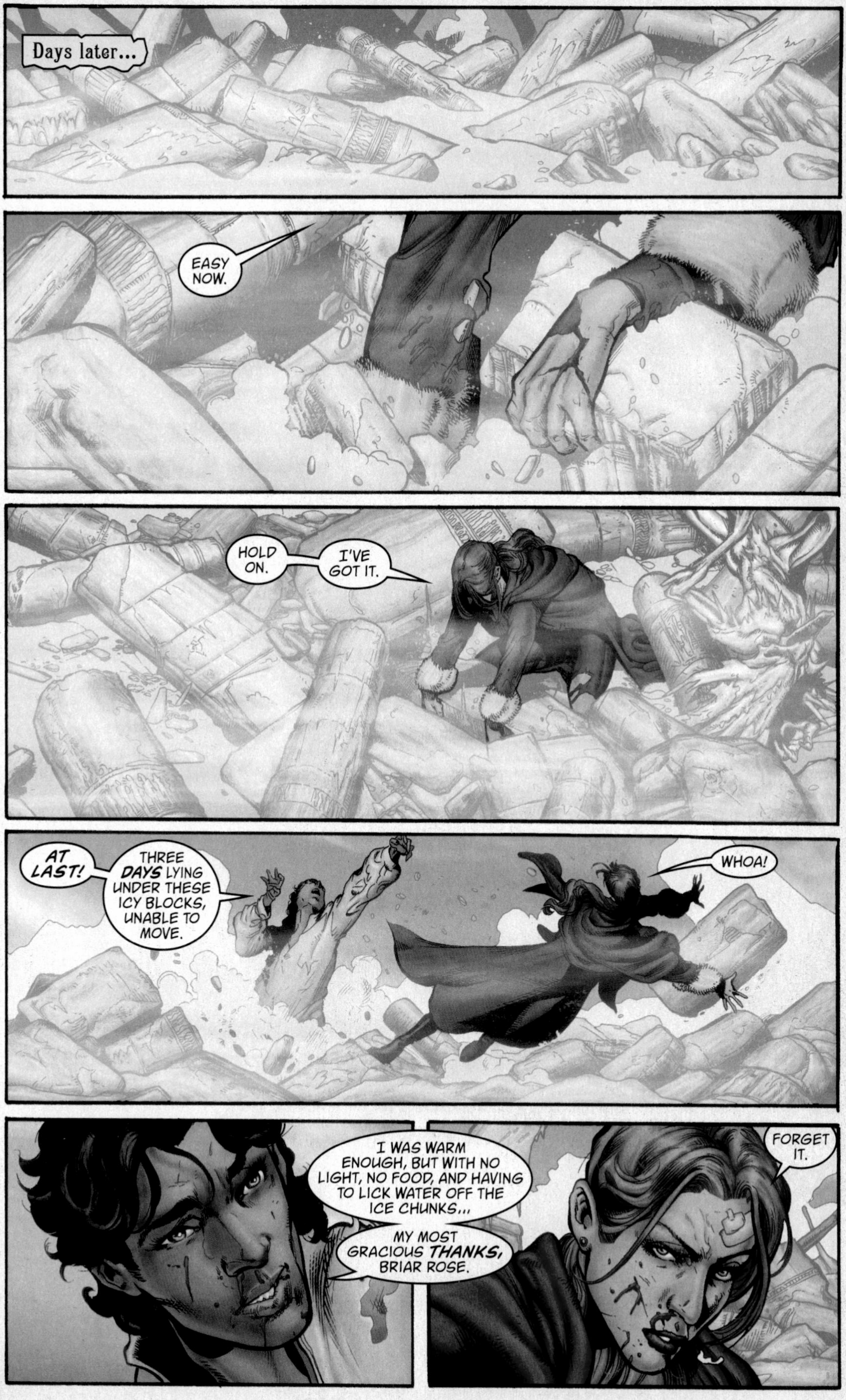
Days later...
EASY NOW.
HOLD ON.
I'VE GOT IT.
AT LAST!
THREE DAYS LYING UNDER THESE ICY BLOCKS, UNABLE TO MOVE.
WHOA!
I WAS WARM ENOUGH, BUT WITH NO LIGHT, NO FOOD, AND HAVING TO LICK WATER OFF THE ICE CHUNKS...
MY MOST GRACIOUS THANKS, BRIAR ROSE.
FORGET IT.

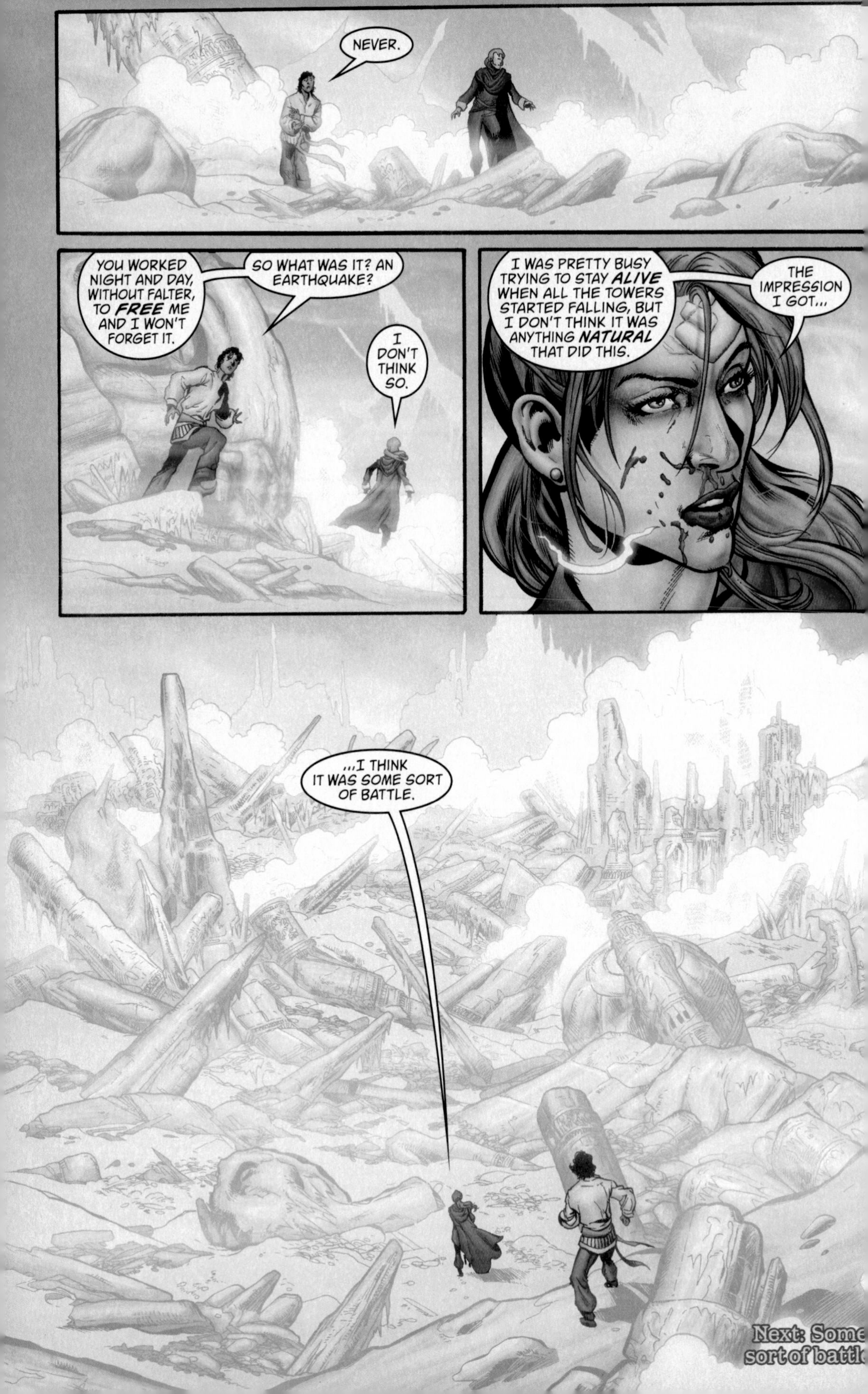
NEVER.
YOU WORKED NIGHT AND DAY, WITHOUT FALTER, TO FREE ME AND I WON'T FORGET IT.
SO WHAT WAS IT? AN EARTHQUAKE?
I DON'T THINK SO.
I WAS PRETTY BUSY TRYING TO STAY ALIVE WHEN ALL THE TOWERS STARTED FALLING, BUT I DON'T THINK IT WAS ANYTHING NATURAL THAT DID THIS.
THE IMPRESSION I GOT...
...I THINK IT WAS SOME SORT OF BATTLE.
Next: Some
sort of battl

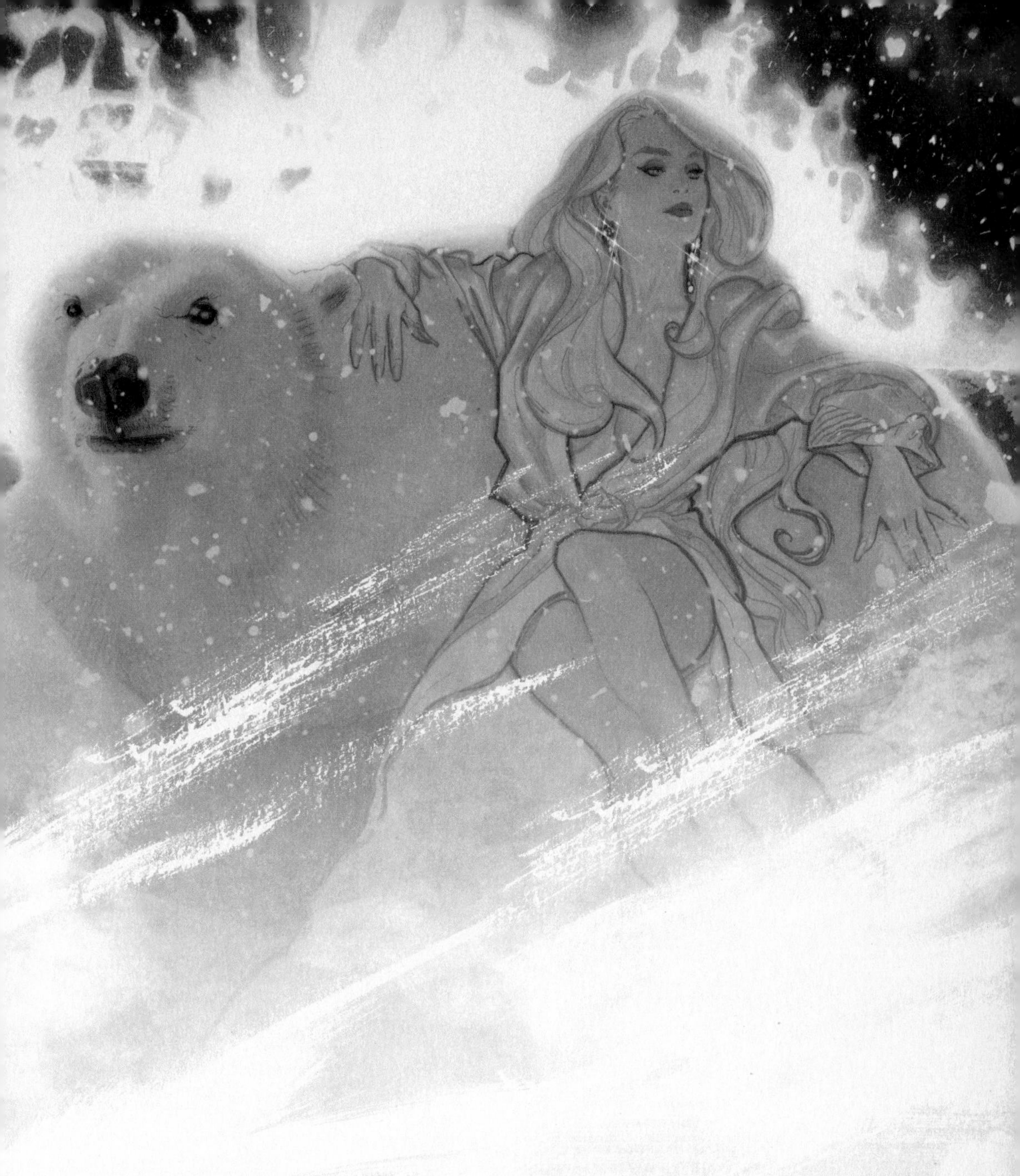

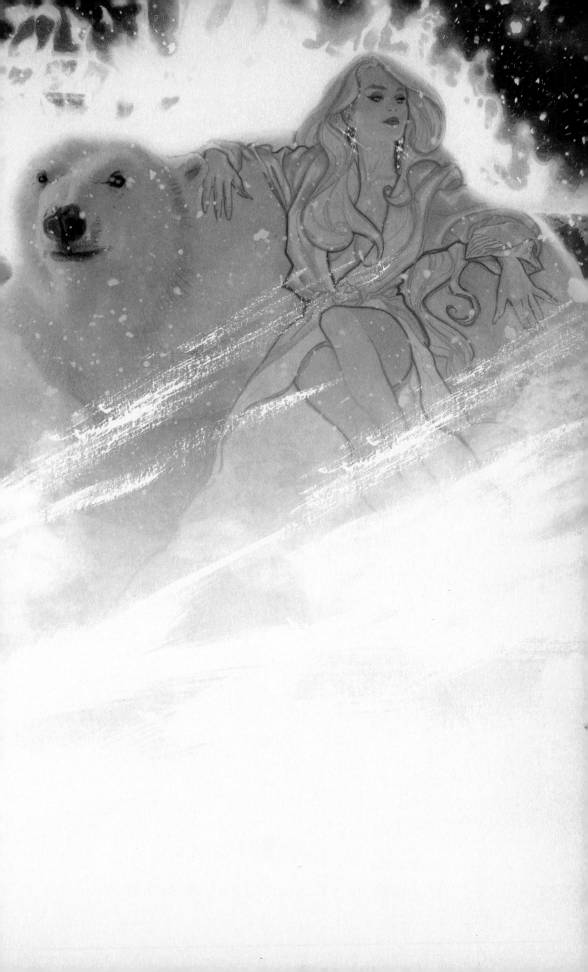

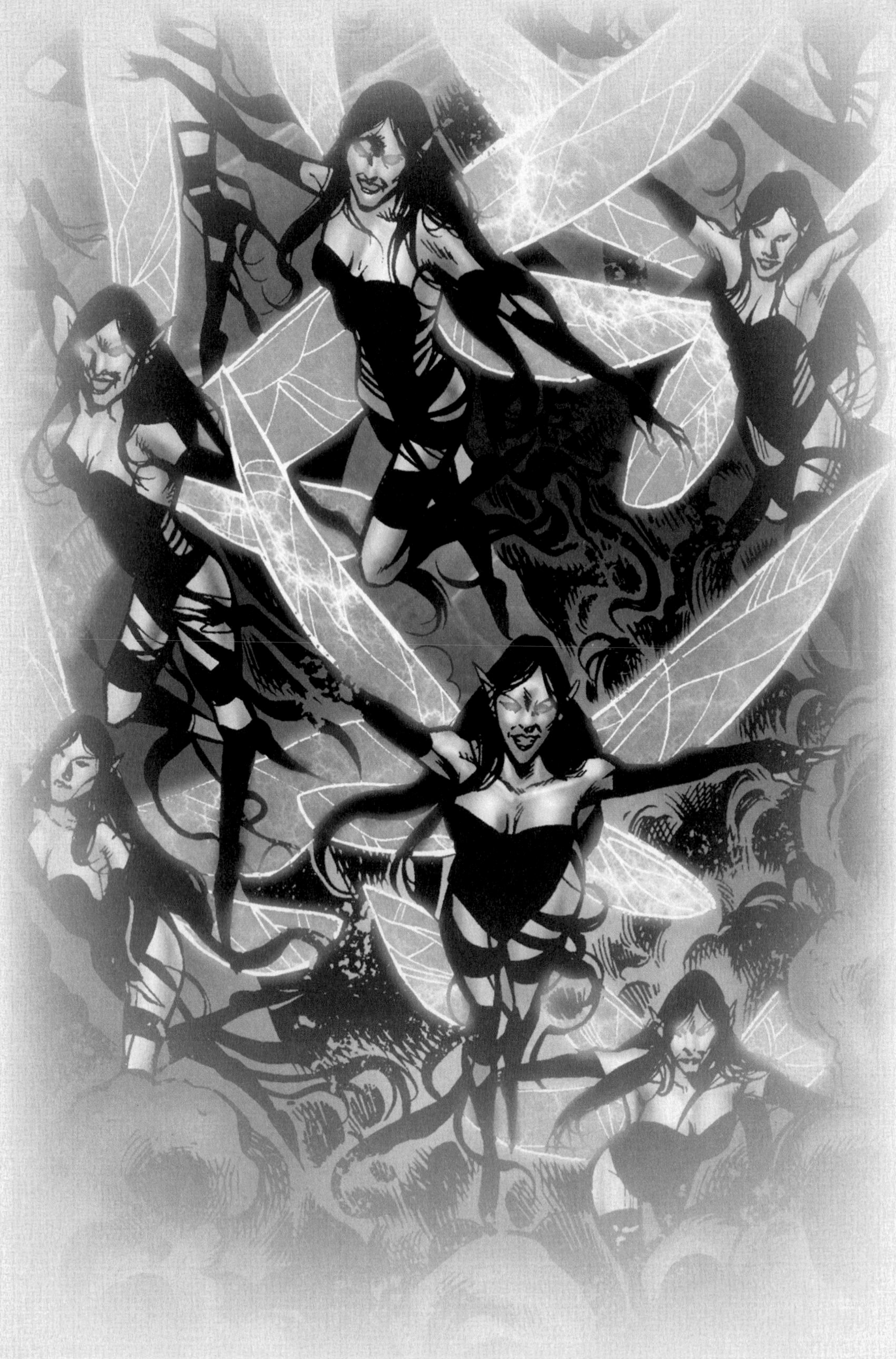

"Women like us should keep in practice."

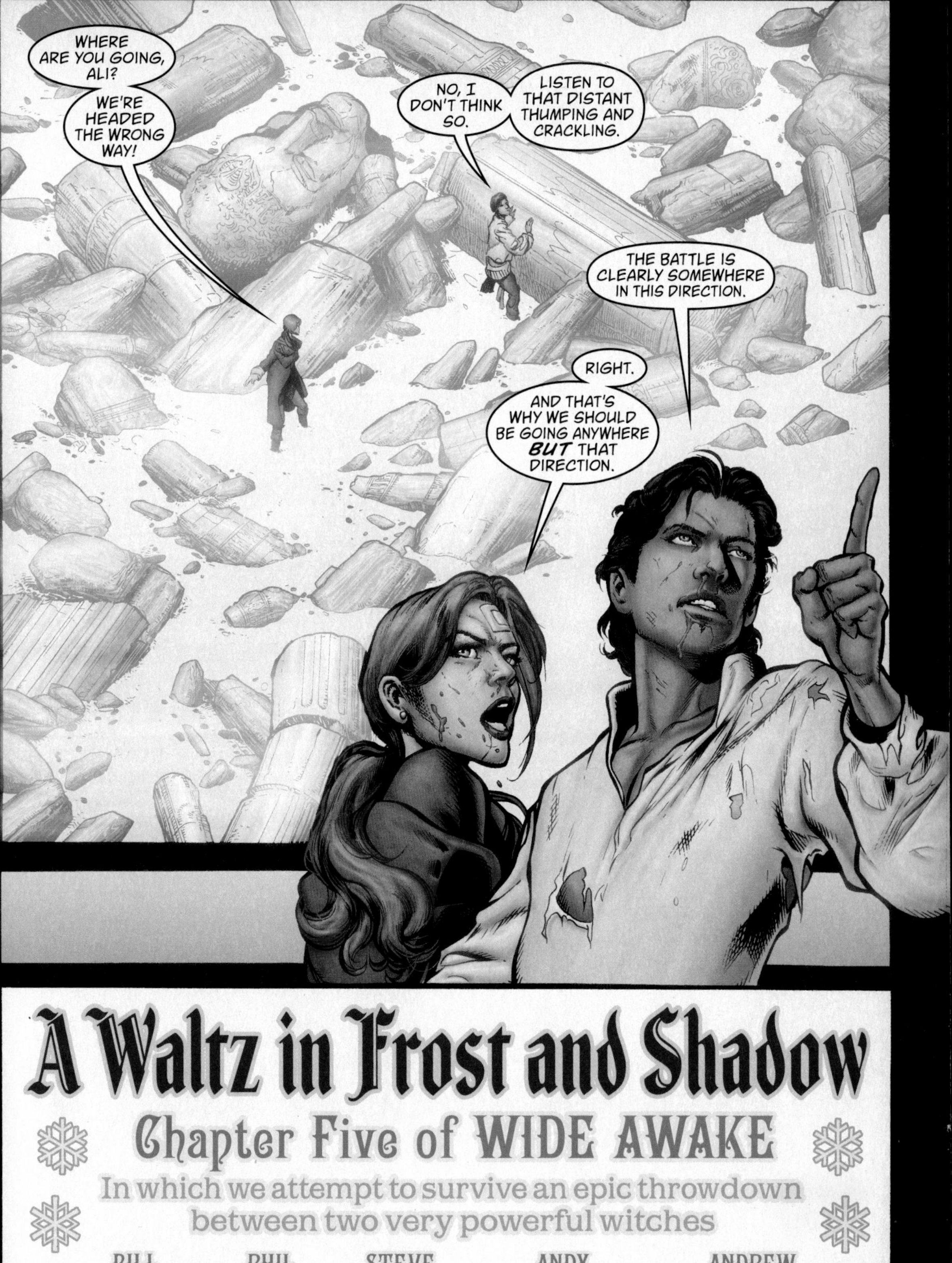

WHERE ARE YOU GOING, ALI?
WE'RE HEADED THE WRONG WAY!
NO, I DON'T THINK SO.
LISTEN TO THAT DISTANT THUMPING AND CRACKLING.
THE BATTLE IS CLEARLY SOMEWHERE IN THIS DIRECTION.
RIGHT.
AND THAT'S WHY WE SHOULD BE GOING ANYWHERE *BUT* THAT DIRECTION.

A Waltz in Frost and Shadow

Chapter Five of WIDE AWAKE

In which we attempt to survive an epic throwdown between two very powerful witches

BILL WILLINGHAM writer
PHIL JIMENEZ pencils
STEVE SADOWSKI pencils: 15,19-20
ANDY LANNING inks: 1,3-9,12-14,17
ANDREW PEPOY inks: 2,10-11,15-16,18-20

ANDREW DALHOUSE colors
TODD KLEIN letters
ADAM HUGHES cover
special thanks to ZANDER CANNON
GREGORY LOCKARD asst. ed.
SHELLY BOND editor
FAIREST is created by Bill Willingham

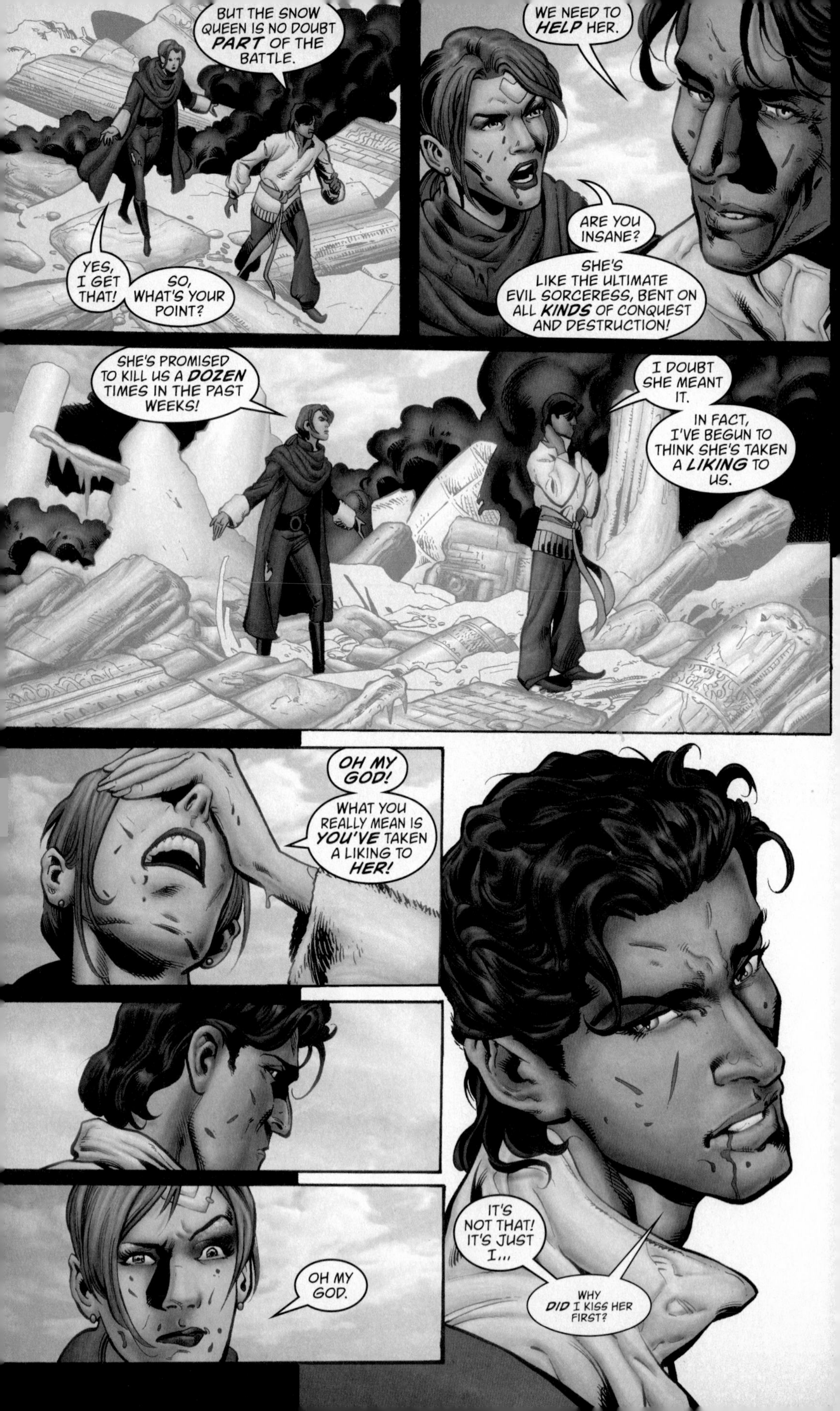
BUT THE SNOW QUEEN IS NO DOUBT **PART** OF THE BATTLE.
YES, I GET THAT!
SO, WHAT'S YOUR POINT?
WE NEED TO **HELP** HER.
ARE YOU INSANE?
SHE'S LIKE THE ULTIMATE EVIL SORCERESS, BENT ON ALL **KINDS** OF CONQUEST AND DESTRUCTION!
SHE'S PROMISED TO KILL US A **DOZEN** TIMES IN THE PAST WEEKS!
I DOUBT SHE MEANT IT.
IN FACT, I'VE BEGUN TO THINK SHE'S TAKEN A **LIKING** TO US.
OH MY GOD!
WHAT YOU REALLY MEAN IS **YOU'VE** TAKEN A LIKING TO **HER!**
OH MY GOD.
IT'S NOT THAT! IT'S JUST I...
WHY **DID** I KISS HER FIRST?

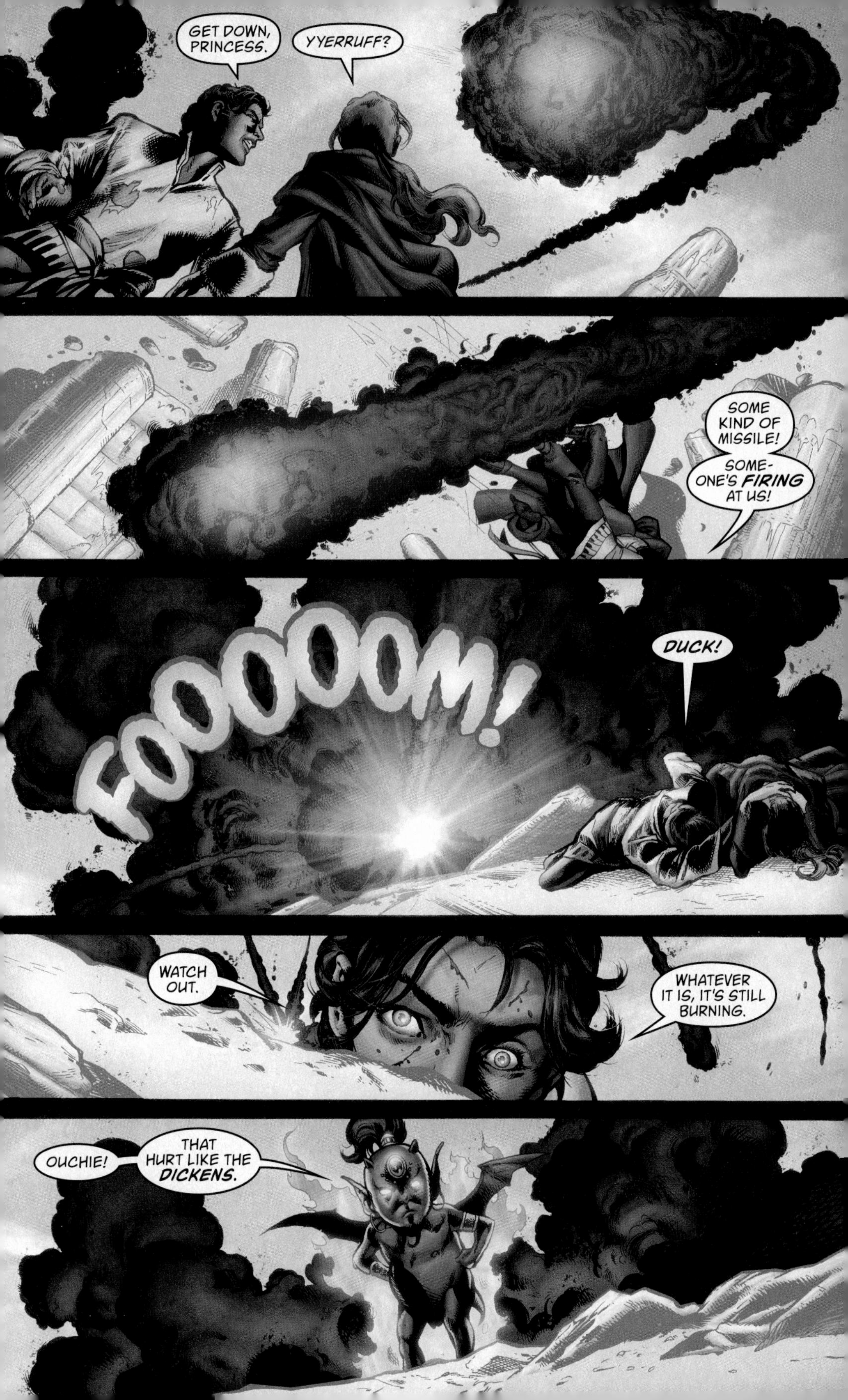
GET DOWN, PRINCESS.
YYERRUFF?
SOME KIND OF MISSILE!
SOME-ONE'S FIRING AT US!
FOOOOOM!
DUCK!
WATCH OUT.
WHATEVER IT IS, IT'S STILL BURNING.
OUCHIE!
THAT HURT LIKE THE DICKENS.

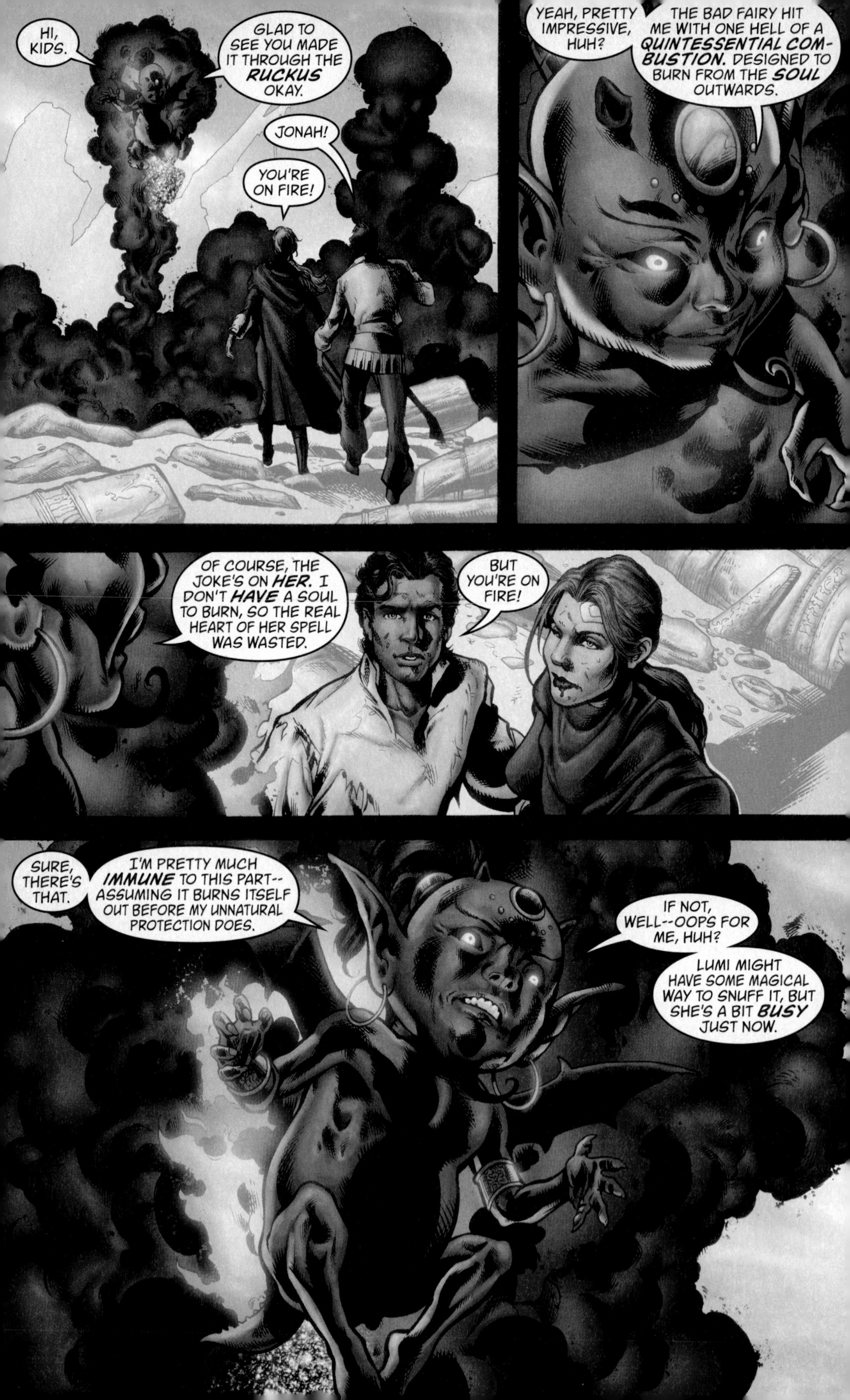
HI, KIDS.
GLAD TO SEE YOU MADE IT THROUGH THE RUCKUS OKAY.
JONAH!
YOU'RE ON FIRE!
YEAH, PRETTY IMPRESSIVE, HUH?
THE BAD FAIRY HIT ME WITH ONE HELL OF A QUINTESSENTIAL COMBUSTION. DESIGNED TO BURN FROM THE SOUL OUTWARDS.
OF COURSE, THE JOKE'S ON HER. I DON'T HAVE A SOUL TO BURN, SO THE REAL HEART OF HER SPELL WAS WASTED.
BUT YOU'RE ON FIRE!
SURE, THERE'S THAT.
I'M PRETTY MUCH IMMUNE TO THIS PART--ASSUMING IT BURNS ITSELF OUT BEFORE MY UNNATURAL PROTECTION DOES.
IF NOT, WELL--OOPS FOR ME, HUH?
LUMI MIGHT HAVE SOME MAGICAL WAY TO SNUFF IT, BUT SHE'S A BIT BUSY JUST NOW.

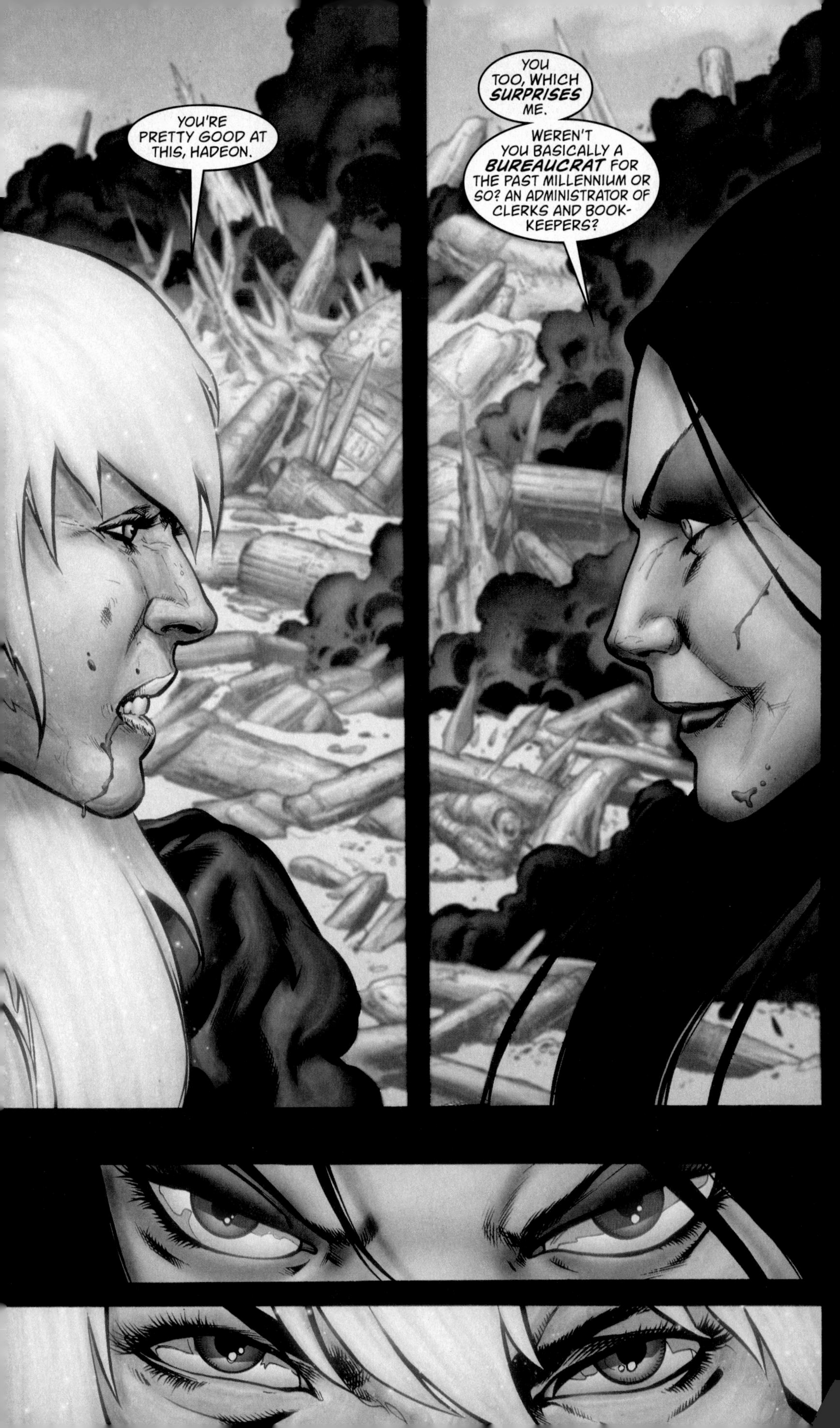
YOU'RE PRETTY GOOD AT THIS, HADEON.
YOU TOO, WHICH SURPRISES ME.
WEREN'T YOU BASICALLY A BUREAUCRAT FOR THE PAST MILLENNIUM OR SO? AN ADMINISTRATOR OF CLERKS AND BOOK-KEEPERS?

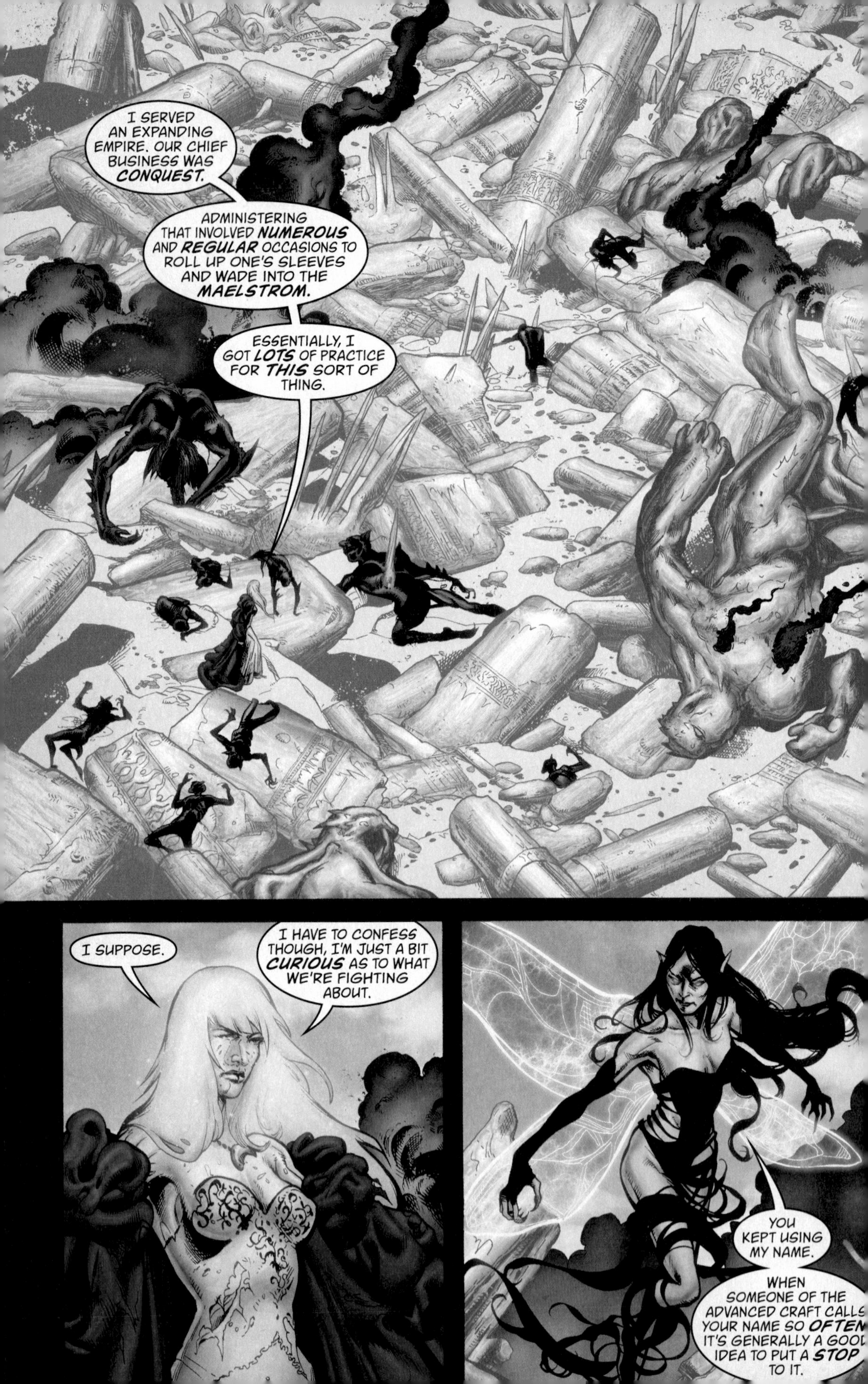
I SERVED AN EXPANDING EMPIRE. OUR CHIEF BUSINESS WAS **CONQUEST.**
ADMINISTERING THAT INVOLVED **NUMEROUS** AND **REGULAR** OCCASIONS TO ROLL UP ONE'S SLEEVES AND WADE INTO THE **MAELSTROM.**
ESSENTIALLY, I GOT **LOTS** OF PRACTICE FOR **THIS** SORT OF THING.
I SUPPOSE.
I HAVE TO CONFESS THOUGH, I'M JUST A BIT **CURIOUS** AS TO WHAT WE'RE FIGHTING ABOUT.
YOU KEPT USING MY NAME.
WHEN SOMEONE OF THE ADVANCED CRAFT CALLS YOUR NAME SO **OFTEN** IT'S GENERALLY A GOOD IDEA TO PUT A **STOP** TO IT.

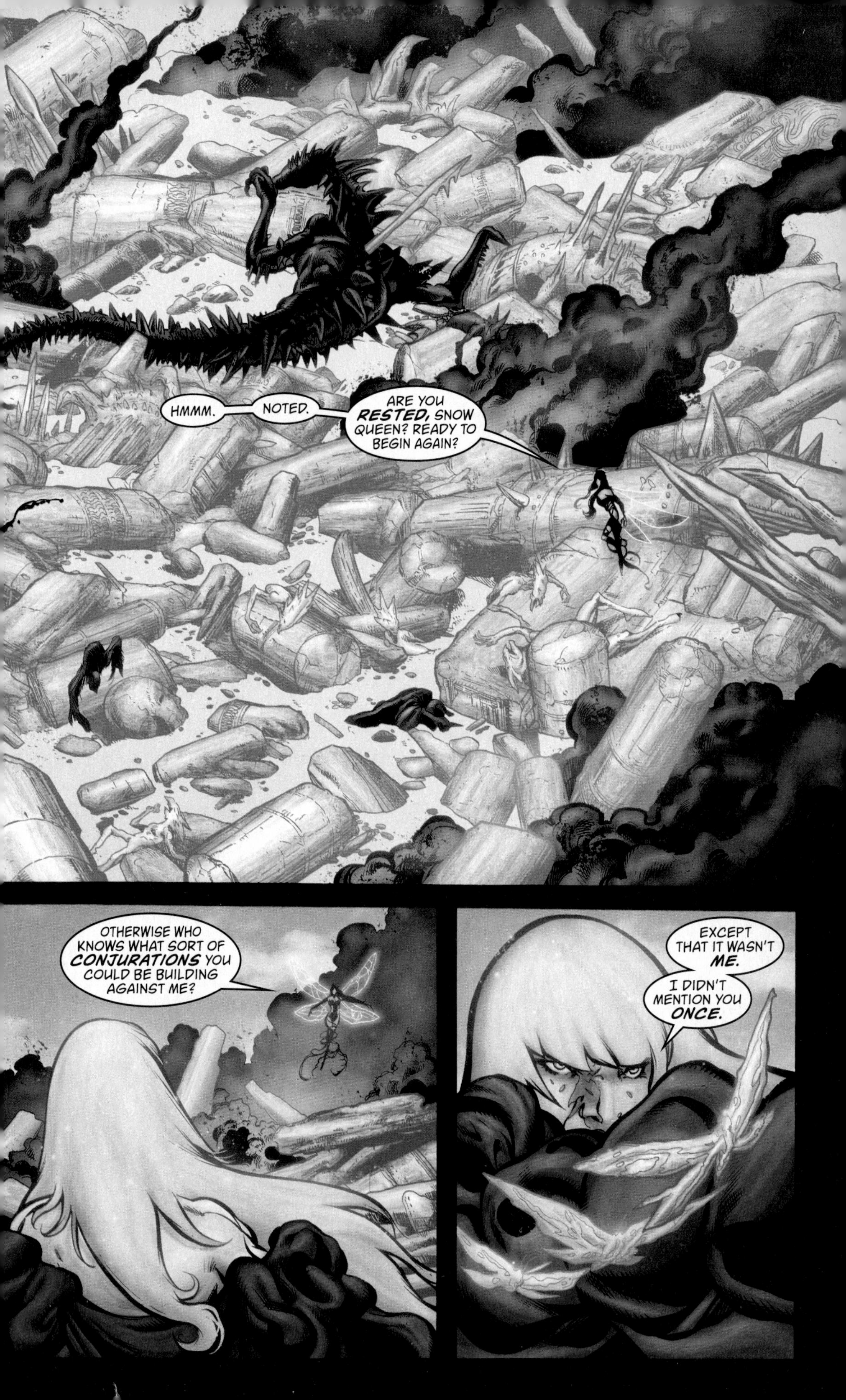
HMMM.
NOTED.
ARE YOU RESTED, SNOW QUEEN? READY TO BEGIN AGAIN?
OTHERWISE WHO KNOWS WHAT SORT OF CONJURATIONS YOU COULD BE BUILDING AGAINST ME?
EXCEPT THAT IT WASN'T ME.
I DIDN'T MENTION YOU ONCE.

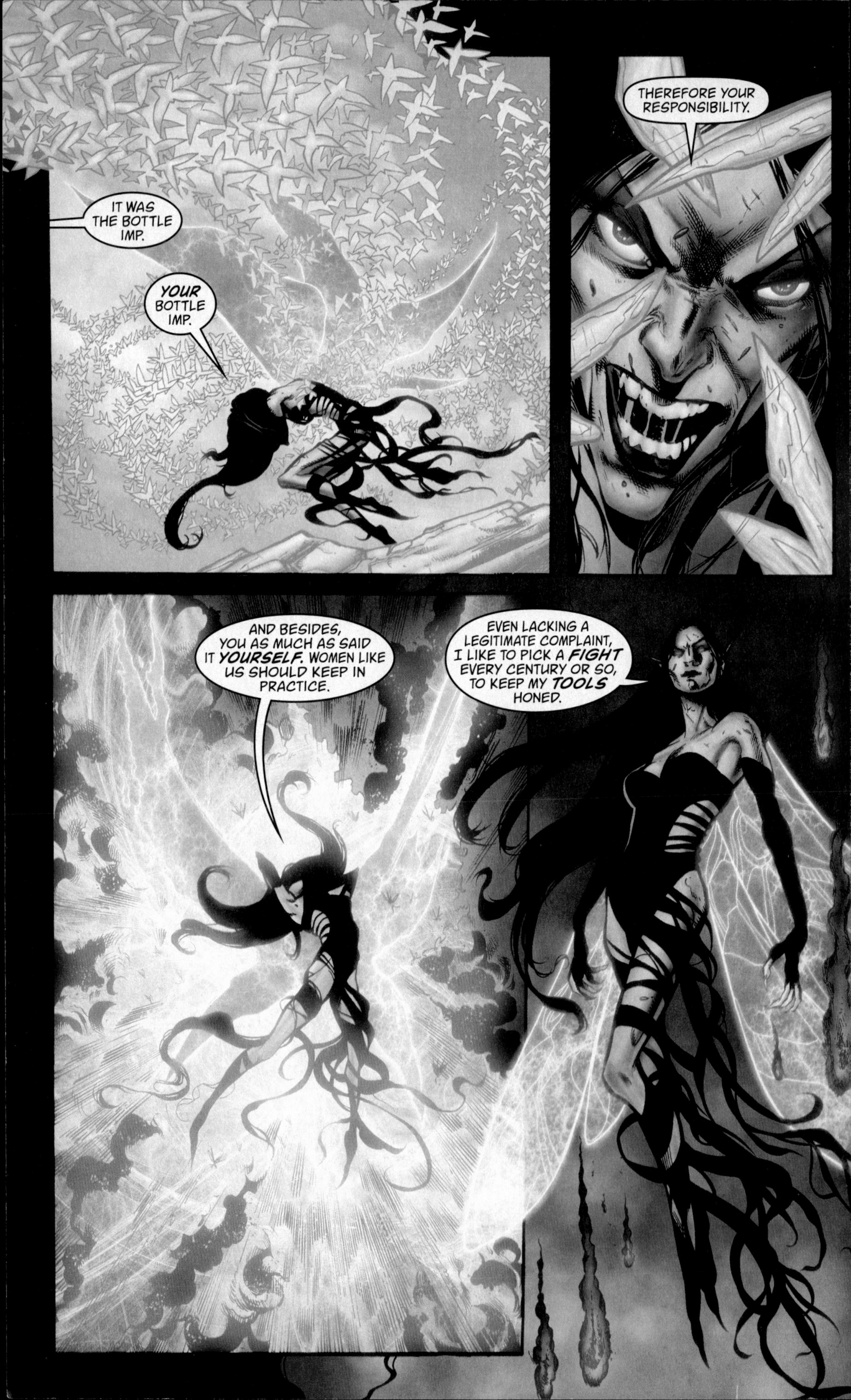
IT WAS THE BOTTLE IMP.
YOUR BOTTLE IMP.
THEREFORE YOUR RESPONSIBILITY.
AND BESIDES, YOU AS MUCH AS SAID IT YOURSELF. WOMEN LIKE US SHOULD KEEP IN PRACTICE.
EVEN LACKING A LEGITIMATE COMPLAINT, I LIKE TO PICK A FIGHT EVERY CENTURY OR SO, TO KEEP MY TOOLS HONED.

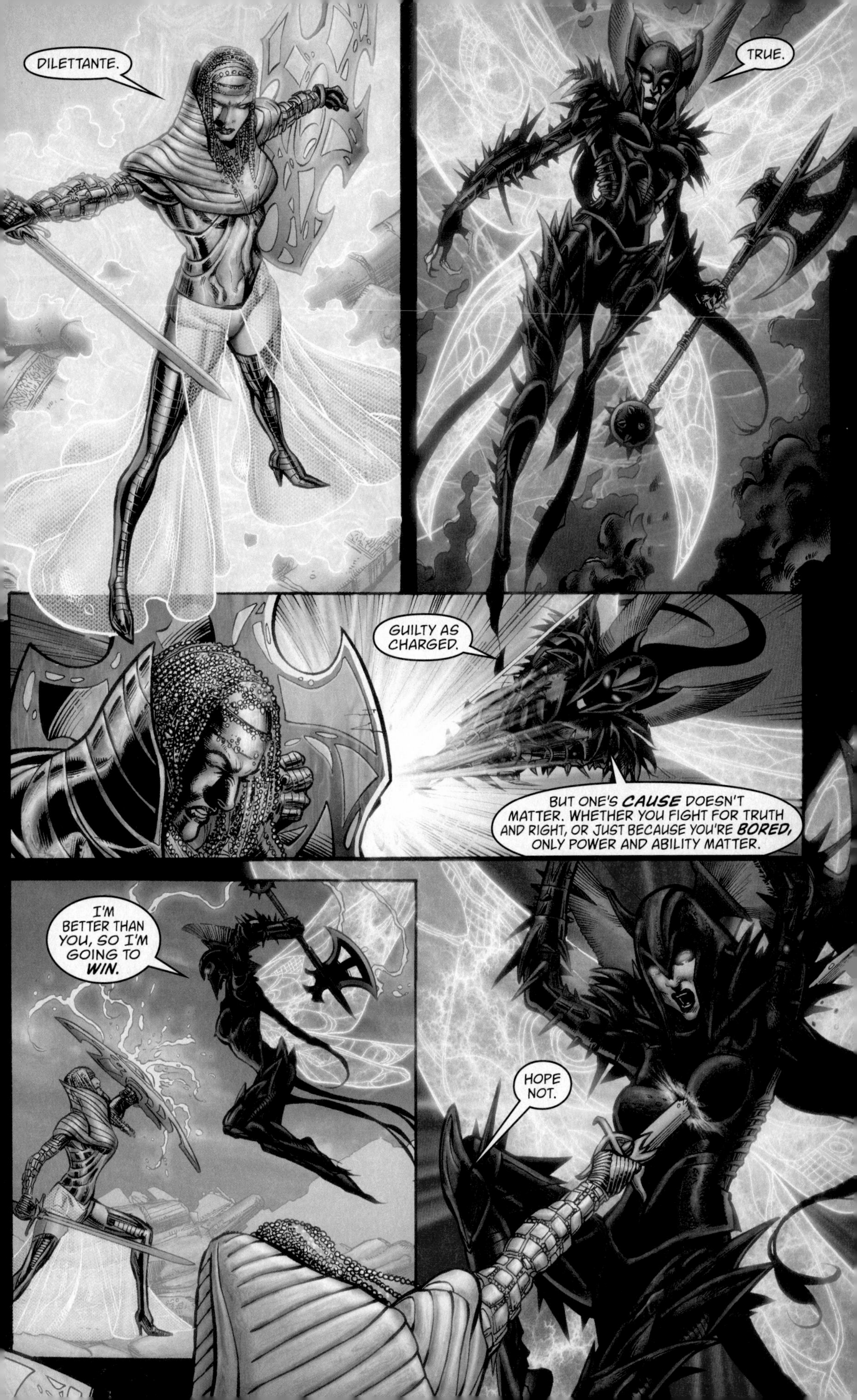
DILETTANTE.
TRUE.
GUILTY AS CHARGED.
BUT ONE'S **CAUSE** DOESN'T MATTER. WHETHER YOU FIGHT FOR TRUTH AND RIGHT, OR JUST BECAUSE YOU'RE **BORED,** ONLY POWER AND ABILITY MATTER.
I'M BETTER THAN YOU, SO I'M GOING TO **WIN.**
HOPE NOT.

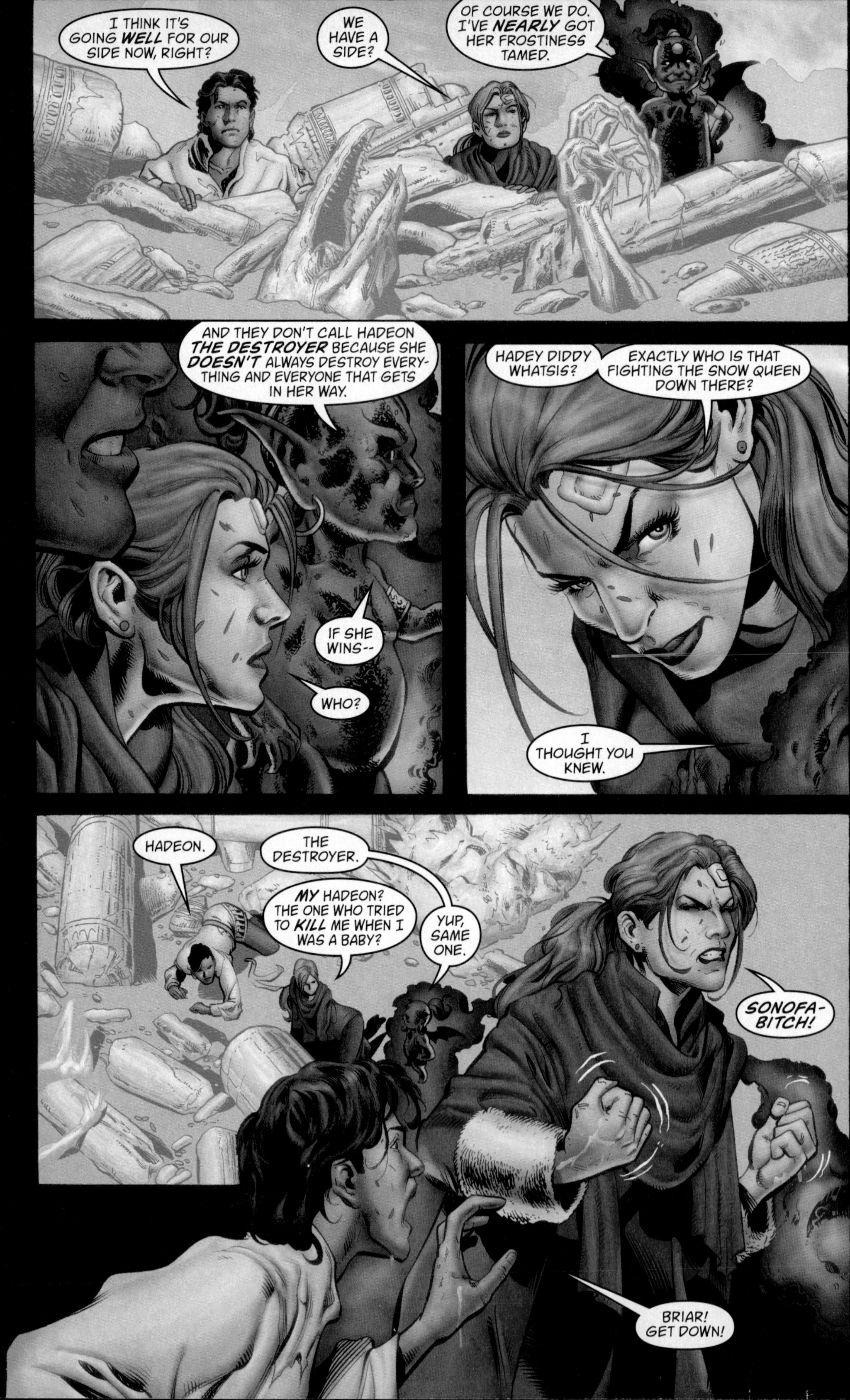

I THINK IT'S GOING **WELL** FOR OUR SIDE NOW, RIGHT?
WE HAVE A SIDE?
OF COURSE WE DO. I'VE **NEARLY** GOT HER FROSTINESS TAMED.
AND THEY DON'T CALL HADEON **THE DESTROYER** BECAUSE SHE **DOESN'T** ALWAYS DESTROY EVERYTHING AND EVERYONE THAT GETS IN HER WAY.
IF SHE WINS--
WHO?
HADEY DIDDY WHATSIS?
EXACTLY WHO IS THAT FIGHTING THE SNOW QUEEN DOWN THERE?
I THOUGHT YOU KNEW.
HADEON.
THE DESTROYER.
MY HADEON? THE ONE WHO TRIED TO *KILL* ME WHEN I WAS A BABY?
YUP, SAME ONE.
SONOFA-BITCH!
BRIAR! GET DOWN!

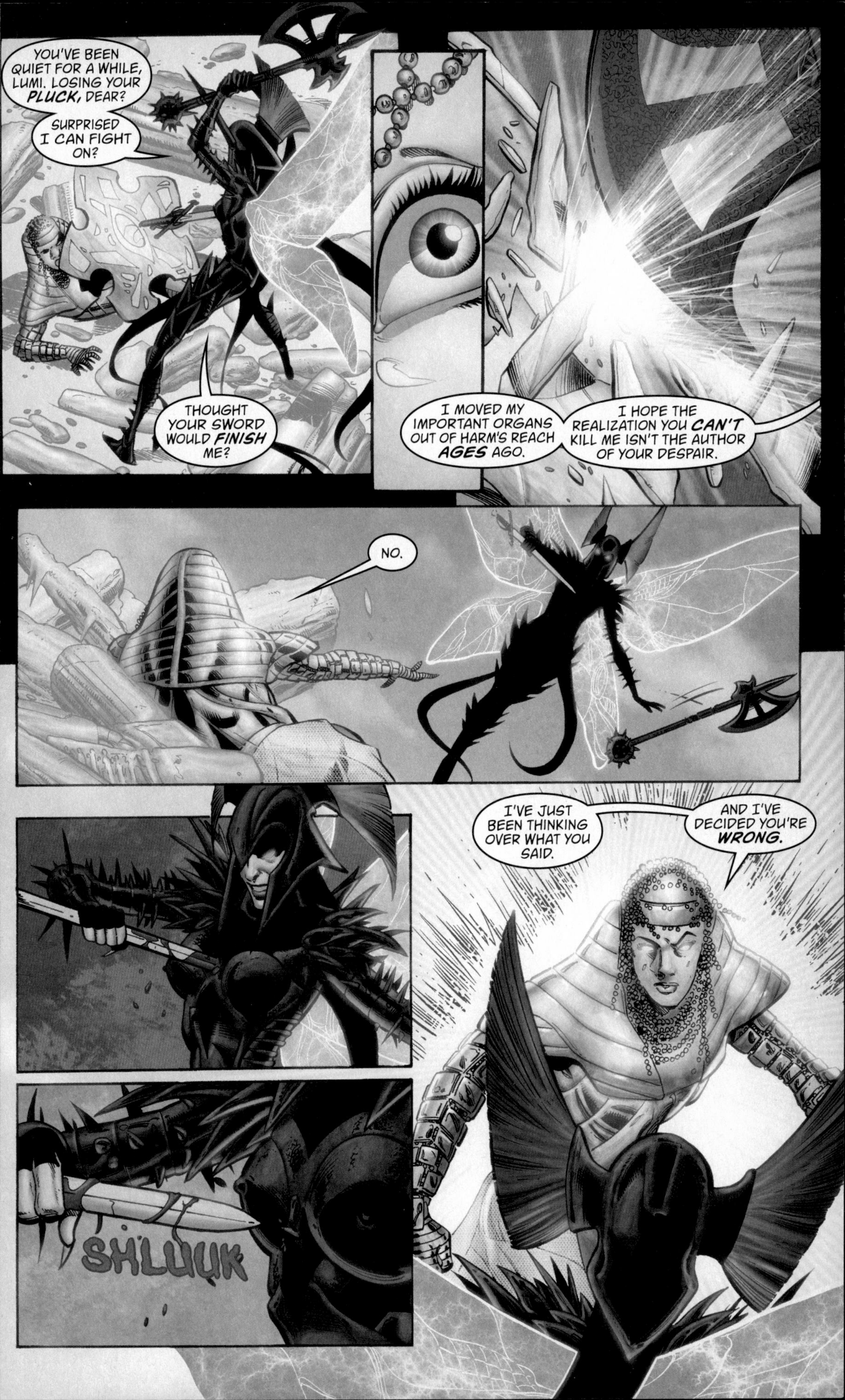
YOU'VE BEEN QUIET FOR A WHILE, LUMI. LOSING YOUR PLUCK, DEAR?
SURPRISED I CAN FIGHT ON?
THOUGHT YOUR SWORD WOULD FINISH ME?
I MOVED MY IMPORTANT ORGANS OUT OF HARM'S REACH AGES AGO.
I HOPE THE REALIZATION YOU CAN'T KILL ME ISN'T THE AUTHOR OF YOUR DESPAIR.
NO.
I'VE JUST BEEN THINKING OVER WHAT YOU SAID.
AND I'VE DECIDED YOU'RE WRONG.
SHLUUK

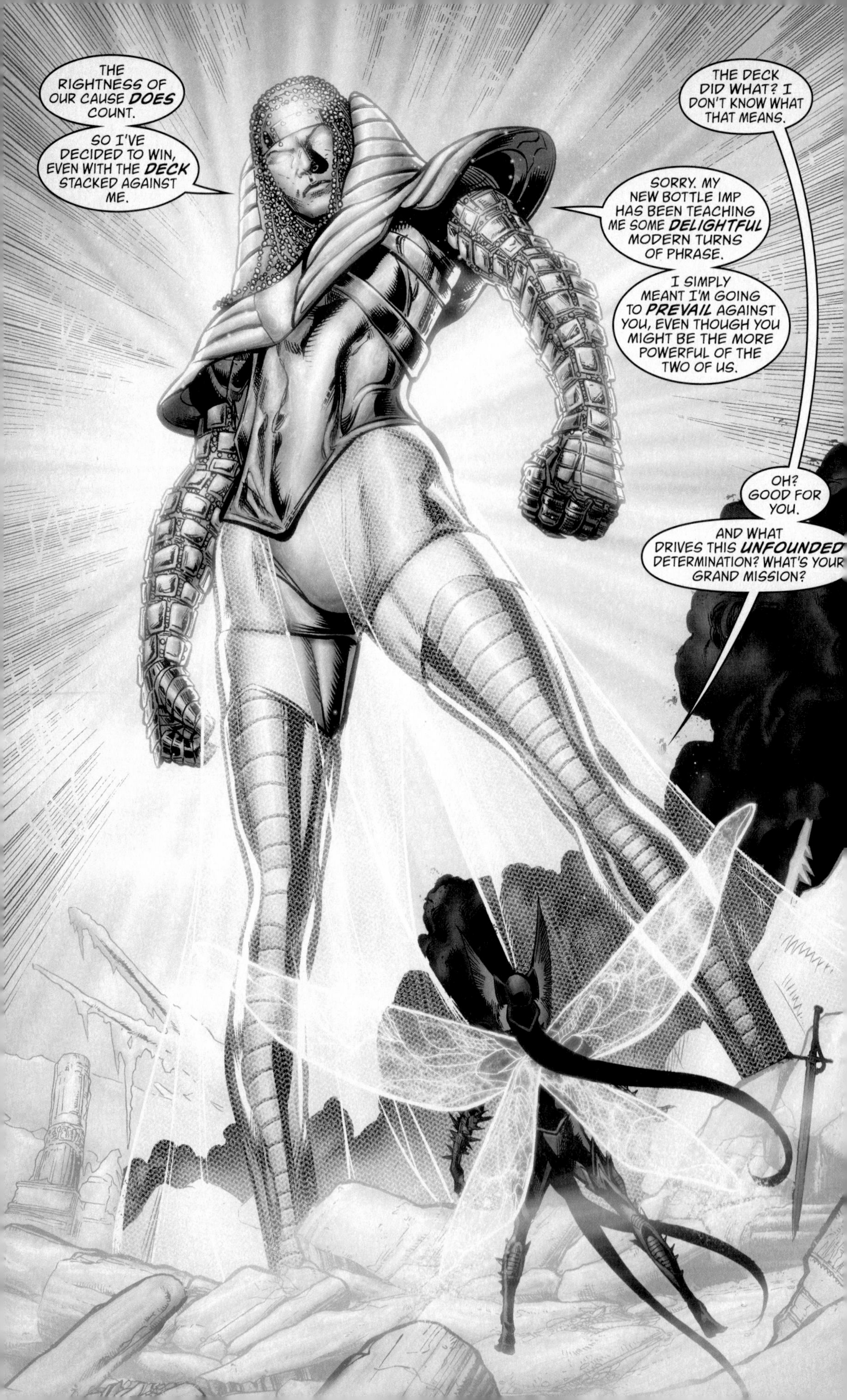
THE RIGHTNESS OF OUR CAUSE DOES COUNT.
SO I'VE DECIDED TO WIN, EVEN WITH THE DECK STACKED AGAINST ME.
THE DECK DID WHAT? I DON'T KNOW WHAT THAT MEANS.
SORRY. MY NEW BOTTLE IMP HAS BEEN TEACHING ME SOME DELIGHTFUL MODERN TURNS OF PHRASE.
I SIMPLY MEANT I'M GOING TO PREVAIL AGAINST YOU, EVEN THOUGH YOU MIGHT BE THE MORE POWERFUL OF THE TWO OF US.
OH? GOOD FOR YOU.
AND WHAT DRIVES THIS UNFOUNDED DETERMINATION? WHAT'S YOUR GRAND MISSION?

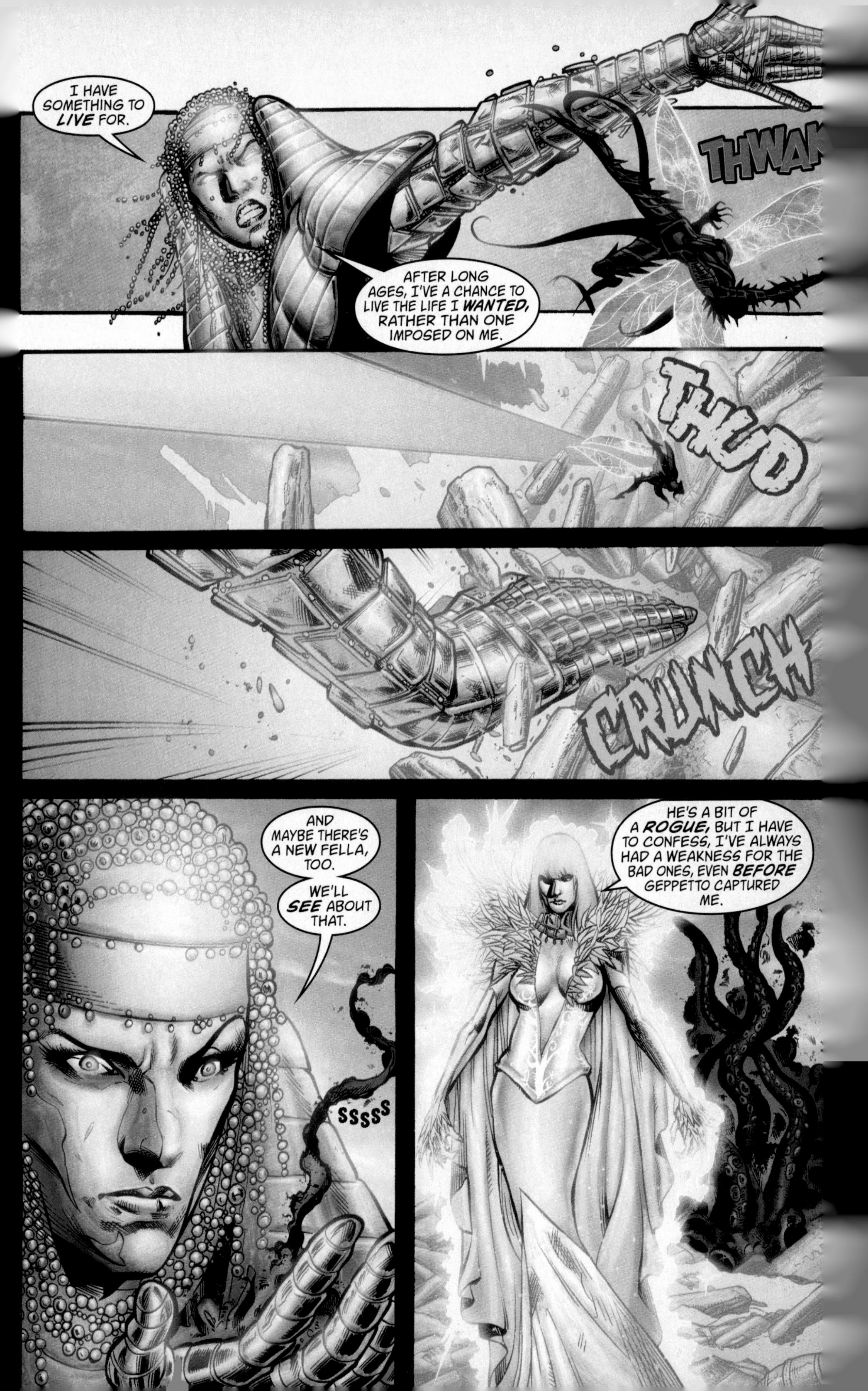
I HAVE SOMETHING TO LIVE FOR.
THWAK
AFTER LONG AGES, I'VE A CHANCE TO LIVE THE LIFE I WANTED, RATHER THAN ONE IMPOSED ON ME.
THUD
CRUNCH
AND MAYBE THERE'S A NEW FELLA, TOO.
WE'LL SEE ABOUT THAT.
SSSSS
HE'S A BIT OF A ROGUE, BUT I HAVE TO CONFESS, I'VE ALWAYS HAD A WEAKNESS FOR THE BAD ONES, EVEN BEFORE GEPPETTO CAPTURED ME.

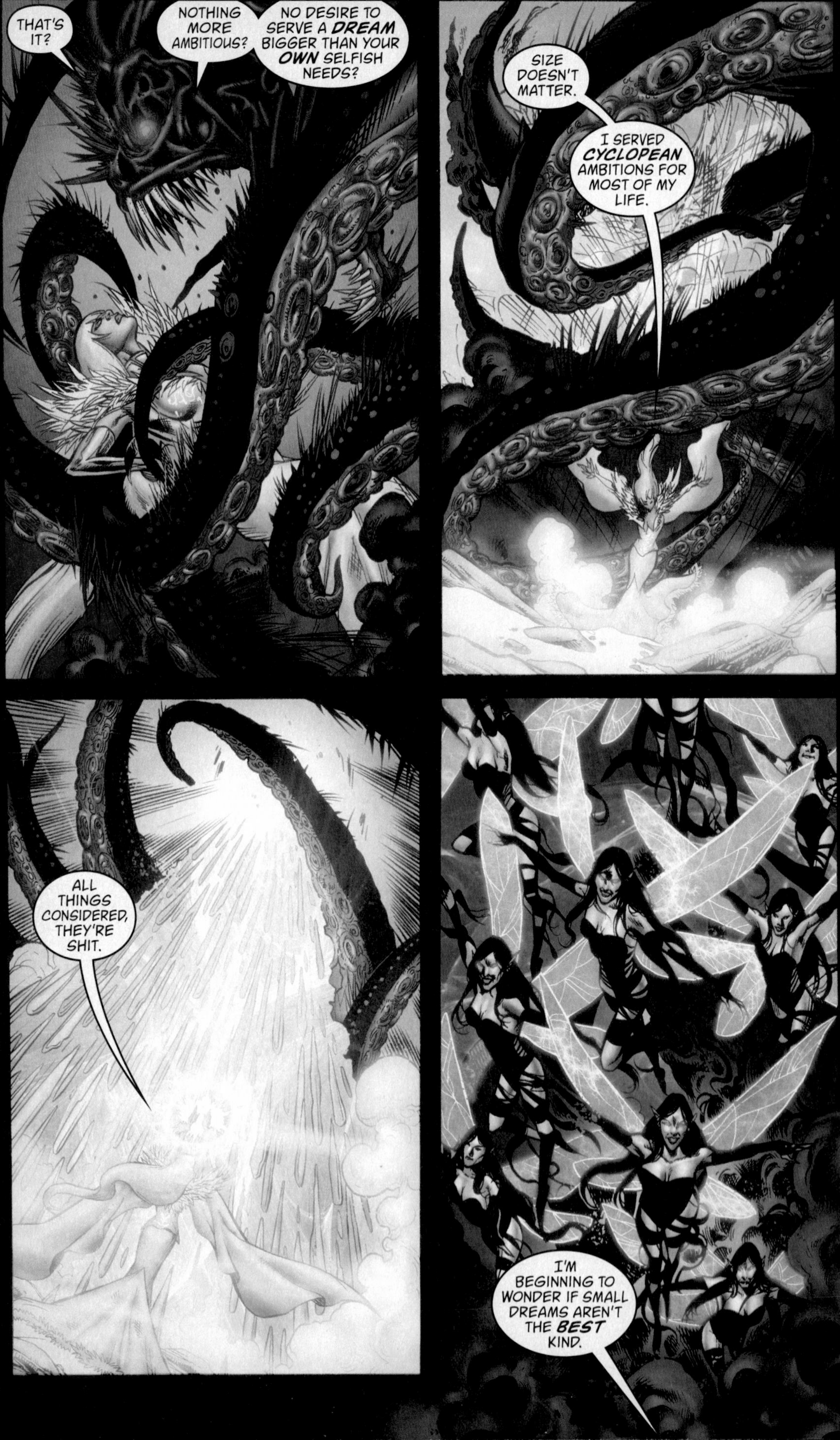

THAT'S IT?
NOTHING MORE AMBITIOUS?
NO DESIRE TO SERVE A DREAM BIGGER THAN YOUR OWN SELFISH NEEDS?
SIZE DOESN'T MATTER.
I SERVED CYCLOPEAN AMBITIONS FOR MOST OF MY LIFE.
ALL THINGS CONSIDERED, THEY'RE SHIT.
I'M BEGINNING TO WONDER IF SMALL DREAMS AREN'T THE BEST KIND.

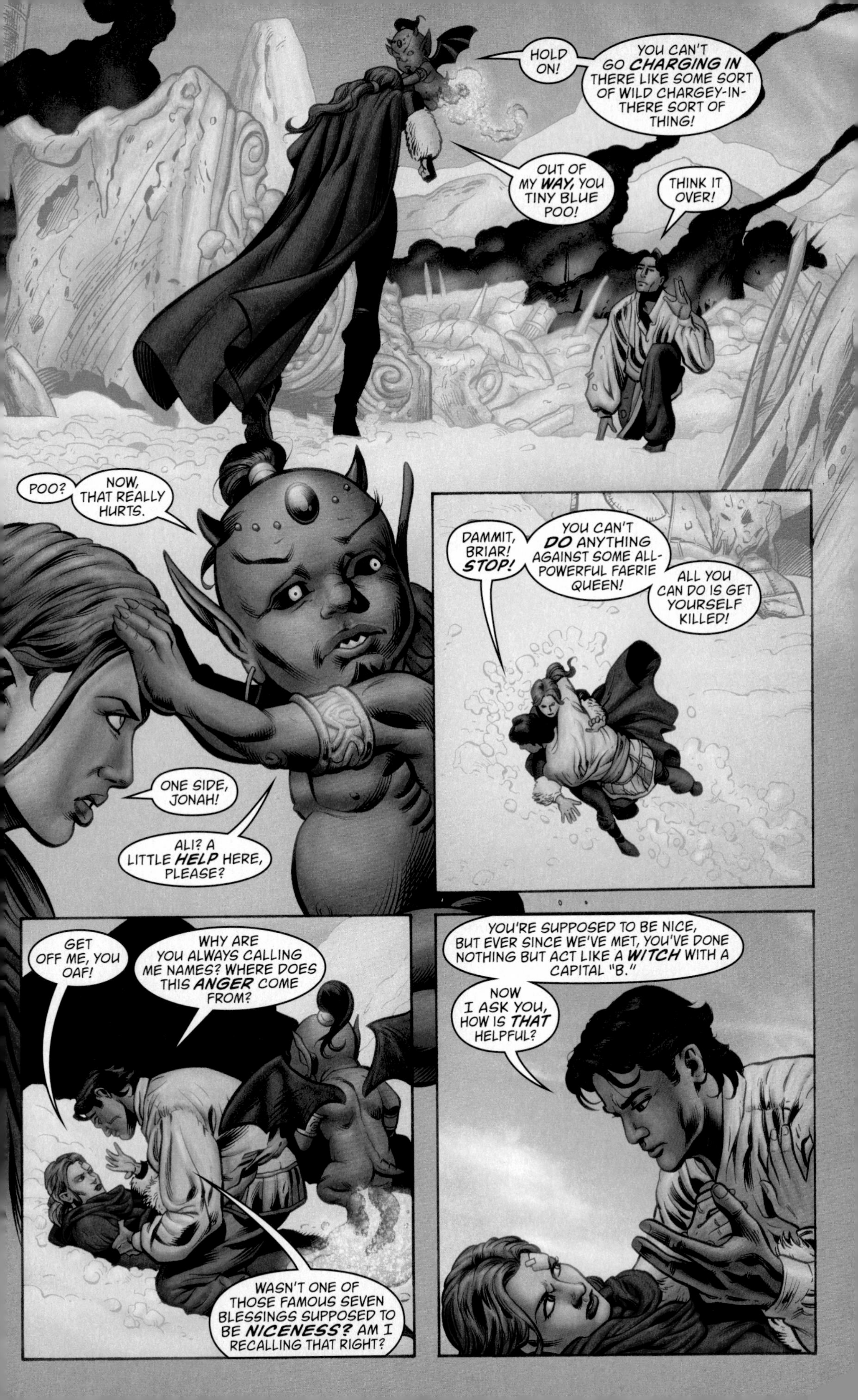
HOLD ON!
YOU CAN'T GO CHARGING IN THERE LIKE SOME SORT OF WILD CHARGEY-IN-THERE SORT OF THING!
OUT OF MY WAY, YOU TINY BLUE POO!
THINK IT OVER!
POO?
NOW, THAT REALLY HURTS.
ONE SIDE, JONAH!
ALI? A LITTLE HELP HERE, PLEASE?
DAMMIT, BRIAR! STOP!
YOU CAN'T DO ANYTHING AGAINST SOME ALL-POWERFUL FAERIE QUEEN!
ALL YOU CAN DO IS GET YOURSELF KILLED!
GET OFF ME, YOU OAF!
WHY ARE YOU ALWAYS CALLING ME NAMES? WHERE DOES THIS ANGER COME FROM?
WASN'T ONE OF THOSE FAMOUS SEVEN BLESSINGS SUPPOSED TO BE NICENESS? AM I RECALLING THAT RIGHT?
YOU'RE SUPPOSED TO BE NICE, BUT EVER SINCE WE'VE MET, YOU'VE DONE NOTHING BUT ACT LIKE A WITCH WITH A CAPITAL "B."
NOW I ASK YOU, HOW IS THAT HELPFUL?

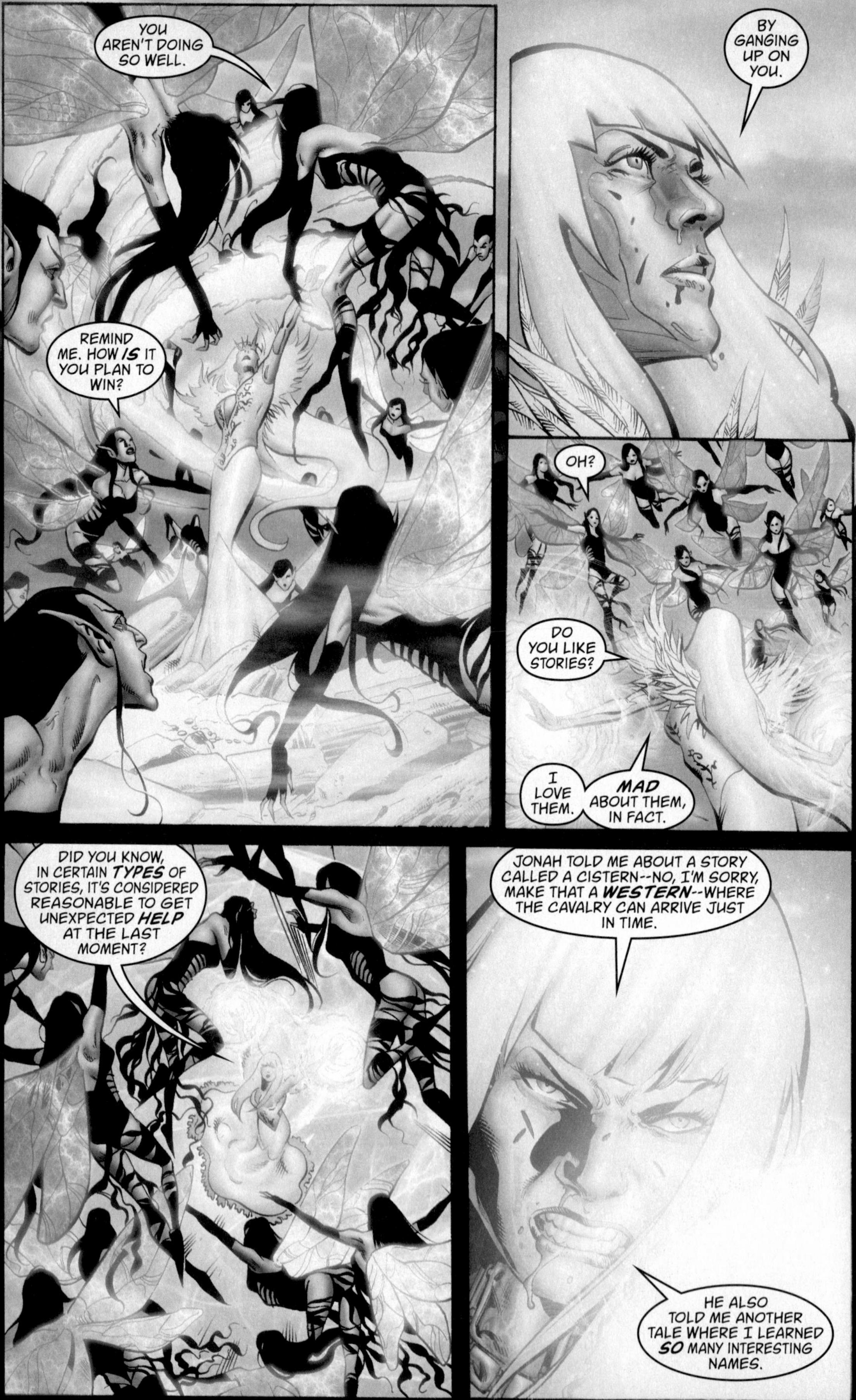
YOU AREN'T DOING SO WELL.
BY GANGING UP ON YOU.
REMIND ME. HOW *IS* IT YOU PLAN TO WIN?
OH?
DO YOU LIKE STORIES?
I LOVE THEM.
MAD ABOUT THEM, IN FACT.
DID YOU KNOW, IN CERTAIN *TYPES* OF STORIES, IT'S CONSIDERED REASONABLE TO GET UNEXPECTED *HELP* AT THE LAST MOMENT?
JONAH TOLD ME ABOUT A STORY CALLED A CISTERN--NO, I'M SORRY, MAKE THAT A *WESTERN*--WHERE THE CAVALRY CAN ARRIVE JUST IN TIME.
HE ALSO TOLD ME ANOTHER TALE WHERE I LEARNED *SO* MANY INTERESTING NAMES.

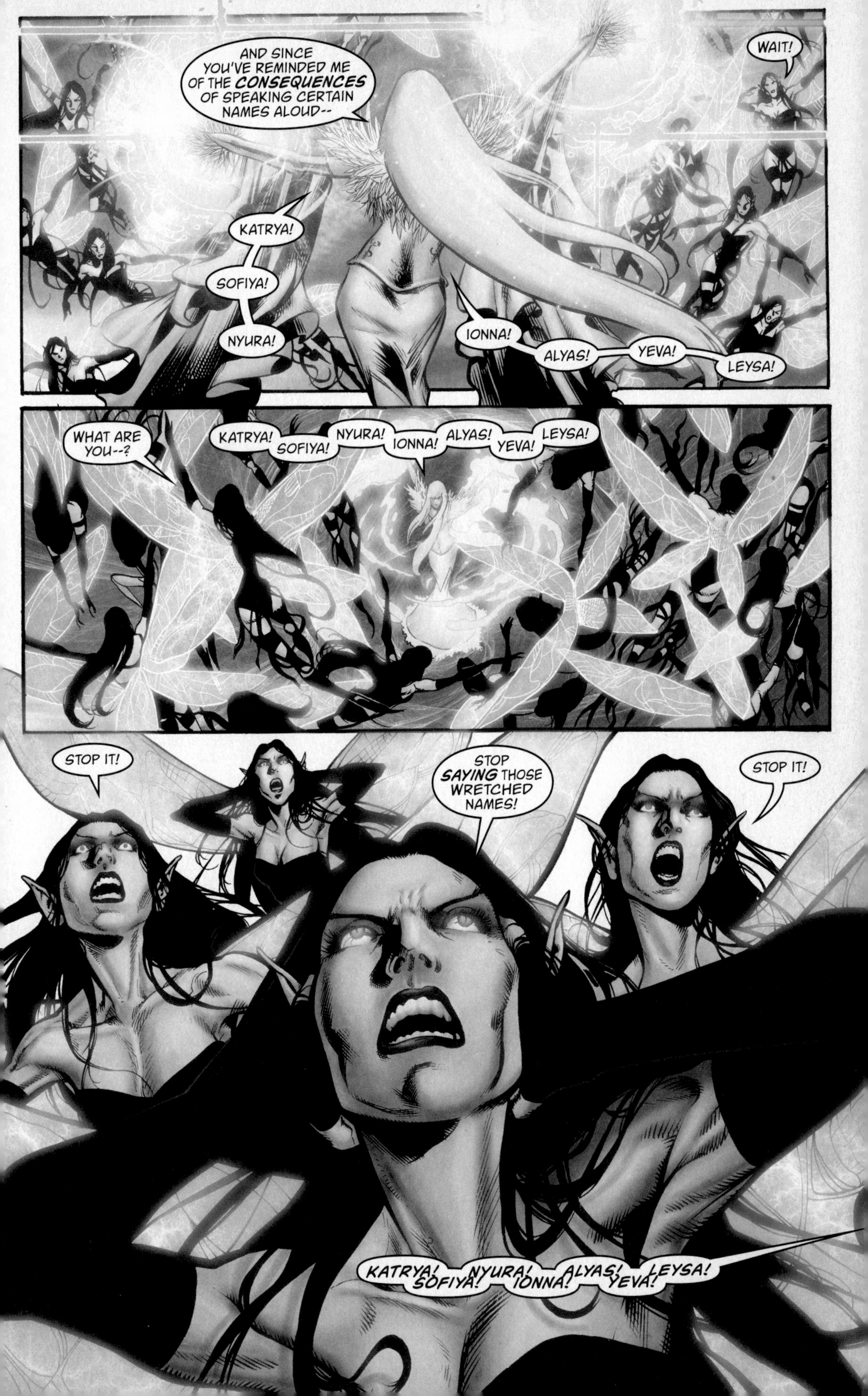
AND SINCE YOU'VE REMINDED ME OF THE CONSEQUENCES OF SPEAKING CERTAIN NAMES ALOUD--
WAIT!
KATRYA!
SOFIYA!
NYURA!
IONNA!
ALYAS!
YEVA!
LEYSA!
WHAT ARE YOU--?
KATRYA! SOFIYA! NYURA! IONNA! ALYAS! YEVA! LEYSA!
STOP IT!
STOP SAYING THOSE WRETCHED NAMES!
STOP IT!
KATRYA! SOFIYA! NYURA! IONNA! ALYAS! YEVA! LEYSA!

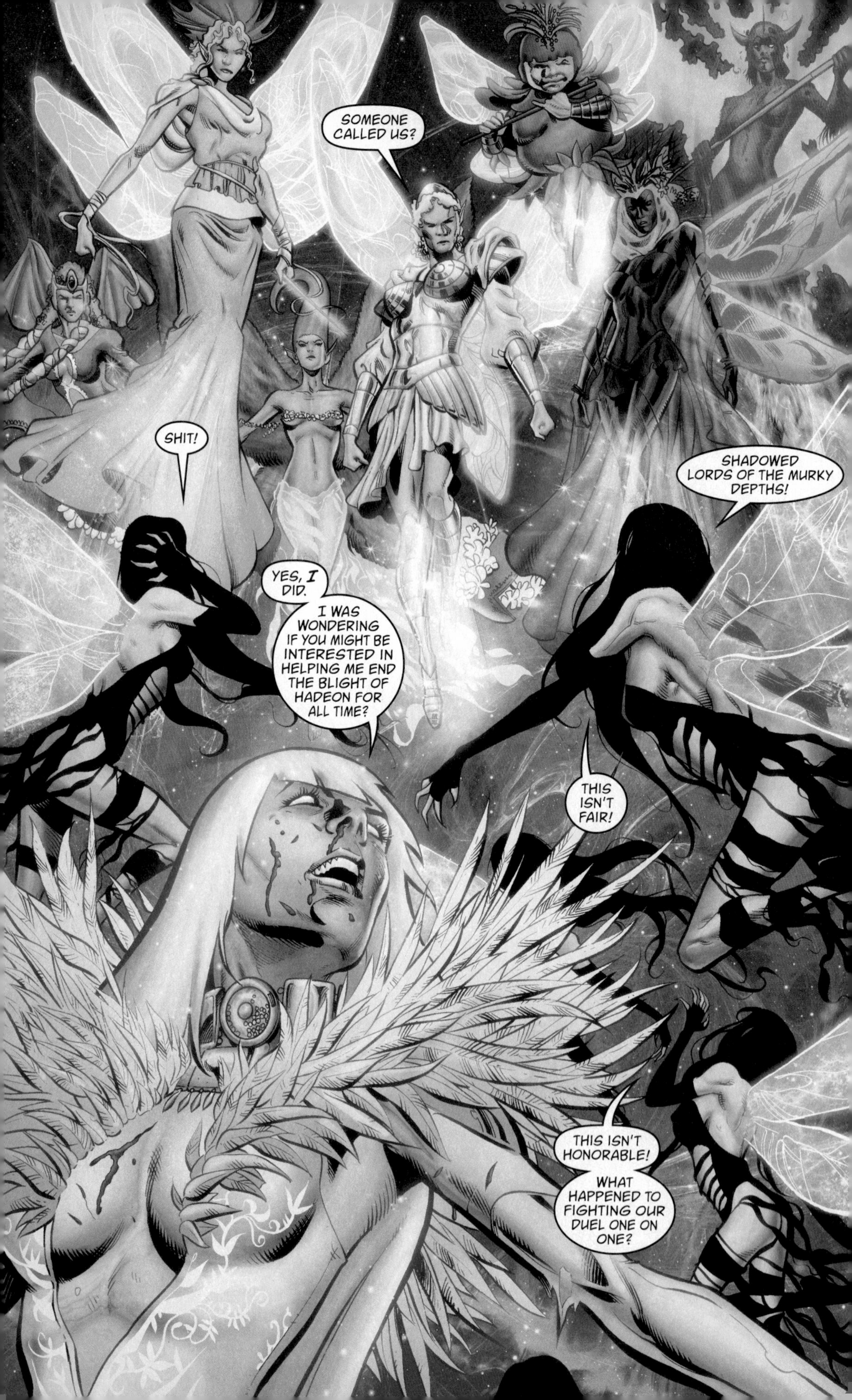
SOMEONE CALLED US?
SHIT!
SHADOWED LORDS OF THE MURKY DEPTHS!
YES, I DID.
I WAS WONDERING IF YOU MIGHT BE INTERESTED IN HELPING ME END THE BLIGHT OF HADEON FOR ALL TIME?
THIS ISN'T FAIR!
THIS ISN'T HONORABLE!
WHAT HAPPENED TO FIGHTING OUR DUEL ONE ON ONE?

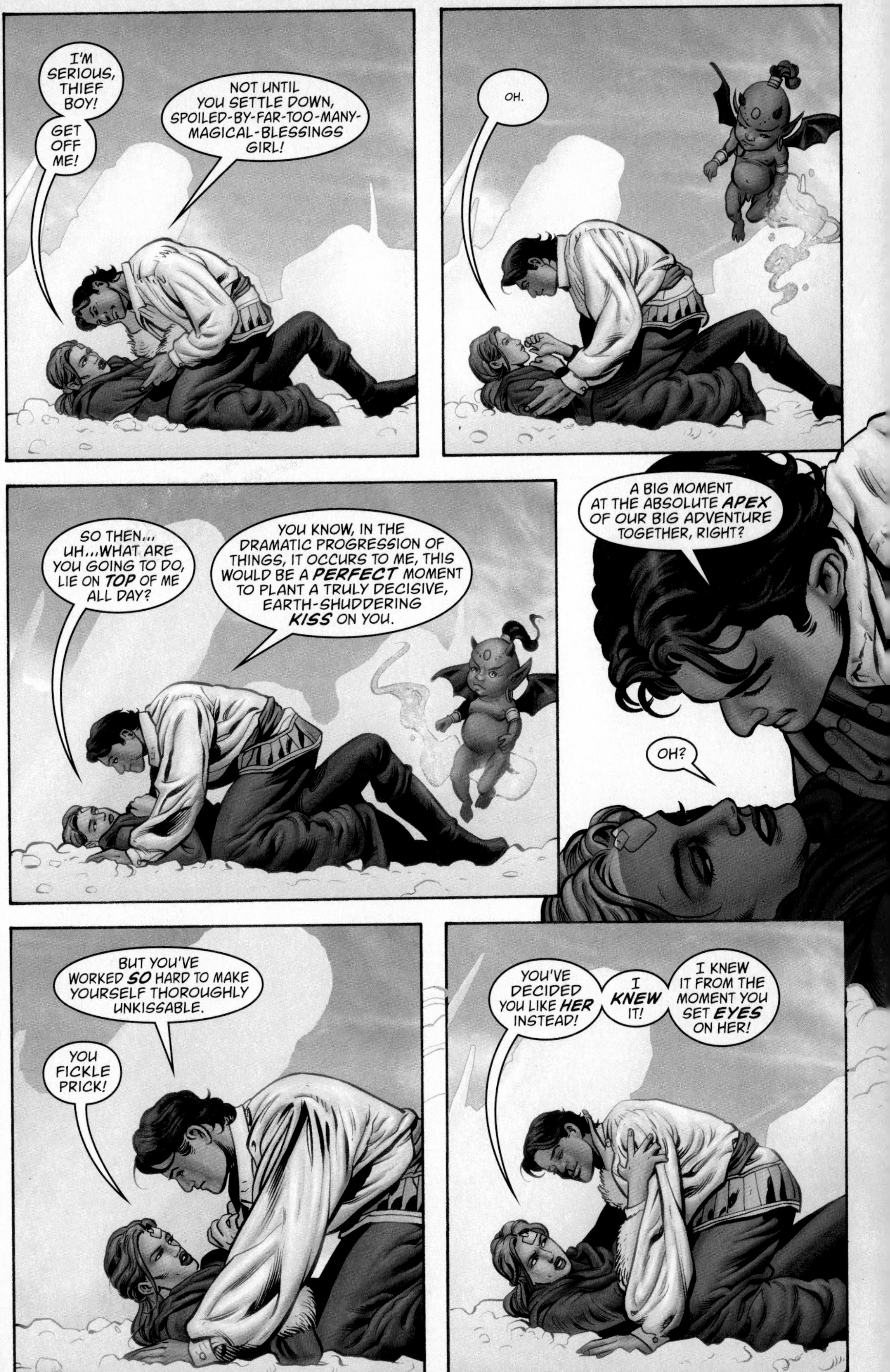
I'M SERIOUS, THIEF BOY!
GET OFF ME!
NOT UNTIL YOU SETTLE DOWN, SPOILED-BY-FAR-TOO-MANY-MAGICAL-BLESSINGS GIRL!
OH.
SO THEN... UH...WHAT ARE YOU GOING TO DO, LIE ON TOP OF ME ALL DAY?
YOU KNOW, IN THE DRAMATIC PROGRESSION OF THINGS, IT OCCURS TO ME, THIS WOULD BE A PERFECT MOMENT TO PLANT A TRULY DECISIVE, EARTH-SHUDDERING KISS ON YOU.
A BIG MOMENT AT THE ABSOLUTE APEX OF OUR BIG ADVENTURE TOGETHER, RIGHT?
OH?
BUT YOU'VE WORKED SO HARD TO MAKE YOURSELF THOROUGHLY UNKISSABLE.
YOU FICKLE PRICK!
YOU'VE DECIDED YOU LIKE HER INSTEAD!
I KNEW IT!
I KNEW IT FROM THE MOMENT YOU SET EYES ON HER!

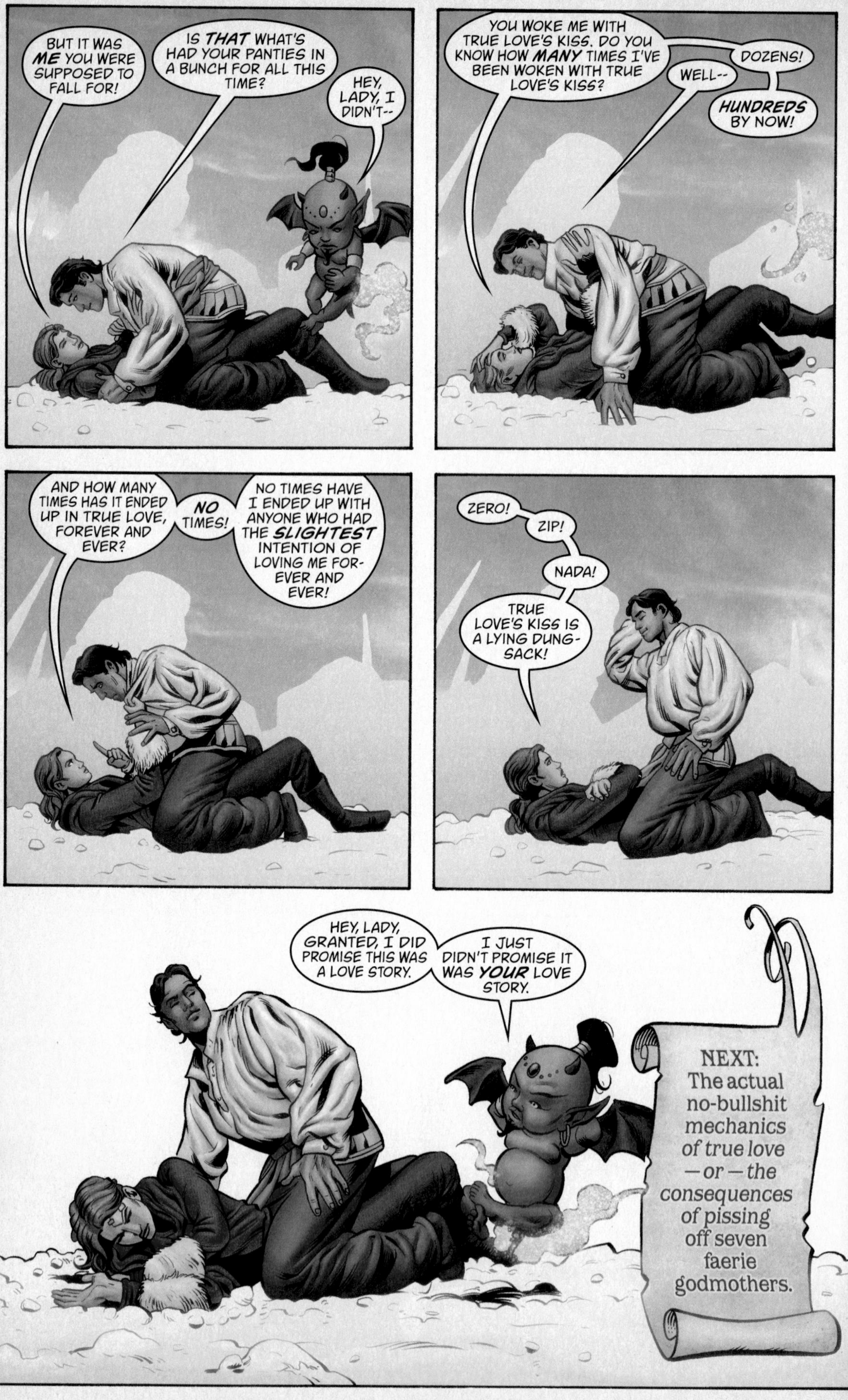
BUT IT WAS ME YOU WERE SUPPOSED TO FALL FOR!
IS THAT WHAT'S HAD YOUR PANTIES IN A BUNCH FOR ALL THIS TIME?
HEY, LADY, I DIDN'T--
YOU WOKE ME WITH TRUE LOVE'S KISS. DO YOU KNOW HOW MANY TIMES I'VE BEEN WOKEN WITH TRUE LOVE'S KISS?
WELL--
DOZENS!
HUNDREDS BY NOW!
AND HOW MANY TIMES HAS IT ENDED UP IN TRUE LOVE, FOREVER AND EVER?
NO TIMES!
NO TIMES HAVE I ENDED UP WITH ANYONE WHO HAD THE SLIGHTEST INTENTION OF LOVING ME FOR-EVER AND EVER!
ZERO!
ZIP!
NADA!
TRUE LOVE'S KISS IS A LYING DUNG-SACK!
HEY, LADY, GRANTED, I DID PROMISE THIS WAS A LOVE STORY.
I JUST DIDN'T PROMISE IT WAS YOUR LOVE STORY.
NEXT:
The actual no-bullshit mechanics of true love —or— the consequences of pissing off seven faerie godmothers.

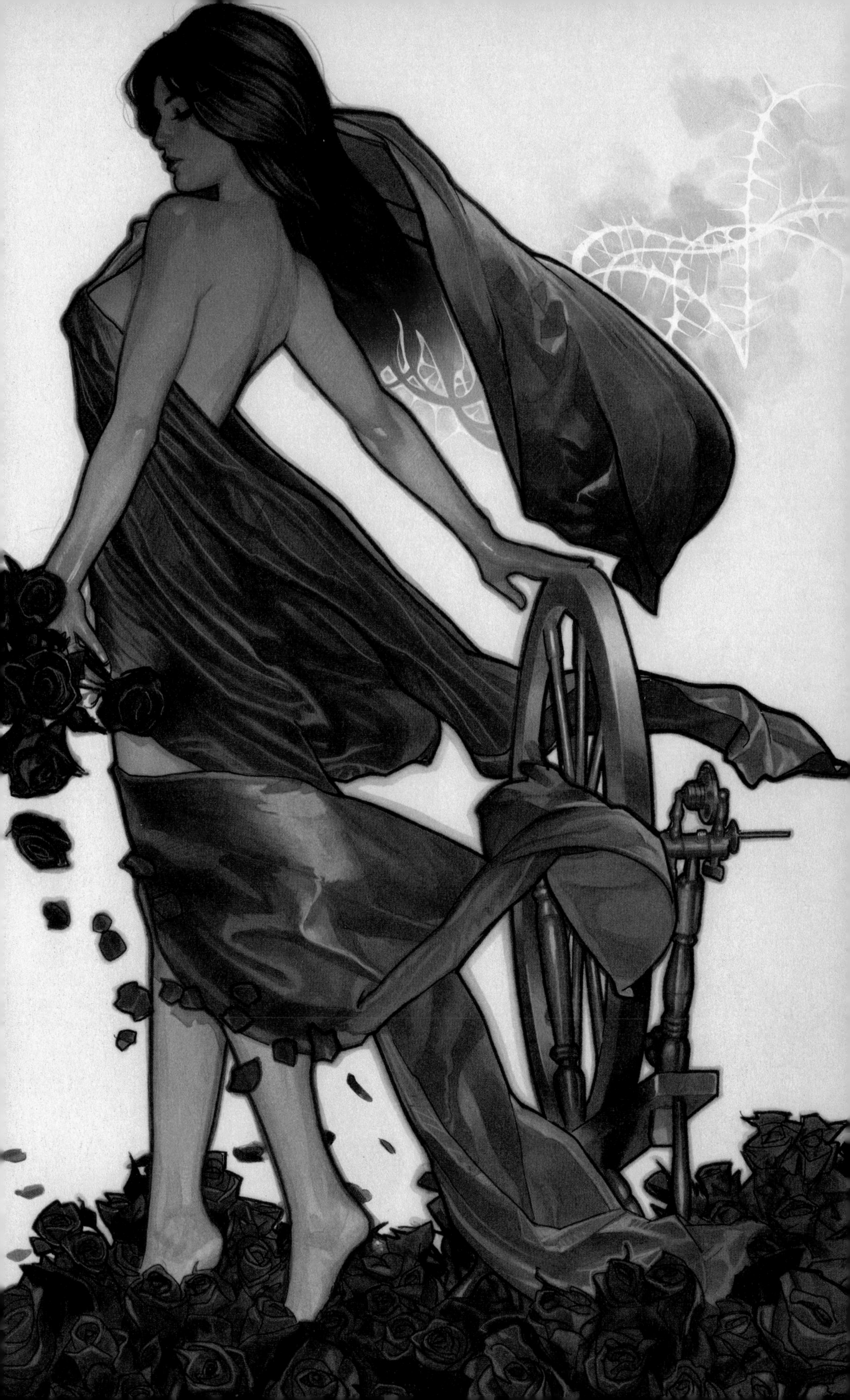

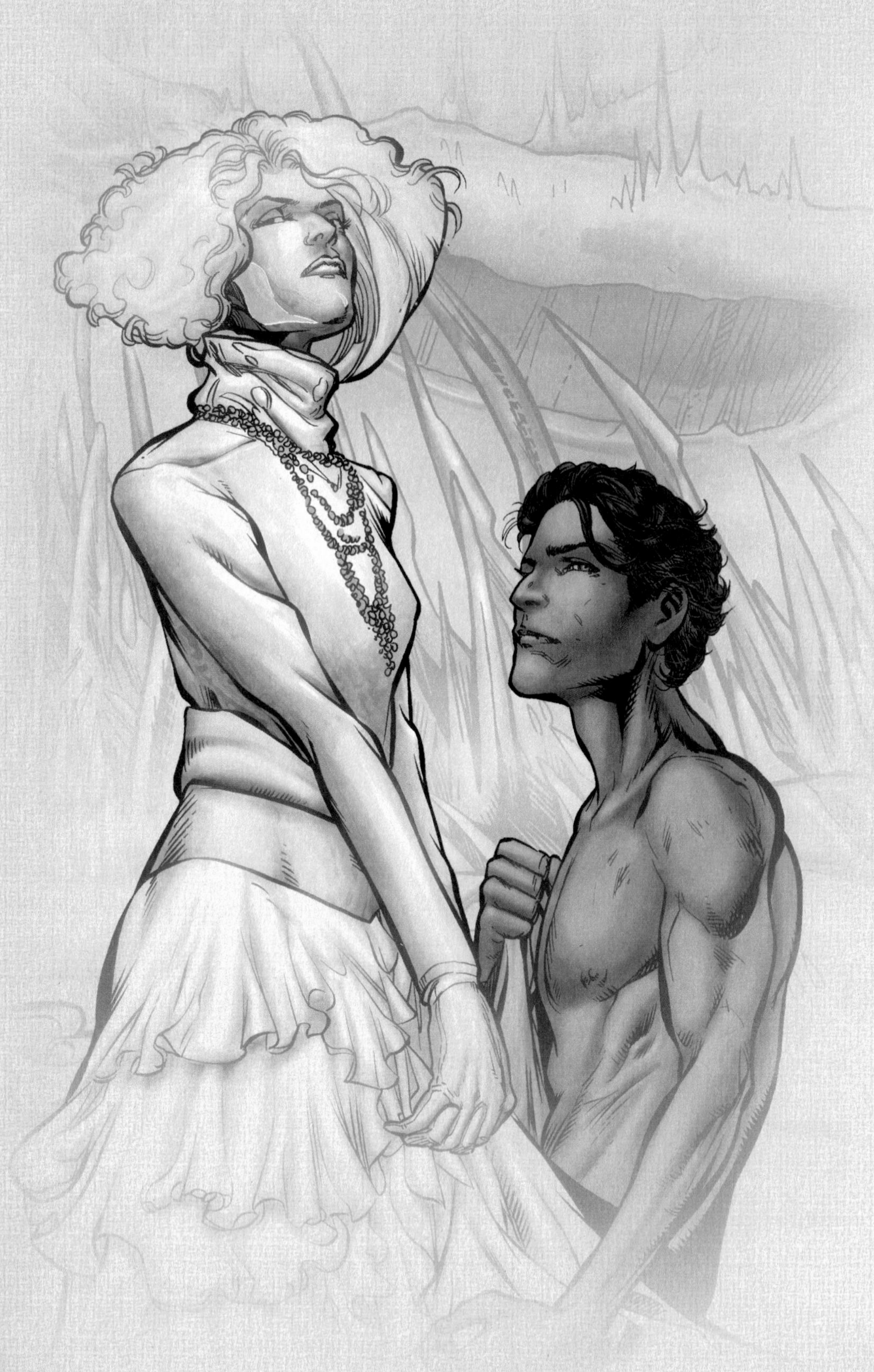

"Please don't turn out to be an asshole."

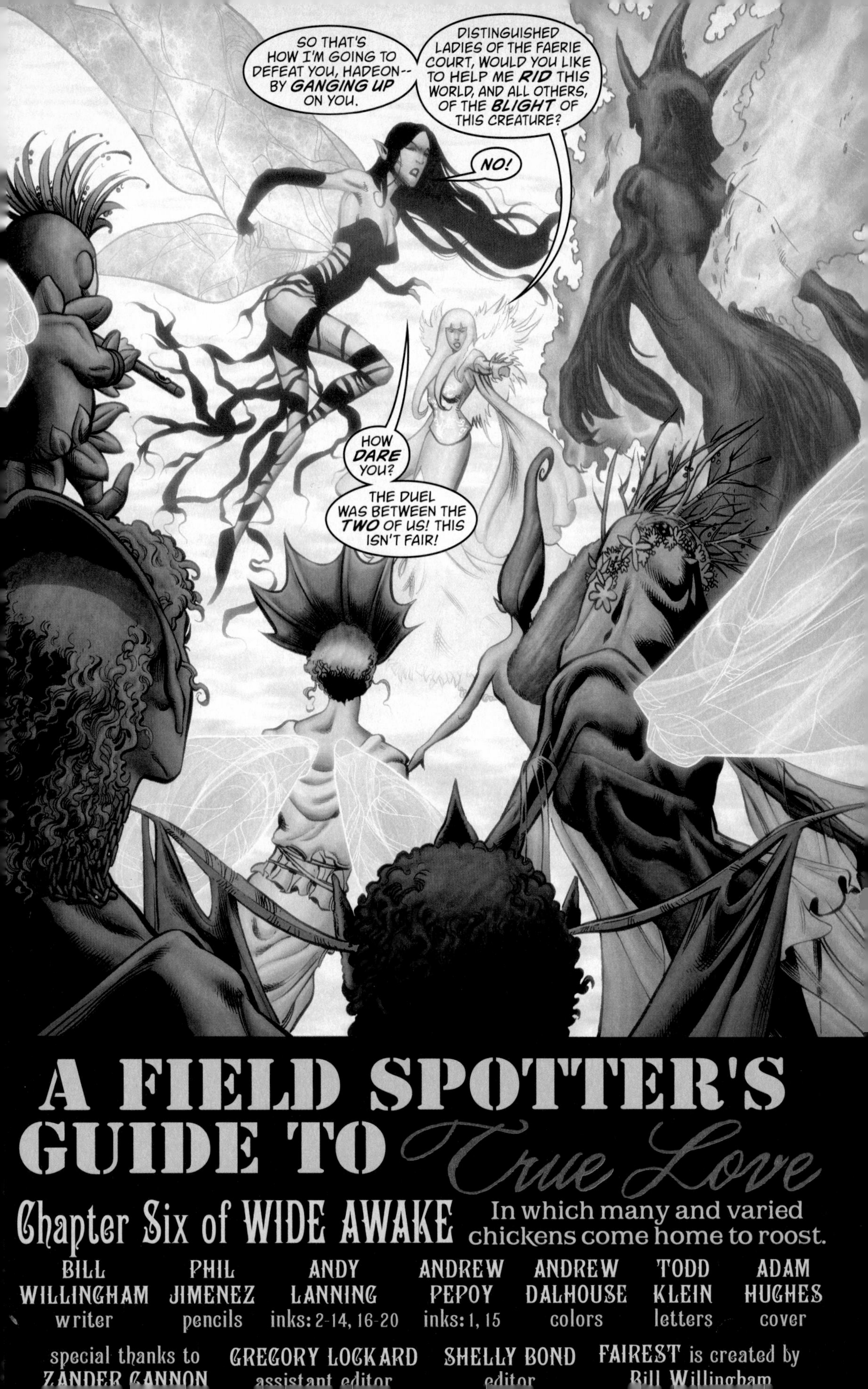
SO THAT'S HOW I'M GOING TO DEFEAT YOU, HADEON-- BY GANGING UP ON YOU.
DISTINGUISHED LADIES OF THE FAERIE COURT, WOULD YOU LIKE TO HELP ME RID THIS WORLD, AND ALL OTHERS, OF THE BLIGHT OF THIS CREATURE?
NO!
HOW DARE YOU?
THE DUEL WAS BETWEEN THE TWO OF US! THIS ISN'T FAIR!

A FIELD SPOTTER'S GUIDE TO *True Love*

Chapter Six of WIDE AWAKE

In which many and varied chickens come home to roost.

BILL WILLINGHAM writer
PHIL JIMENEZ pencils
ANDY LANNING inks: 2-14, 16-20
ANDREW PEPOY inks: 1, 15
ANDREW DALHOUSE colors
TODD KLEIN letters
ADAM HUGHES cover

special thanks to ZANDER CANNON
GREGORY LOCKARD assistant editor
SHELLY BOND editor
FAIREST is created by Bill Willingham

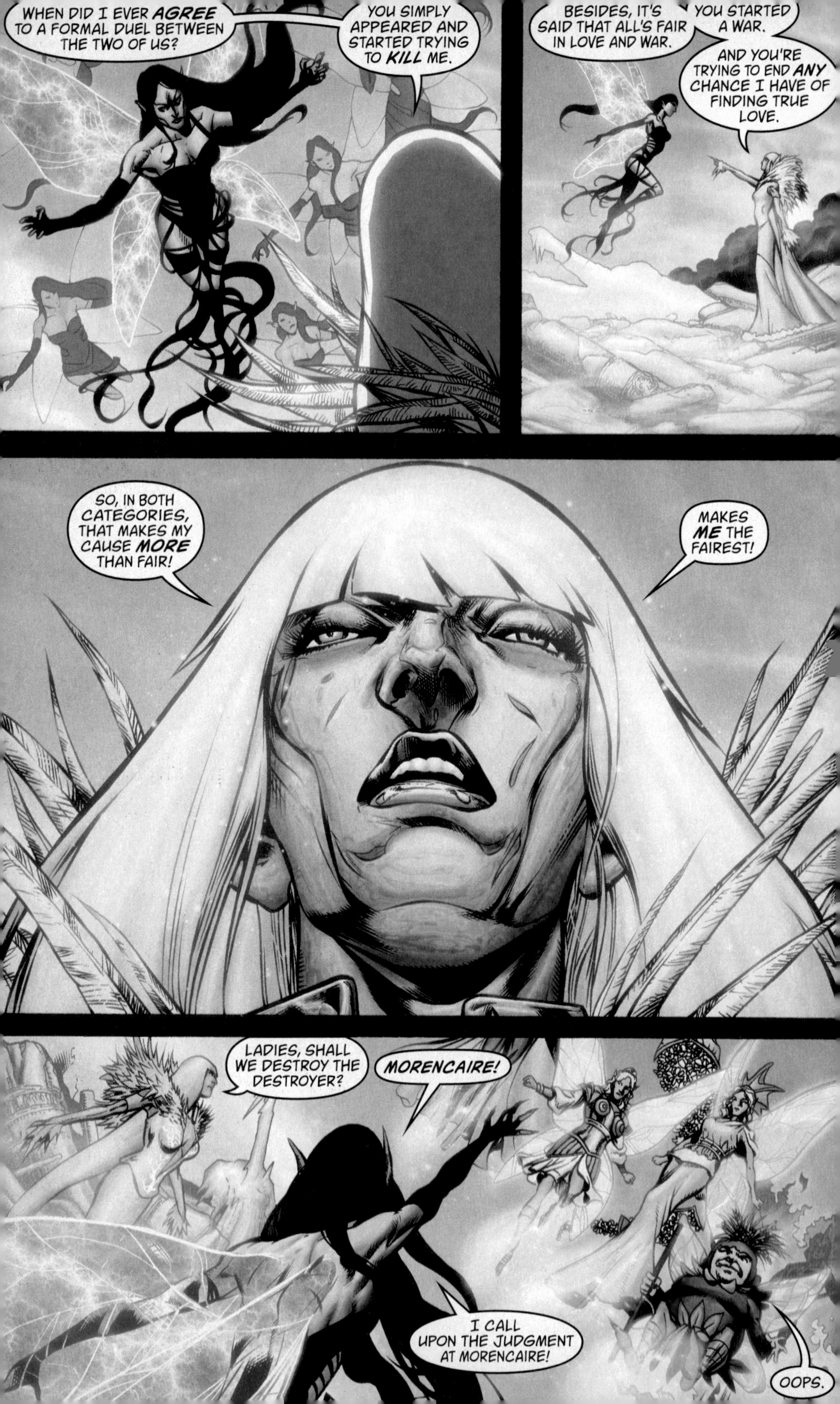

WHEN DID I EVER AGREE TO A FORMAL DUEL BETWEEN THE TWO OF US?
YOU SIMPLY APPEARED AND STARTED TRYING TO KILL ME.
BESIDES, IT'S SAID THAT ALL'S FAIR IN LOVE AND WAR.
YOU STARTED A WAR.
AND YOU'RE TRYING TO END ANY CHANCE I HAVE OF FINDING TRUE LOVE.
SO, IN BOTH CATEGORIES, THAT MAKES MY CAUSE MORE THAN FAIR!
MAKES ME THE FAIREST!
LADIES, SHALL WE DESTROY THE DESTROYER?
MORENCAIRE!
I CALL UPON THE JUDGMENT AT MORENCAIRE!
OOPS.

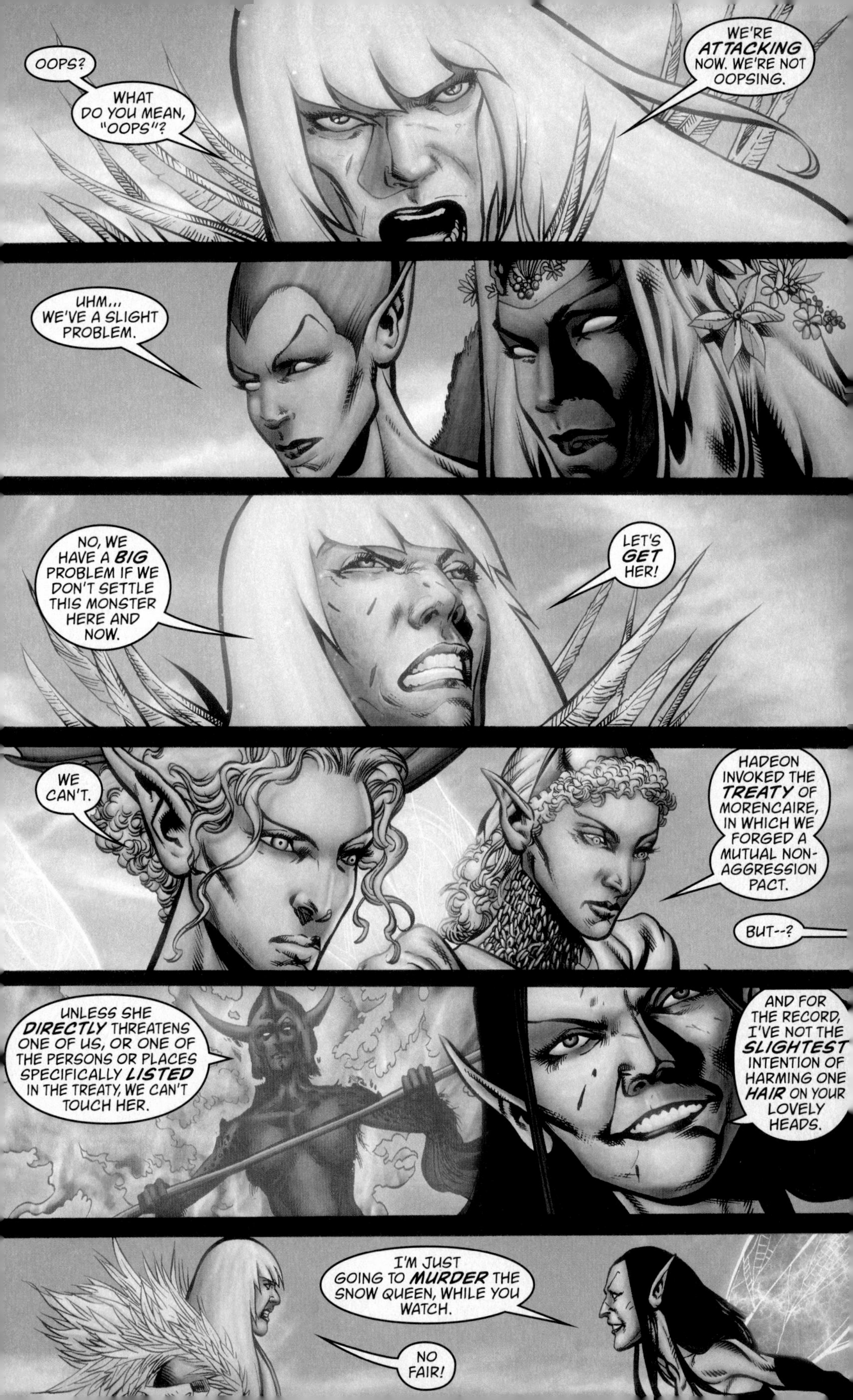
OOPS?
WHAT DO YOU MEAN, "OOPS"?
WE'RE ATTACKING NOW. WE'RE NOT OOPSING.
UHM... WE'VE A SLIGHT PROBLEM.
NO, WE HAVE A BIG PROBLEM IF WE DON'T SETTLE THIS MONSTER HERE AND NOW.
LET'S GET HER!
WE CAN'T.
HADEON INVOKED THE TREATY OF MORENCAIRE, IN WHICH WE FORGED A MUTUAL NON-AGGRESSION PACT.
BUT--?
UNLESS SHE DIRECTLY THREATENS ONE OF US, OR ONE OF THE PERSONS OR PLACES SPECIFICALLY LISTED IN THE TREATY, WE CAN'T TOUCH HER.
AND FOR THE RECORD, I'VE NOT THE SLIGHTEST INTENTION OF HARMING ONE HAIR ON YOUR LOVELY HEADS.
I'M JUST GOING TO MURDER THE SNOW QUEEN, WHILE YOU WATCH.
NO FAIR!

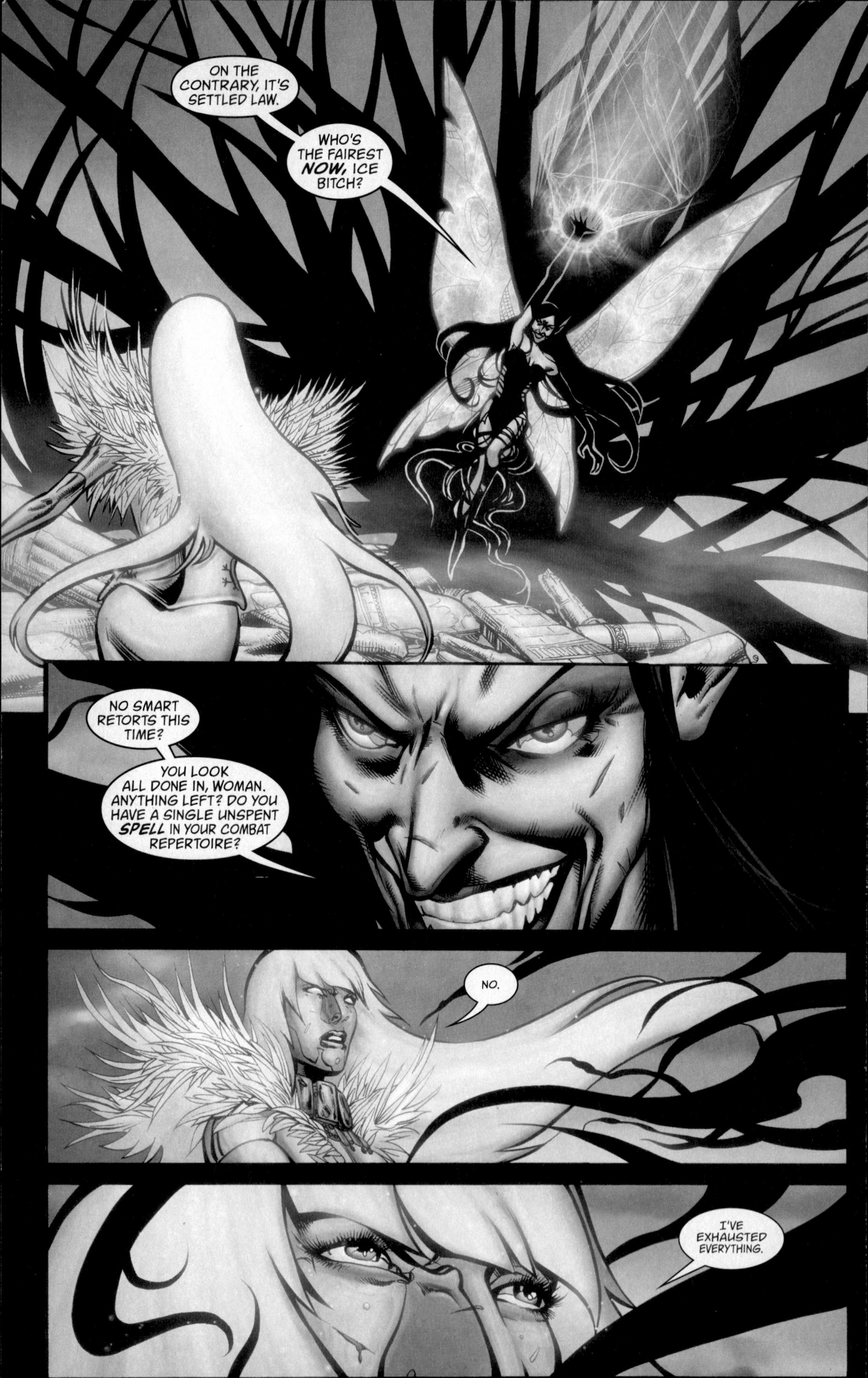
ON THE CONTRARY, IT'S SETTLED LAW.
WHO'S THE FAIREST NOW, ICE BITCH?
NO SMART RETORTS THIS TIME?
YOU LOOK ALL DONE IN, WOMAN. ANYTHING LEFT? DO YOU HAVE A SINGLE UNSPENT SPELL IN YOUR COMBAT REPERTOIRE?
NO.
I'VE EXHAUSTED EVERYTHING.

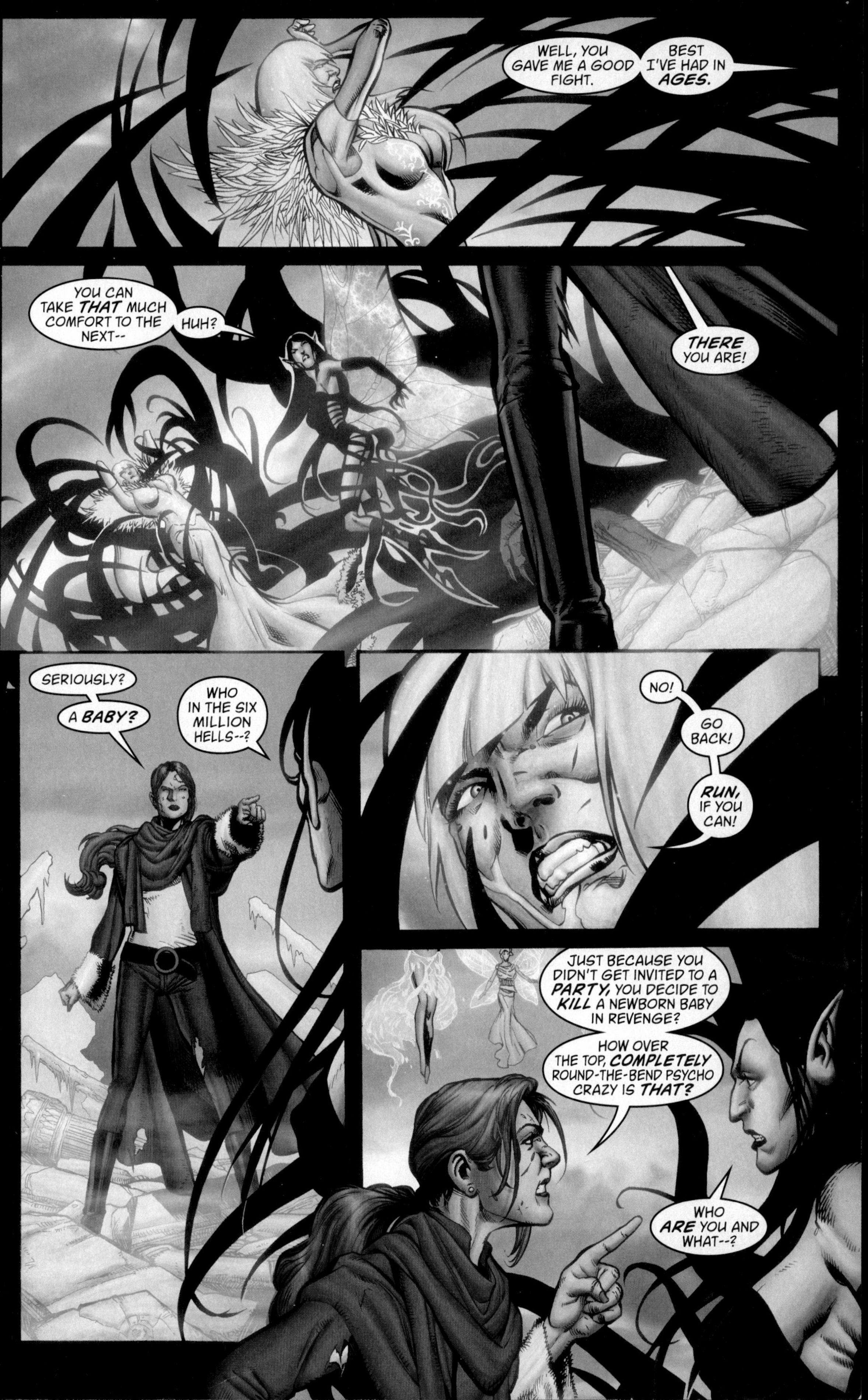

WELL, YOU GAVE ME A GOOD FIGHT.
BEST I'VE HAD IN AGES.
YOU CAN TAKE THAT MUCH COMFORT TO THE NEXT--
HUH?
THERE YOU ARE!
SERIOUSLY?
A BABY?
WHO IN THE SIX MILLION HELLS--?
NO!
GO BACK!
RUN, IF YOU CAN!
JUST BECAUSE YOU DIDN'T GET INVITED TO A PARTY, YOU DECIDE TO KILL A NEWBORN BABY IN REVENGE?
HOW OVER THE TOP, COMPLETELY ROUND-THE-BEND PSYCHO CRAZY IS THAT?
WHO ARE YOU AND WHAT--?

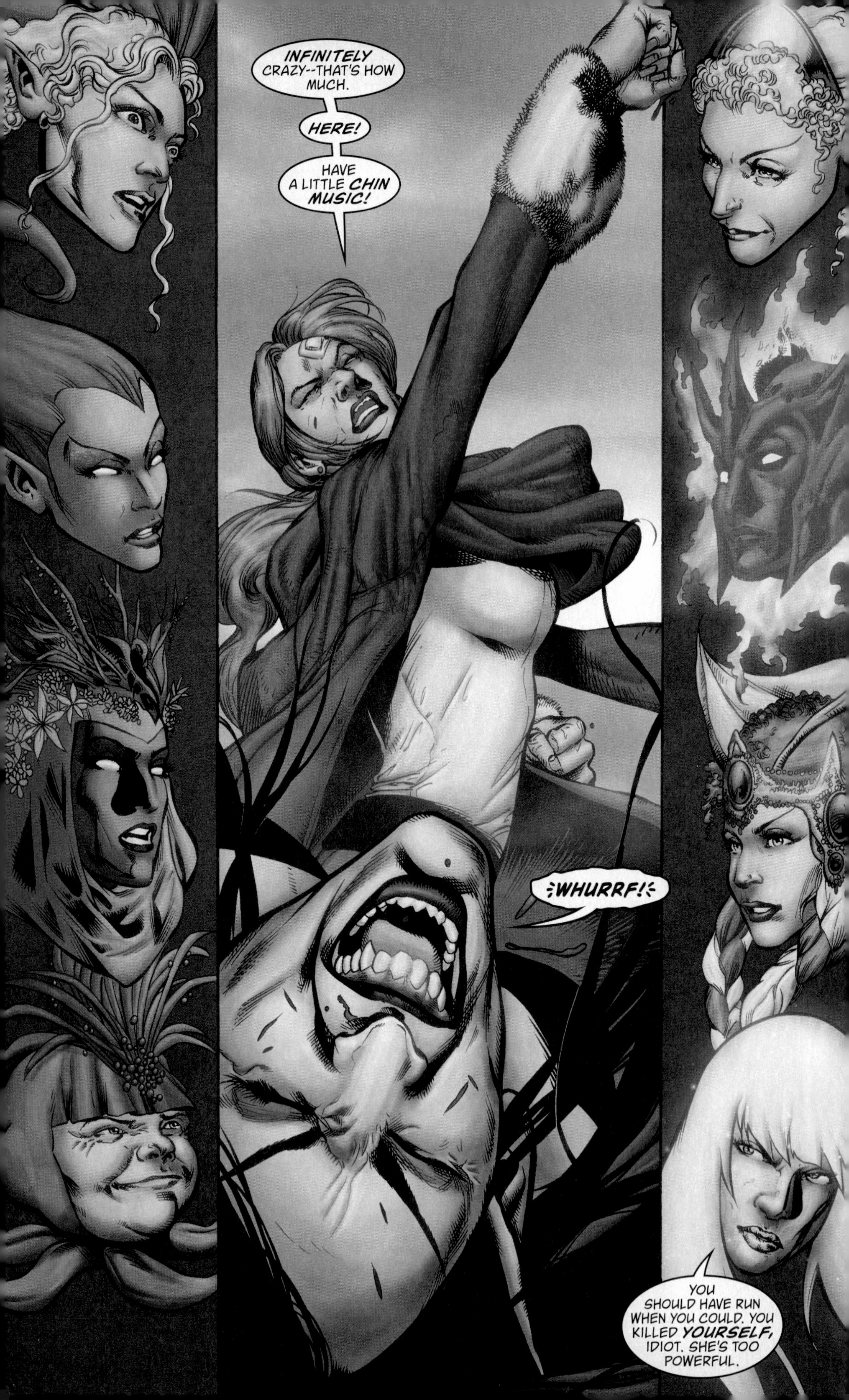
INFINITELY CRAZY--THAT'S HOW MUCH.
HERE!
HAVE A LITTLE CHIN MUSIC!
WHURRF!
YOU SHOULD HAVE RUN WHEN YOU COULD. YOU KILLED YOURSELF, IDIOT. SHE'S TOO POWERFUL.

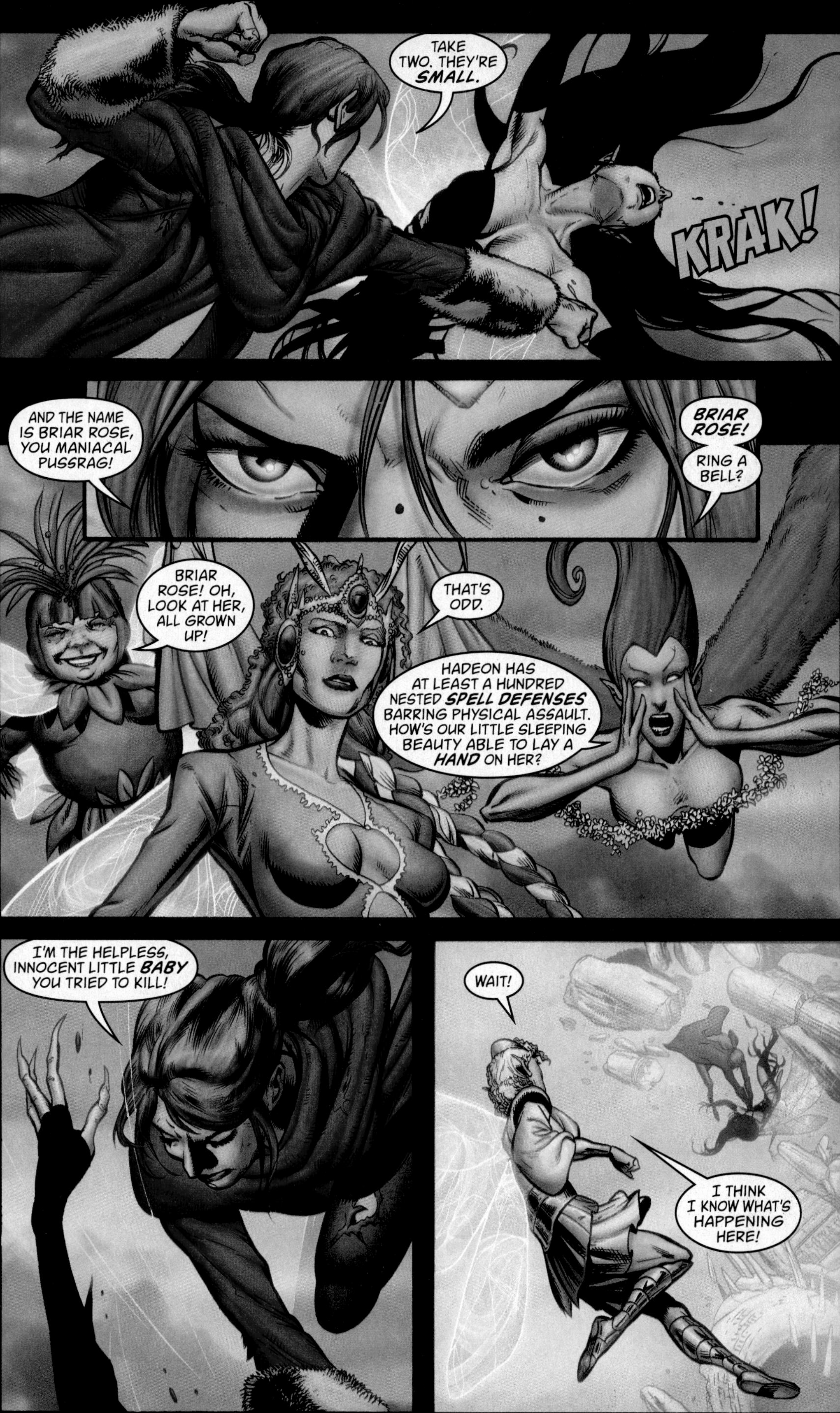
TAKE TWO. THEY'RE SMALL.
KRAK!
AND THE NAME IS BRIAR ROSE, YOU MANIACAL PUSSRAG!
BRIAR ROSE!
RING A BELL?
BRIAR ROSE! OH, LOOK AT HER, ALL GROWN UP!
THAT'S ODD.
HADEON HAS AT LEAST A HUNDRED NESTED SPELL DEFENSES BARRING PHYSICAL ASSAULT. HOW'S OUR LITTLE SLEEPING BEAUTY ABLE TO LAY A HAND ON HER?
I'M THE HELPLESS, INNOCENT LITTLE BABY YOU TRIED TO KILL!
WAIT!
I THINK I KNOW WHAT'S HAPPENING HERE!

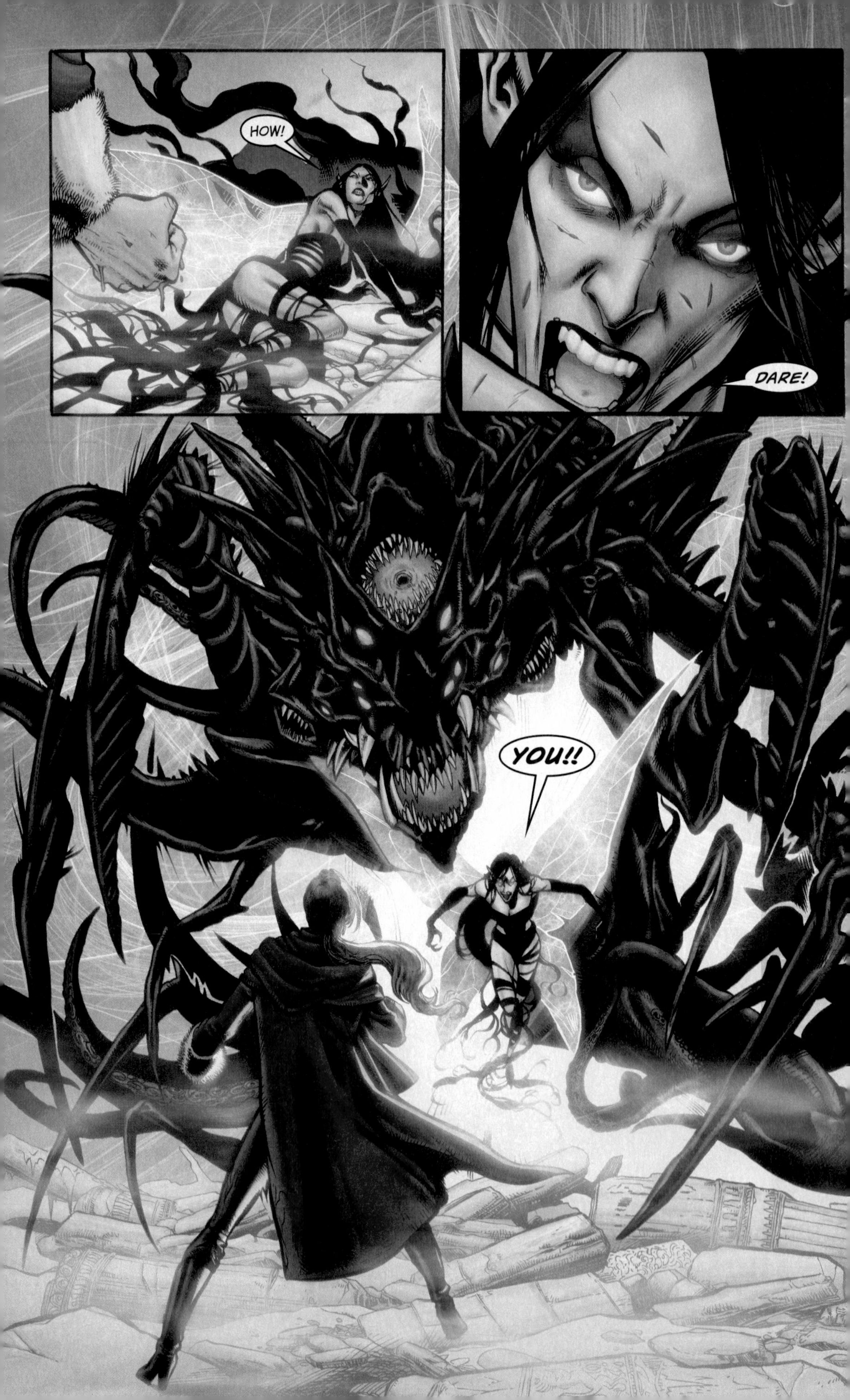
HOW!
DARE!
YOU!!

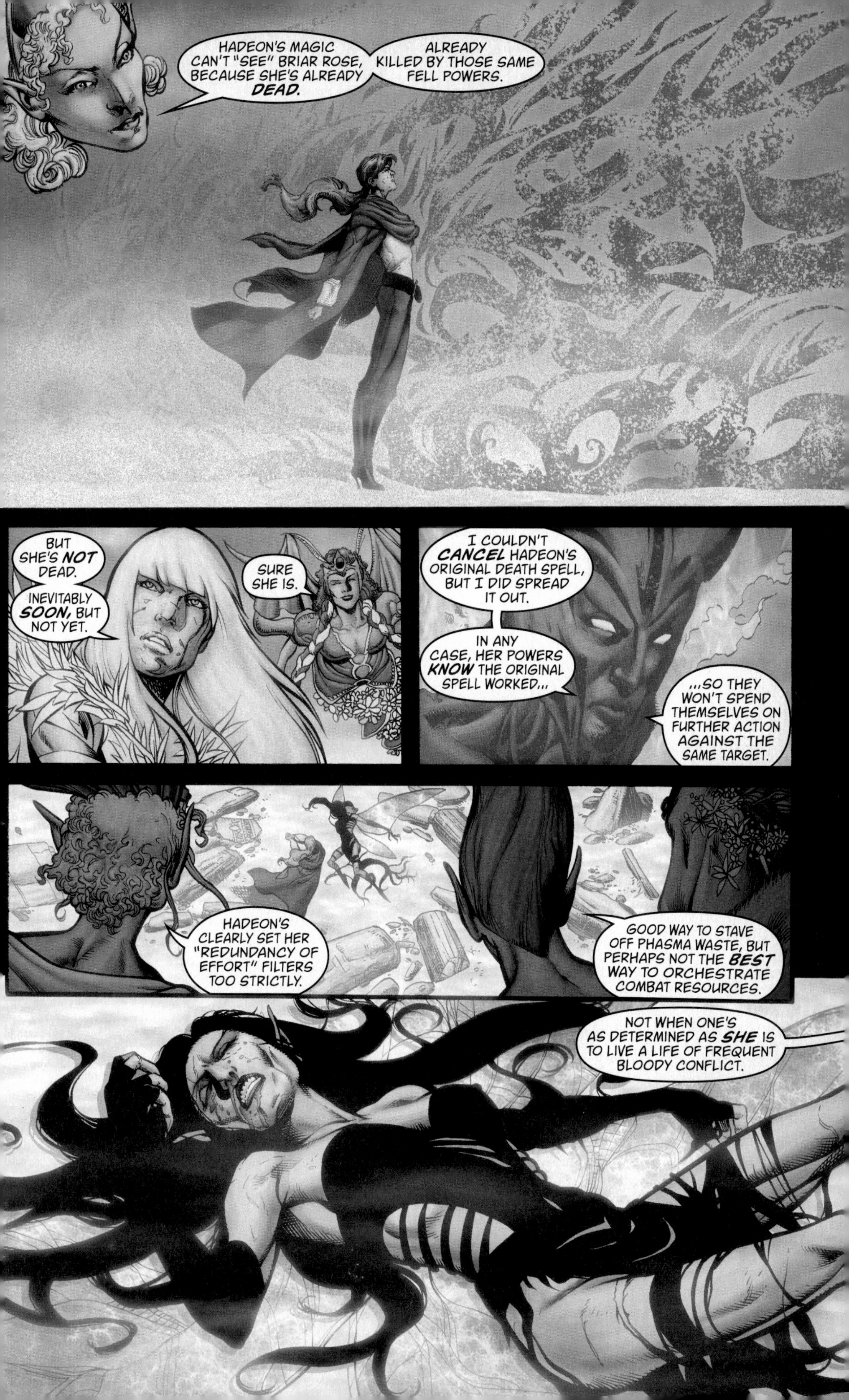
HADEON'S MAGIC CAN'T "SEE" BRIAR ROSE, BECAUSE SHE'S ALREADY DEAD.
ALREADY KILLED BY THOSE SAME FELL POWERS.
BUT SHE'S NOT DEAD.
INEVITABLY SOON, BUT NOT YET.
SURE SHE IS.
I COULDN'T CANCEL HADEON'S ORIGINAL DEATH SPELL, BUT I DID SPREAD IT OUT.
IN ANY CASE, HER POWERS KNOW THE ORIGINAL SPELL WORKED...
...SO THEY WON'T SPEND THEMSELVES ON FURTHER ACTION AGAINST THE SAME TARGET.
HADEON'S CLEARLY SET HER "REDUNDANCY OF EFFORT" FILTERS TOO STRICTLY.
GOOD WAY TO STAVE OFF PHASMA WASTE, BUT PERHAPS NOT THE BEST WAY TO ORCHESTRATE COMBAT RESOURCES.
NOT WHEN ONE'S AS DETERMINED AS SHE IS TO LIVE A LIFE OF FREQUENT BLOODY CONFLICT.

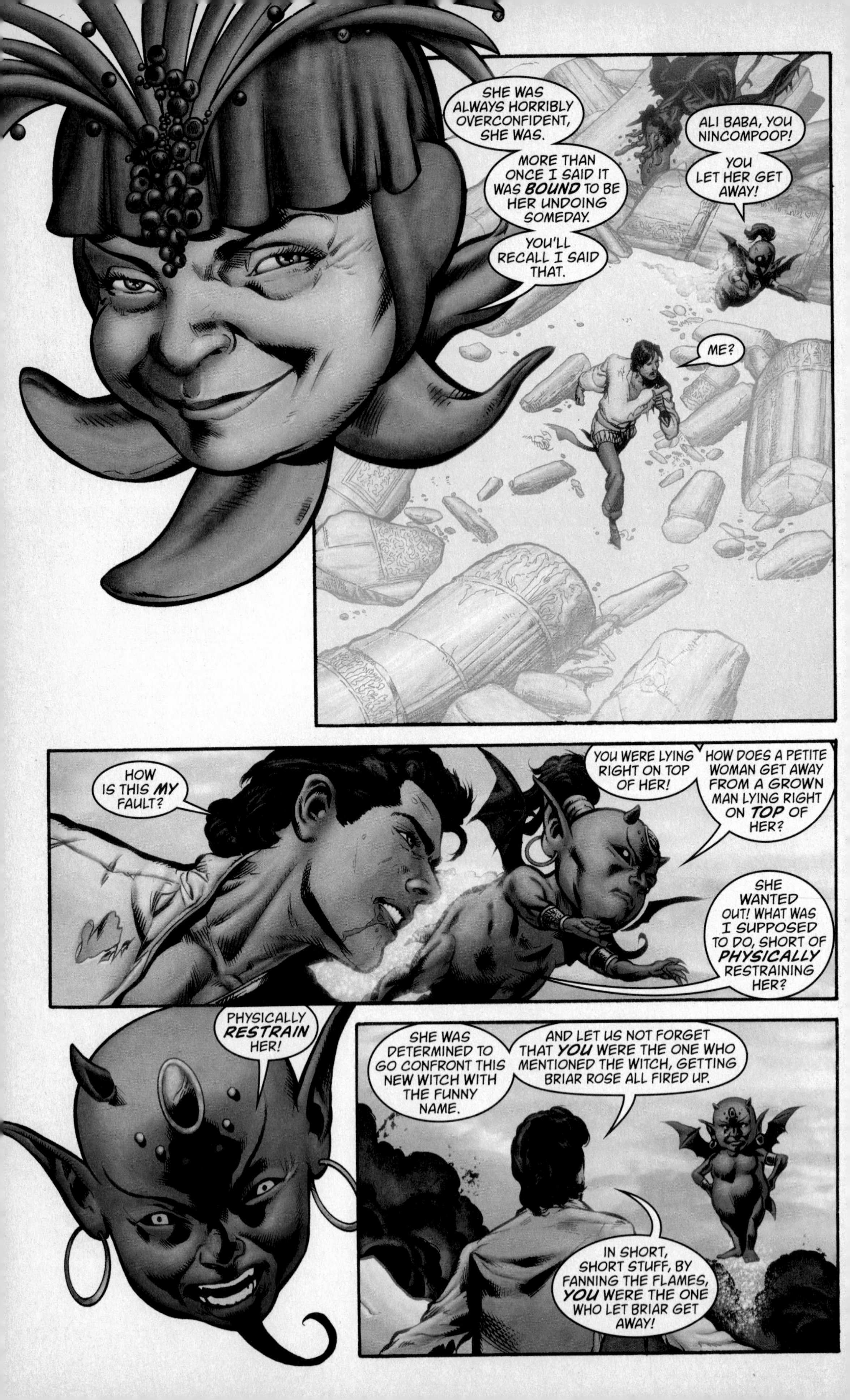
SHE WAS ALWAYS HORRIBLY OVERCONFIDENT, SHE WAS.
MORE THAN ONCE I SAID IT WAS BOUND TO BE HER UNDOING SOMEDAY.
YOU'LL RECALL I SAID THAT.
ALI BABA, YOU NINCOMPOOP!
YOU LET HER GET AWAY!
ME?
HOW IS THIS MY FAULT?
YOU WERE LYING RIGHT ON TOP OF HER!
HOW DOES A PETITE WOMAN GET AWAY FROM A GROWN MAN LYING RIGHT ON TOP OF HER?
SHE WANTED OUT! WHAT WAS I SUPPOSED TO DO, SHORT OF PHYSICALLY RESTRAINING HER?
PHYSICALLY RESTRAIN HER!
SHE WAS DETERMINED TO GO CONFRONT THIS NEW WITCH WITH THE FUNNY NAME.
AND LET US NOT FORGET THAT YOU WERE THE ONE WHO MENTIONED THE WITCH, GETTING BRIAR ROSE ALL FIRED UP.
IN SHORT, SHORT STUFF, BY FANNING THE FLAMES, YOU WERE THE ONE WHO LET BRIAR GET AWAY!

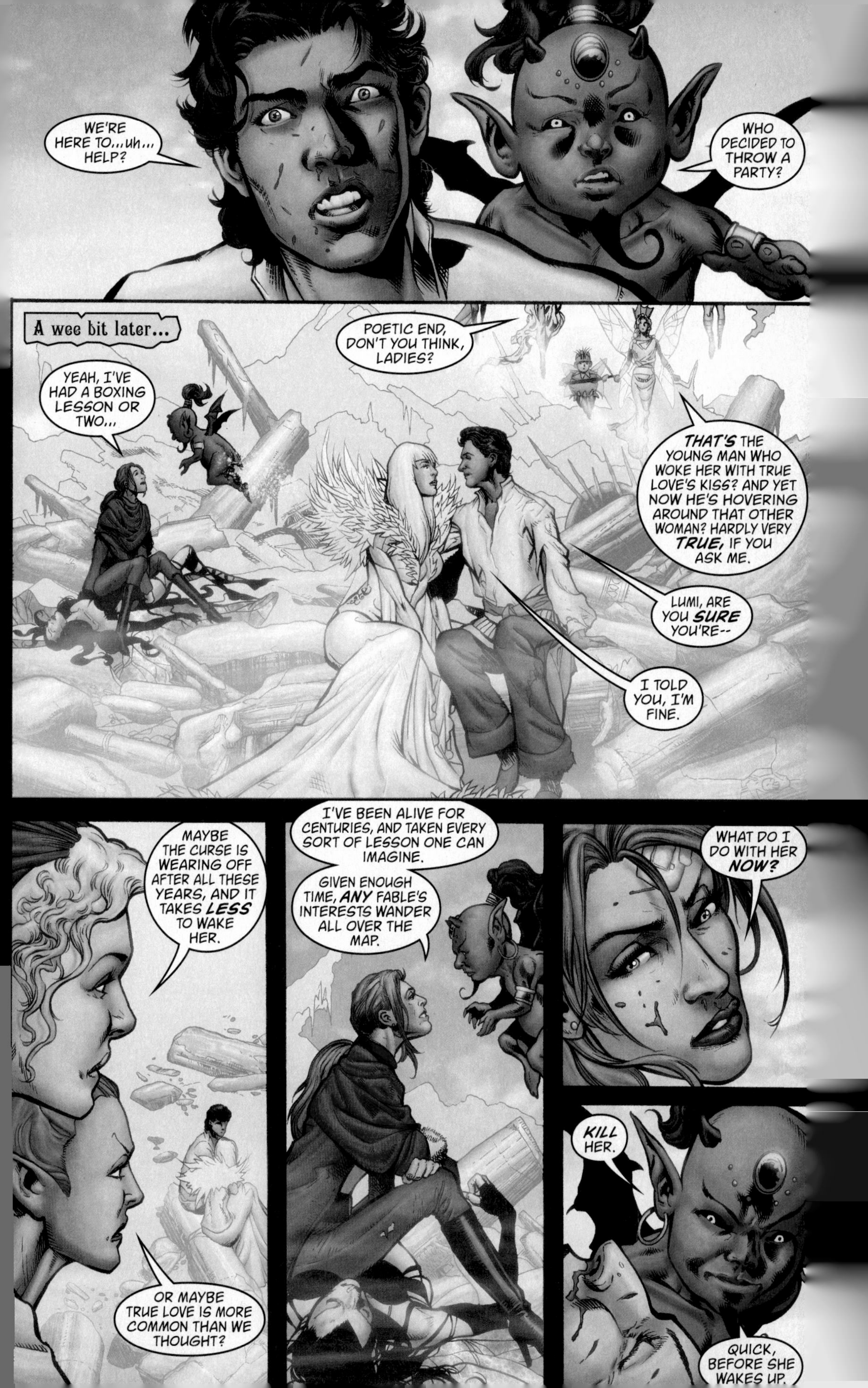
WE'RE HERE TO...uh... HELP?
WHO DECIDED TO THROW A PARTY?
A wee bit later...
POETIC END, DON'T YOU THINK, LADIES?
YEAH, I'VE HAD A BOXING LESSON OR TWO...
THAT'S THE YOUNG MAN WHO WOKE HER WITH TRUE LOVE'S KISS? AND YET NOW HE'S HOVERING AROUND THAT OTHER WOMAN? HARDLY VERY TRUE, IF YOU ASK ME.
LUMI, ARE YOU SURE YOU'RE--
I TOLD YOU, I'M FINE.
MAYBE THE CURSE IS WEARING OFF AFTER ALL THESE YEARS, AND IT TAKES LESS TO WAKE HER.
OR MAYBE TRUE LOVE IS MORE COMMON THAN WE THOUGHT?
I'VE BEEN ALIVE FOR CENTURIES, AND TAKEN EVERY SORT OF LESSON ONE CAN IMAGINE.
GIVEN ENOUGH TIME, ANY FABLE'S INTERESTS WANDER ALL OVER THE MAP.
WHAT DO I DO WITH HER NOW?
KILL HER.
QUICK, BEFORE SHE WAKES UP.

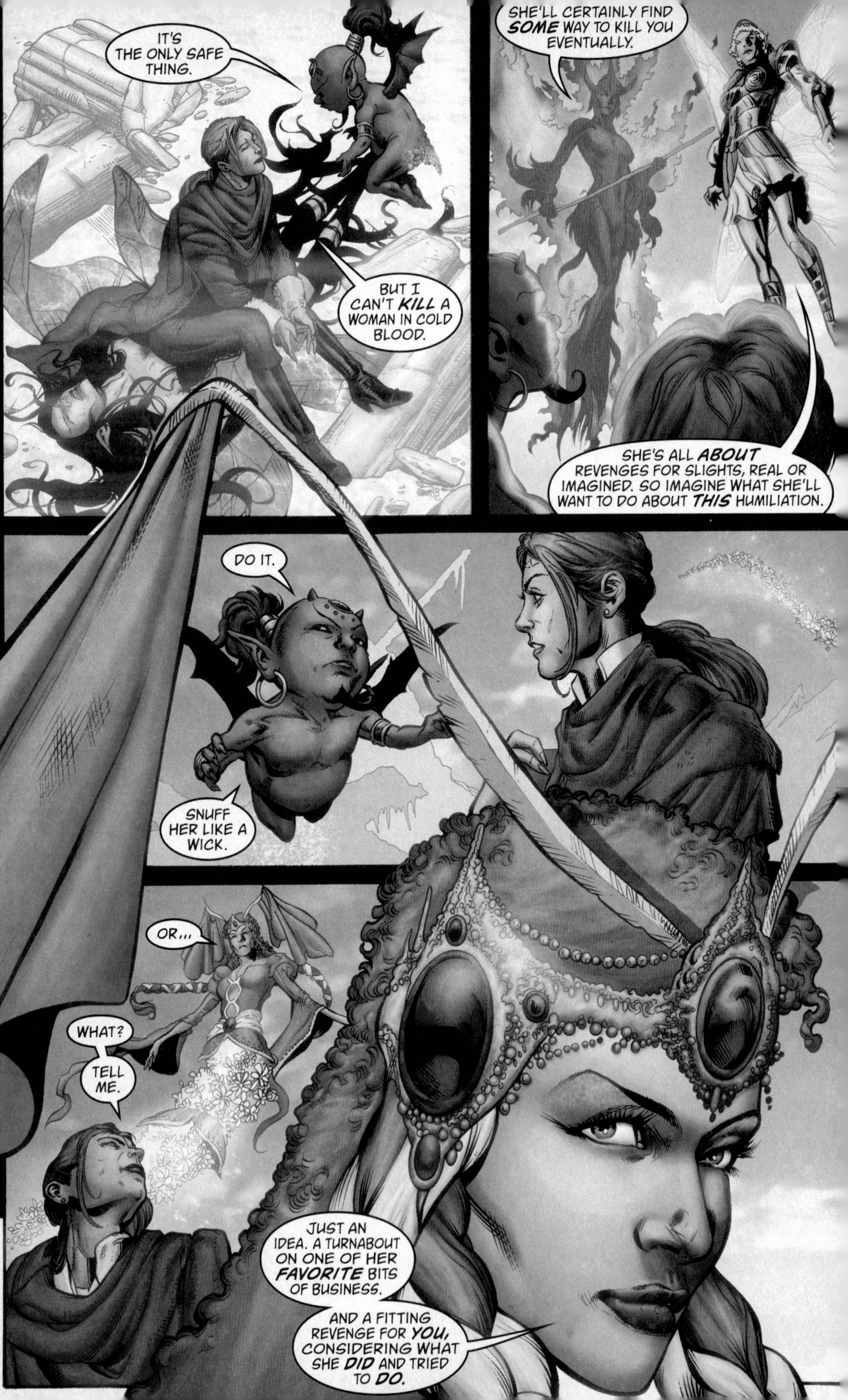
IT'S THE ONLY SAFE THING.
BUT I CAN'T KILL A WOMAN IN COLD BLOOD.
SHE'LL CERTAINLY FIND SOME WAY TO KILL YOU EVENTUALLY.
SHE'S ALL ABOUT REVENGES FOR SLIGHTS, REAL OR IMAGINED. SO IMAGINE WHAT SHE'LL WANT TO DO ABOUT THIS HUMILIATION.
DO IT.
SNUFF HER LIKE A WICK.
OR...
WHAT?
TELL ME.
JUST AN IDEA. A TURNABOUT ON ONE OF HER FAVORITE BITS OF BUSINESS.
AND A FITTING REVENGE FOR YOU, CONSIDERING WHAT SHE DID AND TRIED TO DO.

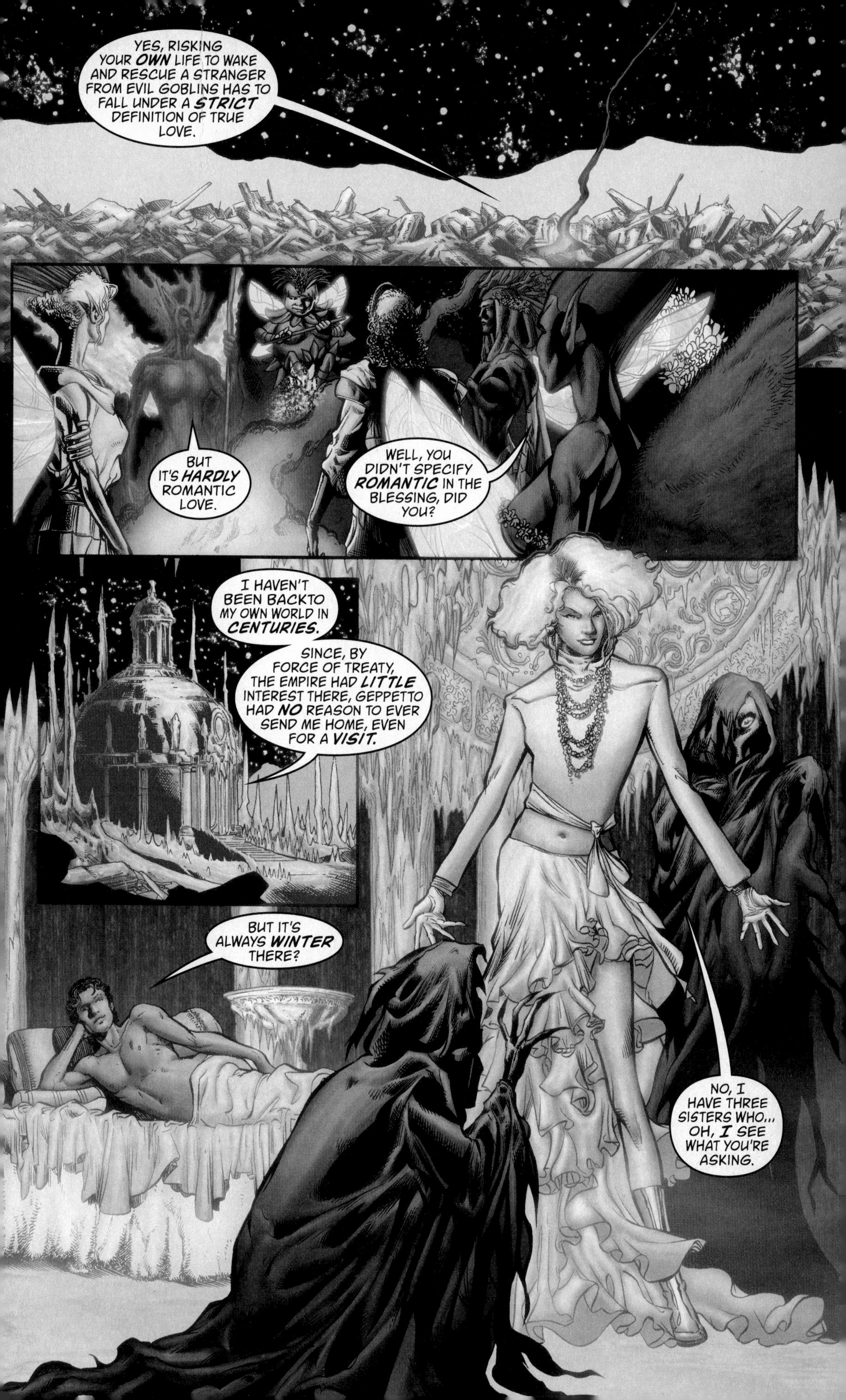

YES, RISKING YOUR OWN LIFE TO WAKE AND RESCUE A STRANGER FROM EVIL GOBLINS HAS TO FALL UNDER A STRICT DEFINITION OF TRUE LOVE.
BUT IT'S HARDLY ROMANTIC LOVE.
WELL, YOU DIDN'T SPECIFY ROMANTIC IN THE BLESSING, DID YOU?
I HAVEN'T BEEN BACKTO MY OWN WORLD IN CENTURIES.
SINCE, BY FORCE OF TREATY, THE EMPIRE HAD LITTLE INTEREST THERE, GEPPETTO HAD NO REASON TO EVER SEND ME HOME, EVEN FOR A VISIT.
BUT IT'S ALWAYS WINTER THERE?
NO, I HAVE THREE SISTERS WHO... OH, I SEE WHAT YOU'RE ASKING.

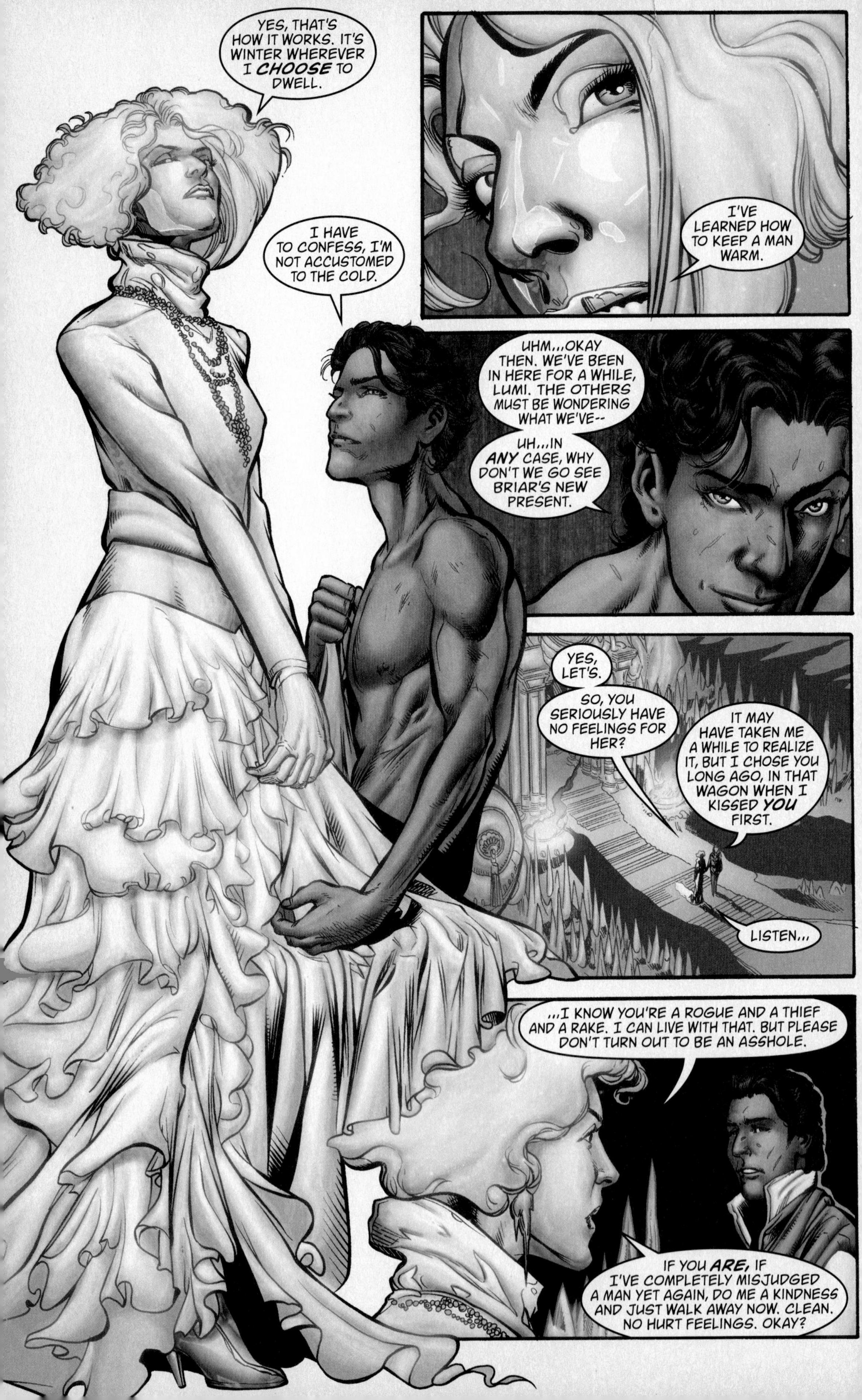
YES, THAT'S HOW IT WORKS. IT'S WINTER WHEREVER I CHOOSE TO DWELL.
I HAVE TO CONFESS, I'M NOT ACCUSTOMED TO THE COLD.
I'VE LEARNED HOW TO KEEP A MAN WARM.
UHM...OKAY THEN. WE'VE BEEN IN HERE FOR A WHILE, LUMI. THE OTHERS MUST BE WONDERING WHAT WE'VE--
UH...IN ANY CASE, WHY DON'T WE GO SEE BRIAR'S NEW PRESENT.
YES, LET'S.
SO, YOU SERIOUSLY HAVE NO FEELINGS FOR HER?
IT MAY HAVE TAKEN ME A WHILE TO REALIZE IT, BUT I CHOSE YOU LONG AGO, IN THAT WAGON WHEN I KISSED YOU FIRST.
LISTEN...
...I KNOW YOU'RE A ROGUE AND A THIEF AND A RAKE. I CAN LIVE WITH THAT. BUT PLEASE DON'T TURN OUT TO BE AN ASSHOLE.
IF YOU ARE, IF I'VE COMPLETELY MISJUDGED A MAN YET AGAIN, DO ME A KINDNESS AND JUST WALK AWAY NOW. CLEAN. NO HURT FEELINGS. OKAY?

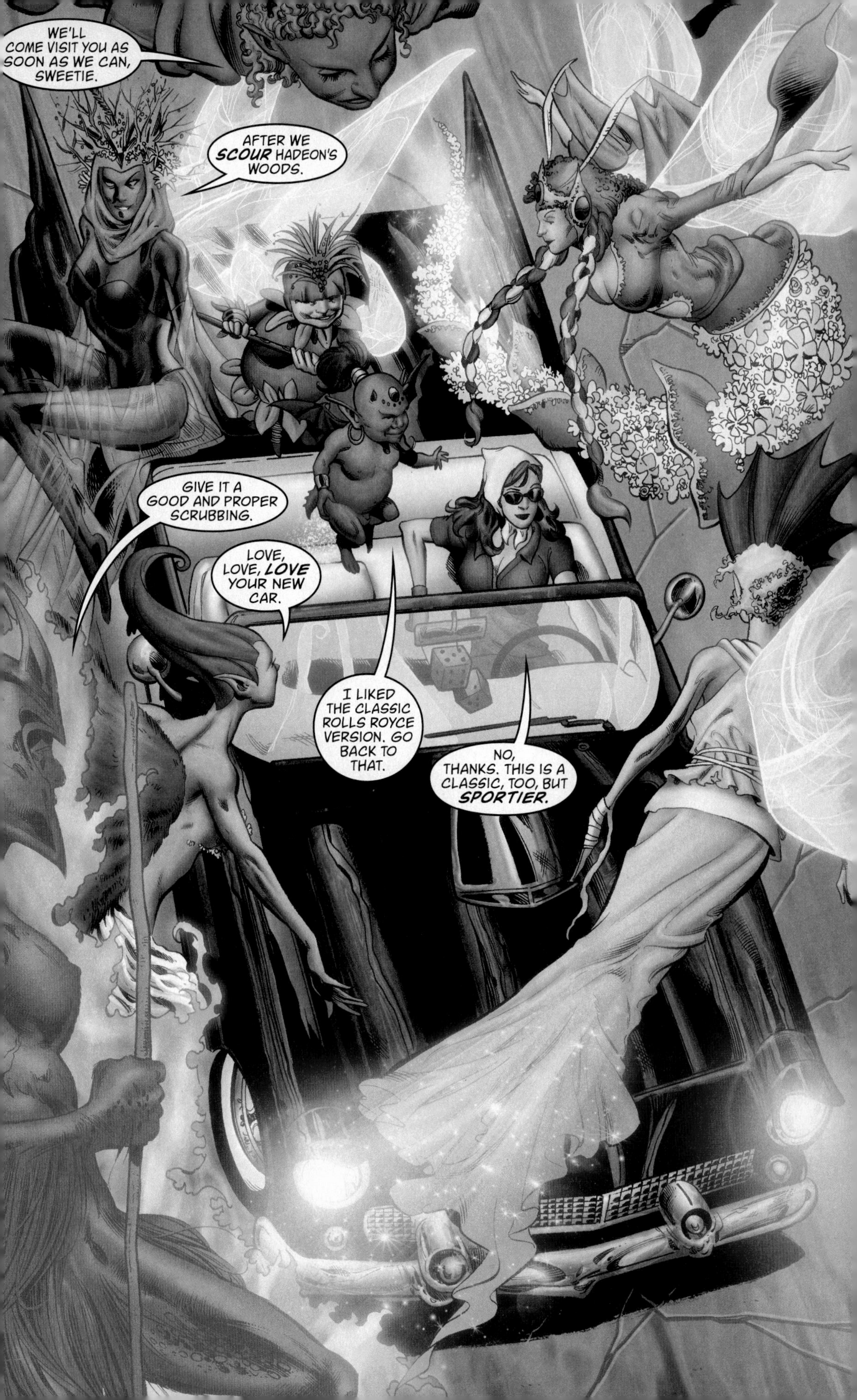
WE'LL COME VISIT YOU AS SOON AS WE CAN, SWEETIE.
AFTER WE **SCOUR** HADEON'S WOODS.
GIVE IT A GOOD AND PROPER SCRUBBING.
LOVE, LOVE, **LOVE** YOUR NEW CAR.
I LIKED THE CLASSIC ROLLS ROYCE VERSION. GO BACK TO THAT.
NO, THANKS. THIS IS A CLASSIC, TOO, BUT **SPORTIER**.

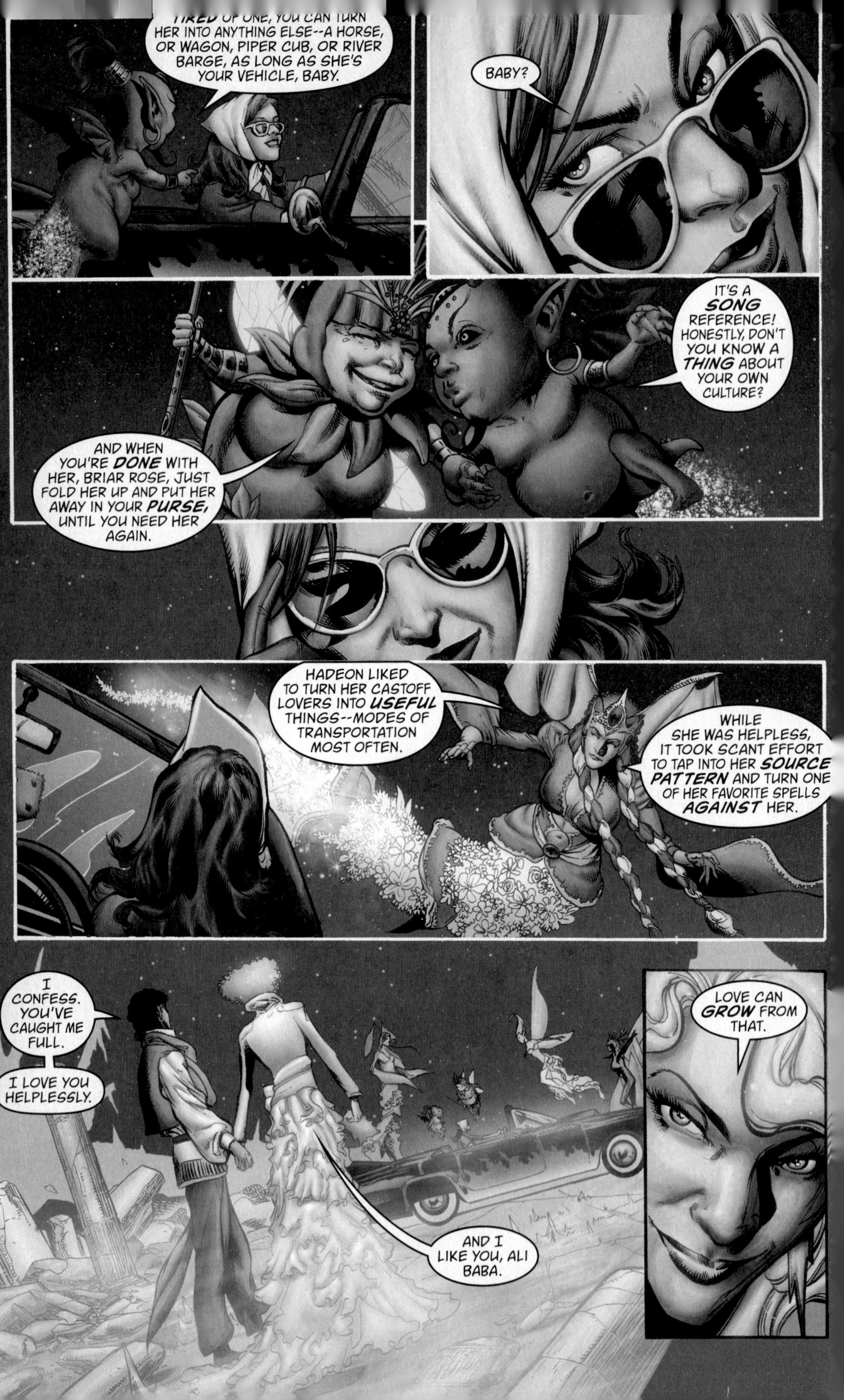
TIRED OF ONE, YOU CAN TURN HER INTO ANYTHING ELSE--A HORSE, OR WAGON, PIPER CUB, OR RIVER BARGE, AS LONG AS SHE'S YOUR VEHICLE, BABY.
BABY?
IT'S A SONG REFERENCE! HONESTLY, DON'T YOU KNOW A THING ABOUT YOUR OWN CULTURE?
AND WHEN YOU'RE DONE WITH HER, BRIAR ROSE, JUST FOLD HER UP AND PUT HER AWAY IN YOUR PURSE, UNTIL YOU NEED HER AGAIN.
HADEON LIKED TO TURN HER CASTOFF LOVERS INTO USEFUL THINGS--MODES OF TRANSPORTATION MOST OFTEN.
WHILE SHE WAS HELPLESS, IT TOOK SCANT EFFORT TO TAP INTO HER SOURCE PATTERN AND TURN ONE OF HER FAVORITE SPELLS AGAINST HER.
I CONFESS. YOU'VE CAUGHT ME FULL.
I LOVE YOU HELPLESSLY.
AND I LIKE YOU, ALI BABA.
LOVE CAN GROW FROM THAT.

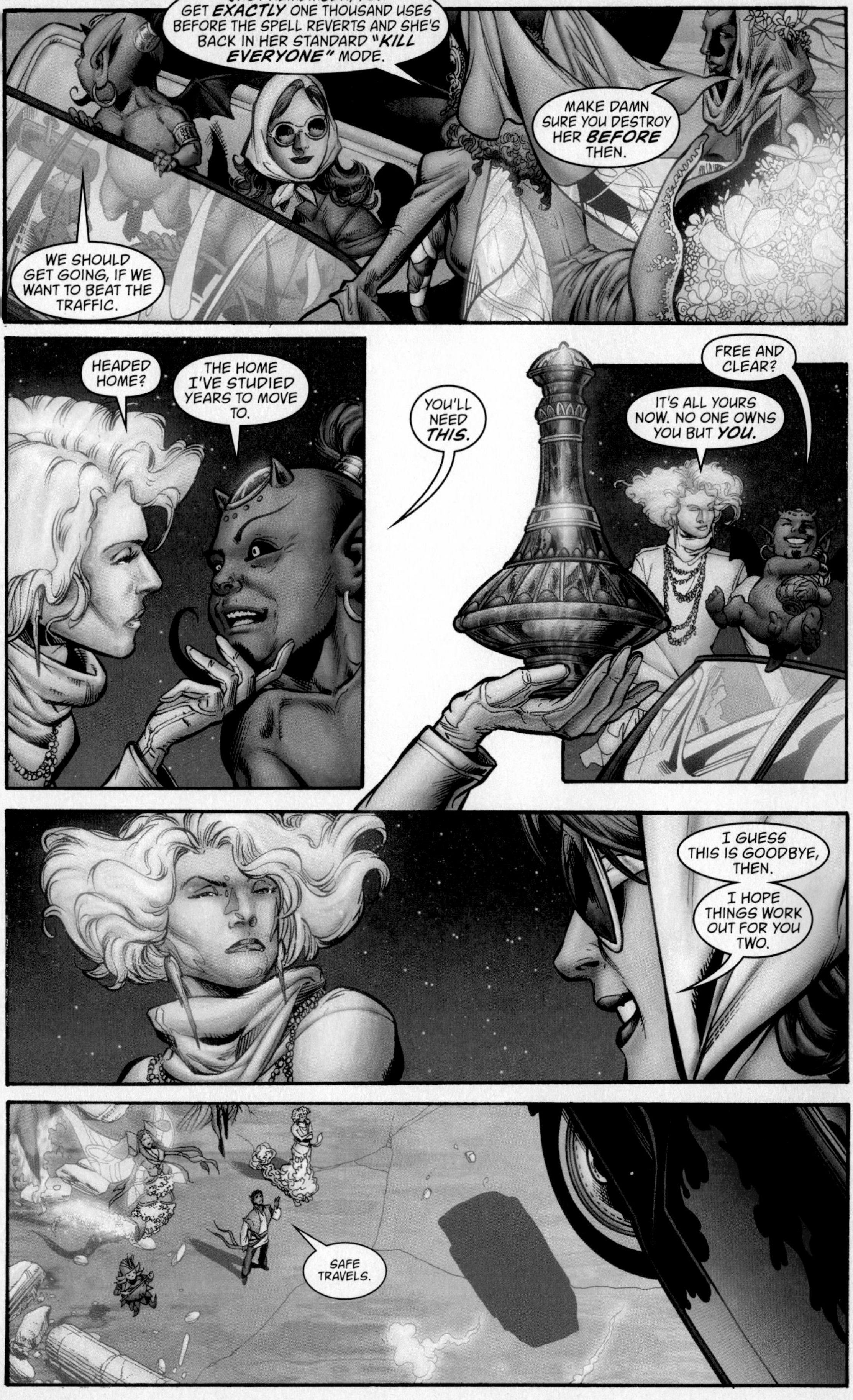
JUST REMEMBER, YOU GET EXACTLY ONE THOUSAND USES BEFORE THE SPELL REVERTS AND SHE'S BACK IN HER STANDARD "KILL EVERYONE" MODE.
MAKE DAMN SURE YOU DESTROY HER BEFORE THEN.
WE SHOULD GET GOING, IF WE WANT TO BEAT THE TRAFFIC.
HEADED HOME?
THE HOME I'VE STUDIED YEARS TO MOVE TO.
YOU'LL NEED THIS.
FREE AND CLEAR?
IT'S ALL YOURS NOW. NO ONE OWNS YOU BUT YOU.
I GUESS THIS IS GOODBYE, THEN.
I HOPE THINGS WORK OUT FOR YOU TWO.
SAFE TRAVELS.

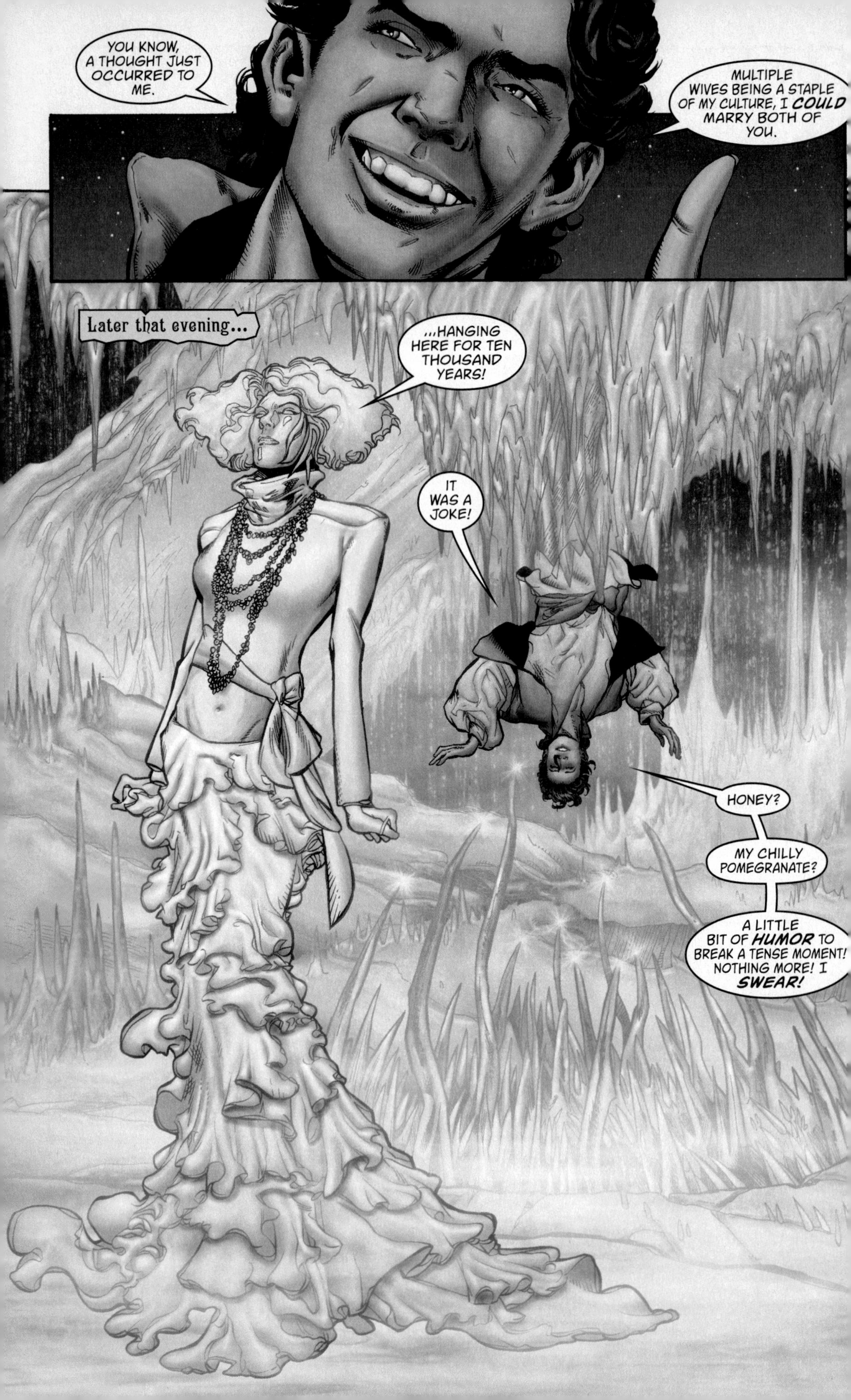
YOU KNOW, A THOUGHT JUST OCCURRED TO ME.
MULTIPLE WIVES BEING A STAPLE OF MY CULTURE, I COULD MARRY BOTH OF YOU.
Later that evening...
...HANGING HERE FOR TEN THOUSAND YEARS!
IT WAS A JOKE!
HONEY?
MY CHILLY POMEGRANATE?
A LITTLE BIT OF HUMOR TO BREAK A TENSE MOMENT! NOTHING MORE! I SWEAR!

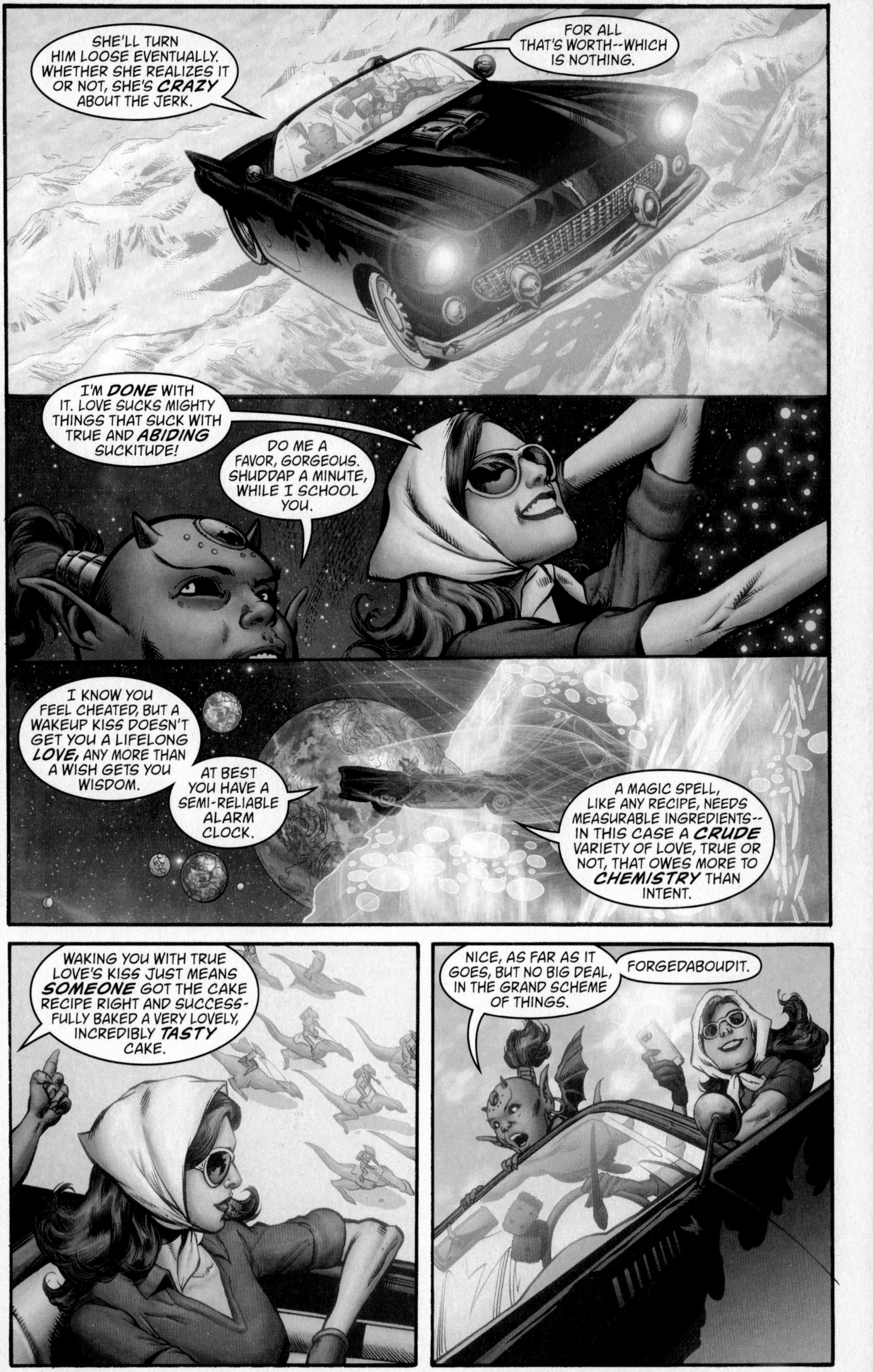
SHE'LL TURN HIM LOOSE EVENTUALLY. WHETHER SHE REALIZES IT OR NOT, SHE'S CRAZY ABOUT THE JERK.
FOR ALL THAT'S WORTH--WHICH IS NOTHING.
I'M DONE WITH IT. LOVE SUCKS MIGHTY THINGS THAT SUCK WITH TRUE AND ABIDING SUCKITUDE!
DO ME A FAVOR, GORGEOUS. SHUDDAP A MINUTE, WHILE I SCHOOL YOU.
I KNOW YOU FEEL CHEATED, BUT A WAKEUP KISS DOESN'T GET YOU A LIFELONG LOVE, ANY MORE THAN A WISH GETS YOU WISDOM.
AT BEST YOU HAVE A SEMI-RELIABLE ALARM CLOCK.
A MAGIC SPELL, LIKE ANY RECIPE, NEEDS MEASURABLE INGREDIENTS-- IN THIS CASE A CRUDE VARIETY OF LOVE, TRUE OR NOT, THAT OWES MORE TO CHEMISTRY THAN INTENT.
WAKING YOU WITH TRUE LOVE'S KISS JUST MEANS SOMEONE GOT THE CAKE RECIPE RIGHT AND SUCCESS-FULLY BAKED A VERY LOVELY, INCREDIBLY TASTY CAKE.
NICE, AS FAR AS IT GOES, BUT NO BIG DEAL, IN THE GRAND SCHEME OF THINGS.
FORGEDABOUDIT.

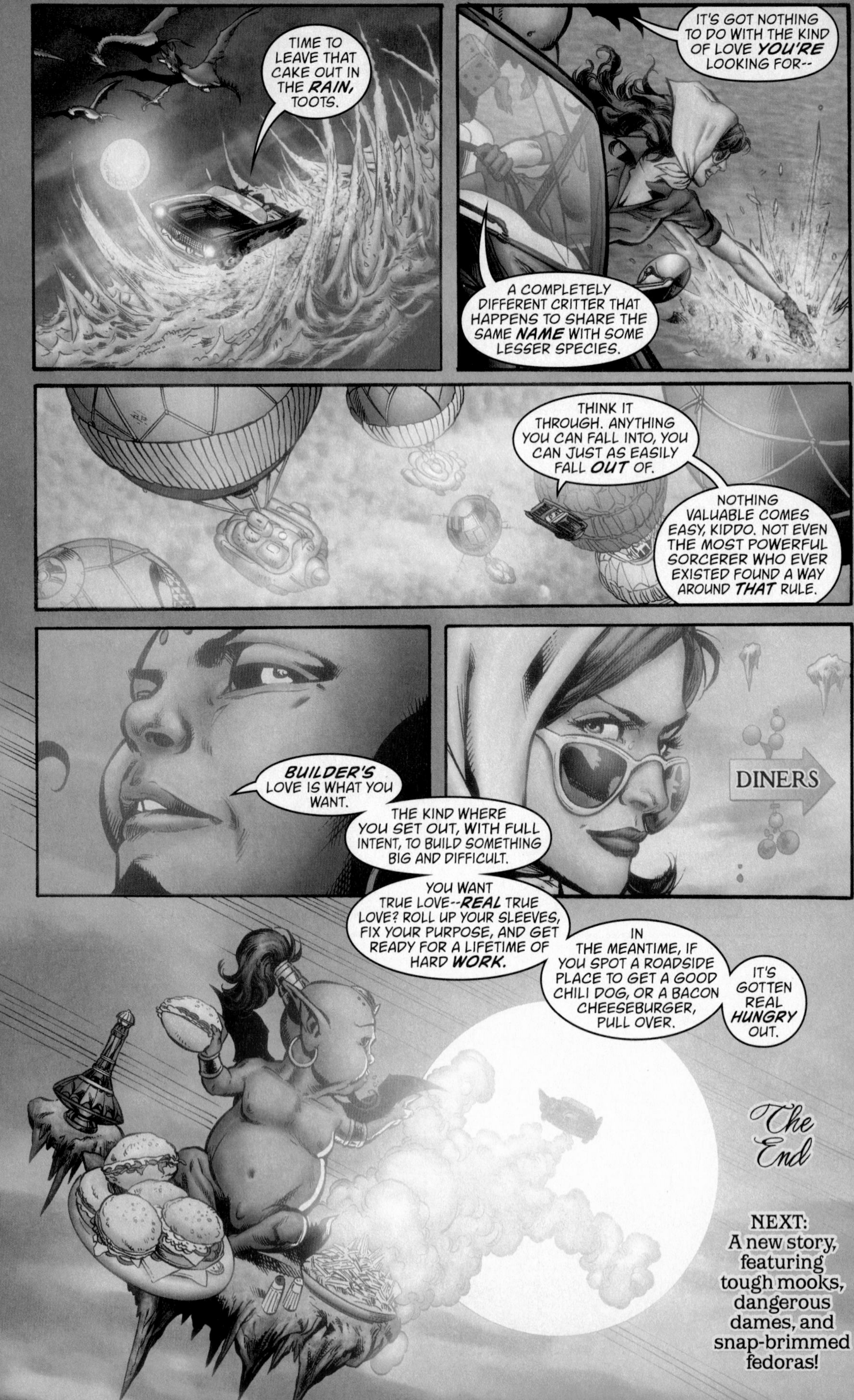
TIME TO LEAVE THAT CAKE OUT IN THE RAIN, TOOTS.
IT'S GOT NOTHING TO DO WITH THE KIND OF LOVE YOU'RE LOOKING FOR--
A COMPLETELY DIFFERENT CRITTER THAT HAPPENS TO SHARE THE SAME NAME WITH SOME LESSER SPECIES.
THINK IT THROUGH. ANYTHING YOU CAN FALL INTO, YOU CAN JUST AS EASILY FALL OUT OF.
NOTHING VALUABLE COMES EASY, KIDDO. NOT EVEN THE MOST POWERFUL SORCERER WHO EVER EXISTED FOUND A WAY AROUND THAT RULE.
BUILDER'S LOVE IS WHAT YOU WANT.
THE KIND WHERE YOU SET OUT, WITH FULL INTENT, TO BUILD SOMETHING BIG AND DIFFICULT.
DINERS
YOU WANT TRUE LOVE--REAL TRUE LOVE? ROLL UP YOUR SLEEVES, FIX YOUR PURPOSE, AND GET READY FOR A LIFETIME OF HARD WORK.
IN THE MEANTIME, IF YOU SPOT A ROADSIDE PLACE TO GET A GOOD CHILI DOG, OR A BACON CHEESEBURGER, PULL OVER.
IT'S GOTTEN REAL HUNGRY OUT.
The End
NEXT: A new story, featuring tough mooks, dangerous dames, and snap-brimmed fedoras!

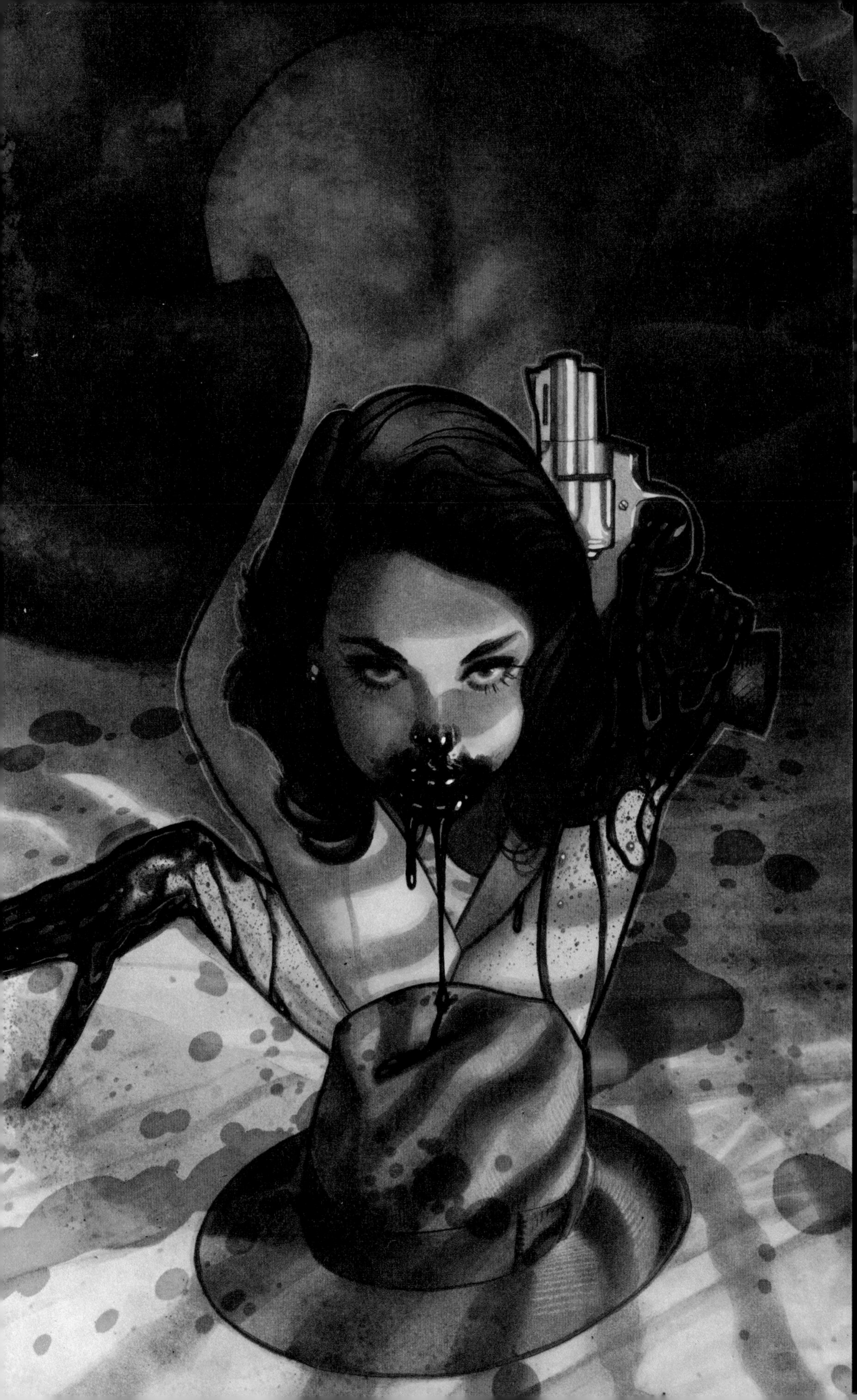

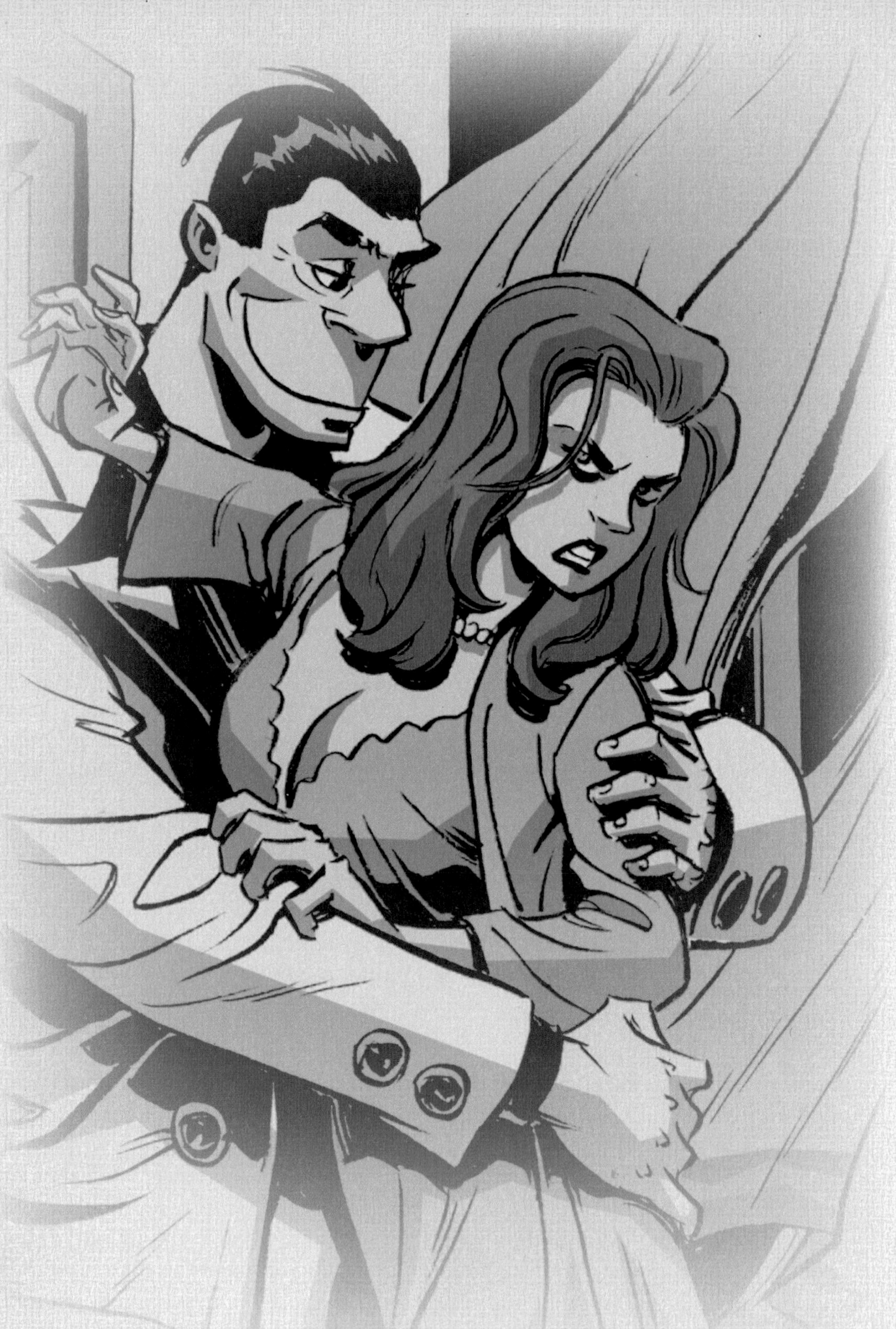

"You gonna play nice,
or do I need to get a little rough?"

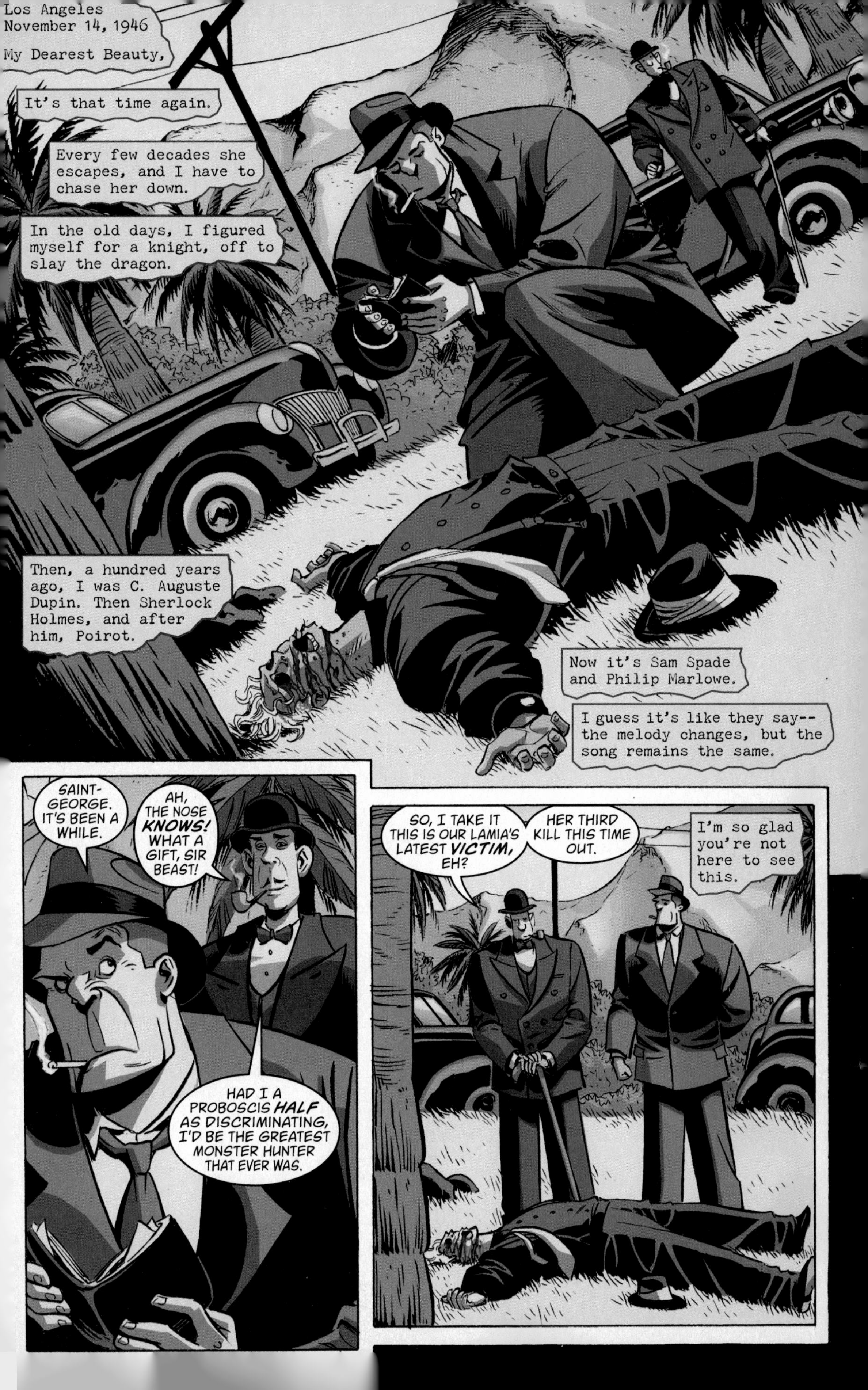
Los Angeles
November 14, 1946
My Dearest Beauty,
It's that time again.
Every few decades she escapes, and I have to chase her down.
In the old days, I figured myself for a knight, off to slay the dragon.
Then, a hundred years ago, I was C. Auguste Dupin. Then Sherlock Holmes, and after him, Poirot.
Now it's Sam Spade and Philip Marlowe.
I guess it's like they say--the melody changes, but the song remains the same.
SAINT-GEORGE. IT'S BEEN A WHILE.
AH, THE NOSE KNOWS! WHAT A GIFT, SIR BEAST!
HAD I A PROBOSCIS HALF AS DISCRIMINATING, I'D BE THE GREATEST MONSTER HUNTER THAT EVER WAS.
SO, I TAKE IT THIS IS OUR LAMIA'S LATEST VICTIM, EH?
HER THIRD KILL THIS TIME OUT.
I'm so glad you're not here to see this.

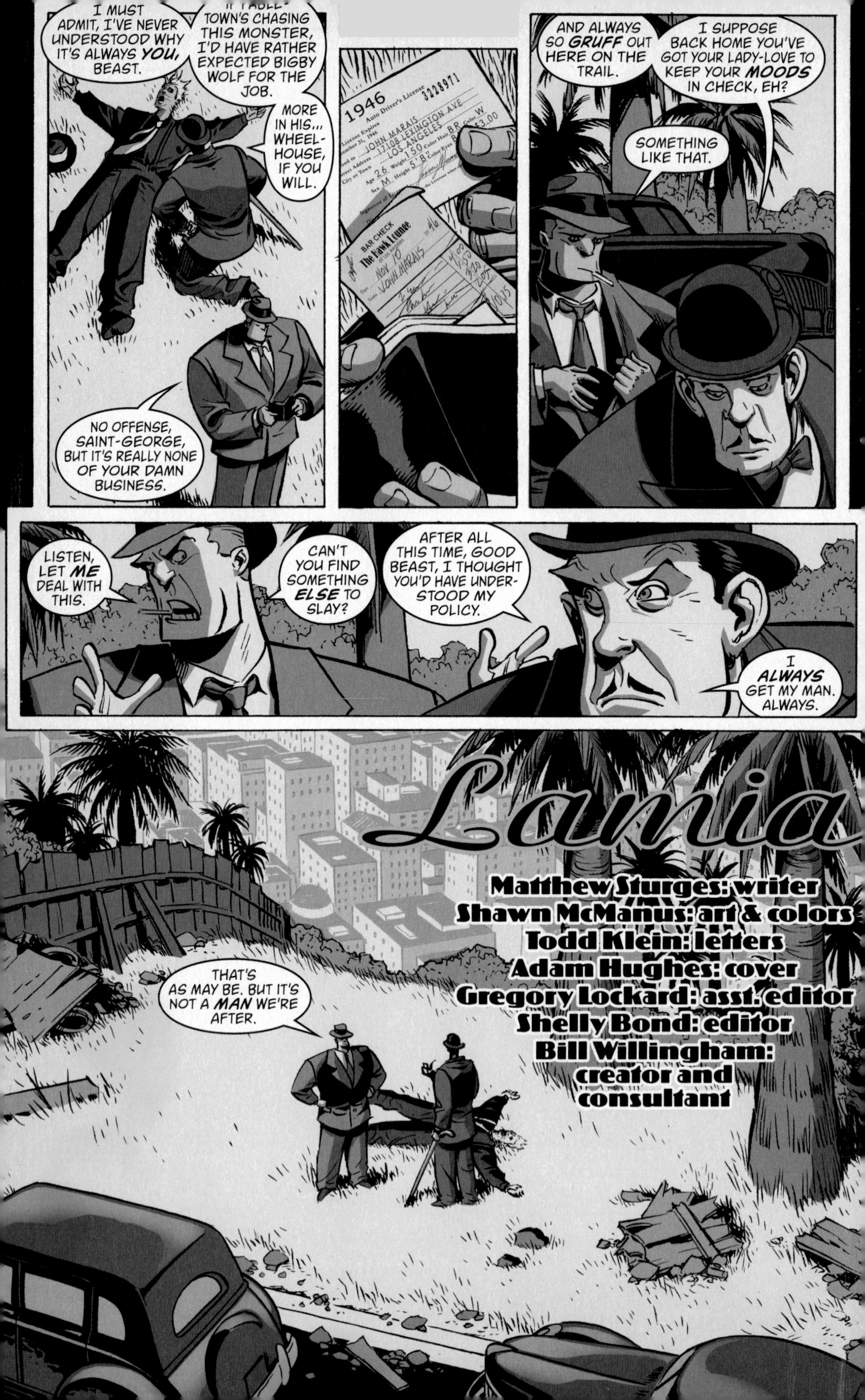

I MUST ADMIT, I'VE NEVER UNDERSTOOD WHY IT'S ALWAYS *YOU,* BEAST.
TOWN'S CHASING THIS MONSTER, I'D HAVE RATHER EXPECTED BIGBY WOLF FOR THE JOB.
MORE IN HIS... WHEEL-HOUSE, IF YOU WILL.
NO OFFENSE, SAINT-GEORGE, BUT IT'S REALLY NONE OF YOUR DAMN BUSINESS.
1946
3228971
JOHN MARAIS
17108 LEXINGTON AVE
LOS ANGELES
BAR CHECK
AND ALWAYS SO *GRUFF* OUT HERE ON THE TRAIL.
I SUPPOSE BACK HOME YOU'VE GOT YOUR LADY-LOVE TO KEEP YOUR *MOODS* IN CHECK, EH?
SOMETHING LIKE THAT.
LISTEN, LET *ME* DEAL WITH THIS.
CAN'T YOU FIND SOMETHING *ELSE* TO SLAY?
AFTER ALL THIS TIME, GOOD BEAST, I THOUGHT YOU'D HAVE UNDERSTOOD MY POLICY.
I *ALWAYS* GET MY MAN. ALWAYS.
Lamia
Matthew Sturges: writer
Shawn McManus: art & colors
Todd Klein: letters
Adam Hughes: cover
Gregory Lockard: asst. editor
Shelly Bond: editor
Bill Willingham: creator and consultant
THAT'S AS MAY BE. BUT IT'S NOT A *MAN* WE'RE AFTER.

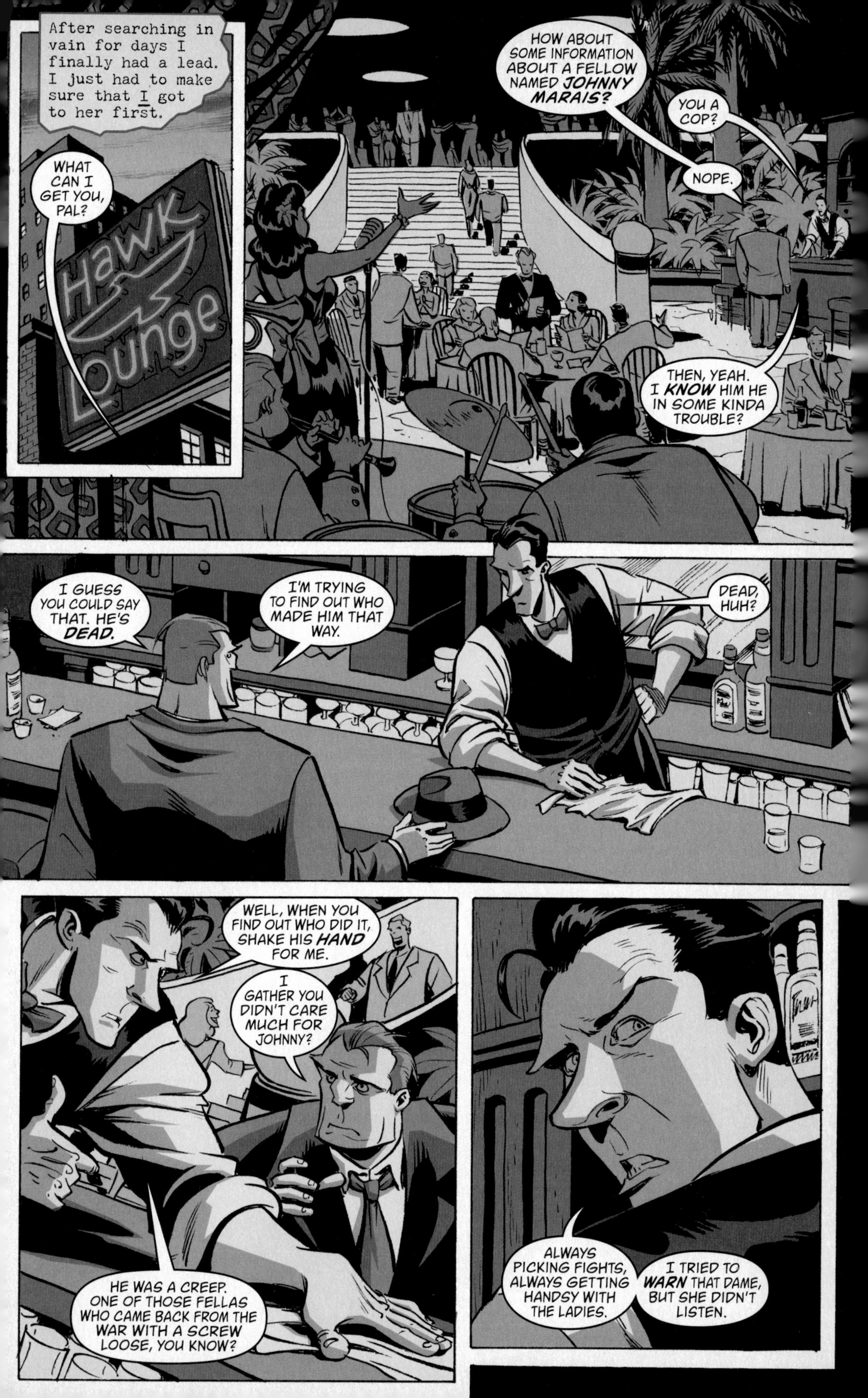
After searching in vain for days I finally had a lead. I just had to make sure that I got to her first.
WHAT CAN I GET YOU, PAL?
HAWK LOUNGE
HOW ABOUT SOME INFORMATION ABOUT A FELLOW NAMED JOHNNY MARAIS?
YOU A COP?
NOPE.
THEN, YEAH. I KNOW HIM. HE IN SOME KINDA TROUBLE?
I GUESS YOU COULD SAY THAT. HE'S DEAD.
I'M TRYING TO FIND OUT WHO MADE HIM THAT WAY.
DEAD, HUH?
WELL, WHEN YOU FIND OUT WHO DID IT, SHAKE HIS HAND FOR ME.
I GATHER YOU DIDN'T CARE MUCH FOR JOHNNY?
HE WAS A CREEP. ONE OF THOSE FELLAS WHO CAME BACK FROM THE WAR WITH A SCREW LOOSE, YOU KNOW?
ALWAYS PICKING FIGHTS, ALWAYS GETTING HANDSY WITH THE LADIES.
I TRIED TO WARN THAT DAME, BUT SHE DIDN'T LISTEN.

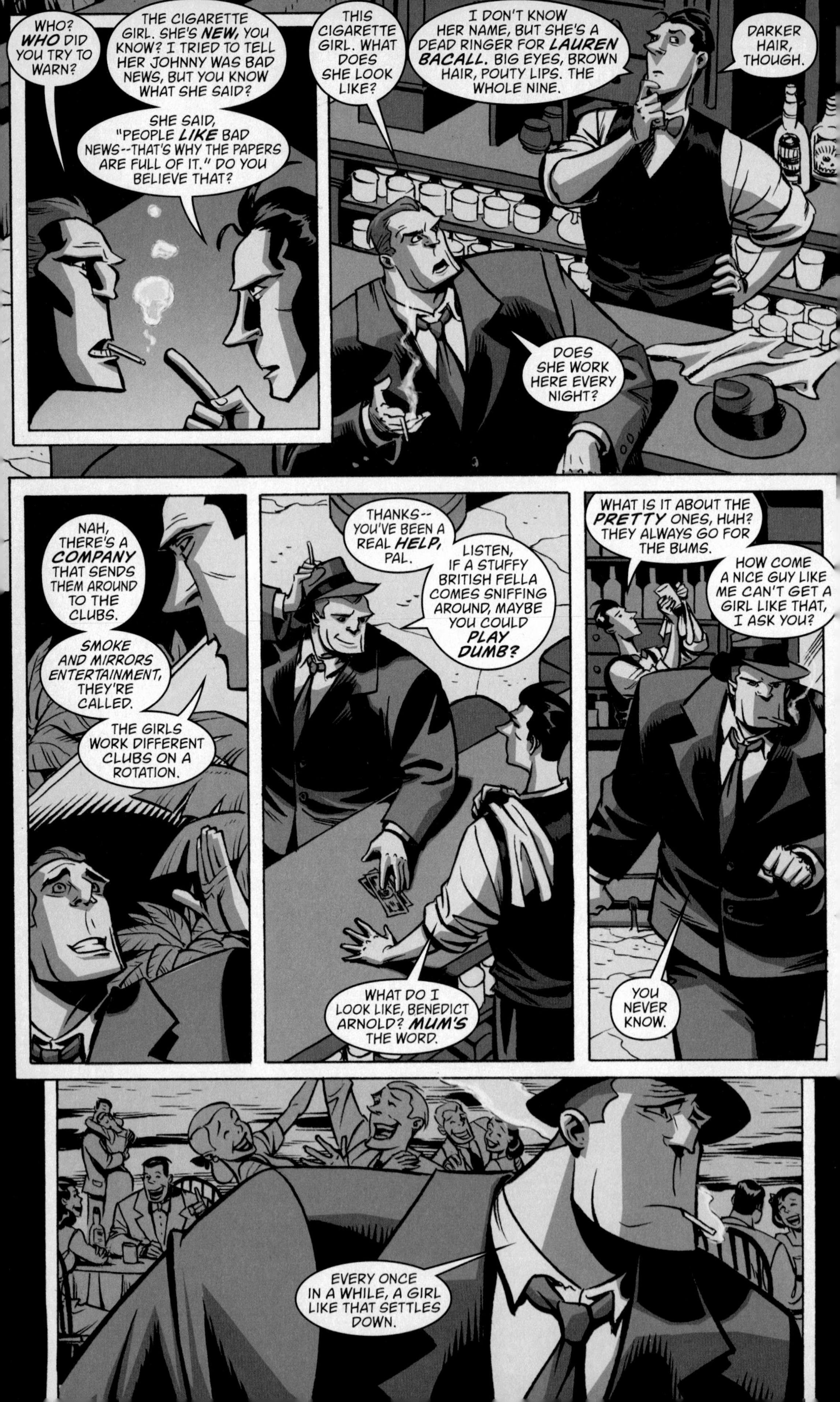
WHO? WHO DID YOU TRY TO WARN?
THE CIGARETTE GIRL. SHE'S NEW, YOU KNOW? I TRIED TO TELL HER JOHNNY WAS BAD NEWS, BUT YOU KNOW WHAT SHE SAID?
SHE SAID, "PEOPLE LIKE BAD NEWS--THAT'S WHY THE PAPERS ARE FULL OF IT." DO YOU BELIEVE THAT?
THIS CIGARETTE GIRL. WHAT DOES SHE LOOK LIKE?
I DON'T KNOW HER NAME, BUT SHE'S A DEAD RINGER FOR LAUREN BACALL. BIG EYES, BROWN HAIR, POUTY LIPS. THE WHOLE NINE.
DARKER HAIR, THOUGH.
DOES SHE WORK HERE EVERY NIGHT?
NAH, THERE'S A COMPANY THAT SENDS THEM AROUND TO THE CLUBS.
SMOKE AND MIRRORS ENTERTAINMENT, THEY'RE CALLED.
THE GIRLS WORK DIFFERENT CLUBS ON A ROTATION.
THANKS-- YOU'VE BEEN A REAL HELP, PAL.
LISTEN, IF A STUFFY BRITISH FELLA COMES SNIFFING AROUND, MAYBE YOU COULD PLAY DUMB?
WHAT DO I LOOK LIKE, BENEDICT ARNOLD? MUM'S THE WORD.
WHAT IS IT ABOUT THE PRETTY ONES, HUH? THEY ALWAYS GO FOR THE BUMS.
HOW COME A NICE GUY LIKE ME CAN'T GET A GIRL LIKE THAT, I ASK YOU?
YOU NEVER KNOW.
EVERY ONCE IN A WHILE, A GIRL LIKE THAT SETTLES DOWN.

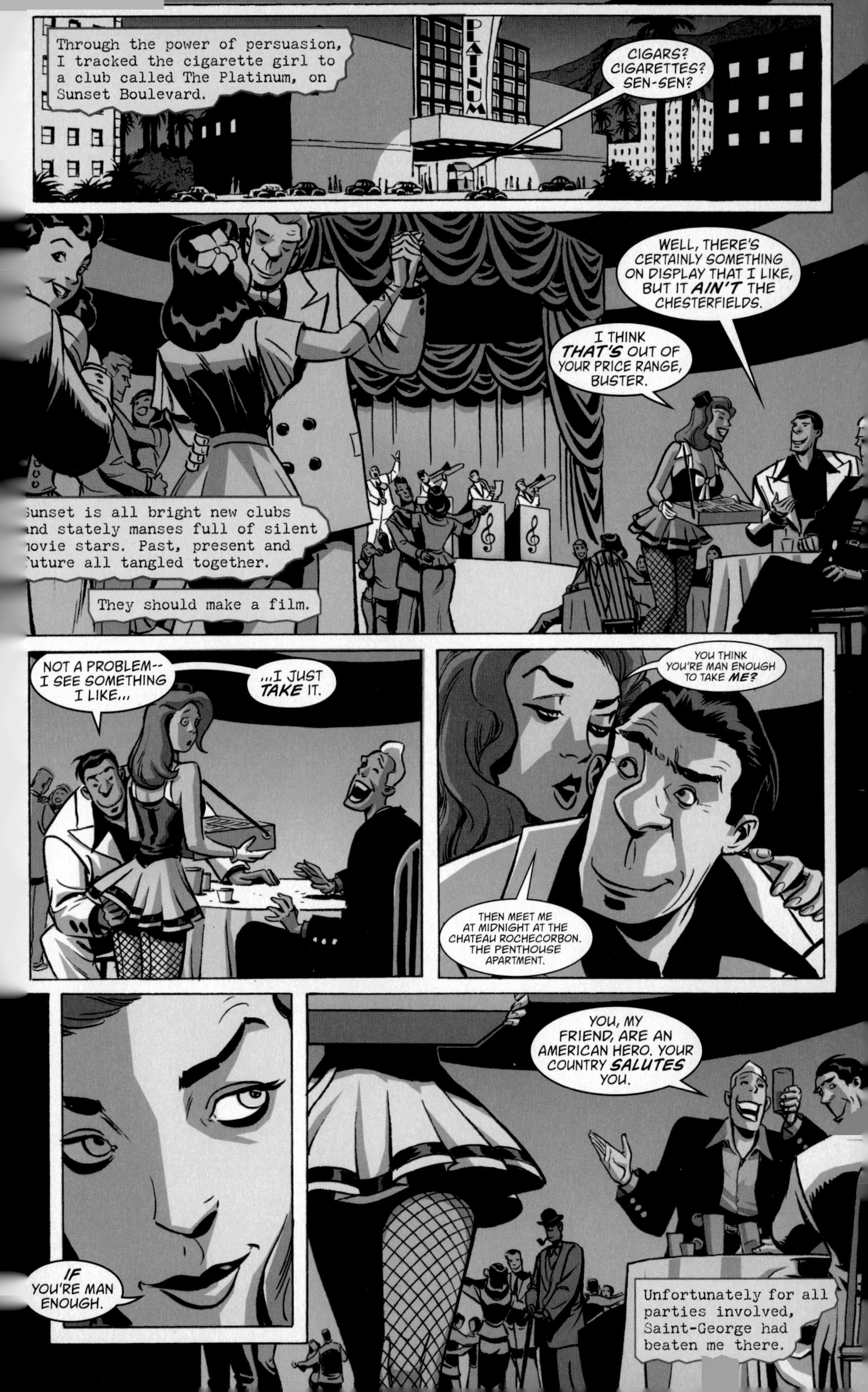
Through the power of persuasion, I tracked the cigarette girl to a club called The Platinum, on Sunset Boulevard.
PLATINUM
CIGARS? CIGARETTES? SEN-SEN?
WELL, THERE'S CERTAINLY SOMETHING ON DISPLAY THAT I LIKE, BUT IT AIN'T THE CHESTERFIELDS.
I THINK THAT'S OUT OF YOUR PRICE RANGE, BUSTER.
Sunset is all bright new clubs and stately manses full of silent movie stars. Past, present and future all tangled together.
They should make a film.
NOT A PROBLEM-- I SEE SOMETHING I LIKE...
...I JUST TAKE IT.
YOU THINK YOU'RE MAN ENOUGH TO TAKE ME?
THEN MEET ME AT MIDNIGHT AT THE CHATEAU ROCHECORBON. THE PENTHOUSE APARTMENT.
IF YOU'RE MAN ENOUGH.
YOU, MY FRIEND, ARE AN AMERICAN HERO. YOUR COUNTRY SALUTES YOU.
Unfortunately for all parties involved, Saint-George had beaten me there.

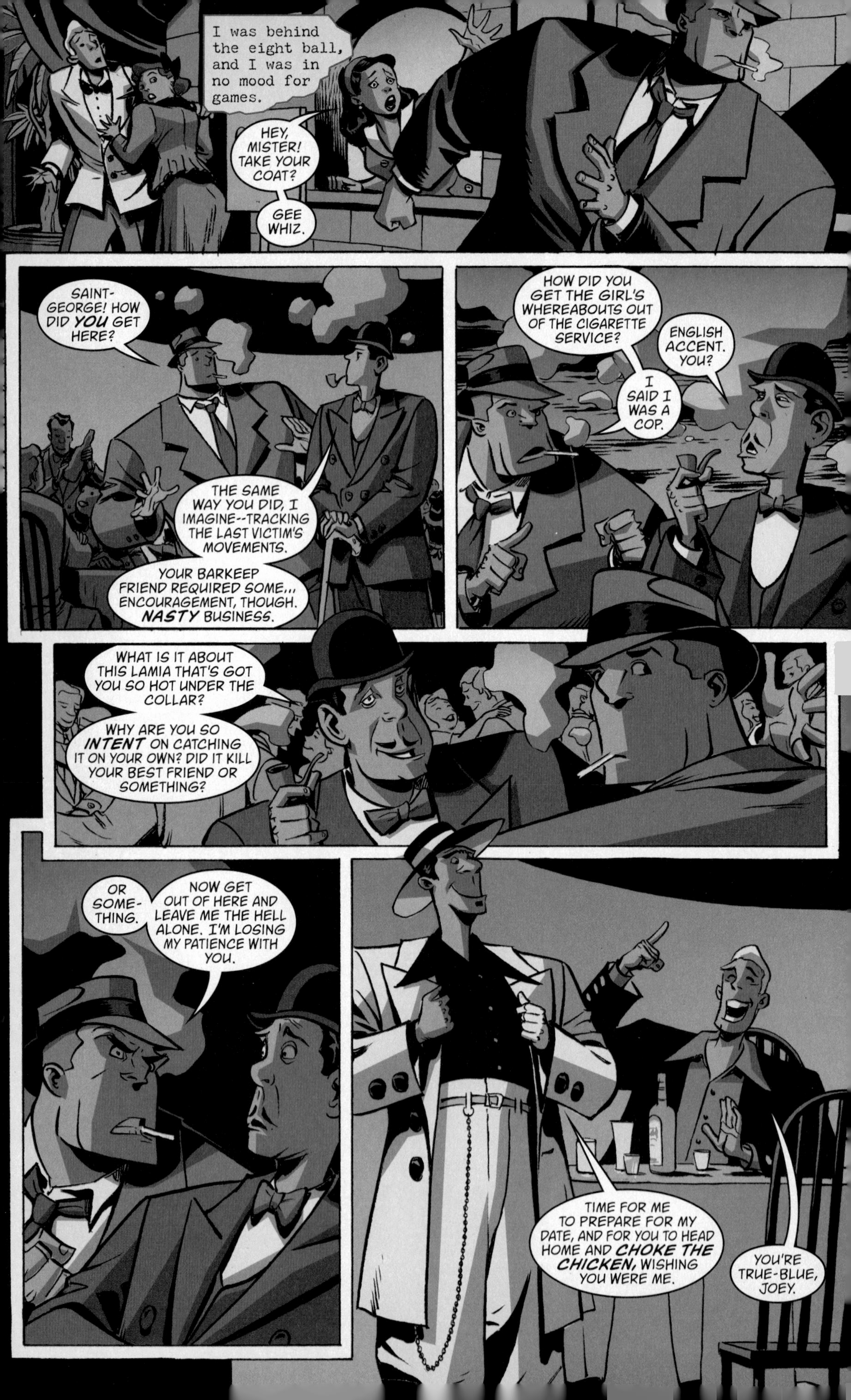
I was behind the eight ball, and I was in no mood for games.
HEY, MISTER! TAKE YOUR COAT?
GEE WHIZ.
SAINT-GEORGE! HOW DID YOU GET HERE?
THE SAME WAY YOU DID, I IMAGINE--TRACKING THE LAST VICTIM'S MOVEMENTS.
YOUR BARKEEP FRIEND REQUIRED SOME... ENCOURAGEMENT, THOUGH. NASTY BUSINESS.
HOW DID YOU GET THE GIRL'S WHEREABOUTS OUT OF THE CIGARETTE SERVICE?
ENGLISH ACCENT. YOU?
I SAID I WAS A COP.
WHAT IS IT ABOUT THIS LAMIA THAT'S GOT YOU SO HOT UNDER THE COLLAR?
WHY ARE YOU SO INTENT ON CATCHING IT ON YOUR OWN? DID IT KILL YOUR BEST FRIEND OR SOMETHING?
OR SOME-THING.
NOW GET OUT OF HERE AND LEAVE ME THE HELL ALONE. I'M LOSING MY PATIENCE WITH YOU.
TIME FOR ME TO PREPARE FOR MY DATE, AND FOR YOU TO HEAD HOME AND CHOKE THE CHICKEN, WISHING YOU WERE ME.
YOU'RE TRUE-BLUE, JOEY.

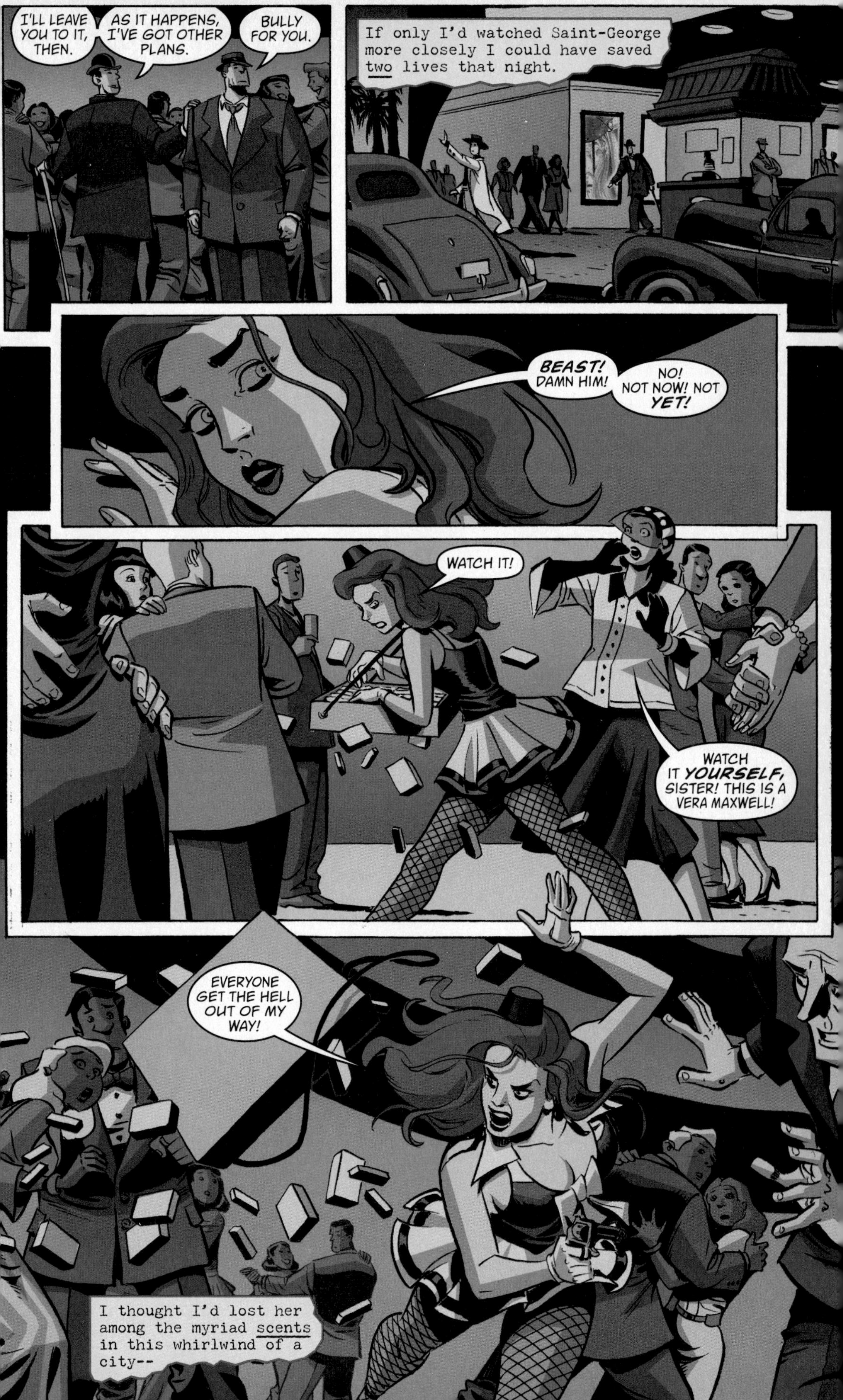
I'LL LEAVE YOU TO IT, THEN.
AS IT HAPPENS, I'VE GOT OTHER PLANS.
BULLY FOR YOU.
If only I'd watched Saint-George more closely I could have saved two lives that night.
BEAST! DAMN HIM!
NO! NOT NOW! NOT YET!
WATCH IT!
WATCH IT YOURSELF, SISTER! THIS IS A VERA MAXWELL!
EVERYONE GET THE HELL OUT OF MY WAY!
I thought I'd lost her among the myriad scents in this whirlwind of a city--

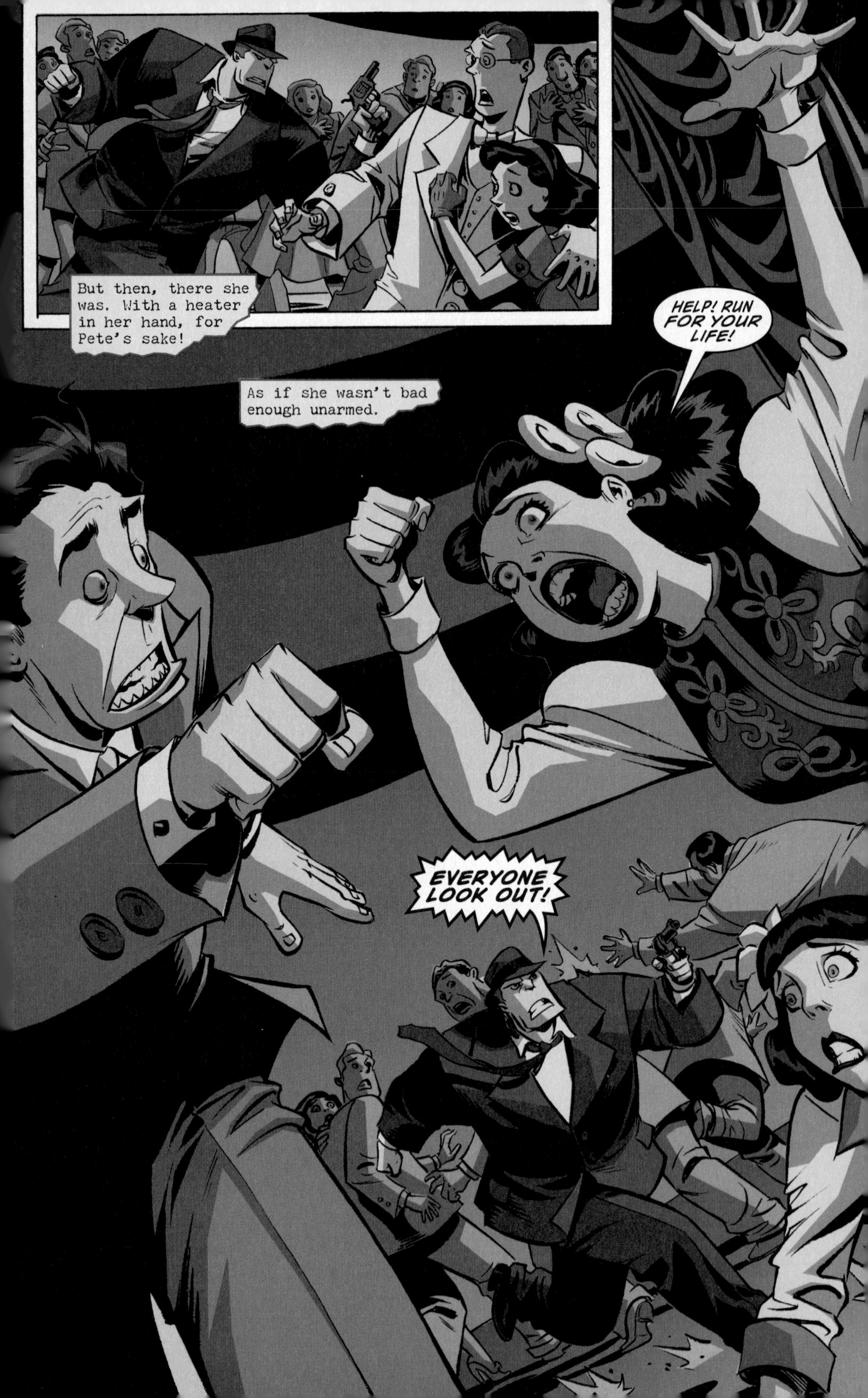
But then, there she was. With a heater in her hand, for Pete's sake!
HELP! RUN FOR YOUR LIFE!
As if she wasn't bad enough unarmed.
EVERYONE LOOK OUT!

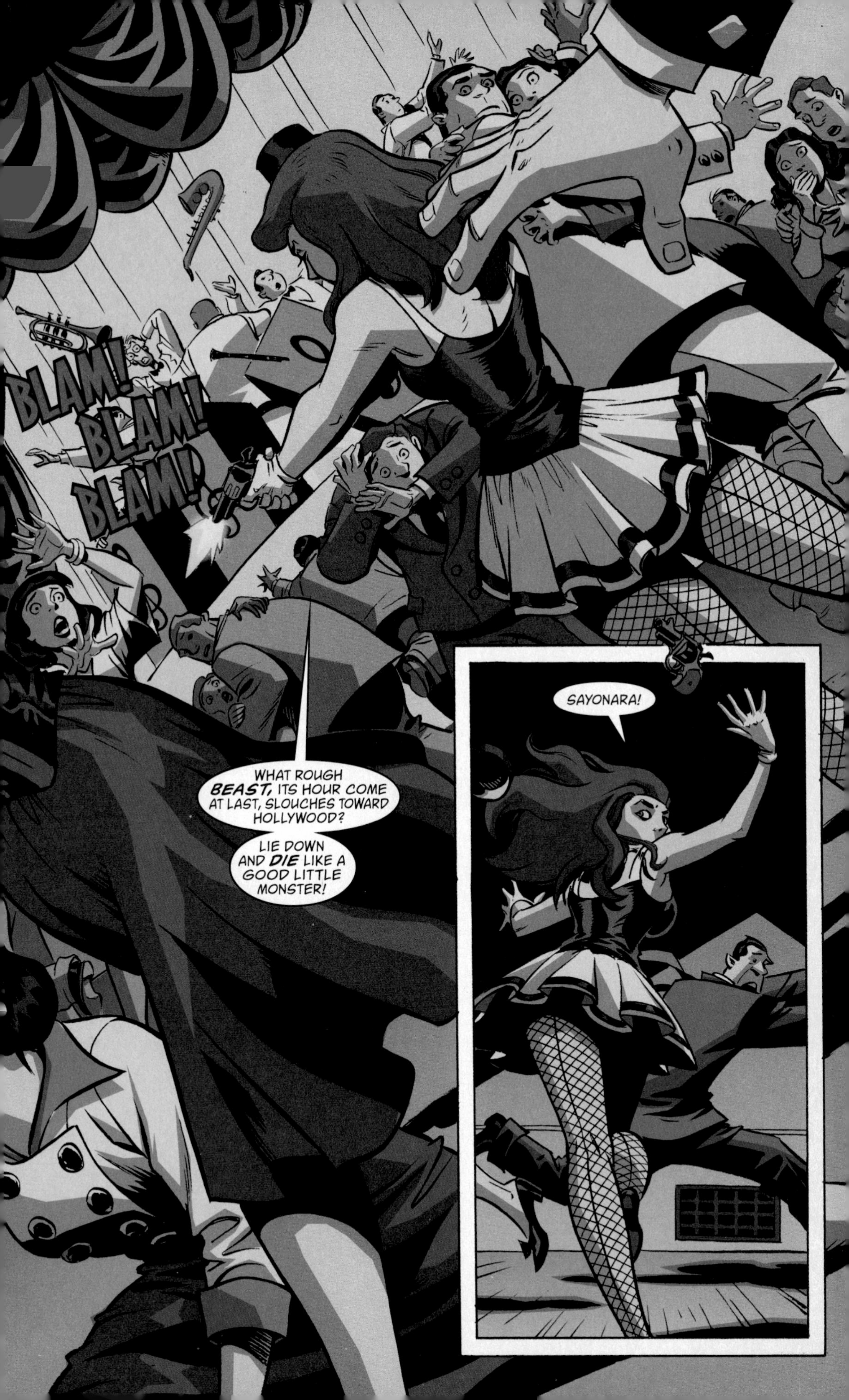
BLAM! BLAM! BLAM!
WHAT ROUGH BEAST, ITS HOUR COME AT LAST, SLOUCHES TOWARD HOLLYWOOD?
LIE DOWN AND DIE LIKE A GOOD LITTLE MONSTER!
SAYONARA!

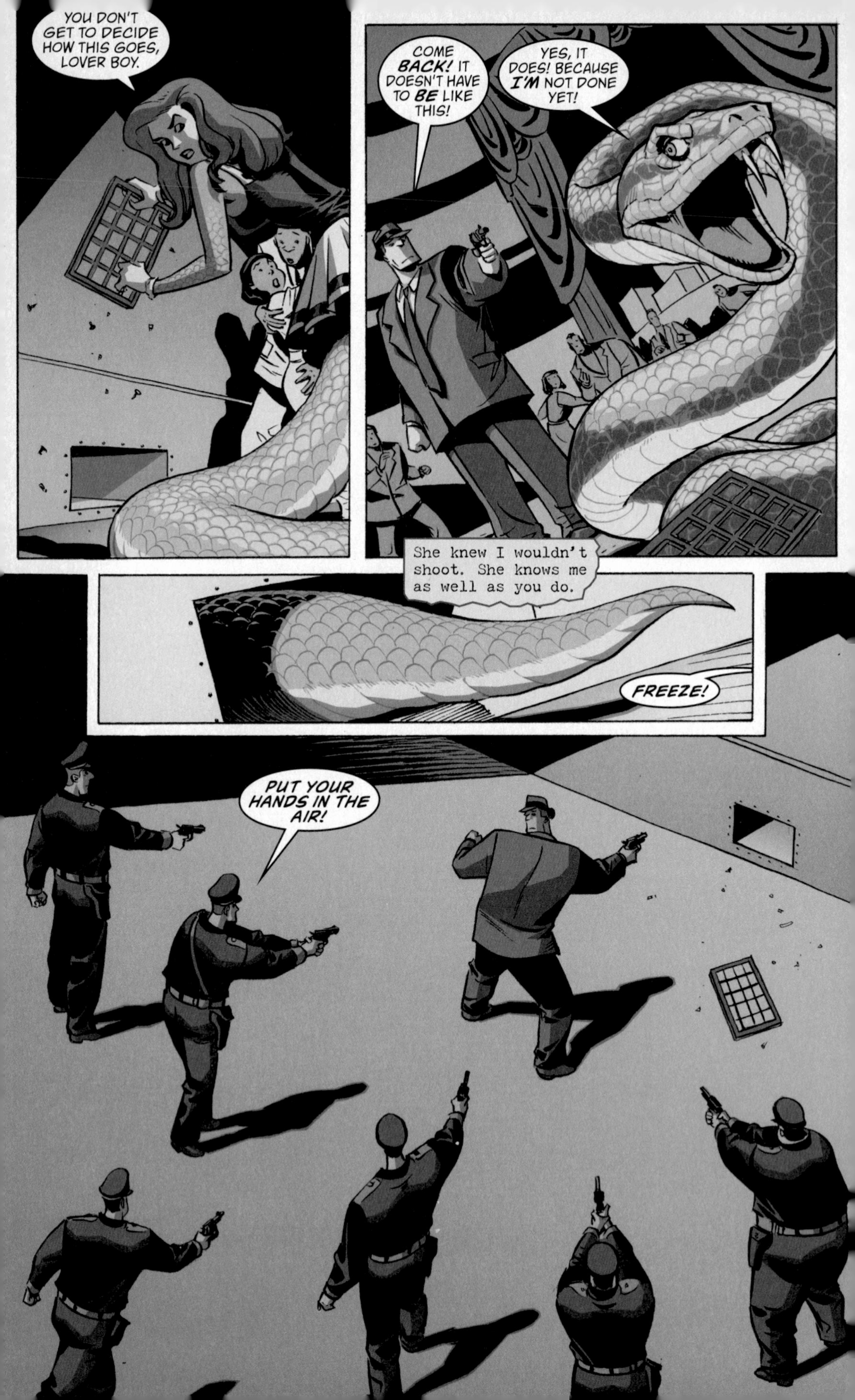
YOU DON'T GET TO DECIDE HOW THIS GOES, LOVER BOY.
COME BACK! IT DOESN'T HAVE TO BE LIKE THIS!
YES, IT DOES! BECAUSE I'M NOT DONE YET!
She knew I wouldn't shoot. She knows me as well as you do.
FREEZE!
PUT YOUR HANDS IN THE AIR!

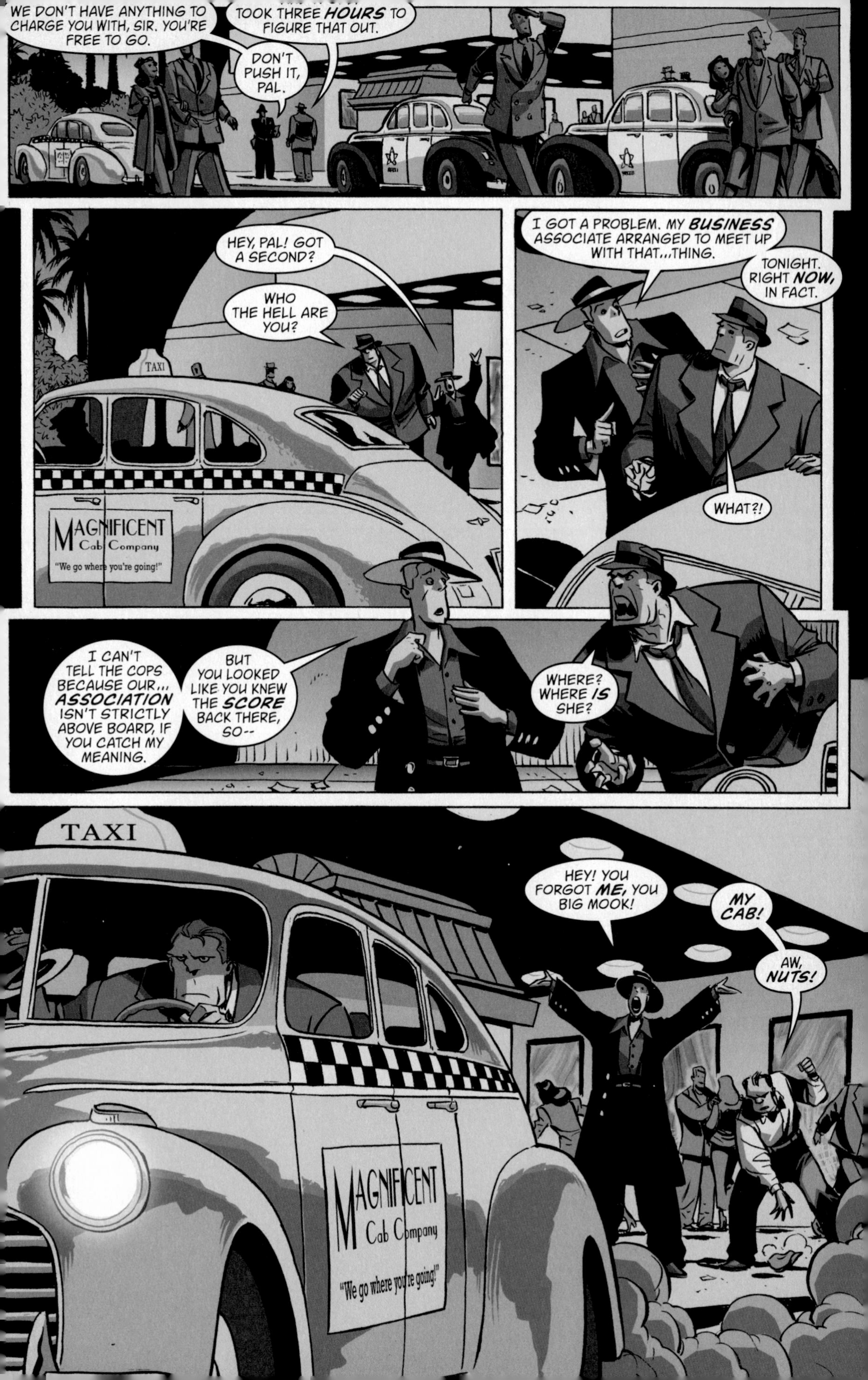
WE DON'T HAVE ANYTHING TO CHARGE YOU WITH, SIR. YOU'RE FREE TO GO.
TOOK THREE HOURS TO FIGURE THAT OUT.
DON'T PUSH IT, PAL.
HEY, PAL! GOT A SECOND?
WHO THE HELL ARE YOU?
TAXI
MAGNIFICENT Cab Company
"We go where you're going!"
I GOT A PROBLEM. MY BUSINESS ASSOCIATE ARRANGED TO MEET UP WITH THAT...THING.
TONIGHT. RIGHT NOW, IN FACT.
WHAT?!
I CAN'T TELL THE COPS BECAUSE OUR... ASSOCIATION ISN'T STRICTLY ABOVE BOARD, IF YOU CATCH MY MEANING.
BUT YOU LOOKED LIKE YOU KNEW THE SCORE BACK THERE, SO--
WHERE? WHERE IS SHE?
TAXI
HEY! YOU FORGOT ME, YOU BIG MOOK!
MY CAB!
AW, NUTS!
MAGNIFICENT Cab Company
"We go where you're going!"

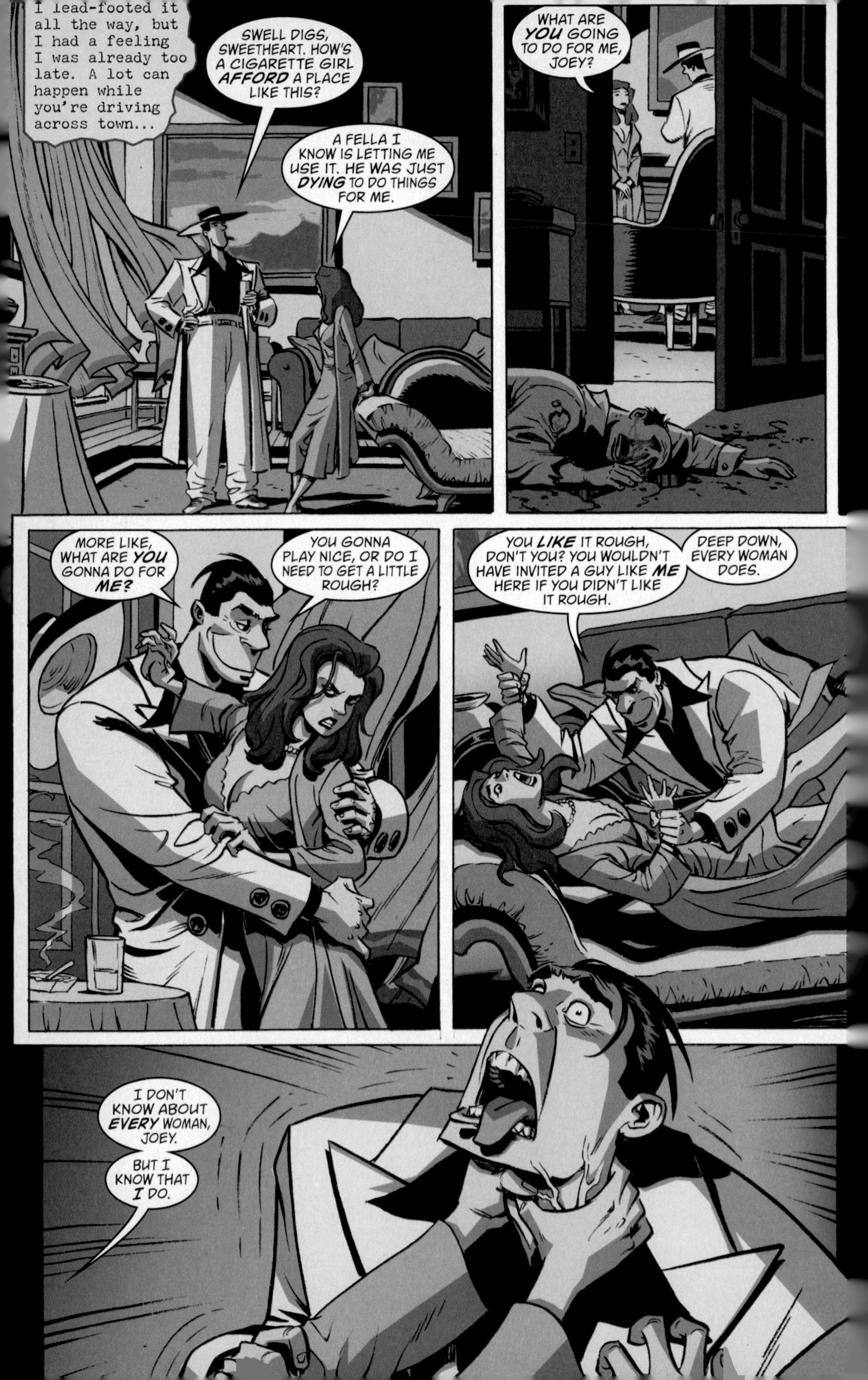
I lead-footed it all the way, but I had a feeling I was already too late. A lot can happen while you're driving across town...
SWELL DIGS, SWEETHEART. HOW'S A CIGARETTE GIRL AFFORD A PLACE LIKE THIS?
A FELLA I KNOW IS LETTING ME USE IT. HE WAS JUST DYING TO DO THINGS FOR ME.
WHAT ARE YOU GOING TO DO FOR ME, JOEY?
MORE LIKE, WHAT ARE YOU GONNA DO FOR ME?
YOU GONNA PLAY NICE, OR DO I NEED TO GET A LITTLE ROUGH?
YOU LIKE IT ROUGH, DON'T YOU? YOU WOULDN'T HAVE INVITED A GUY LIKE ME HERE IF YOU DIDN'T LIKE IT ROUGH.
DEEP DOWN, EVERY WOMAN DOES.
I DON'T KNOW ABOUT EVERY WOMAN, JOEY.
BUT I KNOW THAT I DO.

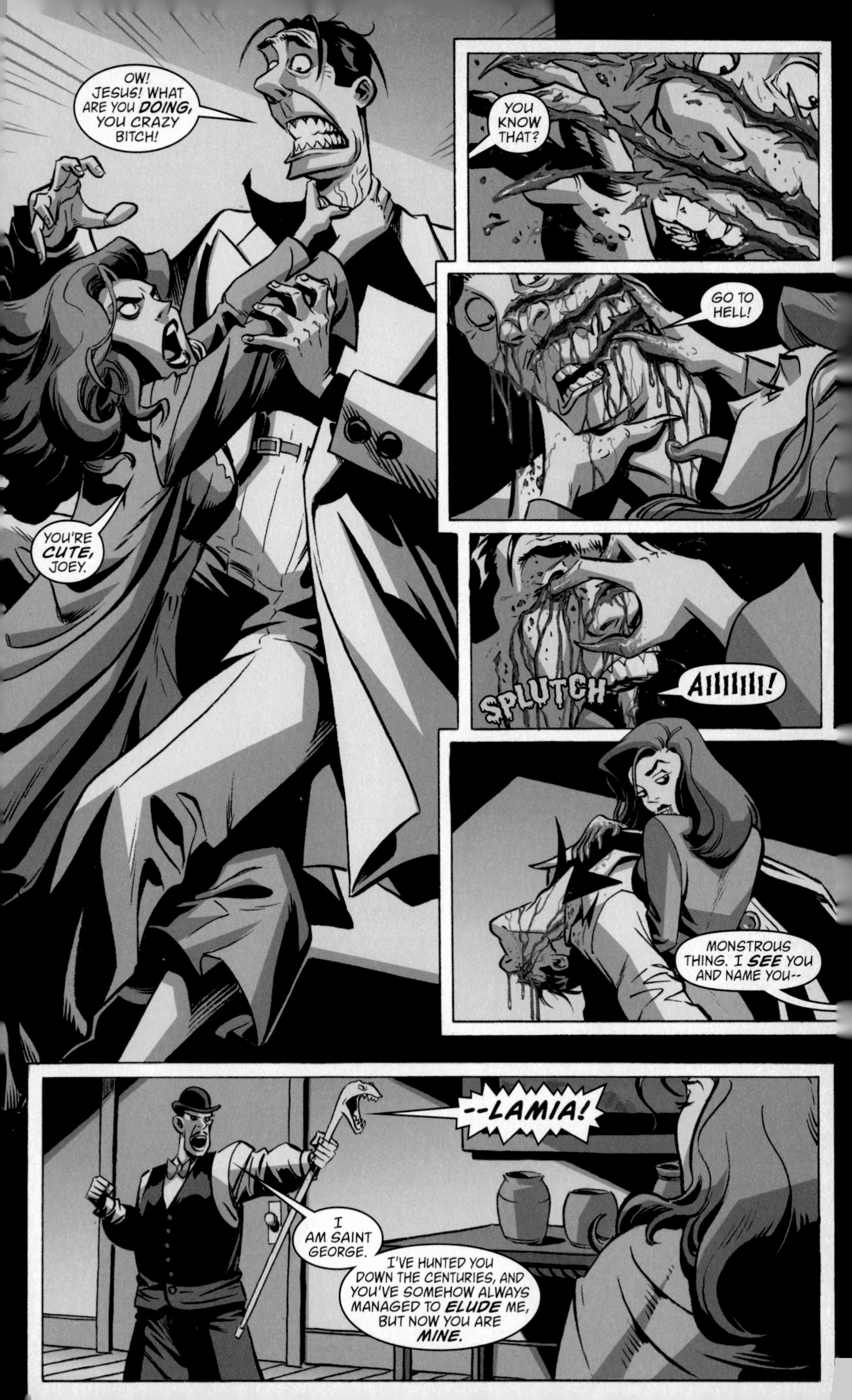
OW! JESUS! WHAT ARE YOU DOING, YOU CRAZY BITCH!
YOU'RE CUTE, JOEY.
YOU KNOW THAT?
GO TO HELL!
SPLUTCH
AIIIIIII!
MONSTROUS THING. I SEE YOU AND NAME YOU--
--LAMIA!
I AM SAINT GEORGE.
I'VE HUNTED YOU DOWN THE CENTURIES, AND YOU'VE SOMEHOW ALWAYS MANAGED TO ELUDE ME, BUT NOW YOU ARE MINE.

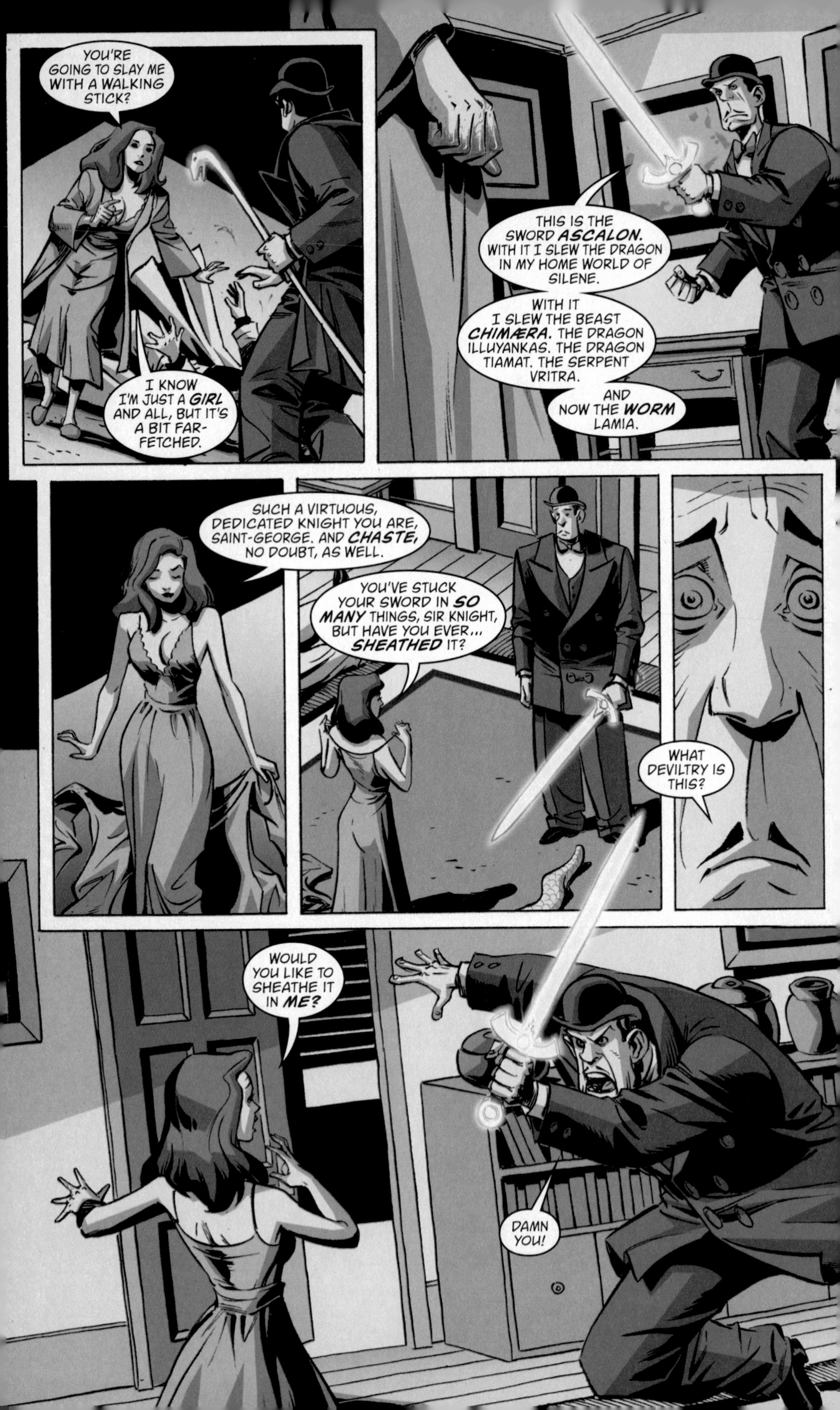
YOU'RE GOING TO SLAY ME WITH A WALKING STICK?
I KNOW I'M JUST A GIRL AND ALL, BUT IT'S A BIT FAR-FETCHED.
THIS IS THE SWORD ASCALON. WITH IT I SLEW THE DRAGON IN MY HOME WORLD OF SILENE.
WITH IT I SLEW THE BEAST CHIMÆRA. THE DRAGON ILLUYANKAS. THE DRAGON TIAMAT. THE SERPENT VRITRA.
AND NOW THE WORM LAMIA.
SUCH A VIRTUOUS, DEDICATED KNIGHT YOU ARE, SAINT-GEORGE. AND CHASTE, NO DOUBT, AS WELL.
YOU'VE STUCK YOUR SWORD IN SO MANY THINGS, SIR KNIGHT, BUT HAVE YOU EVER... SHEATHED IT?
WHAT DEVILTRY IS THIS?
WOULD YOU LIKE TO SHEATHE IT IN ME?
DAMN YOU!

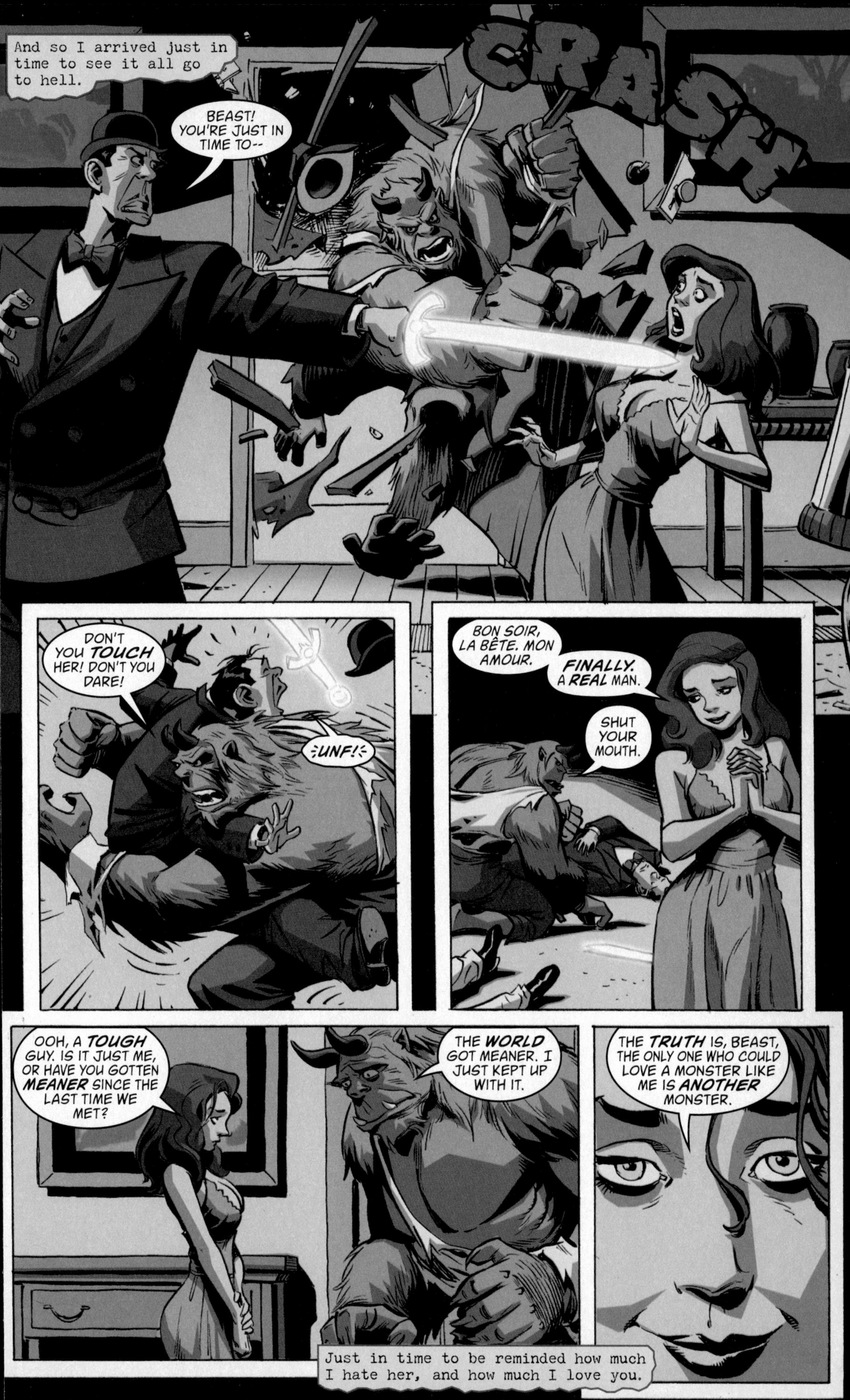
And so I arrived just in time to see it all go to hell.
CRASH
BEAST! YOU'RE JUST IN TIME TO--
DON'T YOU TOUCH HER! DON'T YOU DARE!
UNF!
BON SOIR, LA BÊTE. MON AMOUR.
FINALLY. A REAL MAN.
SHUT YOUR MOUTH.
OOH, A TOUGH GUY. IS IT JUST ME, OR HAVE YOU GOTTEN MEANER SINCE THE LAST TIME WE MET?
THE WORLD GOT MEANER. I JUST KEPT UP WITH IT.
THE TRUTH IS, BEAST, THE ONLY ONE WHO COULD LOVE A MONSTER LIKE ME IS ANOTHER MONSTER.
Just in time to be reminded how much I hate her, and how much I love you.

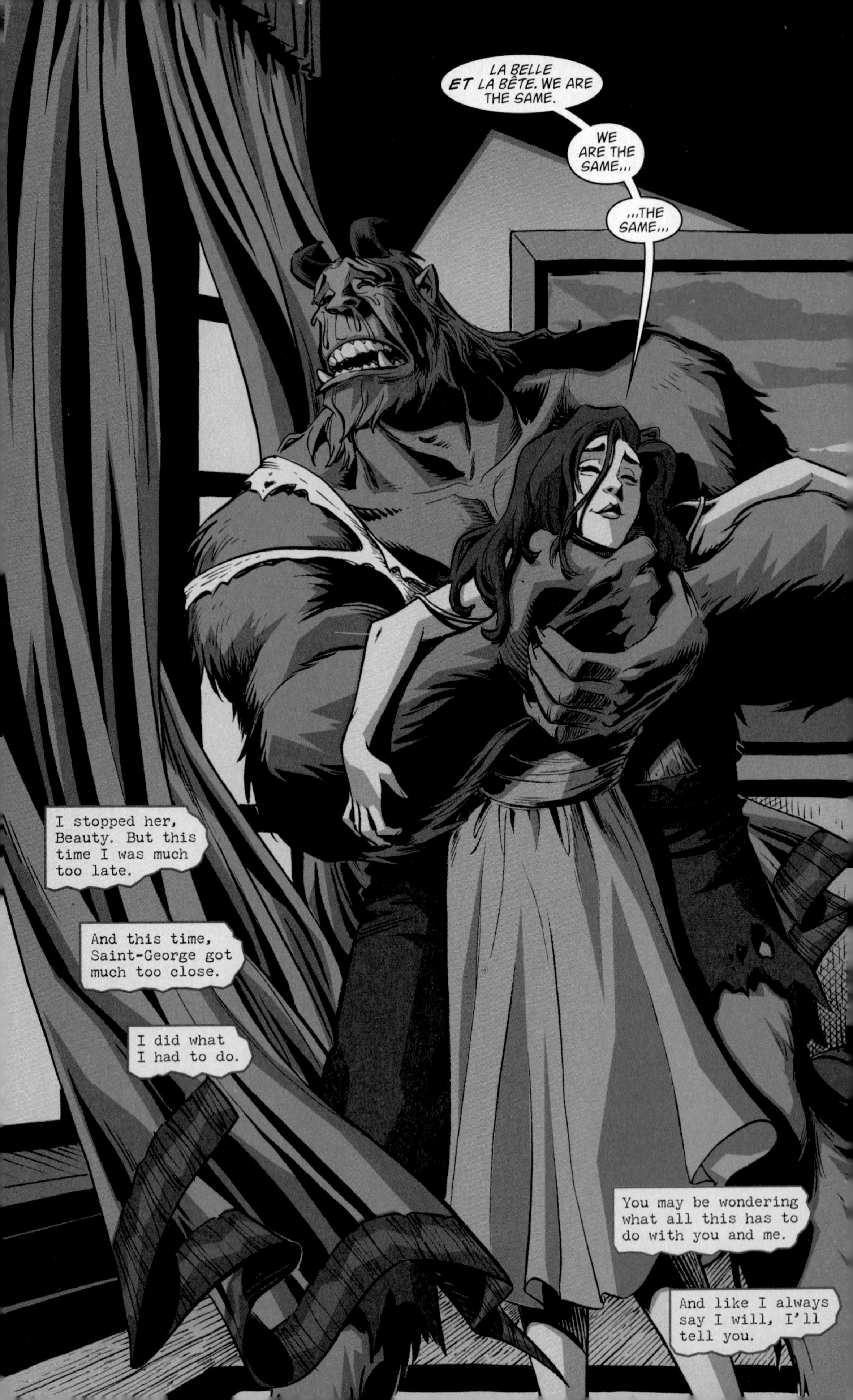
LA BELLE ET LA BÊTE. WE ARE THE SAME.
WE ARE THE SAME...
...THE SAME...
I stopped her, Beauty. But this time I was much too late.
And this time, Saint-George got much too close.
I did what I had to do.
You may be wondering what all this has to do with you and me.
And like I always say I will, I'll tell you.

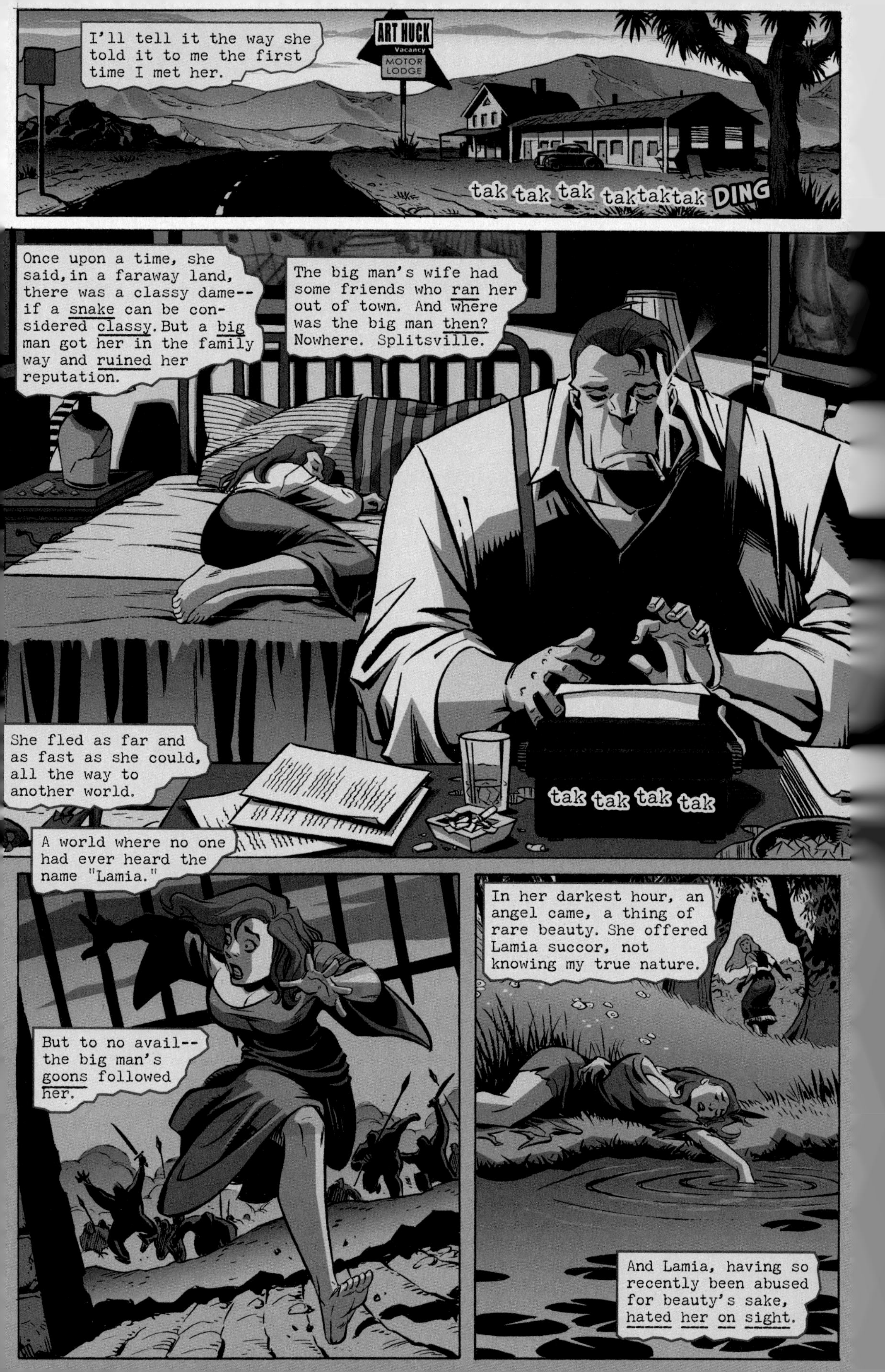
I'll tell it the way she told it to me the first time I met her.
ART HUCK Vacancy MOTOR LODGE
tak tak tak taktaktak DING
Once upon a time, she said, in a faraway land, there was a classy dame--if a snake can be considered classy. But a big man got her in the family way and ruined her reputation.
The big man's wife had some friends who ran her out of town. And where was the big man then? Nowhere. Splitsville.
She fled as far and as fast as she could, all the way to another world.
tak tak tak tak
A world where no one had ever heard the name "Lamia."
But to no avail--the big man's goons followed her.
In her darkest hour, an angel came, a thing of rare beauty. She offered Lamia succor, not knowing my true nature.
And Lamia, having so recently been abused for beauty's sake, hated her on sight.

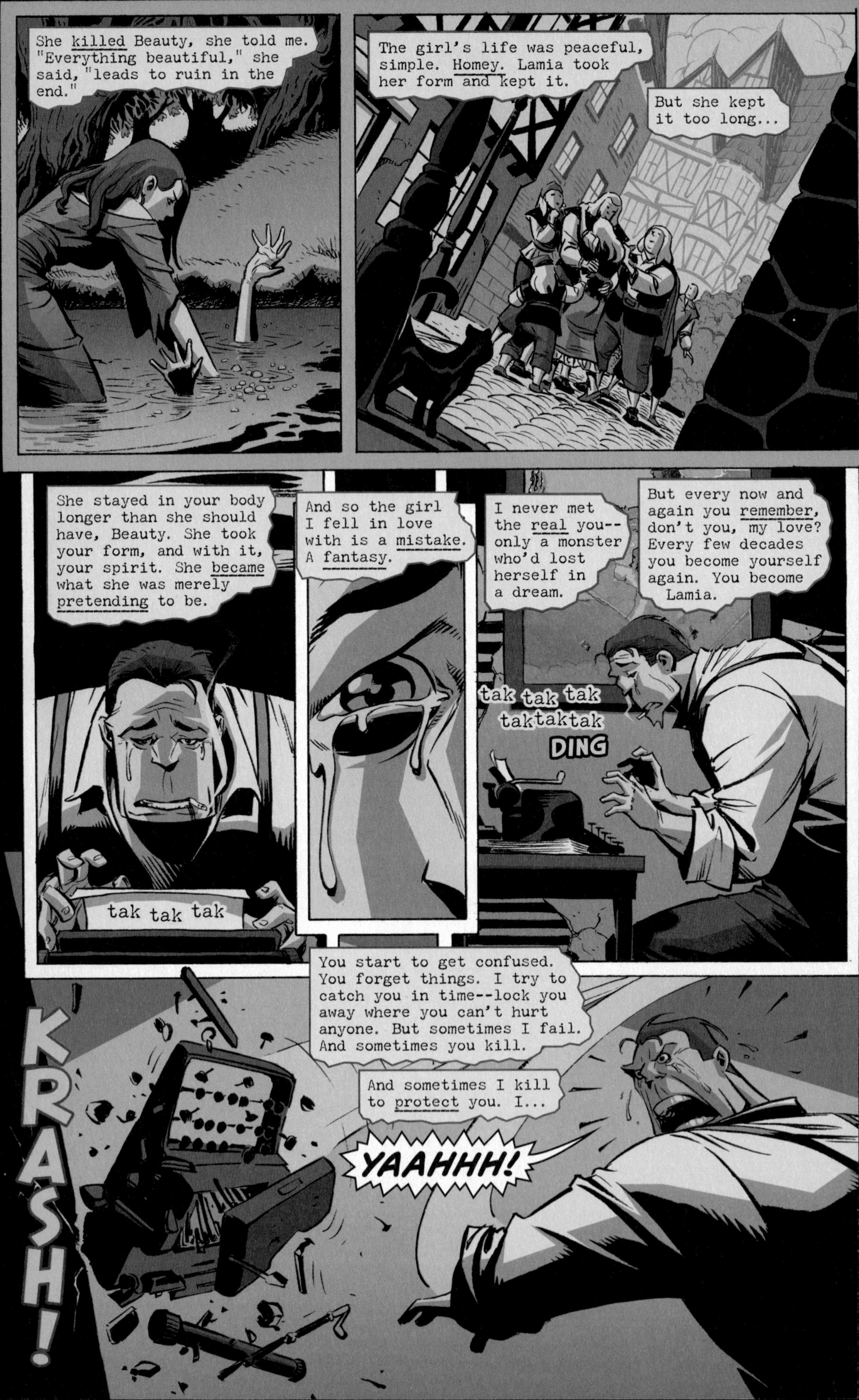

She killed Beauty, she told me. "Everything beautiful," she said, "leads to ruin in the end."
The girl's life was peaceful, simple. Homey. Lamia took her form and kept it.
But she kept it too long...
She stayed in your body longer than she should have, Beauty. She took your form, and with it, your spirit. She became what she was merely pretending to be.
tak tak tak
And so the girl I fell in love with is a mistake. A fantasy.
I never met the real you--only a monster who'd lost herself in a dream.
But every now and again you remember, don't you, my love? Every few decades you become yourself again. You become Lamia.
tak tak tak
taktaktak
DING
You start to get confused. You forget things. I try to catch you in time--lock you away where you can't hurt anyone. But sometimes I fail. And sometimes you kill.
And sometimes I kill to protect you. I...
YAAHHH!
KRASH!

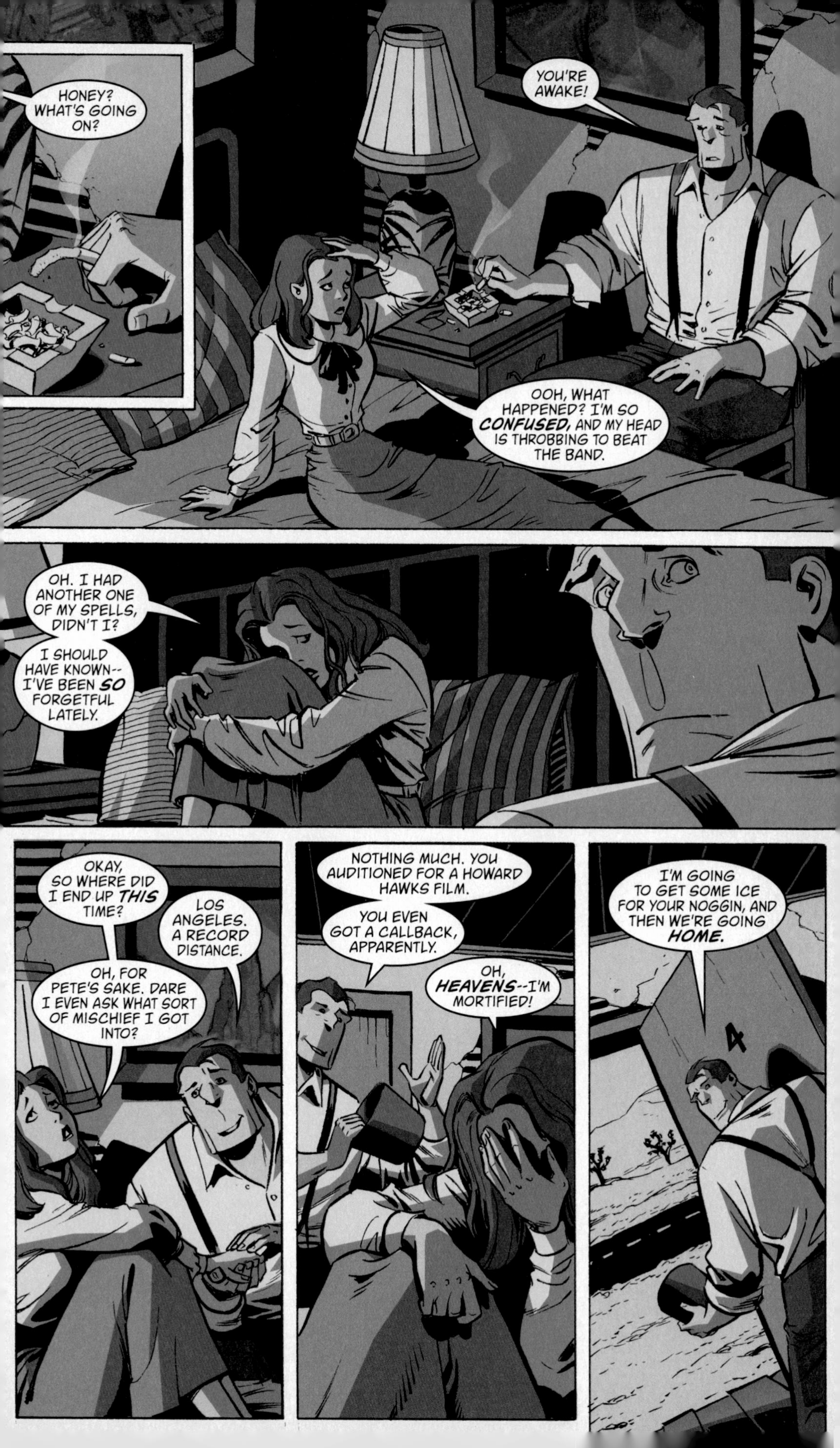
HONEY? WHAT'S GOING ON?
YOU'RE AWAKE!
OOH, WHAT HAPPENED? I'M SO CONFUSED, AND MY HEAD IS THROBBING TO BEAT THE BAND.
OH. I HAD ANOTHER ONE OF MY SPELLS, DIDN'T I?
I SHOULD HAVE KNOWN-- I'VE BEEN SO FORGETFUL LATELY.
OKAY, SO WHERE DID I END UP THIS TIME?
LOS ANGELES. A RECORD DISTANCE.
OH, FOR PETE'S SAKE. DARE I EVEN ASK WHAT SORT OF MISCHIEF I GOT INTO?
NOTHING MUCH. YOU AUDITIONED FOR A HOWARD HAWKS FILM.
YOU EVEN GOT A CALLBACK, APPARENTLY.
OH, HEAVENS--I'M MORTIFIED!
I'M GOING TO GET SOME ICE FOR YOUR NOGGIN, AND THEN WE'RE GOING HOME.
4

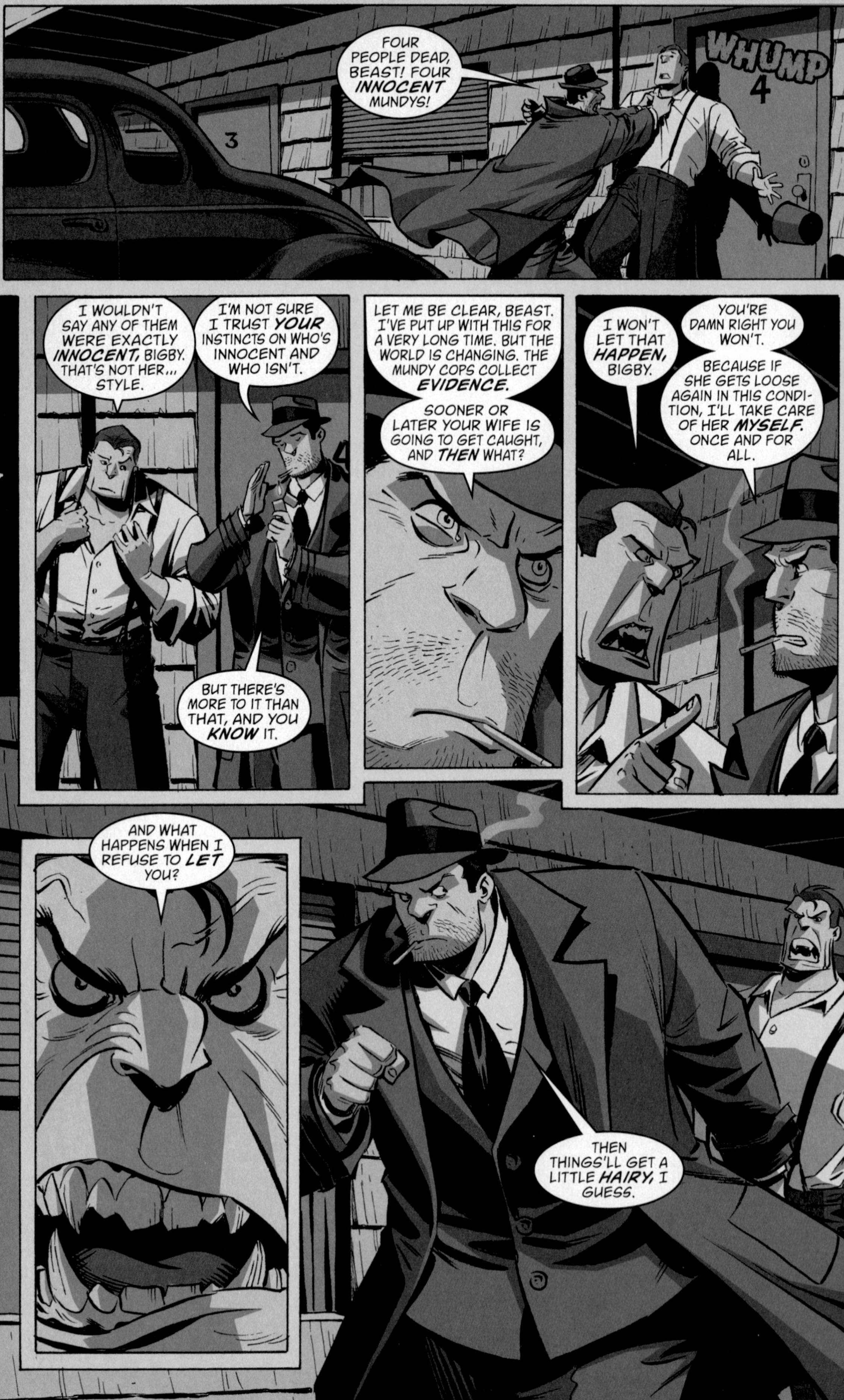
FOUR PEOPLE DEAD, BEAST! FOUR INNOCENT MUNDYS!
WHUMP
4
3
I WOULDN'T SAY ANY OF THEM WERE EXACTLY INNOCENT, BIGBY. THAT'S NOT HER... STYLE.
I'M NOT SURE I TRUST YOUR INSTINCTS ON WHO'S INNOCENT AND WHO ISN'T.
BUT THERE'S MORE TO IT THAN THAT, AND YOU KNOW IT.
LET ME BE CLEAR, BEAST. I'VE PUT UP WITH THIS FOR A VERY LONG TIME. BUT THE WORLD IS CHANGING. THE MUNDY COPS COLLECT EVIDENCE.
SOONER OR LATER YOUR WIFE IS GOING TO GET CAUGHT, AND THEN WHAT?
I WON'T LET THAT HAPPEN, BIGBY.
YOU'RE DAMN RIGHT YOU WON'T.
BECAUSE IF SHE GETS LOOSE AGAIN IN THIS CONDITION, I'LL TAKE CARE OF HER MYSELF. ONCE AND FOR ALL.
AND WHAT HAPPENS WHEN I REFUSE TO LET YOU?
THEN THINGS'LL GET A LITTLE HAIRY, I GUESS.

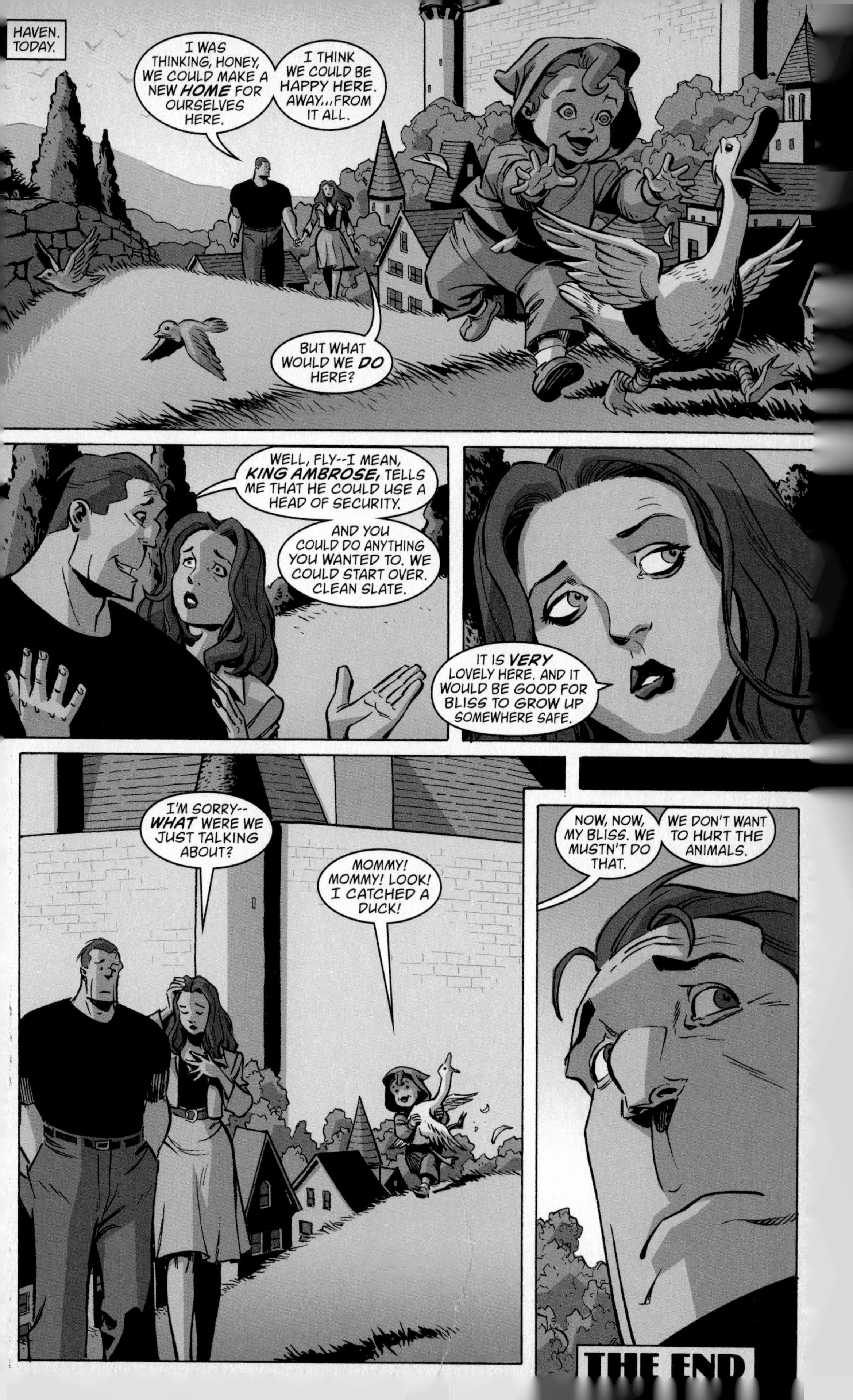
HAVEN. TODAY.
I WAS THINKING, HONEY, WE COULD MAKE A NEW HOME FOR OURSELVES HERE.
I THINK WE COULD BE HAPPY HERE. AWAY...FROM IT ALL.
BUT WHAT WOULD WE DO HERE?
WELL, FLY--I MEAN, KING AMBROSE, TELLS ME THAT HE COULD USE A HEAD OF SECURITY.
AND YOU COULD DO ANYTHING YOU WANTED TO. WE COULD START OVER. CLEAN SLATE.
IT IS VERY LOVELY HERE. AND IT WOULD BE GOOD FOR BLISS TO GROW UP SOMEWHERE SAFE.
I'M SORRY-- WHAT WERE WE JUST TALKING ABOUT?
MOMMY! MOMMY! LOOK! I CATCHED A DUCK!
NOW, NOW, MY BLISS. WE MUSTN'T DO THAT.
WE DON'T WANT TO HURT THE ANIMALS.
THE END

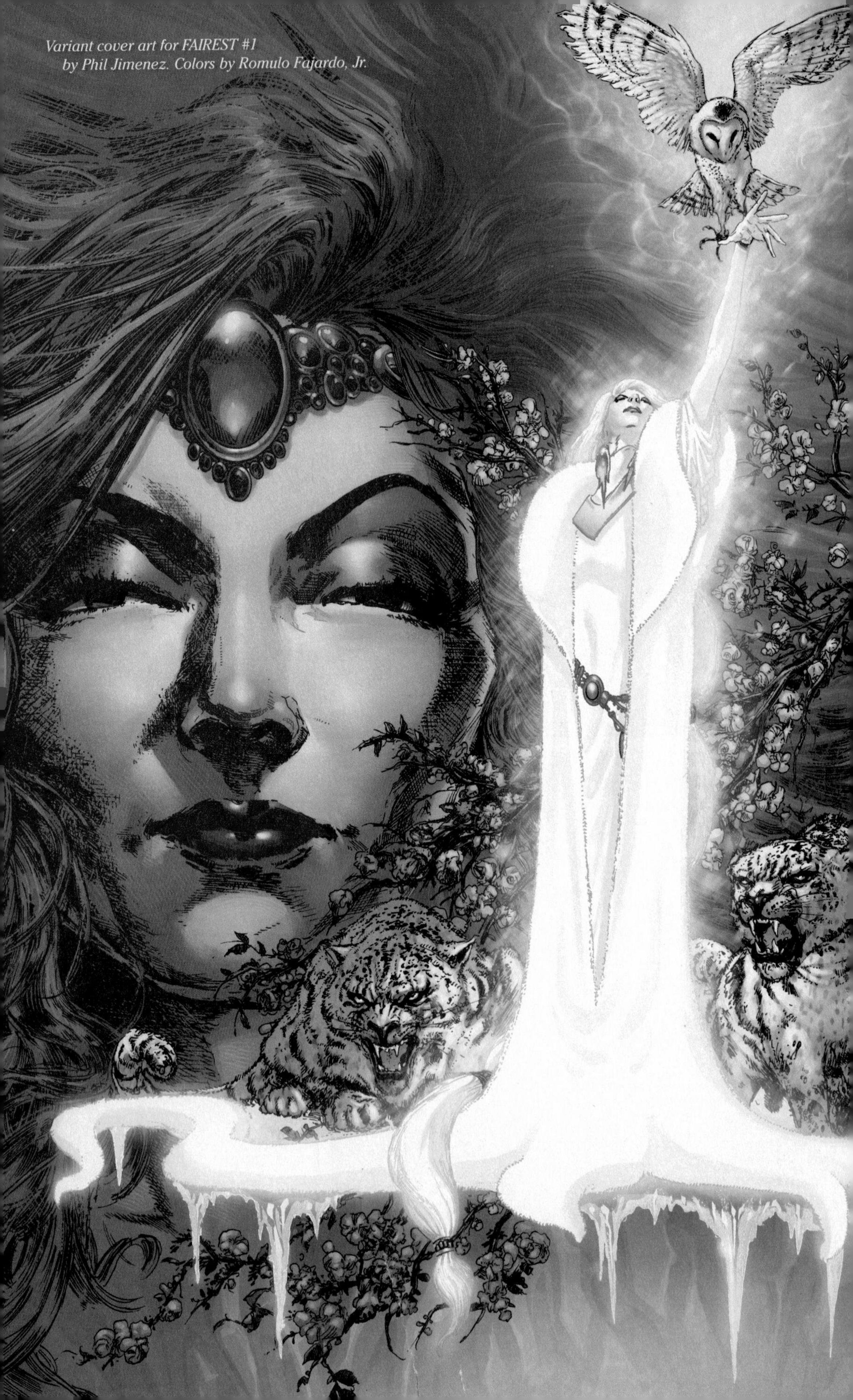

Variant cover art for FAIREST #1 by Phil Jimenez. Colors by Romulo Fajardo, Jr.